The great
book of
Pasta

THUNDER BAY
P·R·E·S·S

The great book of
Pasta

*450 recipes
for every occasion*

By
STELLA DONATI

Translation by
ANDREA JOURDAN

THUNDER BAY
P·R·E·S·S

First published in 2000 by
Thunder Bay Press
An imprint of the Advantage Publishers Group
5880 Oberlin Drive, San Diego, CA 92121-4794
www.advantagebooksonline.com

Direction: Marco Drago, Andrea Boroli
Editorial Director: Cristina Cappa Legora
Editorial Coordinator: Valeria Camaschella
Graphic Coordinator: Marco Volpati

Editorial collaboration: Tiziana Campana
Graphic Design: Gianfranco Fiori
Jacket: Paola Piacco

Nutritionist: Antonella Parolo

*Research into iconography by the Centro Iconografico at the Istituto Geografico De Agostini
directed by Maria Serena Battaglia*
Photos: Archivio I.G.D.A. (N. Banas, L. Chiozzi, I. Feroldi,
P. Ingaldi, K. Kissov, G. Losito, R. Marcialis, P. Martini, U. Marzani, Photographis, G. Pisacane,
Prima Press, L. Rizzi, C. Ruggiero,
M. Sarcina, E. Simion, G. Ummarino, Visual Food)

First published in Italy by Istituto Geografico De Agostini
under the title:
Il grande libro della pasta

Library of Congress Cataloging-in-Publication Data
Great book of pasta
    p.cm.
    Includes index.
    ISBN 1-57145-247-8
    1.Cookery (Pasta)

    TX809.M17 G69 2000
    641.8'22--dc21

Printed in Italy.

1 2 3 4 5 00 01 02 03 04

Preface

When I grew up, we called it "noodles." But it slowly made a name for itself, just as "sandwich," "pizza," or "terrine." It entered our lives and deliberately sneaked in to make a place for itself next to our favorite sauces. After all, everyone likes sauces. What better way to make oneself known than to be associated with an already well acquainted element. So, we do not call it "noodles" anymore, but "pasta," please. And "al dente," if you don't mind. What a long way we've gone together.

My grandmother did not like pasta - no wonder, who would like these long stringy tubes, overboiled and soaking in a plate of tomato juice - but my mother insisted we eat it, for, she said, it would be the food of the future. Little did she know I would write an introduction for a pasta bible!

So, I ate pasta, and I discovered many beautiful ways to use it along the years. But it is only when I lived in Italy that I really discovered the true and only way to treat pasta: with reverence and love! Pasta is easy; pasta is fun; pasta is challenging; pasta is versatile... If I have to use one word, I'd say pasta is ... sexy!

Italians call it "Queen of the meal" - a truly appropriate definition for, after all, it is pasta that conquered the whole world in the name of Italian cuisine. It is the importance pasta has taken in the culinary world that, without doubt, brought this book to life. Full of new and traditional recipes, it provides information that will not only be a precious guide for the beginner but will also be and old friend for the expert chef always striving to find new ideas. A large selection of recipes will hopefully find something for every palate. For every recipe, the degree of difficulty, the preparation time and the calorie count are indicated clearly to simplify the cooks selection.

To facilitate your research in the book, the recipes are divided in the traditional way: long pasta, short, pasta, filled pasta, baked pasta. Within these sections, recipes can be found by alphabetical order. Before entering the kitchen, browsing the section on basic information will help your encounter with the magical world of pasta.

A celebration for your taste: bring the Queen to your table!

Summary

Introduction

Pasta

Pasta is practically a magical word for a simple product that conquered the world. Where, how and when was pasta actually born?

Its long voyage, paralleling Man's evolution, started far away and long ago in times since lost. The way pasta is made, its ingredients, and even the way it is called, have undergone extensive evolution along the centuries.

In some parts of Italy, evidence of pasta making was found in Etruscan tombs. Near the towns of Orvieto and Cerveteri, instruments found are believed to have served in the making of pasta: a rolling pin (called *mattarello* and still used today for home-made pasta), a shaped roller-cutter, a pastry board, a deep spoon for adding small quantities of water and a bag for dusting.

In times closer to us, and well documented, we can find new evidence through literature of Ancient Greece when pasta was called *laganon* and *laganum* in the latin world. It is written that these types of "pasta" were home-made with flour and water. This pasta, similar to our modern "lasagna," was, in those imperial days, fried or cooked on hot coals and served with a sauce. Only later was pasta served in soups and, closer to us, it was understood that it could be boiled. Today, we serve pasta with many different sauces made with ingredients that were completely unknown in the early years of pasta making.

And early document discovered in Baghdad, dated 1226, suggests that pasta was brought to Italy by the Arabs who, pushed by necessity during their long travels through the desert, preferred to bring dried pasta with them since it lasted longer than other perishables.

A document has also been found on which a soldier from Genoa left in his inheritance a "barrel full of macheronis," or dried pasta in 1279.

So, although it is also certain that the same type of pasta existed in China, the idea that Marco Polo imported it to Italy in 1295 is only a legend.

Even in the early days, pasta was long and flat and called *lasagna* or *tagliatelle*. Then appeared the "maccheroni", a name that included all types of dried pasta..

In Southern Italy, the term maccheroni is still used for ziti, perciatelli, penne and other tubular pasta which also includes spaghetti and linguini. In the rest of Italy, types of pasta are differentiated as short, long, tubular, irregular, or smooth.

Surely, the dried pasta of the past was far different from that of today, for its basic ingredients were as different as the methods used for drying. Flour was grown and ground differently and the pasta was dried under the sun.

By the end of the 18th century, the region of Naples, thanks to its climate with perfect conditions of sun, wind and humidity, started the first commercial pasta making

companies. In those years, spaghetti was sometimes eaten with the fingers, as seen in some works of art representing thieves crudely enjoying themselves.

It was also in Naples that our way of eating was transformed forever by Ferdinand II. Insisting on eating pasta during official banquets, he threatened to fire his chamberlain if he did not find a way to eat the pasta in a more dignified manner. The frightened man therefore invented the four-prong fork which is more adapted to eating long pasta than the three prong fork used for meat.

Early in the 19th century, pasta took a cosmic leap when it finally encountered the one ingredient that changed it forever - the tomato, which had been brought to Europe from Central America already in the 16th century.

Italians abandoned their sweet-and-sour and their sweet-savory combinations for pasta "c'a pummarola in coppa" or "co lo pommodoro", as described by Ippolito Cavalcanti di Bonvicino (1787-1859).

From that point on, this dish of pasta and tomato sauce was know as being part of the tradition of the cuisine of Naples. And even today, it is still identified as "the" Italian dish.

Slowly, mostly around Naples but also in Liguria and other Italian regions, each with its own particular climate, there sprang up the first industrial pasta factories. The use of automation permitted to perfect the techniques and to control the manufacturing of pasta. It forced the development of a large industry reproducing countless shapes of pasta and regional specialties.

Metric Conversion Table

The mathematics of the metric system do not always correspond exactly to the English measuring system. The conversions of the measurements in the book have been rounded off and adjusted to avoid decimal points and complicated fractions. Metric measuring cups are available everywhere and metric measurements are clearly labeled on all food cans and pasta packaging.

Multiply	by	to get
liters (l)	4.2	cups
	2.2	pints (pt)
	1,000	milliliters (ml)
	100	centiliters (cl)
	10	deciliters (dl)
	1.05	quarts (qt)
grams (g)	.034	ounces (oz)
	.002	pounds (lb)
	.001	kilograms (k)
kilograms (k)	1,000	grams(g)
	35.3	ounces(oz)
	2.2	pounds (lb)
centimeters (cm)	.3	inches (in)
	10	millimeters(k)

General information:

flour, sugar and liquids ar not measured the same way.

flour	100 g	1 cup
sugar	100 g	1/2 cup
liquids	250 ml (2.5 dl)	1 cup

The Mediterranean diet

For many years, pasta, a totally natural product, was considered a fattening element in our diet. The discovery and the worldwide promotion of the "Mediterranean diet" influenced our choice to go back to pasta with a new vision. Cereals, pasta, bread, extra virgin olive oil, fruits and vegetables, fish, dairy products, meats in limited quantities and wine in moderation have been declared good for us. This type of diet has always been followed by the Mediterraneans and now it has become the modern way to healthy eating by returning to typical dishes, highly varied, changing according to modern tastes and adapted to consumption of proper quantities. Within this diet is included pasta which was once falsely held responsible for gain in weight, but has now justly been exonerated.

Cooked with fresh vegetables; eaten with the ever present extra virgin olive oil or with a sprinkling of grated cheese, pasta is a beneficial addition to our diet. Rich in protein, vitamins and minerals, it is a complex carbohydrate food.

If you consider that 80 grams of pasta is equal to about 285 calories, about one fifth of our daily needs, then it is only logical that the calories in a portion will increase only in relation to the sauce that accompanies the pasta.

Cooking Pasta

To be easily digestible, pasta (dried pasta ought to be made of durum wheat) should not be too "al dente" nor too cooked.

The cooking pot has to be large and preferably with a rounded bottom; enameled pots are better suited for long pasta since the short pasta will tend to stick.

Use abundant water, about 4 cups of water for 4 oz of pasta; in any case, it should not exceed 3/4 of the depth of the pot. For egg pasta, especially for lasagna, you can add some oil to help avoid sticking.

Coarse salt (about 1 tablespoon in 4 cups of water) should be added when the water is hot, or preferably when boiling bubbles start to form.

Throw the pasta into the boiling water and stir immediately to prevent it from sticking to the pot. The flame should be at its highest point, so that boiling will resume as quickly as possible, and the pan should not be covered with a lid. As soon as the boiling resumes, reduce the flame slightly, making sure the boiling continues. Never put a lid on the pan; otherwise the cooking will not be perfect.

From time to time, while the pasta is cooking, stir it well with a long fork, preferably made of wood; short pasta should be mixed with a long handled spoon to keep it from sticking to the bottom.

The cooking time is usually written on the packaging, but the only way to know with any certainty when the pasta is ready, is to taste it often.

Once cooked, the pasta must be drained in a colander so that it does not exceed its ideal cooking time. Shake all the water out of the pasta in the colander, more for short pasta since it tends to hold the water inside because of the different shapes. Drained pasta can be sautéed and mixed with its sauce in a pan or tossed in a preheated bowl. Always serve pasta in warm individual bowls. Long pasta should be tossed with a spoon and fork or with pasta tongs, which are particularly useful to transfer the pasta onto plates; short pasta is best tossed with a large spoon to blend in the sauce.

On the plate, short pasta is gathered up with a fork, several short pieces at a time; long pasta is rolled up with the fork without the help of a spoon.

It should be remembered that, because of water absorption, short pasta increases its original weight up to three times and its volume up to four times when cooked.

Dried pasta can be stored for several months if it is kept away from light in its original packaging in a fresh and ventilated place. However, it is best to use up most of it before the arrival of hot weather. This is especially true for whole wheat pasta. In warmer conditions small insects can fill part of the packaging and they will infest other starchy foods as well. Once a package is opened, it is best to use up all the contents in a short span, storing what is left in clean dry jars.

Marrying shapes to sauces

The shape of the pasta has a great effect on the taste which is affected by the thickness, the surface area and the capacity for absorbing sauces and seasonings.

The qualities of ridged pasta allow it to support cooking better while large shaped pasta increases greatly in volume because of water absorption; the latter serves better if portions need to be reduced as in the case of dieting, so at least the eye is appeased...

Oil based seasonings/sauces
 - *long shapes, moderately fine*
 - *short shapes that hold sauce better; tubular shapes, shells, and similar pasta*

Butter based seasonings/sauces
 - *long shapes of constant thickness*
 - *egg pasta*

Meat based seasonings/sauces
 - *short and large shapes: 'orecchiette' (ear shaped)*
 - *long and pierced shapes: ziti (tubes), toriglioni, fusilli*

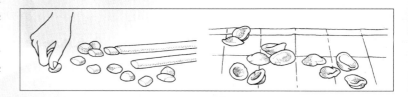

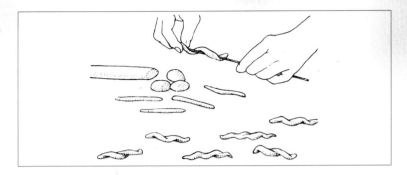

Vegetable based seasonings/sauces
- short pasta shapes, but larger than the pieces of chopped vegetables in the sauce

Here are some suggestions to combine seasonings or sauces with the right pasta:
Simple seasoning
Garlic and oil: spaghetti
Amatriciana: buccatini
Pesto: trenette, linguini, trofie, thin lasagna (in Genoa they are called *mandilli de sea* - silk handkerchiefs)

Sauces and seasonings with eggs, cheese, meat, fish, vegetables
Carbonara: vermicelli
Ragù (meat sauce): egg pasta, short pasta, lightly ridged pasta
Wild game sauces: pappardelle, reginette or mafaldine
Sauces made with sausages: gramignia, malloreddus (Sardinian gnochetti)
Fish sauces: spaghettini, perciatelli, linguini
Vegetable sauces, like cauliflower or turnip greens: orecchiette, fusilli
Baked: lasagne, cannelloni, rigatoni, tortiglioni, ruote, lumaconi rigati

Filled pasta
It was a great moment in history when an unknown genius thought of enveloping a filling between pieces of flat pasta. The earliest texts that mention it appeared in the 13th Century by Salimbene da Parma and in the 15th Century by Maestro Martino da Como. But then, again, perhaps it was a frugal housewife who came up with the idea by recycling leftovers, demonstrating that in the kitchen, nothing should go to waste.

Every region, and sometimes every town, came up with their own unique names: agnolotti in Piedmont, ravioli in Liguria and in lower Piedmont - some maintain that Gavi was the place where filled pasta originated, capelletti in Reggio Emilia, anolini in Parma, casonzei in Brescia and in Val Camonica, cialzons in Friuli, tortellini (disputed, as usual, between Bologna and Modena, as to whom legends credit with the imitation of the navel of Venus). Although filled pasta is also to be found in the southern part of the Peninsula, known by other names, it remains a particularity of the north.
Among this type of pasta there is also cannelloni which can be prepared from thin dough or with dry pasta of the appropriate shape.

Casseroles, Timballo and Pies
These typical molded preparations, mentioned in recipe books of the 14th and 15th Centuries, are often covered by a crust, much like a pie, and usually are the main serving in a midday meal of a certain standing, particularly among table companions who appreciate meals that are rich in flavor and highly nourishing. In a family lunch, for example, it could be the sole dish followed by a salad.
Timballo and pasticcio are terms used equally, especially in regional preparations, and can be enclosed in a pie crust, lightly sugared; in puff pastry dough; or in pate brisée.
Here are a few useful suggestions:
- the crust can be pre-cooked; in this case, when the mold has been prepared, place a sheet of wax paper over it and weigh it down with dried beans. Cook in an oven for 15 minutes at 200°C (about 380°F), then remove the paper and the beans and fill with the contents which can be tortellini, ravioli, etc.
- if you do not pre-cook the crust, once the mold has

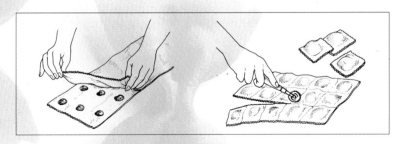

been covered with dough, sprinkle the bottom with bread crumbs which will absorb the fat from the filling, preventing the crust from becoming soggy.

- before taking the casserole/pie out of the mold, whether in a crust or without, wait a few minutes for the pasta to detach itself from the bottom and the sides of the mold; it would be easier to use a spring mold.

- if you are making a casserole without a crust, butter the mold; then butter some wax paper and use it to line the container.

- Preparations without a crust can be cooked in a bain-marie: they will turn out more tender; the cooking time, however, will be doubled.

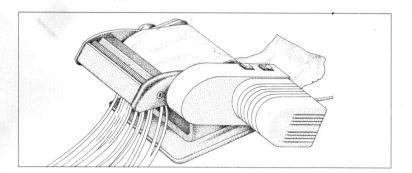

Fresh egg pasta
Basic recipe
Make a mound of sifted flour on the work surface, form a well in the center and break the eggs into it, allowing one egg per 100 grams of flour. Lightly beat the eggs with a fork, then blend the eggs into the flour with your fingers without letting the eggs run out of the mound.
When the flour is completely absorbed, begin to work the mixture with your palms until it is smooth; alternate the mixing with slamming the dough often on the work surface, ever more vigorously, with gusto. When the dough becomes elastic, form a ball, cover with a towel and let it rest for a half hour in a cool place.

To roll out the dough with a rolling pin: lightly flour the work surface and the rolling pin, press out the dough with the palms of your hands and begin to spread it with the rolling pin. From time to time, fold it over and spread it in the opposite direction continuing the process until you get the desired thickness.

To cut the dough by hand: sprinkle the sheet of dough with flour, roll it up not too tightly and cut it with a long, very sharp knife into strips as wide as you need: about 1/4" wide for tagliatelle, about 3/8" for fettuccine or tagliolini. Unroll the sliced rolls of dough on floured towels and spread them out for drying.
Pasta sheets with a machine: as soon as the flour has absorbed the eggs and the paste appears flaky, separate it in-

to large lumps and pass them through the rolls at the maximum opening; gradually reduce the opening until the desired thickness is obtained.
If you wish to make spaghetti "alla chitarra" and don't have the right equipment, roll the sheets to a thickness that, when passed through the cutting attachment, will come out square rather than flat.
These machines are available either manual or electric; of the latter, there are attachments with blades to mix the dough and dies through which a multitude or shapes can be formed.

Filled pasta
Cut the dough into strips.
To make square ravioli, put small amounts of the filling spaced out on one half of the strip, fold over the other half, press the sides together with the tips of your fingers to seal the dough and to eliminate trapped air; cut into squares with a serrated cutting wheel.
If you prefer a half-moon shape, cut the dough sheets with a serrated round stamp, then fill and fold over into a half-moon.
If you like them round, space out the filling, cover with another strip and cut the ravioli using the round stamp. The scrap dough can be reworked and used for more ravioli or for other shapes.
There are trays available that are made to produce 2-3 dozen ravioli at a time. Line the tray with a strip of dough, fill the indentations with the preparation, and cover with another strip of dough; then, press a rolling pin that comes with the device over the top.
Tortellini: cut the dough sheet into squares with a pointed knife or with a serrated cutting wheel; put a nut-size dab

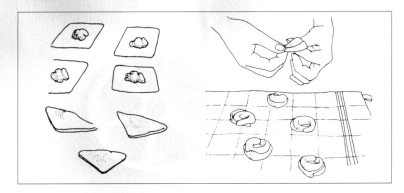

of filling in the center of each square, fold over one of the corners to form a triangle; wrap the triangles over the index finger with the center point upwards and the two lower corners toward the thumb; press together so they remain well sealed: lay out on the work space. *Cappelletti* are made in the same manner, only the dough is cut with a round stamp.

Colored pasta: the most common color is green, obtained with the use of spinach: for 4 cups of flour, use two whole eggs and 7 oz of spinach, boiled, very well drained, and very finely chopped;
- for red, use the same amount of flour and eggs and two spoons of tomato concentrate dissolved in just a bit of water; for a deeper color increase the quantity of the concentrate;
- to make a reddish purple color, use mashed beets;
- for a deep yellow, use a small packet of saffron soaked in a few drops of water; for orange, use a carrot puré.
Brown pasta can be made by sifting the flower with cocoa powder; to get black color, octopus ink is added to the dough (sometimes available in specialty food shops).

Color and flavor: the pasta dough can be flavored by adding a nice bunch of parsley and basil or rosemary and sage or various other herbs as long as they are fresh, go well together, and are uniformly blended with the dough.
For a spicier flavor, it is possible to sift in with the flour powdered red chili peppers in large doses for really hot or in milder doses by mixing the peppers with the eggs. Your guests will remain open-mouthed not just from the reddish color of the pasta!

Using leftovers
Even when the pasta is a great success, some may be left over. There are many ways to use these leftovers.

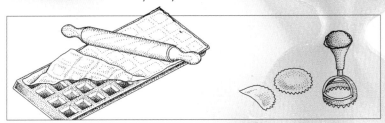

Any type of pasta in a sauce, whether small or medium shapes, can be used to stuff tomatoes and peppers for baking; to make casseroles without a crust, by combining with béchamel sauce and other leftovers of sausages, meat or vegetables, chopped in large pieces; or mixed into dumpling dough, small spoonfuls can be deep fried in hot oil to make delicious fritters.
Long shapes can be pan fried until they become golden and crusty; by adding eggs a delicious frittata can be made which can also be enriched with mozzarella. Add boiled vegetables and, if you like, béchamel sauce, cover it all with bread crumbs, bake it in an oven, and you have a dish for a second course.
Spaghettini, angel hair pasta, tagliolini, can be rolled up on a fork, dipped in beaten eggs, then passed in flour or bread crumbs and fried to make a really delicious dish.
The big shaped pasta like zitoni, rigatoni, tortiglioni, large penne, when sliced into short rings can be used in salads by adding mozzarella, capers, olives, peppers in a dressing of your preferred condiment and extra virgin olive oil. Tofe and lumaconi can be stuffed with a ravioli type filling, covered with béchamel sauce and grated parmigiano then baked until the top is golden.
These are just a few suggestions. Use your imagination for other ideas, since there are virtually no limits with such a popular and varied food. You can find suggestions and pointers in a number of books on the subject, like *L'arte di utilizzare gli avanzi* ("The Art of Using Leftovers") written by Olindo Guerrini, better known as Lorenzo Stecchetti, first published in 1918 and recently reissued in Italy which suggests infinite ways to reuse leftover foods.

Long pasta

Bavette with garlic and olive oil

Difficulty **easy** • *Time needed* **less than 30 minutes** • *Calories per serving* **410**

INGREDIENTS

serves 4

BAVETTE *11 oz*
PINE NUTS *1 tablespoon*
BREAD CRUMBS *3 tablespoons*
PARSLEY *1 bunch*
GARLIC *2 cloves*
EXTRA VIRGIN OLIVE OIL *4 tablespoons*
SALT & PEPPER *to taste*

1 Heat 3 tablespoons of extra virgin olive oil in a pan. Peel the garlic and fry lightly without burning. Add the pine nuts and toast until golden. Remove the pan from the heat and season the ingredients with salt and pepper. Discard the garlic. In a skillet, heat the remaining olive oil and lightly toast the bread crumbs.

2 In the meantime, cook the bavette in abundant boiling salted water. When al dente, drain, transfer the bavette to a serving dish. Clean, rinse, dry and chop the parsley finely. Add the pine nuts, the bread crumbs, and the parsley to the bavette; mix well and serve immediately.

Bavette with mushrooms carbonara

Difficulty **medium** • *Time needed* **less than 30 minutes** • *Calories per serving* **550**

INGREDIENTS

serves 4

BAVETTE *14 oz*
PANCETTA *2 oz*
MUSHROOMS *11 oz*
EGG YOLKS *2*
PARSLEY *1 bunch*
CHILI POWDER *a pinch*
GRATED PARMIGIANO *2 tablespoons*
BUTTER *1 tablespoon*
SALT *to taste*

1 Carefully clean the mushrooms, rinse, pat dry with a kitchen towel and slice. Trim the parsley, rinse, dry and chop. Dice the pancetta and cook in a cast iron pan over high heat until crispy; remove from heat and set aside. In the same pan, leave a tablespoon of cooking fat, discarding the rest, and cook the mushrooms over high heat for 2-3 minutes, stirring from time to time with a wooden spoon; finally, add the chopped parsley.

2 In the meantime, bring abundant water to a boil in a pot, add salt and cook the bavette. Beat the egg yolks with the chili powder. When al dente, drain the bavette and transfer to a pan with 2-3 tablespoons of pasta cooking water; add the butter (at room temperature); mix well and add the pancetta, the mushrooms and the egg yolks.

3 Heat the mixture for a few minutes, mix rapidly to blend the ingredients and serve at once in the same cooking pan, sprinkling generously with the grated parmigiano.

Bavette with savoy cabbage

Difficulty **easy** • *Time needed* **less than 30 minutes** • *Calories per serving* **390**

INGREDIENTS
serves 4

BAVETTE *11 oz*
SAVOY CABBAGE *1, small*
SALTED ANCHOVIES *3*
EXTRA VIRGIN OLIVE OIL *3 tablespoons*
SALT *to taste*

1 Discard the large and hard external leaves from the cabbage and remove the core. Gently rinse the tender leaves, pat dry with a towel and cut into thin strips. Desalt the anchovies by washing under running water, remove the bones, chop finely, and set aside. In abundant boiling salted water, cook the bavette together with the cabbage.

2 In the meantime, heat the oil in a skillet, add the anchovies and melt them over very low heat, stirring with a wooden spoon. When al dente, drain the pasta and the cabbage and transfer to a serving plate; toss with the sauce, mix well and serve hot.

Bavette with sun dried tomatoes

Difficulty **easy** • *Time needed* **less than 30 minutes** • *Calories per serving* **390**

INGREDIENTS
serves 4

BAVETTE *12 oz*
SUN DRIED TOMATOES *2 oz*
TOMATO SAUCE *1 tablespoon*
PARSLEY *1 bunch*
GARLIC *1 clove*
HOT CHILI POWDER
a pinch
EXTRA VIRGIN OLIVE OIL *3 tablespoons*
SALT & PEPPER *to taste*

1 Trim the parsley, rinse, dry and chop them finely; chop the sun dried tomatoes, setting aside 2 whole ones for decoration; peel the garlic and chop finely. In a large pot, bring abundant water to a boil, add salt, drop in the bavette and cook until al dente. When ready, drain, reserving 3 tablespoons of the cooking water, and put the bavette back in the same pot.

2 Pour the extra virgin olive oil over the pasta, add the sun dried tomatoes, the tomato sauce, the garlic, the chili powder, a pinch of salt, a dash of fresh ground pepper, and the reserved cooking water. Cook the pasta for a few minutes, tossing and mixing with a large fork. Pour into a serving bowl, garnish with the reserved dried tomatoes and the chopped parsley. Serve immediately.

Bavette with vegetables

Difficulty **medium** • *Time needed* **under an hour** • *Calories per serving* **540**

INGREDIENTS
serves 4

BAVETTE *14 oz*
SHELLED PEAS *4 tablespoons*
YELLOW PEPPER *1/2*
PEELED TOMATOES *7 oz*
CELERY *1 stalk*
CARROT *1*
GARLIC *1 clove*
ONION *1*
OREGANO *a pinch*
VEGETABLE STOCK CUBE *1/2*
DRY WHITE WINE *1/4 cup*
GRATED PECORINO *2 tablespoons*
GRATED PARMIGIANO *1 tablespoon*
EXTRA VIRGIN OLIVE OIL *4 tablespoons*
SALT & PEPPER *to taste*

1 Trim and rinse the vegetables. Coarsely chop the garlic clove, the onion, the carrot, the celery stalk, and the pepper; heat the oil in a cast iron pot, and fry all the chopped vegetables. When the mixture begins to brown, add the peas, and the tomatoes; cook for 1-2 minutes and add 1/2 cup of hot water.

2 Reduce the sauce over low heat, add the bouillon cube (crushed), a pinch of salt and a dash of fresh ground pepper, a generous dash of oregano and the white wine. Cover and let the sauce reduce slowly over low heat.

3 In the meantime, cook the bavette al dente in abundant boiling salted water.

Drain and transfer the bavette to a soup tureen; sprinkle with a little grated pecorino and parmigiano and pour over a few spoonfuls of the sauce; continue to add the ingredients, alternating, to thoroughly mix in the sauce. Serve hot.

Bigoli with baby sardines

Difficulty **easy** • *Time needed* **over an hour** • *Calories per serving* **500**

INGREDIENTS
serves 4

For the pasta
UNBLEACHED FLOUR *3 cups*
EGGS *2*
SALT *to taste*

For the sauce
SARDINES *14 oz*
GARLIC *1 clove*
PARSLEY *1 bunch*
EXTRA VIRGIN OLIVE OIL *5 tablespoons*
SALT & PEPPER *to taste*

1 Prepare the pasta. Sift the flour on the work surface and make a mound. Break the eggs in the center, add a dash of salt and work the ingredients, adding enough water (or milk) to make a smooth and homogenous dough. Cover with plastic wrap and let rest for 30 minutes.

2 At the end of this time, roll out the pasta and pass through the appropriate attachment to make the bigoli; lay them out on the flour dusted work surface. Clean the sardines, scale them, remove the heads, the fins and the fish bones,

wash, dry and cut into small pieces.

3 Peel the garlic, rinse, dry and crush; clean the parsley, rinse, dry and chop finely. In a pan, cook the garlic with the oil without browning; add the pieces of sardines and cook for 4-5 minutes over moderate heat. Season with a pinch of salt and fresh ground pepper; sprinkle with the chopped parsley.

4 Cook the bigoli in abundant boiling salted water. When al dente, drain well and mix with the sardine sauce. Serve while hot.

Bigoli with shellfish

*Difficulty **medium*** • *Time needed **over an hour*** • *Calories per serving **600***

INGREDIENTS
serves 4

BIGOLI *11 oz*
MUSSELS *1 1/4 lbs*
CLAMS *1 1/4 lbs*
SHRIMP *5 oz*
SCAMPI *5 oz*
ZUCCHINI *3*
YELLOW PEPPER *1*
EGG PLANT *1*
ONION *1, small*
PARSLEY *1 bunch*
BASIL *1 bunch*
GARLIC *2 cloves*
DRY WHITE WINE *1/4 cup*
BUTTER *2 tablespoons*
EXTRA VIRGIN OLIVE OIL *6 tablespoons*
SALT & PEPPER *to taste*

1 Scrape the mussels, wash well and drain. Wash the clams, leave immersed in abundant salted water to get rid of any sand, then drain. Remove the tails and devein the shrimp, rinse and cut into pieces.

2 Peel and crush the garlic; clean and chop the parsley. In two separate pans, cook the mussels and the clams together with a garlic clove, half the parsley, 2 tablespoons of oil and half the white wine. Cover the pans and cook over high heat to open the shells.

3 Cut the ends of the eggplant and cut into small pieces; sprinkle with a little salt and let rest in a colander for 30 minutes to lose the vegetal water; briefly rinse under running water, drain well and pat dry. Drain the clams and the mussels (discard any that remain closed) and separate the meat from the shells; filter the cooking liquid and reserve in one bowl. Trim the zucchini, rinse and cut into small pieces. Remove the seeds and the white parts of the pepper, rinse, dry and cut into pieces.

4 Peel the onion, chop finely and cook in a pan with the remaining oil and butter until transparent. Add the scampi and shrimp pieces and simmer for 2 minutes; drain and cover to keep hot. In the same pan, fry the pepper for 2 minutes; add the eggplant and the zucchini and brown over high heat for several minutes, stirring with a wooden spoon.

5 Season with a pinch of salt and fresh ground pepper, lower the heat, cover, and continue cooking for about 15 minutes. Add the seafood, the scampi and the shrimp, a few tablespoons of the reserved cooking liquid, the basil and the remaining chopped parsley.

6 In the meantime, cook the bigoli in abundant boiling salted water; when al dente, drain and mix with the prepared sauce. Serve at once.

Bigoli with sardines

Difficulty **easy** • *Time needed* **under an hour** • *Calories per serving* **580**

INGREDIENTS
serves 4

For the pasta
UNBLEACHED FLOUR *4 cups*
EGGS *4*
SALT *to taste*

For the sauce
SARDINES *6*
PARSLEY *2 oz*
GARLIC *1 clove*
EXTRA VIRGIN OLIVE OIL *3 tablespoons*
SALT *to taste*

1 Sift the flour into a mound on the work surface; in the center, break the eggs and add the salt. Work the ingredients vigorously for 15 minutes. Make a ball with the dough and flatten it with the palm of your hand.

2 Dust the work surface with flour and roll out the dough into a sheet, not too thin. With a rotary cutter or a very sharp knife, cut the dough into spaghetti like lengths.

3 Wash the sardines thoroughly; discard the innards, the fins and the head; wash again, dry and cut into pieces.

4 Heat the oil in a casserole; add the sardines, stir gently with a wooden spoon, and cook for 15 minutes until completely done. Clean and crush the garlic. Trim the parsley, rinse and chop. Add the garlic, the parsley and a pinch of salt to the sardines. Mix well and after a few moments remove from the heat.

5 Cook the bigoli, drain when al dente and pour into the casserole with the sardines along with a few tablespoons of cooking water; mix well, let the flavors blend with the pasta, and serve.

SUGGESTION
To concentrate the taste, dissolve 1 or 2 salted anchovies in the sauce.

Bigoli with duck ragù

*Difficulty **medium*** • *Time needed **under an hour*** • *Calories per serving **560***

INGREDIENTS
serves 4

For the pasta
UNBLEACHED FLOUR *4 cups*
EGGS *2*
WATER *or* **MILK** *as needed*
SALT *to taste*

For the sauce
DUCK BREAST *11 oz*
TOMATOES *14 oz, ripe and firm*
CARROT *1*
CELERY *1 stalk*
ONION *1*
GARLIC *1 clove*
BAY LEAVES *1 leaf*
THYME *1 sprig*
PARSLEY *1 small bunch*
BRANDY *2 tablespoons*
BUTTER *2 tablespoons*
EXTRA VIRGIN OLIVE OIL *2 tablespoons*
SALT & PEPPER *to taste*

1 Prepare the pasta. Sift the flour into a mound on the work surface; break the eggs in the center, add a pinch of salt and work the ingredients adding enough water or milt to make an elastic and homogenous dough. Cover with plastic wrap and let rest 30 minutes.

2 When rested, roll out the pasta and use the appropriate cutter to make the bigoli; lay them out on the work surface dusted with flour. Prepare the sauce. Scald the tomatoes in boiling water, drain, peel, squeeze out the seeds and the water and dice coarsely. Rinse the duck breast, dry and cut into cubes.

3 Peel the onion and the garlic; cut the ends of the carrot and peel; clean the celery, removing the large filaments; rinse the vegetables, dry and chop. Clean and rinse the parsley, dry and chop finely. Heat the butter in a pan with the oil; add the bay leaf, the thyme, the parsley. Add the chopped onion, garlic, celery and carrot; cook without browning.

4 Add the meat cubes and brown all over on high heat; pour on the brandy and let evaporate. Add the diced tomatoes, season with salt and pepper; cover and continue cooking over moderate heat for 20-30 minutes, mixing from time to time. Cook the bigoli in abundant boiling salted water. When al dente, drain and mix with the sauce. Serve immediately.

SUGGESTION
A variation of this recipe: Heat 3 tablespoons of oil in a skillet and brown the meat all over; add the brandy, let evaporate; season with salt and pepper and reserve the meat. Prepare the sauce following the recipe and add cubes of duck breast just before the cooking is done.

Bucatini with hake

Difficulty **medium** • *Time needed* **less than 30 minutes** • *Calories per serving* **460**

INGREDIENTS
serves 4

BUCATINI *14 oz*
HAKE *5 oz*
TOMATOES *2*
ONION *1/2*
BASIL *3 leaves*
EXTRA VIRGIN OLIVE OIL *3 tablespoons*
SALT & PEPPER *to taste*

1 Peel the tomatoes, remove the seeds and dice the pulp. Chop the onion and cook in a pan with the oil until transparent. Cut the hake fillets into pieces. Add the tomatoes and the hake to the onion.

2 Cook over low heat for 10-15 minutes. Shred the basil leaves and add with salt and pepper to the mixture just before the cooking is done.

3 In the meantime, cook the pasta al dente in abundant boiling salted water.

Drain and mix with the sauce in the pan; toss for a few minutes and serve hot.

Bucatini all'amatriciana

Difficulty **easy** • *Time needed* **less than 30 minutes** • *Calories per serving* **650**

INGREDIENTS
serves 4

BUCATINI *14 oz*
PANCETTA *5 oz*
GRATED PECORINO *3 tablespoons*
HOT CHILI PEPPER *1 small piece*
SALT *to taste*

1 With a very sharp knife, cut the pancetta into 1/2 inch cubes.

2 Cook the pancetta in a skillet over high heat without adding flavoring, stirring now and then with a wooden spoon. Crush the chili pepper and add to the pancetta.

3 Cook the pasta in abundant boiling salted water. Drain when al dente.

Transfer to a serving bowl and add the pancetta. Sprinkle with the grated pecorino and serve.

SUGGESTION
Many variations can be made from this classic recipe, including a particularly tasty one made by adding onions and tomatoes.

Bucatini, Calabrian style

Difficulty **medium** • *Time needed* **under an hour** • *Calories per serving* **610**

INGREDIENTS
serves 4

BUCATINI *12 oz*
GROUND BEEF *4 oz*
SPICY SAUSAGE *4 oz*
MUSHROOMS *5 oz*
TOMATOES *14 oz, ripe and firm*
PARSLEY *1 bunch*
ONION *1*
CHILI PEPPER *1 small piece*
OREGANO *1 pinch*
GRATED PARMIGIANO *4 tablespoons*
EXTRA VIRGIN OLIVE OIL *4 tablespoons*
SALT *to taste*

1 Scald the tomatoes in boiling water; drain, peel, remove the seeds and the water; dice coarsely. Rinse the parsley, dry and chop; remove the skin from the sausage and chop finely.

2 Clean the mushrooms, removing the dirt, rinse briefly in cold water, pat dry with a kitchen towel and cut into slices. Peel the onion and chop it; in an ample saucepan, heat the olive oil and cook the onion until transparent.

3 Add the ground beef, and cook over high heat to brown it all over. Add the sausage and the mushrooms; continue cooking for 2 minutes, stirring with a wooden spoon. Add the tomatoes, the chili pepper, a pinch of salt and cook for 20 minutes over moderate heat; add a pinch of oregano.

4 In the meantime, cook the bucatini in abundant boiling salted water until al dente; drain and mix with the sauce. Clean, rinse, dry, and chop the parsley. Sprinkle the pasta with the parsley and the grated parmigiano and serve hot.

Bucatini, Mediterranean style

Difficulty **medium** • *Time needed* **under an hour** • *Calories per serving* **460**

INGREDIENTS
serves 4

BUCATINI *12 oz*
YELLOW PEPPER *1*
EGG PLANT *1*
TOMATOES *4*
BLACK OLIVES *4 oz*
CAPERS *1 tablespoon*
BASIL *a few leaves*
EXTRA VIRGIN OLIVE OIL *3 tablespoons*
SALT *to taste*

1 Clean the pepper, removing the seeds and the white parts; rinse and dice. Rinse and dice the egg plant. Rinse the capers under running water. In a small skillet, heat the oil and add the diced pepper and egg plant, the capers and the olives.

2 Cook the vegetables for a few minutes, add a dash of salt, mix again and remove from the heat. Cook the bucatini in abundant boiling salted water; when al dente, drain and blend with the prepared mixture adding a few shredded basil leaves. Transfer to four individual deep serving plates.

3 Rinse the tomatoes, remove the seeds and the water and cut into slices. Add 1 tomato per portion, mix gently and serve at once.

Bucatini, Capri style

Difficulty **medium** • *Time needed* **under an hour** • *Calories per serving* **520**

INGREDIENTS
serves 4

BUCATINI *14 oz*
CHERRY TOMATOES *2 lbs*
YELLOW PEPPER *1*
BLACK OLIVES *30*
BASIL *1 bunch*
GARLIC *1 clove*
GRATED PARMIGIANO *4 tablespoons*
EXTRA VIRGIN OLIVE OIL *3 tablespoons*
SALT & PEPPER *to taste*

1 Scald the tomatoes in boiling water for a few seconds, drain, peel, and squeeze out the seeds and the water; chop coarsely. Peel and crush the garlic; clean the pepper, eliminate the seeds and the white parts and dice. Heat the oil in a casserole, add the garlic and cook until lightly golden; discard and add the diced pepper.

2 Fry the diced pepper for a few minutes, add the diced tomato, mix well and simmer for about 10 minutes over moderate heat. Season with a pinch of salt and a little fresh ground pepper; add the olives, the basil and finish cooking the sauce over low heat.

3 Cook the pasta in a pot with abundant boiling salted water; drain when al dente, pour the sauce over, sprinkle with the grated parmigiano and serve immediately.

Bucatini, country style

Difficulty **medium** • *Time needed* **over an hour** • *Calories per serving* **680**

INGREDIENTS
serves 4

BUCATINI *12 oz*
CANNELLINI BEANS *5 oz*
PANCETTA *3 oz*
ONION *1*
GARLIC *1 clove*
SAGE *1 leaf*
PARSLEY *1 bunch*
BAY LEAVES *1 leaf*
ROSEMARY *2 branches*
HOT CHILI PEPPER *1*
GRATED PECORINO *2 tablespoons*
EXTRA VIRGIN OLIVE OIL *4 tablespoons*
SALT *to taste*

1 Rinse the beans and soak in abundant cold water for 12 hours. Drain and rinse under running water. Transfer to a pot, cover with abundant water, add the bay leaf and a branch of rosemary.

2 Bring to a boil, then cook the beans for about an hour over very low heat, adding, if needed, hot water and seasoning with salt after about 30 minutes. In the meantime, cut the pancetta into thin strips; peel the onion and the garlic, rinse and chop with the remaining rosemary, the sage, and the parsley.

3 Heat the oil in a skillet with the chili pepper, the chopped onion, the garlic, and the herbs and cook without browning; add the pancetta strips and fry briefly, stirring with a wooden spoon. Drain the cooked beans and add to the skillet; cover and cook for about 10 minutes over medium heat. Discard the chili pepper.

4 Cook the bucatini in a pot with abundant boiling salted water. When al dente, drain and mix with the bean ragù. Serve hot, sprinkled with the remaining parsley and the grated pecorino.

Bucatini, Sicilian style

Difficulty **medium** • *Time needed* **less than 30 minutes** • *Calories per serving* **440**

INGREDIENTS
serves 4

BUCATINI *12 oz*
SALTED ANCHOVIES *4*
DAY OLD BREAD *1 slice*
GARLIC *1 clove*
EXTRA VIRGIN OLIVE OIL *4 tablespoons*
SALT & PEPPER *to taste*

1 Debone the anchovies and wash thoroughly under running water to remove the salt; pat dry and cut into small pieces. If the bread is still a little soft, toast in a hot oven to dry; then remove the crust and grate the rest.

2 In a skillet, heat 2 tablespoons of oil, peel the garlic and fry until golden. Add the anchovies and cook briefly to dissolve them. Remove the skillet from the heat and season with a pinch of fresh ground pepper. Lightly oil a cast iron pan and toast the grated bread, stirring often with a wooden spoon.

3 In the meantime, boil abundant water in a pot and add salt. Cook the bucatini al dente and drain. Add 3 tablespoons of cooking water to the sauce. Mix the bucatini with the anchovy sauce and the grated bread crumbs.

Bucatini with anchovies and mushrooms

Difficulty **medium** • *Time needed* **under an hour** • *Calories per serving* **610**

INGREDIENTS
serves 4

BUCATINI *14 oz*
ANCHOVY FILLETS *3*
FRESH MUSHROOMS *11 oz*
GARLIC *2 cloves*
ROMA TOMATOES *11 oz*
OREGANO *a pinch*
WORCESTER SAUCE *1 tablespoon*
CHOPPED PARSLEY *1 tablespoon*
EXTRA VIRGIN OLIVE OIL *10 tablespoons*
SALT & PEPPER *to taste*

1 Peel and crush the garlic. Heat the oil in a large saucepan and cook the garlic until it begins to turn golden.

2 Peel the tomatoes and pass through a vegetable mill. Debone and desalt the anchovies and cut into small pieces; add to the garlic and dissolve over medium heat, then add the tomato purée.

3 Clean the mushrooms well and add to the sauce. Mix, continue cooking; season with salt, pepper, oregano, and finally, add the Worcester sauce.

4 Cook over moderate heat for 20 minutes, stirring often; when done, sprinkle with finely chopped parsley. Cook the bucatini in abundant boiling salted water, drain and transfer to a serving bowl with the sauce. Toss well and serve at once.

Bucatini with sweet peppers

Difficulty **medium** • *Time needed* **under an hour** • *Calories per serving* **450**

INGREDIENTS
serves 4

BUCATINI *12 oz*
RED PEPPERS *11 oz*
YELLOW PEPPERS *3 oz*
TOMATOES *1 1/4 lbs*
ONION *1*
GARLIC *1 clove*
BASIL *2 bunches*
EXTRA VIRGIN OLIVE OIL *4 tablespoons*
SALT & PEPPER *to taste*

1 Scald the tomatoes in boiling water, peel, squeeze gently to remove the seeds, then dice. Peel the onion, rinse and chop; peel the garlic clove and chop; rinse and shred the basil; rinse the peppers, remove the seeds and the white parts and slice into strips.

2 In a skillet, heat 2 tablespoons of oil, fry the onion and half the garlic until the onion is transparent, stirring from time to time with a wooden spoon; add tomatoes, half the basil, a pinch of salt, a dash of fresh ground pepper and cook over moderate heat for 20 minutes.

3 In another pan, heat the remaining olive oil, add the peppers and, stirring now and again, let cook for 10-12 minutes. At the end of the cooking, add the chopped garlic and the remaining basil; mix thoroughly.

4 In the meantime, cook the bucatini in a pot with abundant boiling salted water. When al dente, transfer to a serving bowl, add the tomato sauce, cover with the peppers and sprinkle with the rest of the shredded basil. Serve immediately.

Bucatini primavera

Difficulty **medium** • *Time needed* **under an hour** • *Calories per serving* **430**

INGREDIENTS
serves 4

BUCATINI *12 oz*
ZUCCHINI *7 oz, small*
CARROT *1*
ONION *1*
BASIL *a few leaves*
GRATED PARMIGIANO *3 tablespoons*
EXTRA VIRGIN OLIVE OIL *3 tablespoons*
SALT & PEPPER *to taste*

1 Peel the onion, rinse and slice. Cut the ends of the carrot and the zucchini, rinse and cut into round slices. Heat the oil in a casserole and fry the onion and the carrot.

2 Add the zucchini, season with salt, and cook over moderate heat for 5-6 minutes, stirring now and then with a wooden spoon. Rinse, dry and shred the basil; add to the casserole and cook another 2 minutes.

3 In the meantime, in a pot, bring abundant water to a boil; add salt and cook the bucatini. When al dente, drain and pour into the casserole with the vegetables; add a dash of fresh ground pepper and the grated parmigiano. Mix quickly and serve at once.

Capellini with tomato sauce and garlic

Difficulty **medium** • *Time needed* **under an hour** • *Calories per serving* **550**

INGREDIENTS
serves 4

For the pasta
UNBLEACHED FLOUR *4 cups*
EGGS *4*
SALT *to taste*

For the sauce
ROMA TOMATOES *14 oz*
PARSLEY *2 oz*
GARLIC *2 cloves*
EXTRA VIRGIN OLIVE OIL *5 tablespoons*
SALT & PEPPER *to taste*

1 Sift the flour in a mound on the work surface, add salt and the eggs and work vigorously to make smooth and elastic dough. Roll out into a thin sheet, then roll onto itself and cut into very fine strips which you let rest on a towel.

2 Heat the olive oil in a casserole. Peel and crush the garlic; fry in the casserole until golden. Pass the tomatoes in a vegetable mill, pour into the casserole, mix and cook for 18 minutes.

3 Trim and clean the parsley, rinse, dry, chop, and add to the tomatoes. Cook for another 2 minutes; season the preparation with salt and fresh ground pepper.

4 Cook the capellini in a pot with abundant boiling salted water. Drain, transfer to a serving bowl. Discard the garlic from the sauce and pour over the pasta. Mix well and serve.

Ciriole with mushrooms

Difficulty **medium** • *Time needed* **over an hour** • *Calories per serving* **430**

INGREDIENTS
serves 4

For the pasta
UNBLEACHED FLOUR *3 1/2 cups*
EGG WHITES *1*
SALT *a pinch*

For the sauce
FRESH MUSHROOMS *7 oz*
TOMATO SAUCE *11 oz*
GARLIC *2 cloves*
PARSLEY *1 bunch*
EXTRA VIRGIN OLIVE OIL *4 tablespoons*
SALT & PEPPER *to taste*

1 Form a mound with the flour on the work surface and, in the center, place the salt, the egg white and half a cup of lukewarm water; work the ingredients well, adding enough water until the dough becomes firm and elastic.

2 With a rolling pin, roll out the dough into a sheet about 1/16 inch thick; dust with flour and roll around itself; finally, cut thin strips, about 1/16 inch wide and lay them out on a dusted surface to dry out for about half an hour.

3 Clean the mushrooms, wipe them with a moist towel, and, if necessary, pass them quickly under running water and spat dry; cut into slices, put into a pan, cover and cook for 8-10 minutes over high heat.

4 Peel the garlic, trim, rinse and dry the parsley, and chop them together. Heat the oil in a casserole and fry the chopped garlic and parsley mixture; add the tomato sauce, season with salt and pepper; cover and cook over low heat for about half an hour, stirring from time to time.

5 In the meantime, cook the pasta in a pot with abundant boiling salted water, drain and toss with the prepared sauce. Serve hot, without adding any cheese.

Fettuccine with pancetta

Difficulty **medium** • *Time needed* **under an hour** • *Calories per serving* **690**

INGREDIENTS
serves 4

EGG FETTUCINE *14 oz*
PANCETTA *4 oz*
ONION *1*
PARSLEY *1 bunch*
BASIL *a few leaves*
GRATED PECORINO *6 tablespoons*
EXTRA VIRGIN OLIVE OIL *3 tablespoons*
SALT & PEPPER *to taste*

1 Peel and chop the onion; dice the pancetta and fry both ingredients in a pan with the oil. In the meantime, trim, rinse, and dry the parsley, chop with the basil, then add to the pan.

2 Season with salt and pepper and cook over low heat for about 15 minutes, adding a little hot water, now and then to thin the sauce, stirring from time to time with a wooden spoon.

3 In the meantime, cook the fettuccine in abundant boiling salted water until al dente; drain and transfer to a serving bowl and toss with the prepared sauce; serve with the grated pecorino on the side.

Fettuccine with black olive sauce

Difficulty **easy** • *Time needed* **under an hour** • *Calories per serving* **540**

INGREDIENTS
serves 4

For the pasta
UNBLEACHED FLOUR *3 cups*
EGGS *3*
EXTRA VIRGIN OLIVE OIL *1 tablespoon*
SALT *to taste*

For the sauce
BLACK OLIVES *7 oz, small*
CAPERS *1/2 tablespoon*
GRATED PEEL OF 1/2 LEMON
LEMON JUICE *1 tablespoon*
BUTTER *3 tablespoons*
EXTRA VIRGIN OLIVE OIL *2 tablespoons*
SALT & PEPPER *to taste*

1 Prepare the pasta dough. Sift the flour on the work surface and form a mound; in the center, put the eggs, the oil and the salt; work the ingredients, kneading until the dough becomes smooth and elastic. Cover with plastic wrap and let it rest for at least 30 minutes.

2 After this time, roll out the pasta with a rolling pin (or in a pasta machine) into a thin sheet; roll upon itself and with a very sharp knife, cut into long fettuccine strips.

3 Prepare the olive sauce. Place the butter in a bowl, break up into pieces and let it soften at room temperature. During this time, remove the kernels with an appropriate tool, rinse repeatedly with cold water, drain, and dry with a very clean towel; chop finely or blend in a food processor.

4 Rinse the capers in running water, drain, dry and chop finely. Work the butter with a wooden spoon until it swells and is foamy; add the chopped olives, the chopped capers, the grated lemon rind, the oil, the lemon juice and a pinch of salt and pepper. Mix vigorously until the ingredients are will blended and creamy.

5 Cook the fettuccine in a pot with abundant boiling salted water. Add 2 tablespoons of the cooking water to the olive cream and mix well. Drain the fettuccine when al dente, toss with the olive sauce and serve.

Fettuccine with oyster mushrooms

Difficulty **easy** • *Time needed* **under an hour** • *Calories per serving* **410**

INGREDIENTS
serves 4

For the pasta
UNBLEACHED FLOUR *3 cups*
SALT *to taste*

For the sauce
OYSTER MUSHROOMS *11 oz*
TOMATOES *8 oz, ripe and firm*
PARSLEY *1 bunch*
BASIL *1 bunch*
GARLIC *2 cloves*
EXTRA VIRGIN OLIVE OIL *6 tablespoons*
SALT & PEPPER *to taste*

1 Prepare the pasta dough. Sift the flour and form a mound on the work surface; add a pinch of salt and enough luke-warm water to make a dough that is smooth and elastic; cover with plastic wrap and let rest for about 30 minutes.

2 In the meantime, prepare the sauce. Carefully clean the mushrooms, removing the earth, rinse quickly in cold water, drain, pat dry and cut into pieces. Scald the tomatoes in boiling water, drain, peel, squeeze gently to remove the seeds and the water and chop the flesh coarsely.

3 Rinse the parsley and the basil; dry and chop the parsley and cut the basil into strips. Peel the garlic and crush. Heat 3 tablespoons of olive oil in a skillet and cook 1 garlic clove with a little chopped parsley without browning. Add the mushrooms and fry for 2-3 minutes, stirring with a wooden spoon; season with salt and pepper.

4 In another pan, heat the remaining oil and cook the other garlic clove without browning. Add the chopped tomatoes, a dash of salt and pepper, and continue cooking over high heat for about 5 minutes. Add the mushrooms and cook another 2-3 minutes.

5 Roll out the pasta with a rolling pin into a thin sheet; cut into strips about 2 inch long. Fold the pasta strips over a stick a little thicker than a match and let dry. Boil abundant water, add salt and cook the pasta. When al dente, drain, mix with the mushroom sauce, sprinkle with the remaining chopped parsley and with the basil strips; serve immediately.

Fettuccine alla romana

Difficulty **easy** • *Time needed* **under an hour** • *Calories per serving* **580**

INGREDIENTS
serves 4

For the pasta
UNBLEACHED FLOUR *4 cups*
EGGS *3*
SALT *to taste*

For the sauce
CHICKEN LIVERS & GIBLETS *7 oz*
DRIED MUSHROOMS *1 oz*
ONION *1*
SAGE *1 leaf*
GRATED PARMIGIANO *2 tablespoons*
BUTTER *3 tablespoons*
EXTRA VIRGIN OLIVE OIL *4 tablespoons*
SALT & PEPPER *to taste*

1 Soak the dried mushrooms in a little lukewarm water. Prepare the pasta dough. Sift the flour and form a mound on the work surface; add a pinch of salt and enough lukewarm water to make a dough that is smooth and elastic; cover with plastic wrap and let rest for about 30 minutes.

2 With a rolling pin, roll out the pasta into a thin sheet, roll it around itself, and , with a very sharp knife, cut the fettuccine about 3/8 inch wide. Lay out the fettuccine on a flour dusted surface and let dry.

3 Prepare the sauce. Clean the chicken livers and the giblets, rinse and dry them and cut into pieces. Peel the onion, rinse, dry and chop finely. In a skillet, heat half the oil with half the butter, add the chopped chicken livers and giblets and cook for 2-3 minutes, until lightly browned.

4 Season with a pinch of salt and fresh ground pepper, drain and set apart. In another pan, heat the remaining oil and butter, and cook the chopped onion with the sage until transparent. Drain and pat dry the mushrooms and dice. Put the mushrooms in the pan and cook over moderate heat for 2-3 minutes; season with salt and fresh ground pepper.

5 Add the chicken livers and giblets set apart, simmer for a minute and remove the pan from the heat. In the meantime, cook the pasta in abundant boiling salted water, drain when al dente and mix with the liver and mushroom sauce. Serve the fettuccine accompanied with grated parmigiano.

Fettuccine with vegetables

Difficulty **medium** • *Time needed* **under an hour** • *Calories per serving* **440**

INGREDIENTS
serves 4

FETTUCCINE *14 oz*
ZUCCHINI *8 oz*
TOMATOES *14 oz*
CELERY *1 stalk*
PARSLEY *1 tablespoon*
ONION *1*
GARLIC *1 clove*
EXTRA VIRGIN OLIVE OIL *3 tablespoons*
SALT & PEPPER *to taste*

1 Peel the tomatoes and remove the seeds and vegetal water; dice coarsely. Rinse the zucchini and the celery, removing the coarse fibers and cut both in julienne.

2 Trim, rinse, dry and chop the parsley together with the garlic clove. Peel the onion, slice and cook in a saucepan with the oil until transparent, stirring with a wooden spoon for about 2-3 minutes.

3 To the onion, add the zucchini, the celery, the tomatoes, the chopped parsley with the garlic, and a pinch of salt and pepper. Mix well and continue cooking for about 25 minutes.

4 In a large pot, boil about 4 quarts of water; add salt and drop in the fettuccine. When al dente, drain and pour into the pan with the sauce, blending carefully.

5 Replace the saucepan on the heat and toss the mixture for 2 or 3 minutes always stirring, then transfer to a serving bow and bring to the table at once.

Fettuccine with cream, peas and ham

Difficulty **easy** • *Time needed* **under an hour** • *Calories per serving* **600**

INGREDIENTS
serves 4

EGG FETTUCINE *11 oz*
COOKED HAM *5 oz, in two slices*
FRESH PEAS *11 oz*
HEAVY CREAM *1/4 cup*
BUTTER *2 tablespoons*
SALT *to taste*

1 Shell the peas, rinse them and cook in a pot with abundant salted water. In the meantime, cut the prosciutto into strips and cook in a skillet with the butter.

2 When the peas are cooked, drain, add the cooked ham and cook for 3 or 4 minutes, then add the cream and mix well to blend the ingredients.

3 When the fettuccine are cooked al dente, drain well and pour into the sauce which, by now, should be reduced. Toss in the pan still over the heat for a minute before serving.

Fried tagliatelle

Difficulty **medium** • *Time needed* **under an hour** • *Calories per serving* **400**

INGREDIENTS
serves 4

NESTS OF TAGLIATELLE *7 oz*
UNBLEACHED FLOUR *2 tablespoons*
EGGS *2*
MILK *to taste*
VEGETABLE BROTH *4 cups*
GRATED PARMIGIANO *4 tablespoons*
EXTRA VIRGIN OLIVE OIL *enough for frying*
SALT & PEPPER *to taste*

1 In a large casserole, heat the vegetable broth and as soon as it starts to boil, drop in the pasta taking care to not undo the nests while stirring and stopping the cooking when al dente.

2 In a large bowl, break the eggs, beat lightly and add the grated parmigiano, a pinch of salt, a dash of pepper, a little milk; then add the flour, sprinkling it and stirring continually to avoid lumps.

3 As soon as the pasta is cooked, be careful to not undo the nests. Heat abundant oil in the pot or in the deep fryer. Dip the pasta nests in the batter and drop into the heated oil.

4 Fry the tagliatelle until they are uniformly golden, dry on paper towels to remove the excess oil and place on a serving dish. Serve immediately.

Mushroom pasta with tomato sauce

Difficulty **medium** • *Time needed* **over an hour** • *Calories per serving* **570**

INGREDIENTS
serves 4

For the pasta
UNBLEACHED FLOUR **4 cups**
EGGS *1*
FRESH MUSHROOMS *11 oz*
VEGETABLE BROTH *1 cup*

For the sauce
PEELED TOMATOES *7 oz*
PANCETTA *2 oz*
SAGE *a few leaves*
BASIL *a few leaves*
GARLIC *1 clove*
GRATED PARMIGIANO *to taste*
EXTRA VIRGIN OLIVE OIL *2 tablespoons*
SALT & PEPPER *to taste*

1 Thoroughly clean the mushrooms and cook them in a casserole for 10 minutes with the vegetable broth; blend in a food processor, setting aside a little cooking broth. Sift the flour into a mound on the work surface; in the center, add the blended mushrooms, the egg and a little of the cooking broth.

2 Work the dough until it is smooth and elastic and let rest for about 20 minutes in a cool place, then roll out into a thin sheet and cut into 1 inch wide strips (called 'fungucce').

3 Dice the pancetta; peel and crush the garlic. Rinse and dry the basil. In a skillet, heat the oil and cook the pancetta with the crushed garlic; add the peeled tomatoes, the sage leaves, and the basil; season with salt and finish the cooking of the sauce over low heat.

4 Cook the pasta al dente in abundant boiling salted water; drain and season with a little pepper, grated parmigiano and mix with the tomato sauce. Serve at once.

SUGGESTION
In the preparation of the sauce, the pancetta can also be eliminated: in this case, remember to add a tablespoon of extra virgin olive oil to the measure indicated in the ingredients.

Fusilli with tofu ragù

Difficulty **medium** • *Time needed* **under an hour** • *Calories per serving* **470**

INGREDIENTS
serves 4

FUSILLI *14 oz*
TOFU *8 oz*
SOY SAUCE *1 tablespoon*
LEEK *1*
VEGETABLE BROTH *1 cup*
TAHINI *1 tablespoon*
SESAME SEED OIL *2 tablespoons*

1 Cut off the roots from the leek and remove the tougher green parts, rinse the remainder and chop finely with a sharp knife. Heat the oil in a casserole, add the chopped leek and cook slowly without browning. Break up the tofu into small pieces and add to the casserole, mix thoroughly and cook for several minutes.

2 Season the mixture with a teaspoon of soy sauce, add the vegetable broth and cook over moderate heat for 20 minutes, stirring now and then. As soon as the sauce is cooked, add the tahini. Cook the fusilli in abundant boiling salted water; when al dente, drain and pour into a tureen, add the sauce, mix and serve at once.

Seafood pasta salad

Difficulty **medium** • *Time needed* **under an hour** • *Calories per serving* **560**

INGREDIENTS
serves 4

LASAGNETTE *12 oz*
ASSORTED SEAFOOD *4 lbs*
(mussels, clams, razor clams, scampi, sea snails, shrimp)
ZUCCHINI *1*
PEPPER *1, small*
TOMATO *1, ripe and firm*
PARSLEY *1 bunch*
GARLIC *3 cloves*
SAFFRON *a pinch*
DRY WHITE WINE *4 tablespoons*
WINE VINEGAR *2 tablespoons*
EXTRA VIRGIN OLIVE OIL *4 tablespoons*
SALT & PEPPER *to taste*

1 Wash the clams, the razor clams, the scampi, the sea snails, and the shrimps; immerse them separately in abundant cold water for several hours in order to lose any sand inside them; scrape the mussels and wash them. Shell the shrimp and the scampi, remove the black veins and steam for 3-4 minutes; drain and set apart in a bowl.

2 Peel the garlic cloves; trim the zucchini, rinse and cut into pieces; was the tomato, remove the seeds and chop coarsely. Clean the pepper, removing the seeds and the white parts, rinse, dry and dice; rinse the parsley, dry it and chop finely.

3 Drain the sea snails, put in a pan with a garlic clove, add the chopped tomato and a little of the chopped parsley; cook over moderate heat for about 10 minutes. Drain, remove the meat from the shells with a match stick and add to the shrimp and scampi. In another pan, cook the clams, the razor clams, and the mussels with half garlic clove, a tablespoon of white wine and a little chopped parsley over medium heat, shaking the pan from time to time.

4 Drain the shellfish, eliminate those that have remained closed, remove the meat from the shells and add to the shrimp and snail mixture. Steam the zucchini for 2-3 minutes and put in a bowl; add the diced pepper and mix well.

5 In a large pot, bring abundant water to a boil, add salt and the saffron, and cook the pasta. When al dente, drain and transfer to a bowl, drizzle with 2 tablespoons of oil, mix well and let cool. In a mixing bowl, pour in the vinegar and the remaining oil, add a dash of salt and pepper and beat with a fork; add the remaining chopped parsley and season the zucchini and pepper mixture with a spoon of the dressing. Transfer the pasta into a serving bowl, add all the seafood and the vegetables, drizzle with the remaining dressing, mix carefully and serve the pasta cold.

Spaghetti salad

Difficulty **easy** • *Time needed* **less than 30 minutes** • *Calories per serving* **550**

INGREDIENTS
serves 4

SPAGHETTI *14 oz*
TUNA IN OLIVE OIL *5 oz*
GREEN & BLACK OLIVES *4 oz*
CAPERS PRESERVED IN SALT *2 oz*
CHILI PEPPER *1*
EXTRA VIRGIN OLIVE OIL *2 tablespoons*
SALT & PEPPER *to taste*

1 Cook the spaghetti al dente in abundant boiling salted water and drain; replace in the pot and drizzle with a little oil to avoid sticking. Crumble the tuna; remove the pits from the olives and chop into pieces. Rinse the capers to remove the salt and chop. Chop the chili pepper.

2 Pour all these ingredients onto the spaghetti, season with pepper and the chopped chili pepper and mix thoroughly. Transfer to a bowl and serve. If you like, leave the pasta in a cool place for a few hours to serve it cold.

> **SUGGESTION**
> *To make this pasta salad, you can also use other ingredients you like, preferably vegetables in julienne and vegetables preserved in vinegar.*

Spaghettini salad with arugula

Difficulty **easy** • *Time needed* **less than 30 minutes** • *Calories per serving* **430**

INGREDIENTS
serves 4

SPAGHETTINI *12 oz*
ARUGULA *7 oz*
TOMATOES *8*
RED ONION *1*
SALT *to taste*

For the dressing
CIDER VINEGAR *2 tablespoons*
GARLIC *1 clove*
EXTRA VIRGIN OLIVE OIL *4 tablespoons*
SALT & PEPPER *to taste*

1 Prepare the salad dressing. Peel the garlic and cut into thin pieces. In a mixing bowl, add the salt, the cider vinegar and the pepper; mix until all the salt is completely dissolved. Add the olive oil, the garlic and beat lightly with a fork until the dressing is well amalgamated.

2 Scald the tomatoes in boiling water, drain, remove the peel, the seeds and the vegetal water, and dice. Peel the onion, rinse, dry and chop. Rinse the arugula, dry and slice into strips.

3 Cook the spaghettini in abundant boiling salted water. When al dente, drain and transfer to a bowl; add the tomatoes, the onion and the arugula; toss with the dressing, mix quickly and serve.

> **SUGGESTION**
> *You can add a tablespoon of grated fresh ginger to the dressing as prepared in the recipe.*

Lagane and beans

Difficulty **medium** • *Time needed* **over an hour** • *Calories per serving* **470**

INGREDIENTS
serves 4

For the pasta
UNBLEACHED FLOUR 4 cups
SALT *to taste*

For the sauce
FRESH BEANS *12 oz*
GARLIC *2 cloves*
HOT CHILI PEPPER
1 small piece
EXTRA VIRGIN OLIVE OIL *4 tablespoons*
SALT *to taste*

1 Shell the beans, rinse and cook in a pot with salted cold water for about an hour and a half, from the start of boiling. In the meantime, prepare the pasta: on the work surface, make a mound with the flour and pour a dash of salt and enough lukewarm water to make a firm dough.

2 Knead the dough vigorously for 15 minutes; then make a ball, flatten lightly with your hands and roll out into a thin sheet with the aid of a rolling pin. Let the pasta dry for 15 minutes on the work surface and cut into strips about 1 1/4 inches wide.

3 Cook the "lagane" in abundant boiling salted water. During this time, peel the garlic and cook until golden in a skillet with the oil and a piece of chili pepper; remove from heat.

4 When al dente, drain the pasta, pour into a serving dish. Drain the cooked beans and add to the pasta with the cooked garlic and chili pepper; mix well and serve immediately.

SUGGESTION
The lagane can also be prepared with chickpeas or lentils, following the same instructions, but keeping in mind that they need to be soaked in water before cooking.

Laganelle with chickpeas

Difficulty **medium** • *Time needed* **over an hour** • *Calories per serving* **640**

INGREDIENTS
serves 4

LAGANELLE *14 oz*
CHICKPEAS *7 oz*
GARLIC *1 clove*
OREGANO *a generous pinch*
EXTRA VIRGIN OLIVE OIL *6 tablespoons*
SALT & PEPPER *to taste*

1 Soak the chickpeas in a bowl of water for 24 hours. Drain well, transfer to a pot and cover with at least 2 inches of water; cover the pot and cook over low heat for about 2 1/2 hours, adding a little hot water, if necessary.

2 About 10 minutes before the end of cooking, season with salt, add the laganelle and mix. Peel and crush the garlic; in a small pan, lightly brown with oil and oregano. The chickpeas and the laganelle should have absorbed all the water. Pour the garlic and oregano over the pasta and chickpeas, mix, season with pepper and serve.

Lasagne with poppy seeds

Difficulty **medium** • *Time needed* **over an hour** • *Calories per serving* **570**

INGREDIENTS
serves 4

UNBLEACHED FLOUR *4 cups*
POPPY SEEDS *1 oz*
EGGS *4*
SUGAR *1 oz*
BUTTER *4 tablespoons*
SALT *to taste*

1 Sift the flour onto the work surface and make a well in the center; add the eggs and a pinch of salt. Work the ingredients vigorously until the dough is smooth and elastic. Then with the aid of a rolling pin, roll out the dough into very thin sheets and cut into 1/2 inch wide strips. Lay out the lasagne delicately and let dry for at least an hour in a cool place.

2 Boil abundant water in a large pot to cook the pasta; in the meantime, grind the poppy seeds and the sugar with a mortar and pestle; melt the butter in a small skillet. Cook the pasta; when al dente, drain and toss with the ground poppy seeds and the melted butter. Serve at once.

Lasagne from Alba

Difficulty **medium** • *Time needed* **over an hour** • *Calories per serving* **770**

INGREDIENTS
serves 4

For the pasta
UNBLEACHED FLOUR *4 cups*
EGGS *2*
EXTRA VIRGIN OLIVE OIL *1 tablespoon*
SALT *to taste*

For the sauce
SWEETBREADS *7 oz*
SAUSAGE *5 oz*
PROSCIUTTO FAT *2 oz*
HEAVY CREAM *1/2 cup*
ONION *1/2, finely chopped*
CHOPPED PARSLEY *1 tablespoon*
ROSEMARY *the leaves of 1 branch, chopped*
BUTTER *1 tablespoon*
SALT *to taste*

1 Sift the four on the work surface; in the center, add the eggs, the oil, a few tablespons of water and pinch of salt. Work the ingredients vigorously until the dough is firm, adding more water, if necessary. Roll out the dough with a rolling pin into a thin sheet.

2 With a rotary cutter, cut the lasagne about 5 inches long and 3/4 inch wide. Dust the work surface with flour and lay out the lasagne to dry.

3 Prepare the sauce. Scald the sweetbreads in boiling water, remove skin and cut into pieces; remove skin from the sausage. Melt butter in a small casserole and cook the onion, the parsley, the rosemary and the prosciutto fat.

4 When the onion is golden, add the sausage and the sweetbreads. Season with a pinch of salt, cover and cook over low heat for about 30 minutes.

5 Cook the lasagne al dente in abundant boiling salted water. Carefully drain, mix with the cream and add the sauce; mix thoroughly. Transfer to a serving bowl and serve at once.

SUGGESTION
In you want to lighten the taste of this preparation, eliminate the sausage, the prosciutto fat and the cream.

Lasagne with anchovy and tomato sauce

Difficulty **medium** • *Time needed* **over an hour** • *Calories per serving* **560**

INGREDIENTS
serves 4

For the pasta
UNBLEACHED FLOUR *4 cups*
EGGS *4*
SALT *to taste*

For the sauce
LEEKS *8*
TOMATO SAUCE *11 oz*
SALTED ANCHOVIES *5*
BUTTER *2 tablespoons*
SALT *to taste*

1 Sift the flour on the work surface, add a pinch of salt in the middle with the eggs and mix the ingredients slowly; knead the dough vigorously for 15 minutes until it is smooth and elastic.

2 Form a ball, flatten it gently and, using a rolling pin, roll out into a thin sheet; dust with flour and roll onto itself; with a sharp knife, cut the lasagne about 1 1/2 inches wide and let rest for 30 minutes.

3 Rinse the leeks, cut the roots and the tough green parts and cut into thin slices; desalt and debone the anchovies. Put the leeks and the anchovies in a pan with the butter and cook the leeks lightly and let the anchovies dissolve stirring with a wooden spoon. Add the tomato sauce, season with salt, cover and cook over low heat for 20 minutes.

4 In the meantime, cook the lasagne in abundant boiling salted water; drain when al dente. Toss with the sauce and serve at once.

Linguini with sea urchins

Difficulty **medium** • *Time needed* **less than 30 minutes** • *Calories per serving* **460**

INGREDIENTS
serves 4

LINGUINI *12 oz*
SEA URCHINS *2 lbs*
CHIVES *1 bunch*
PARSLEY *1 bunch*
EXTRA VIRGIN OLIVE OIL *4 tablespoons*
SALT *to taste*

1 Rinse the chives and the parsley, dry gently, then cut the chives crosswise and chop the parsley. Open the sea urchins, extract the pulp with a spoon, put in a bowl and set apart.

2 In a large pot, cook the linguini in abundant boiling salted water; drain when al dente, reserving 3 tablespoons of the cooking water. In the meantime, heat the oil in a skillet with a tablespoonful of chives and one of parsley, add the sea urchins, the cooked linguini, and the reserved pasta cooking water.

3 Unite the flavors, mixing delicately with pasta tongs. Remove the pan from the heat, add the remaining chives and the parsley, mix gently and serve immediately.

Linguini with savoy cabbage

Difficulty **easy** • *Time needed* **under an hour** • *Calories per serving* **400**

INGREDIENTS
serves 4

LINGUINI *11 oz*
FRESH ANCHOVIES *5 oz*
SAVOY CABBAGE *1/2*
LEMON *1*
GARLIC *1 clove*
CHILI PEPPER *1 small piece, crushed*
WHITE WINE VINEGAR *2 tablespoons*
EXTRA VIRGIN OLIVE OIL *4 tablespoons*
SALT & PEPPER *to taste*

1 Press the lemon and pour the juice into a bowl. Clean the anchovies; discard the innards, debone, remove the heads, rinse in abundant cold water, drain and pat dry with a kitchen towel. Lay them out in a deep dish, sprinkle with salt and the chili pepper and pour the lemon juice over them. Let marinate for about 2 hours; after one hour, sprinkle with 2 tablespoons of olive oil.

2 Discard the large and hard outer leaves of the savoy cabbage, cut out the stem and slice the tender leaves into thin strips. Rinse in abundant cold water. Transfer into a saucepan with the remaining oil and the garlic; pour in the vinegar and water to just cover; season with salt and pepper. Slowly bring to a boil, cover and continue cooking for about 20 minutes over medium heat, stirring from time to time. About 2 minutes before the end of cooking, drain the anchovies and add to the cabbage, mixing well.

3 In the meantime, cook the linguini in abundant boiling salted water until al dente. Drain and toss with the prepared sauce. Serve immediately.

Linguini alla parmigiana

Difficulty **easy** • *Time needed* **less than 30 minutes** • *Calories per serving* **500**

INGREDIENTS
serves 4

LINGUINI *12 oz*
COOKED HAM *3 oz, in 1 slice*
CARROT *1*
CELERY *1 stalk*
GRATED PARMIGIANO *3 tablespoons*
BUTTER *3 tablespoons*
SALT & PEPPER *to taste*

1 Trim and peel the carrot; clean the celery, removing the larger filaments. Rinse the carrot and the celery, dry and chop finely. Dice the cooked ham and set apart. Melt the butter in a skillet, add the chopped celery and carrot and cook without browning.

2 Season with a pinch of salt and fresh ground pepper, add 2-3 tablespoons of water, cover and continue cooking over moderate heat for 8-10 minutes, stirring from time to time with a wooden spoon. A few minutes before done, add the diced ham to the sauce.

3 In the meantime, boil abundant water in a large pot, add salt and cook the pasta. When al dente, drain and add to the sauce in the pan. Sprinkle the linguini with half the grated parmigiano, mixing with a large fork to blend the flavors. Serve the pasta hot accompanied with the remaining parmigiano.

Linguini with mushrooms and walnuts

Difficulty **medium** • *Time needed* **over an hour** • *Calories per serving* **450**

INGREDIENTS
serves 4

LINGUINI *11 oz*
MUSHROOMS *8 oz*
SHELLED WALNUTS *2 oz*
TOMATOES *1 lb*
ONION *1*
GARLIC *1 clove*
CHOPPED PARSLEY *1 tablespoon*
CINNAMON *1 teaspoon*
ALLSPICE *1 teaspoon*
GRATED GINGER *1 teaspoon*
EXTRA VIRGIN OLIVE OIL *3 tablespoons*
SALT & PEPPER *to taste*

1 Peel and chop the onion; peel and crush the garlic clove. Heat a tablespoon of oil in a skillet and cook the onion, the garlic and the spices until the onion is transparent.

2 Clean the mushrooms, rinse, dry and dice them. Add the mushrooms to the skillet, cover and cook for 10 minutes, stirring from time to time. Peel the tomatoes, remove the seeds and the water and cut into pieces; add to the skillet, season with salt and pepper and cook for another 10 minutes.

3 Chop the walnuts coarsely and cook in another pan with the rest of the oil for 4-5 minutes until they start to brown. Add half the walnuts to the sauce.

4 Cook the linguini in abundant boiling salted water until al dente. Drain, transfer to a serving bowl, add the sauce and toss well. Sprinkle with the remaining walnuts and the chopped parsley. Serve immediately.

Linguini with clams and anchovies

Difficulty **medium** • *Time needed* **under an hour** • *Calories per serving* **520**

INGREDIENTS
serves 4

LINGUINI *12 oz*
CLAMS *11 oz*
FRESH ANCHOVIES *11 oz*
TOMATOES *14 oz, ripe and firm*
CAPERS PRESERVED IN SALT *1 tablespoon*
GARLIC *1 clove*
CHILI PEPPER *1 small piece*
OREGANO *to taste*
EXTRA VIRGIN OLIVE OIL *5 tablespoons*
SALT *to taste*

1 Leave the clams in abundant cold water for a few hours so they lose any sand. Scald the tomatoes in boiling water, drain, peel, and remove the seeds and the water; dice the tomato flesh.

2 Clean the anchovies, discard the head and the innards, rinse thoroughly, pat dry with a kitchen towel and cut into pieces. Rinse the capers under running water, removing all the salt and dry them.

3 Drain the clams and put in a saucepan, add the crushed garlic, a tablespoon of oil, cover and cook over high heat shaking the pan from time to time to open the shells. Remove from heat and set apart; discard the clams that remain closed.

4 In a pan, heat the remaining oil with the chili pepper, add the anchovies, season with a pinch of salt and cook for about 2 minutes; drain and set apart. In the same pan, cook the tomatoes and the capers for about 10 minutes over moderate heat, stirring from time to time. Add the reserved anchovies, the clams and season with a pinch of oregano.

5 In the meantime, cook the linguini in abundant boiling salted water; drain when al dente, mix with the prepared sauce and serve immediately.

SUGGESTION
Without a doubt, pasta served with the clams in the shell is very attractive, but also inconvenient to consume. In fact, the time it takes to extract the flesh from the shells lets the pasta cool and the final taste suffers. It is therefore advisable to discard the shells or, at least, leave only one as an indication of the freshness of the dish.

Maccheroni alla chitarra with meat sauce

Difficulty **medium** • *Time needed* **over an hour** • *Calories per serving* **630**

INGREDIENTS
serves 6

For the pasta
UNBLEACHED FLOUR *4 cups*
EGGS *1*
SALT *to taste*

For the sauce
PORK *4 oz*
VEAL *4 oz*
LAMB *4 oz*
PANCETTA *2 oz, in 1 slice*
CARROTS *1*
CELERY *1 stalk*
ONION *1/2*
RED WINE *1/4 cup*
HOT CHILI PEPPER *1*
GRATED PECORINO *2 tablespoons*
EXTRA VIRGIN OLIVE OIL *3 tablespoons*
SALT & PEPPER *to taste*

1 Prepare the pasta. Sift the flour on the work surface and make a mound; in the center break the egg, add a pinch of salt and enough lukewarm water to make a dough smooth and elastic. Cover the dough in plastic wrap and let rest for 30 minutes.

2 Prepare the sauce. Grind the pork, the veal and the lamb. Also dice the pancetta. Peel the onion, trim the carrot and peel it, clean the celery and remove the large fibers. Rinse the vegetables and chop. Heat the oil in a large pan, add the pancetta and cook briefly, add the onion, the celery and the carrot and cook, stirring from time to time with a wooden spoon.

3 Add the ground meat and cook over high heat until browned all over. Season with salt and pepper; pour on the wine and let it evaporate over high heat. Add the chili pepper, cover and cook the sauce over medium heat for about an hour.

4 Roll out the pasta with a rolling pin into a sheet 1/8 inch thick; cut the sheet to the size of the "chitarra". Dust with flour, lay out over the "chitarra" and pass over with the rolling pin, pressing strong enough to make the "maccheroni" drop onto the work surface.

5 Cook the maccheroni in abundant boiling salted water; when al dente, drain and toss with the prepared sauce. Transfer to a serving bowl and serve at once, accompanied with the grated pecorino.

SUGGESTION
The "chitarra" is a real instrument with keys and chords, commonly sold in Abruzzo, particularly in the province of Chieti. It is the small rolling pin that, pressed over the sheet of dough over the strings, makes the "maccheroni" drop onto the inclined surface below. If a "chitarra" is not available, you can use a normal pasta machine, set to make tagliolini.

Maccheroni alla chitarra with lamb ragù

Difficulty **medium** • *Time needed* **over an hour** • *Calories per serving* **520**

INGREDIENTS
serves 4

For the pasta
UNBLEACHED FLOUR *4 cups*
EGGS *3*
EXTRA VIRGIN OLIVE OIL *2 tablespoons*
SALT *a pinch*

For the sauce
LAMB *7 oz*
TOMATOES *11 oz, ripe and firm*
PARSLEY *1 bunch*
GARLIC *1 clove*
HOT CHILI PEPPER *1*
DRY WHITE WINE *1/2 cup*
GRATED PECORINO *2 tablespoons*
EXTRA VIRGIN OLIVE OIL *3 tablespoons*
SALT & PEPPER *to taste*

1 Prepare the pasta. Sift the flour into a mound on the work surface; in the center break the eggs, add the oil, the salt and work the ingredients vigorously until the dough becomes smooth and elastic.

2 Roll the dough into a sheet 1/8 inch thick; cut into the size of the "chitarra", dust with flour, lay over the strings and press with the rolling pin; press well to make the "maccheroni" fall onto the work surface.

3 Prepare the ragù. With a very sharp knife, chop the lamb into small pieces. Heat the oil in a skillet, add the crushed garlic, the diced lamb and cook over high heat until evenly browned; season with a pinch of salt and a dash of pepper. Add the white wine and let it evaporate.

4 Pass the tomatoes in a food mill and add to the skillet with the chili pepper; cover and cook the ragù over medium heat for about an hour. About 5 minutes before the end of cooking, add the chopped parsley.

5 Cook the "maccheroni" in abundant boiling salted water; drain when al dente and toss with the lamb ragù. Serve at once, accompanied with the grated pecorino.

Maltagliati with tuna and zucchini

Difficulty **easy** • *Time needed* **under an hour** • *Calories per serving* **490**

INGREDIENTS
serves 4

For the pasta
UNBLEACHED FLOUR *4 cups*
EGGS *3*
SALT *to taste*

For the sauce
TOMATOES *11 oz, ripe and firm*
TUNA IN OLIVE OIL *4 oz*
ZUCCHINI *7 oz, small*
ONION *1*
GARLIC *1 clove*
PARSLEY *1 bunch*
EXTRA VIRGIN OLIVE OIL *4 tablespoons*
SALT & PEPPER *to taste*

1 Prepare the pasta. Sift the flour on the work surface into a mound; in the center, break the eggs, add a pinch of salt and work the ingredients until the dough is smooth and elastic; cover with plastic wrap and let rest for at least 30 minutes.

2 Roll out the pasta in a thin sheet and, with an indented rotary cutter, cut the "maltagliati"; lay out on the work surface and let dry.

3 Prepare the sauce. Scald the tomatoes in boiling water, drain, peel, remove the seeds and the water, dice the flesh. Drain the tuna and crumble into pieces. Trim the zucchini, rinse, dry and cut into slices.

4 Peel the onion and the garlic, rinse, dry and chop; rinse the parsley, dry and chop finely. Heat the oil in a pan and cook the garlic and the onion until transparent; add the zucchini and cook for 2-3 minutes.

5 Add the tomatoes, season with a pinch of salt and fresh ground pepper and continue cooking for 7-8 minutes over medium heat. About 3 minutes before the end, add the tuna; finally, sprinkle with the chopped parsley.

6 Cook the "maltagliati" in abundant boiling salted water; drain when al dente, toss with the ragù and serve immediately.

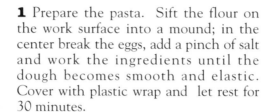
Maltagliati with porcini mushrooms and zucchini

Difficulty **medium** • *Time needed* **under an hour** • *Calories per serving* **510**

INGREDIENTS
serves 4

For the pasta
UNBLEACHED FLOUR *4 cups*
EGGS *3*
SALT *to taste*

For the sauce
PORCINI MUSHROOMS *11 oz*
TOMATOES *11 oz, ripe and firm*
ZUCCHINI *2*
ONION *1*
PARSLEY *1 bunch*
GARLIC *2 cloves*
GRATED PARMIGIANO *3 tablespoons*
EXTRA VIRGIN OLIVE OIL *5 tablespoons*
SALT & PEPPER *to taste*

1 Prepare the pasta. Sift the flour on the work surface into a mound; in the center break the eggs, add a pinch of salt and work the ingredients until the dough becomes smooth and elastic. Cover with plastic wrap and let rest for 30 minutes.

2 In the meantime, prepare the sauce. Clean the mushrooms, removing the earthy and hard parts, rinse quickly under cold water, drain, pat dry carefully with a kitchen towel and cut into slices; rinse, dry and chop the parsley.

3 Trim the zucchini, rinse and cut into slices; peel the garlic and the onion, chop the onion with one garlic clove and crush the other clove. Scald the tomatoes in boiling water, drain, remove the peel, the seeds, the water and dice coarsely.

4 Heat 3 tablespoons of oil in a skillet and cook the crushed garlic clove; add the zucchini and cook for about 2-3 minutes. Add the diced tomatoes, season

with a pinch of salt and pepper and continue cooking for 5-6 minutes over medium heat.

5 In another pan, heat the remaining oil and cook the chopped onion and the garlic until transparent; add the sliced mushrooms and cook for 2-3 minutes. Season with a pinch of salt and pepper, sprinkle with the chopped parsley and add to the mixture of zucchini and tomatoes.

6 Roll out the pasta in a thin sheet and cut into 1 1/4 inch wide strips; cook in abundant boiling salted water; when al dente, drain and toss with the zucchini and mushroom sauce. Sprinkle the pasta with the grated parmigiano and serve at once.

SUGGESTION
You can use a different type of pasta if you like; for example, pappardelle (as seen in the photo below).

Spaghetti with cauliflower

Difficulty **medium** • *Time needed* **over an hour** • *Calories per serving* **440**

INGREDIENTS
serves 4

SPAGHETTI *12 oz*
CAULIFLOWER *1, about 1 1/2 lbs*
TOMATO PASTE *1 teaspoon*
CELERY *1 stalk*
PARSLEY *1 bunch*
GARLIC *1 clove*
GRATED PECORINO *4 tablespoons*
EXTRA VIRGIN OLIVE OIL *2 tablespoons*
SALT & PEPPER *to taste*

1 Rinse the cauliflower and cut into small pieces. Peel the garlic; trim and rinse the parsley; trim the celery stalk and rinse it; then chop these 3 ingredients and cook in a casserole with the oil.

2 When the mixture is nicely golden, dilute the tomato paste in 1/2 cup of hot water and add to the casserole; reduce the liquid a little and add the cauliflower; season with salt and continue cooking for about an hour adding a little water or vegetable broth from time to time. When cooked, the cauliflower should be completely undone and should have the appearance of a dense cream.

3 In the meantime, cook the pasta in abundant boiling salted water. When al dente, drain, pour into the casserole with the cauliflower and, stirring continually, leave it on the heat; finally, add the pecorino, season with pepper and serve immediately.

Spinach and egg pasta with peas

Difficulty **easy** • *Time needed* **under an hour** • *Calories per serving* **510**

INGREDIENTS
serves 4

GREEN TAGLIATELLE 5 oz
EGG TAGLIATELLE 5 oz
SHELLED PEAS 7 oz
COOKED HAM 4 oz
SAGE a few leaves
HEAVY CREAM 2 tablespoons
GRATED PARMIGIANO 3 tablespoons
BUTTER 1 tablespoon
SALT to taste

1 Heat the butter with the sage in a skillet; add the cream and bring to a boil. Add the peas and continue cooking for about 15 minutes. In the meantime, cook the tagliatelle in abundant boiling salted water.

2 Cut the ham into thin strips. When al dente, drain the pasta and transfer to a serving dish; add the ham, the prepared sauce and the grated parmigiano. Mix well and serve at once.

> **SUGGESTION**
> *You can substitute the heavy cream with 4 oz of natural yogurt.*

Spinach and egg pasta with ricotta

Difficulty **easy** • *Time needed* **less than 30 minutes** • *Calories per serving* **570**

INGREDIENTS
serves 4

PAGLIA E FIENO 14 oz
RICOTTA 11 oz
NUTMEG a pinch
GRATED PARMIGIANO 2 oz
BUTTER 2 tablespoons
SALT & PEPPER to taste

1 Melt the butter in a skillet. In a large pot, bring abundant water to a boil, add salt and cook the pasta al dente.

2 In the meantime, in a bowl, mix the melted butter with the ricotta (if needed, add a few tablespoons of the pasta cooking water), a few tablespoons of grated parmigiano, a pinch of salt, a dash of fresh ground pepper and the nutmeg.

3 When the pasta is ready, drain well, pour into the bowl with the prepared sauce, toss well and serve immediately.

> **SUGGESTION**
> *You could also prepare the ricotta and butter sauce by adding a little dried herbs or some freshly chopped parsley.*

Pappardelle with hare ragù

Difficulty **medium** • *Time needed* **over an hour** • *Calories per serving* **750**

INGREDIENTS
serves 4-6

FRESH PAPPARDELLE *11 oz*
HARE *1, small, cleaned*
ONION *1*
GARLIC *1 clove*
ROSEMARY *1 branch*
JUNIPER BERRIES *4-5*
CINNAMON *1 small piece*
CLOVES *2*
BEEF BROTH *1/2 cup*
DRY RED WINE *1/2 cup*
BUTTER *1 tablespoon*
EXTRA VIRGIN OLIVE OIL *3 tablespoons*
SALT & PEPPER *to taste*

1 Wash the hare, dry with a kitchen towel and cut into pieces. Peel the onion and slice; peel the garlic clove and lightly crush; chop the rosemary; grind the cinnamon.

2 Heat the butter and 2 tablespoons of oil in a skillet, add the chopped rosemary, the crushed garlic, the juniper berries, the ground cinnamon, the sliced onion and the cloves; cook until the onion is transparent. Pour the mixture into a bowl and set apart.

3 Pour the remaining oil in the same pan, add the pieces of hare and cook over high heat browning evenly all over. In a small pot, bring the beef broth to a boil and keep hot.

4 Drizzle the hare with the red wine and let evaporate a little; add the mixture of onion and herbs reserved, the hot beef broth, and season everything with a pinch of salt and some fresh ground pepper. Cover and continue cooking over medium heat for about an hour, stirring from time to time with a wooden spoon.

5 Cook the pappardelle in abundant boiling salted water; when al dente, drain, mix with 1/3 of the hare ragù; transfer to a serving plate and pour the remaining ragù with the pieces of hare over the pasta.

Pappardelle with duck

Difficulty **medium** • *Time needed* **over an hour** • *Calories per serving* **680**

INGREDIENTS
serves 4

For the pasta
UNBLEACHED FLOUR *3 cups*
EGGS *3*
SALT *to taste*

For the sauce
DUCK BREAST *11 oz*
PROSCIUTTO *3 oz, in 1 slice*
TOMATOES *11 oz, ripe and firm*
CARROT *1*
CELERY *1 stalk*
ONION *1*
SAGE *1 leaf*
PARSLEY *1 bunch*
BASIL *1 bunch*
BAY LEAVES *1*
DRY WHITE WINE *1/4 cup*
GRATED PARMIGIANO *2 tablespoons*
BUTTER *1 tablespoon*
EXTRA VIRGIN OLIVE OIL *4 tablespoons*
SALT & PEPPER *to taste*

1 Prepare the pasta. Sift the flour on the work surface and make a mound; in the center, break the eggs, add the salt and work the ingredients until the dough becomes elastic and homogenous; cover with plastic wrap and let rest for about 30 minutes.

2 In the meantime, wash the duck breast, pat dry and cut into pieces, setting aside 2 or 3 of the biggest pieces. Dice the cooked ham; cut the ends of the carrot and peel it; peel the onion and remove the large fibers from the celery. Rinse the vegetables and chop finely; rinse the sage, the parsley, the basil and the bay leaf; dry them all. Chop the basil and the parsley.

3 Scald the tomatoes in boiling water; drain, peel, remove the seeds and the vegetal water and dice. Heat the butter and the oil in a skillet, add the bay leaf, the sage, a little of the parsley and the basil, the chopped onion, the carrot and the celery; cook until the onion is transparent.

4 Add the ham and cook briefly; add the pieces of duck breast and brown all over; pour in the white wine and let it evaporate over high heat. Add the tomatoes, 1/4 cup of water, season with a pinch of salt and pepper; cover and continue cooking for 40-50 minutes over medium heat; stirring from time to time. When done, discard the bay leaf and the sage.

5 Roll out the pasta with rolling pin to a thickness of about 1/16 inch; with an indented roller, cut into 3/4 inch wide strips (or roll the pasta onto itself and cut thin strips with a sharp knife).

6 Cook the pappardelle in abundant boiling salted water; when al dente, drain and toss with the duck ragù. Sprinkle with the remaining chopped parsley and basil. Top with the grated parmigiano and serve at once.

Green pappardelle with shrimp and baby cuttlefish

Difficulty **easy** • *Time needed* **under an hour** • *Calories per serving* **480**

INGREDIENTS
serves 4

For the pasta
UNBLEACHED FLOUR *3 cups*
SPINACH *8 oz*
EGGS *2*
SALT *to taste*

For the sauce
SHRIMP *7 oz*
BABY CUTTLEFISH *11 oz*
TOMATOES *7 oz, ripe and firm*
GARLIC *1 clove*
EXTRA VIRGIN OLIVE OIL *4 tablespoons*
SALT & PEPPER *to taste*

1 Prepare the pasta. Clean the spinach, rinse in abundant cold water, drain and cook in a non-stick pan for about 3 minutes. Chop the spinach finely, return to the pan and cook to dry over moderate heat, stirring with a wooden spoon; drain, transfer to a mixing bowl and let cool.

2 Sift the flour on the work surface into a mound; in the center, place the spinach, the eggs, a pinch of salt and work the ingredients until the dough is smooth and elastic. Cover with plastic wrap and let rest for about 30 minutes in a cool place.

3 In the meantime, prepare the sauce. Scald the tomatoes in boiling water, drain, remove the skin, squeeze to remove the seeds and the water and dice the pulp. Shell the shrimp, rinse and dry; peel the garlic and chop finely.

4 Clean the baby cuttlefish, wash and cut into pieces. Heat the oil in a skillet and cook the garlic without browning. Add the baby cuttlefish and cook for 2-3 minutes; add the shrimp, cook for 2 minutes, add the tomatoes, season with salt and pepper and continue cooking for another 4-5 minutes.

5 Roll out the pasta in a thin sheet and cut into pappardelle. Cook the pappardelle in abundant boiling salted water; when al dente, drain and toss with the prepared mixture. Serve at once.

Pasta with anchovy and tomato sauce

Difficulty **medium** • *Time needed* **under an hour** • *Calories per serving* **480**

INGREDIENTS
serves 4

For the pasta
UNBLEACHED FLOUR *4 cups*
EGGS *3*
SALT *to taste*

For the sauce
TOMATOES *1 lb, ripe and firm*
SALTED ANCHOVIES *4*
BREAD CRUMBS *2 oz*
GARLIC *1 clove*
PARSLEY *1 bunch*
EXTRA VIRGIN OLIVE OIL *4 tablespoons*
SALT & PEPPER *to taste*

1 Prepare the pasta. Sift the flour on the work surface into a mound; in the center, break the eggs, add a pinch of salt and work the ingredients until the dough is smooth and elastic; cover with plastic wrap and let rest for 30 minutes.

2 At the end of this time, roll out the dough into a thin sheet; dust with a little flour, roll onto itself and, with a sharp knife, cut the pappardelle to a width of about 1/2 inch; lay out on a flour dusted surface and let dry.

3 In the meantime, prepare the sauce. Scald the tomatoes in boiling water, drain, remove the skin, squeeze gently to remove the seeds and the water and chop coarsely. Peel the garlic, rinse, dry and chop it; rinse the parsley, dry and chop finely.

4 Rinse the anchovies under running water to eliminate all the salt; debone, dry and cut into pieces. Heat the oil in a skillet and cook the chopped garlic with a little parsley without browning; add the anchovies and cook briefly, stirring with a wooden spoon. Add the tomatoes, season with a pinch of salt and pepper and continue cooking the sauce for about 15 minutes over moderate heat.

5 In a large pot, bring abundant water to a boil, add salt and cook the pasta. Cook the bread crumbs in a non-stick pan and, stirring with a wooden spoon, lightly brown them; remove from the heat. When al dente, drain the pasta, toss with the prepared sauce, sprinkle with the bread crumbs, the remaining chopped parsley and serve at once.

Pasta alla Norma

Difficulty **easy** • *Time needed* **under an hour** • *Calories per serving* **480**

INGREDIENTS
serves 4

SPAGHETTI *11 oz*
EGGPLANT *11 oz*
CRUSHED TOMATOES *11 oz*
BASIL *a few leaves*
GARLIC *1 clove*
GRATED AGED RICOTTA *2 oz*
EXTRA VIRGIN OLIVE OIL *to taste*
SALT & PEPPER *to taste*

1 Trim and clean the eggplant; cut into slices and put in layers in a colander, generously sprinkling with coarse salt. Place a weight on top and let the vegetation water drain off for 30 minutes. At the end of this time, rinse the eggplant in running water.

2 Heat 2 tablespoons of oil in a shallow casserole with two handles. Peel and crush the garlic clove and cook in the casserole. After 2-3 minutes discard the garlic, add the crushed tomatoes, season with a pinch of salt and cook over low heat for 15 minutes.

3 Heat abundant oil in a saucepan and when hot but not smoking, put in the eggplant; fry until golden on both side. When done, drain and put on absorbent kitchen towels.

4 Cook the spaghetti in abundant boiling salted water until al dente; drain and toss with the tomato sauce. Separate into individual serving plates; sprinkle with the grated ricotta and garnish with the eggplant and the basil.

SUGGESTION
You can also prepare the tomato sauce using an onion instead of the garlic.

Pasta with sardines

Difficulty **medium** • *Time needed* **under an hour** • *Calories per serving* **570**

INGREDIENTS
serves 4

PERCIATELLI *12 oz*
FRESH SARDINES *14 oz*
WILD FENNEL *3 bulbs*
RAISINS *1 tablespoon*
SARDINES PRESERVED IN SALT *3*
ONION *1*
PINE NUTS *1 tablespoon*
GARLIC *1 clove*
SAFFRON *1 sachet*
EXTRA VIRGIN OLIVE OIL *6 tablespoons*
SALT & PEPPER *to taste*

1 Soak the raisins in a bowl of lukewarm water. Clean the sardines by cutting off the heads and deboning; wash, dry and cut into 2 or 3 pieces. Clean the wild fennel, rinse and cook in abundant boiling salted water; drain remove with a perforated ladle to save the cooking water; chop coarsely.

2 Rinse the sardine fillets with running water to eliminate all the salt; cut into small pieces. Peel the garlic and the onion; rinse and chop finely. Heat 3 tablespoons of oil in a skillet and cook the chopped onion and garlic without browning.

3 Add the desalted sardine pieces and cook briefly stirring with a wooden spoon. Pat dry the raisins and add to the pan; add the wild fennel, the pine nuts and cook for a minute; dissolve the saffron in 1/4 cup of water and add to the mixture; season with salt and pepper.

4 Heat the remaining oil in a pan and cook the fresh sardines, add to the wild fennel sauce and cook for about 2 minutes. Cook the perciatelli in boiling salted water; when al dente, drain and toss with the sauce. Serve immediately.

SUGGESTION

In some areas of Sicily there is a delicious variation of this dish: after cooking the pasta, toss with half the prepared sauce and place in layers in a baking dish, alternating with the remaining sauce. Gratinée in the oven and serve as you prefer, hot, warm or cold.

Fresh pasta with lemon

Difficulty **medium** • *Time needed* **under an hour** • *Calories per serving* **370**

INGREDIENTS
serves 4

For the pasta
UNBLEACHED FLOUR *2 cups*
UNTREATED LEMON *1*
EGGS *2*
GRATED PARMIGIANO *2 tablespoons*
SALT *a pinch*

For the sauce
NUTMEG *a pinch*
GRATED PARMIGIANO *3 tablespoons*
BUTTER *3 tablespoons*

1 Prepare the pasta dough. Rinse the lemon, dry it and grate the rind (only the yellow part). Sift the flour onto the work surface in a mound. Break the eggs in the center, add the grated lemon rind, the grated parmigiano, and the salt.

2 Work the ingredients and knead the dough until it is smooth and elastic; cover with a lightly floured kitchen towel and let rest for half an hour. With a rolling pin, roll out the dough into a thin sheet. Dust the surface with flour, roll onto itself and, with a very sharp knife, cut the tagliatelle about 1/4 inch wide. Stretch out the tagliatelle on the work surface and let dry.

3 Cook the tagliatelle in abundant boiling salted water until al dente. Melt the butter with the nutmeg in a small pan. Drain the tagliatelle, transfer to a deep dish, drizzle with the flavored butter and serve with the grated parmigiano.

Pasta with sausage and pancetta

Difficulty **easy** • *Time needed* **under an hour** • *Calories per serving* **660**

INGREDIENTS
serves 4

For the pasta
UNBLEACHED FLOUR *4 cups*
EGGS *3*
SALT *to taste*

For the sauce
SAUSAGE *4 oz*
PANCETTA *3 oz*
EGGS *2*
ONION *1*
PARSLEY *1 bunch*
BASIL *1 bunch*
MILK *5 tablespoons*
GRATED PECORINO *2 tablespoons*
EXTRA VIRGIN OLIVE OIL *2 tablespoons*
SALT & PEPPER *to taste*

1 Prepare the pasta. Sift the flour onto the work surface into a mound; break the eggs in the center, add a pinch of salt and work the ingredients until the dough becomes smooth and elastic; cover with plastic wrap and let rest for at least 30 minutes.

2 In the meantime, remove the skin from the sausage and break into pieces; dice the pancetta. Rinse the parsley and the basil, dry delicately with a kitchen towel and chop finely; peel the onion, rinse and chop finely.

3 Roll out the pasta dough into a sheet not too thin; dust the surface with a little flour, roll the sheet onto itself and, with a sharp knife, slice the tagliatelle about 3/4 inch wide; lay out on the flour dusted work surface and let dry a little.

4 Cook the diced pancetta in a non-stick pan, letting it brown all over; Drain and set apart; in the same pan, cook the sausage, letting it brown uni-formly; then drain it. In a large saucepan, heat the oil and cook the onion until transparent; add the diced pancetta and the sausage and cook for a couple of minutes.

5 In the meantime, cook the pasta in abundant boiling salted water. Put the eggs in a bowl, add the grated pecorino, the milk, a pinch of salt and pepper, and lightly beat with a fork.

6 When al dente, drain the pasta, reserving a few tablespoons of cooking water; transfer the pasta into the saucepan with the pancetta and sausage mixture and add a few tablespoons of the cooking water. Remove the pan from the heat, add the mixture of eggs and cheese, season with a pinch of salt and fresh ground pepper; return the pan to moderate heat for a few seconds and mix well to blend the ingredients; the sauce should be soft and creamy. Sprinkle the pasta with the parsley and shredded basil. Serve at once.

Perciatelli with vegetables

Difficulty **easy** • *Time needed* **under an hour** • *Calories per serving* **460**

INGREDIENTS
serves 4

PERCIATELLI *12 oz*
EGG PLANT *1*
TOMATOES *11 oz, ripe and firm*
YELLOW PEPPER *1*
SALTED ANCHOVIES *2*
BLACK OLIVES *2 oz*
CAPERS *1 tablespoon*
BASIL *1 bunch*
GARLIC *2 cloves*
EXTRA VIRGIN OLIVE OIL *4 tablespoons*
SALT & PEPPER *to taste*

1 Clean the eggplant, dice and set aside in a colander. Add salt and let rest for 30 minutes. Clean the yellow pepper, cut it and discard all white parts. Dice the pepper. Peel the garlic and crush. Clean the basil, dry and tear in small pieces.

2 Scald the tomatoes, drain, peel and press them gently to remove all seeds; slice thinly. Rinse the anchovies under running water to remove some salt and chop finely.

3 In a skillet, heat 1 tablespoon of extra virgin olive oil and a garlic clove and cook on low heat for 3-4 minutes. Add a pinch of salt and pepper. Set aside. Rinse the eggplants and dry on paper towels.

4 In a pan, heat 4 tablespoons of extra virgin olive oil. Add the anchovies and one garlic clove. On low heat, cook for a few minutes. Add the eggplants and cook for 3 minutes, on medium heat. Add the tomatoes. Taste and add salt and pepper as needed. Cook for 10 minutes, stirring. Add the capers and cook another 5 minutes. Add the chopped olives, the diced peppers and the basil. Mix well and cook for 5 minutes.

5 Cook the pasta in abundant boiling salted water until al dente. Drain and transfer to a large serving bowl. Pour the sauce over the pasta and toss well until all ingredients are well mixed. Serve immediately.

Perciatelli with broccoli and pancetta

Difficulty **easy** • *Time needed* **less than 30 minutes** • *Calories per serving* **650**

INGREDIENTS
serves 4

PERCIATELLI *12 oz*
YOUNG BROCCOLI *1 1/4 lbs*
PANCETTA *4 oz*
TOMATO PASTE *1 tablespoon*
ONION *1*
GARLIC *1 clove*
VEGETABLE BROTH *1/2 cup*
GRATED PARMIGIANO *3 tablespoons*
EXTRA VIRGIN OLIVE OIL *3 tablespoons*
SALT & PEPPER *to taste*

1 Separate the broccoli in florets, discard the stems, rinse with cold water and drain. Peel and chop the garlic and the onion. Dice the pancetta.

2 In a large pan, heat the extra virgin olive oil and sauté the pancetta until just golden. Drain and set aside. In the same pan, add the chopped onions and garlic and cook until the onions are transparent. Return the pancetta to the pan; add the tomato paste and the veg-etable broth. Cook on medium heat for 10 minutes. Taste and add salt and pepper.

3 During this time, in abundant boiling salted water, cook the pasta for 4 minutes. Add the broccoli florets to the pasta water and cook with the pasta, until the pasta is al dente. Drain and transfer to the large pan. Toss well and serve with the grated parmigiano cheese on the side.

Fettuccine with pesto

Difficulty **easy** • *Time needed* **over an hour** • *Calories per serving* **530**

INGREDIENTS
serves 4

For the pasta
UNBLEACHED FLOUR *4 cups*
EGGS *2*
SALT *to taste*

For the pesto
BASIL *40 leaves*
PINE NUTS *1 tablespoon*
GARLIC *1 clove*
GRATED PECORINO *1 tablespoon*
GRATED PARMIGIANO *1 tablespoon*
EXTRA VIRGIN OLIVE OIL *8 tablespoons*
SALT *to taste*

1 Sift the flour into a mound on the work surface; in the center, break the eggs, add a pinch of salt and work the ingredients, adding lukewarm water little by little, until the dough becomes smooth and elastic. Knead vigorously for about 10 minutes, then roll out the dough into a thin sheet. Roll the sheet onto itself and with a sharp knife, cut the fettuccine about 1/2 inch wide; let them dry for at least an hour.

2 In the meantime, prepare the pesto. Rinse and delicately pat dry the basil leaves, toast the pine nuts in the oven and peel the garlic. Blend these ingredients in a food processor; add the two grated cheeses, season with salt and pour in the oil little by little, blending the ingredients with a wooden spoon.

3 Cook the fettuccine in abundant boiling salted water; drain and pour into a serving plate. Dilute the pesto with just a little bit of pasta cooking water and toss with the pasta. Serve immediately.

SUGGESTION
A variant of this preparation is to add 7 oz of fresh crushed tomatoes or a cup of tomato sauce to the traditional pesto.

Green fettuccine with oil and parmigiano

Difficulty **medium** • *Time needed* **over an hour** • *Calories per serving* **510**

INGREDIENTS
serves 4

UNBLEACHED FLOUR *3 1/2 cups*
BORAGE & WILD HERBS *8 oz*
SAUSAGE *2 oz*
EGGS *1*
GRATED PARMIGIANO *4 tablespoons*
EXTRA VIRGIN OLIVE OIL *4 tablespoons*
SALT *to taste*

1 Clean the borage and the wild herbs carefully, then rinse several times under running water, drain and cook in pan with only the water remaining from the rinse for about 15 minutes.

2 When done, drain, shred and chop finely. Chop the sausages. Sift the flour in a mound on a working surface. Make a well in the middle and add the egg, a pinch of salt and the chopped greens; also add the chopped sausages and one tablespoon of grated parmigiano.

3 Work all ingredients, adding about 1 cup of lukewarm water, little by little, at a time. Knead the dough until smooth and elastic. Roll the dough into a thick sheet and cover with plastic wrap. Set aside for 30 minutes.

4 At the end of this time, roll the sheet of dough onto itself and with a sharp knife, cut into 1/2 inch slices. Unroll, dust with flour and let dry for 40 minutes.

5 Cook the fettuccine in abundant boiling salted water for about 10 minutes. When al dente, drain and transfer to a serving plate. Drizzle with the extra virgin olive oil and sprinkle with the grated parmigiano. Serve at once.

Tuscan pici (thick spaghetti)

Difficulty **medium** • *Time needed* **under an hour** • *Calories per serving* **340**

INGREDIENTS
serves 4

UNBLEACHED FLOUR *4 cups*
SALT *to taste*

1 On a work surface, sift the flour in a mound and make a well in the middle. In the center, add the salt and the warm water. Mix the ingredients and work vigorously for 15 minutes, adding a little water, if needed, until the dough becomes smooth and firm.

2 Divide the dough into 10 small pieces. Roll each piece with the palm of the hand to form cylinders. Every cylinder must be separated into several pieces and rolled again into long spaghettoni (thick spaghetti) as thick as a pencil and longer than normal spaghetti: these are the pici.

3 In abundant boiling salted water, cook the pici until al dente. Stir gently from time to time. Drain and transfer to a serving bowl. Serve with any sauce (tomato or ragù) or with the traditional 'sugo finto toscano.'

SUGGESTION

To make the 'sugo finto toscano' or Tuscan sauce, in a skillet with a few tablespoons of extra virgin olive oil, cook lots of chopped onions, carrots, celery and basil. Add some chopped tomatoes and cook for 15 minutes.

Spaghetti balls

Difficulty **medium** • *Time needed* **under an hour** • *Calories per serving* **800**

INGREDIENTS
serves 4

SPAGHETTI *14 oz*
COOKED HAM *5 oz, chopped*
MOZZARELLA *2 oz, diced*
GRATED EMMENTAL *6 tablespoons*
EGGS *3*
BREAD CRUMBS *3 tablespoons*
EXTRA VIRGIN OLIVE OIL *1 tablespoon*
BUTTER *6 tablespoons*
SALT & PEPPER *to taste*

1 Break the spaghetti into small pieces and boil in salted water until al dente. Drain, transfer to a bowl and let cool. Add the chopped ham, both cheeses, the eggs, the salt and the pepper.

2 Mix the preparation thoroughly with a wooden spoon; form oval balls and slightly flatten them. In a skillet, heat the oil and butter, and add the spaghetti balls. Cook until evenly golden.

3 Remove the balls from the oil, transfer to paper towels to absorb the fat. Place on a warm serving dish and serve.

SUGGESTION

This recipe can be made with any leftover pasta.

Reginette with pork and bitter chocolate

Difficulty **easy** • *Time needed* **over an hour** • *Calories per serving* **500**

INGREDIENTS
serves 4

REGINETTE *11 oz*
DARK CHOCOLATE *1 oz*
GROUND PORK *11 oz*
TOMATO PASTE *2 tablespoons*
ONION *1*
RED WINE *3/4 cup*
SUGAR *1 tablespoon*
POWDERED CINNAMON *1 pinch*
EXTRA VIRGIN OLIVE OIL *4 tablespoons*
SALT & PEPPER *to taste*

1 Peel the onion and chop finely. Heat the oil in a pan over medium heat and cook the onion until transparent. Add the ground pork and brown. Add the wine and evaporate over high heat. Add the tomato purée, 3 tablespoons of warm water, a pinch of salt and pepper to taste.

Cover and cook on very low heat for one hour (if needed, add a little water). Add the chocolate, the cinnamon and the sugar. Mix well.

2 During this time, cook the reginette in abundant boiling salted water until al dente. Drain and transfer to a large pasta bowl. Add the hot sauce and toss well. Serve.

SUGGESTION
The reginette can be replaced with egg pappardelle.

Reginette with red pesto

Difficulty **easy** • *Time needed* **less than 30 minutes** • *Calories per serving* **530**

INGREDIENTS
serves 4

REGINETTE *12 oz*
PESTO *5 oz*
TOMATO PASTE *4 tablespoons*
HOT CHILI PEPPER *1, crushed*
GRATED PARMIGIANO *to taste*
EXTRA VIRGIN OLIVE OIL *1 tablespoon*
SALT *to taste*

1 Cook the pasta al dente in abundant boiling salted water. In the meantime, in a large saucepan, heat the oil and the chili pepper; after a few minutes, add the tomato sauce and mix well with a wooden spoon.

2 When thoroughly blended, discard the chili pepper and add the pesto; mix again with a wooden spoon to blend the ingredients well and, after 5 minutes, remove from the heat. Drain the pasta and toss with the prepared sauce; sprinkle generously with the grated parmigiano.

Livorno style reginette

Difficulty **easy** • *Time needed* **less than 30 minutes** • *Calories per serving* **730**

INGREDIENTS
serves 4

REGINETTE *12 oz*
BASIL *4 oz*
SHELLED WALNUTS *3 oz*
PECORINO *5 oz*
EXTRA VIRGIN OLIVE OIL *7 tablespoons*
SALT *to taste*

1 Clean the basil leaves, dry delicately on a clean dish towel. In the bowl of a food processor, mix the walnuts and a pinch of salt. Add the basil leaves, mix again. Mixing constantly, add the extra virgin olive oil slowly until the preparation is smooth.

2 Transfer the preparation into a large bowl. Add the grated pecorino sardo and mix with a wooden spoon. Cook the reginette in abundant boiling salted water until al dente. Drain, reserving 4 tablespoons of the cooking water. Mix the reserved cooking water into the pesto sauce. Transfer to a serving bowl and toss with the reginette. Serve at once.

Roman style reginette

Difficulty **easy** • *Time needed* **less than 30 minutes** • *Calories per serving* **530**

INGREDIENTS
serves 4

REGINETTE *11 oz*
DRIED MUSHROOMS *2 oz*
TOMATOES *11 oz, ripe and firm*
PANCETTA *2 oz, in 1 slice*
ONION *1*
PARSLEY *1 bunch*
GRATED PARMIGIANO *3 tablespoons*
BUTTER *1 tablespoon*
EXTRA VIRGIN OLIVE OIL *3 tablespoons*
SALT & PEPPER *to taste*

1 Soak the dry mushrooms in a little lukewarm water. When softened, dry with paper towels and chop finely. Scald the tomatoes in boiling water; drain, remove the skin, the seeds and the juice and pass through a strainer.

2 Peel the onion and chop finely; dice the pancetta; rinse the parsley, dry gently and chop. Heat the oil in a skillet and cook the onion until transparent.

3 Add the diced pancetta and cook briefly stirring with a wooden spoon; mix in the mushrooms and simmer for 1 minute. Finally, add the tomatoes, season with salt and pepper and continue cooking for about 15 minutes, stirring from time to time.

4 In the meantime, cook the reginette in abundant boiling salted water. When al dente, drain, reserving 2 tablespoons of the cooking water, transfer to the pot with the sauce, add the reserved cooking water and simmer for 1 minute; add the butter and the grated cheese, remove the pasta from the heat and stir well to blend the ingredients..

5 Transfer the pasta to a serving plate, sprinkle with the chopped parsley and serve immediately.

Reginette Capresi

Difficulty **medium** • *Time needed* **under an hour** • *Calories per serving* **550**

INGREDIENTS
serves 4

REGINETTE *12 oz*
TOMATOES *12 oz*
MOZZARELLA *2 pieces*
ONION *1*
BASIL *1 bunch*
EXTRA VIRGIN OLIVE OIL *3 tablespoons*
SALT *to taste*

1 Scald the tomatoes. Drain, peel and squeeze out the seeds and mince. Slice the onion. In a saucepan, heat the oil with the onions. Cook until transparent. Add tomatoes, a pinch of salt and the basil leaves. Cook for 15 minutes over medium heat. Pass the sauce in a food mill (or processor). Return to saucepan and cook for 10 to 15 minutes, to reduce the sauce.

2 During this time, cook the reginette in abundant salted boiling water until al dente. Drain and transfer to a large serving bowl. Pour the sauce over and toss well. Dice the mozzarella and add to the pasta. Toss and serve immediately.

> **SUGGESTION**
> *Instead of the typical curly edged reginette, you can also use egg pappardelle.*

Reginette with lamb ragù

Difficulty **medium** • *Time needed* **over an hour** • *Calories per serving* **480**

INGREDIENTS
serves 4

REGINETTE *12 oz*
LAMB *7 oz*
TOMATOES *11 oz, ripe and firm*
PARSLEY *1 bunch*
GARLIC *1 clove*
HOT CHILI PEPPER *1/2*
DRY WHITE WINE *1/4 cup*
GRATED PECORINO *2 tablespoons*
EXTRA VIRGIN OLIVE OIL *3 tablespoons*
SALT *to taste*

1 Trim, rinse, dry and finely chop the parsley. Cut the lamb into small pieces. Scald the tomatoes in boiling water, drain, peel, squeeze to remove the seeds and the water; dice the pulp.

2 In a pan, heat the oil with the garlic and the chili pepper, add the diced lamb and sauté over high heat until the meat is evenly browned. Remove the garlic. Add white wine and let it evaporate.

3 Add the minced tomatoes, the chili pepper, and a pinch of salt; cover and cook the ragù on medium heat for about 1 hour, stirring with a wooden spoon from time to time. About 5 minutes before done, add the chopped parsley.

4 In the meantime, cook the reginette in abundant boiling salted water until al dente. Drain and transfer to a serving bowl. Toss well and serve with grated pecorino cheese on the side.

Spaghetti "cacio e pepe"

Difficulty **easy** • *Time needed* **less than 30 minutes** • *Calories per serving* **370**

INGREDIENTS
serves 4

SPAGHETTI *11 oz*
GRATED PECORINO *6 tablespoons*
SALT & PEPPER *to taste*

1 Cook the spaghetti in abundant boiling salted water until al dente. Drain, reserving 1/2 cup of the cooking water.

2 Transfer the pasta into a serving bowl. Add the grated pecorino and a generous helping of fresh ground pepper. Toss and gradually add the reserved water so the preparation does not turn out too dry. Here, the spaghetti are expected to be a little softer. Serve in individual preheated bowls.

Spaghetti with wild asparagus

Difficulty **easy** • *Time needed* **under an hour** • *Calories per serving* **570**

INGREDIENTS
serves 4

SPAGHETTI *14 oz*
WILD ASPARAGUS *2 lbs*
TOMATO SAUCE *14 oz*
GRATED PARMIGIANO *4 tablespoons*
EXTRA VIRGIN OLIVE OIL
4 tablespoons
SALT *to taste*

1 Clean the asparagus and cut off the tips. Heat the oil in a skillet and cook the asparagus tips for 3-4 minutes, stirring with a wooden spoon.

2 Add the tomato sauce, a pinch of salt, cover the pan and cook on low heat for 20 minutes, stirring from time to time. Make sure the sauce does not thicken too much. If this happens, add a few tablespoons of hot water and lower the heat.

3 Cook the spaghetti until al dente. Drain and transfer to a serving bowl. Add the grated parmigiano and toss well. Divide the pasta into 4 warm bowls and pour the sauce over each serving.

Spaghetti with olive oil, garlic and chili pepper

Difficulty **easy** • *Time needed* **less than 30 minutes** • *Calories per serving* **410**

INGREDIENTS
serves 6

SPAGHETTI *1 1/4 lbs*
GARLIC *6 cloves*
HOT CHILI PEPPER *1*
EXTRA VIRGIN OLIVE OIL *5 oz*
SALT *to taste*

1 Cook the spaghetti in abundant boiling salted water. Stir several times during the cooking so they do not stick to each other. When al dente, drain.

2 During this time, peel and crush the garlic. In a large skillet, heat the oil with the garlic and the chili pepper (use chili powder, if you like it spicier) over low heat.

3 Do not let the garlic brown, or it will give a bitter taste to the oil. Transfer the pasta to the skillet and toss very well. Remove from heat and serve immediately.

Spaghetti with capers

Difficulty **easy** • *Time needed* **under an hour** • *Calories per serving* **460**

INGREDIENTS
serves 4

SPAGHETTI *14 oz*
CAPERS PRESERVED IN SALT *1 oz*
PEELED TOMATOES *14 oz*
PARSLEY *1 bunch*
GARLIC *1 clove*
OREGANO *a pinch*
VEGETABLE EXTRACT *1 teaspoon*
EXTRA VIRGIN OLIVE OIL *4 tablespoons*
SALT & PEPPER *to taste*

1 Crush the peeled tomatoes. Rinse, dry and chop the parsley. Peel and crush the garlic. In a saucepan, heat the oil, add the tomatoes, the garlic and the vegetable extract. Cook for 10 minutes.

2 Add the capers, a pinch of salt and some fresh ground pepper. Cook over medium heat for another 10 minutes. Add the parsley and the oregano, stir and remove from heat.

3 In abundant boiling salted water, cook the spaghetti until al dente. Drain and transfer to a warm serving bowl. Pour the sauce over the spaghetti and toss well. Serve.

SUGGESTION
*In Spring and in Summer,
use fresh garden tomatoes.*

Spaghetti with shellfish

Difficulty **easy** • *Time needed* **under an hour** • *Calories per serving* **430**

INGREDIENTS
serves 4

SPAGHETTI *11 oz*
SHRIMPS *7 oz*
CLAMS *7 oz*
MUSSELS *14 oz*
CRUSHED TOMATOES *7 oz*
PARSLEY *1 oz*
GARLIC *2 cloves*
EXTRA VIRGIN OLIVE OIL *4 tablespoons*
SALT & PEPPER *to taste*

1 Clean and devein the shrimp; rinse and soak the clams to remove excess sand; scrape the mussels. In a covered pan, cook the mussels and the clams over high heat shaking the pan a few times until all are open. Remove the shellfish meat from the shells and set aside.

2 Peel and crush the garlic. Heat the extra virgin olive oil in a large saucepan over low heat. Add the shrimps, the mussels, the clams and the garlic. Sauté for 5 minutes. Rinse, dry and chop the parsley. In another saucepan, cook the tomatoes with salt and pepper to 10 minutes. Add the shrimps, the shellfish and the chopped parsley. Mix well and cook for 2 minutes on high heat. Cook the spaghetti in abundant boiling salted water; until al dente. Drain and transfer to the pan. Toss well and serve.

SUGGESTION
The tomato can be eliminated from the sauce and substituted with the shellfish cooking water, properly strained.

Spaghetti with pine nuts

Difficulty **easy** • *Time needed* **less than 30 minutes** • *Calories per serving* **580**

INGREDIENTS
serves 4

SPAGHETTI *12 oz*
PINE NUTS *4 oz*
BASIL *2 oz*
CELERY *2 stalks*
GARLIC *1 clove*
GRATED PARMIGIANO *4 tablespoons*
EXTRA VIRGIN OLIVE OIL *5 tablespoons*
SALT & PEPPER *to taste*

1 Cook the spaghetti in abundant boiling salted water until al dente. In the meantime, mix the basil leaves in a food processor with the pine nuts, the garlic, the grated parmigiano and the extra virgin olive oil. Add a pinch of salt and pepper to taste. Mix until the preparation is creamy. Chop the celery stalks very finely. Transfer the basil preparation and the chopped celery to a large serving bowl.

2 Drain the spaghetti and transfer to a serving bowl. Toss until sauce is absorbed by the pasta and serve.

SUGGESTION
This sauce can be used with all types of pasta. The pine nuts can be replaced by walnuts, almonds or hazelnuts.

Spaghetti with basil

Difficulty **easy** • *Time needed* **less than 30 minutes** • *Calories per serving* **620**

INGREDIENTS
serves 4

SPAGHETTI *14 oz*
BASIL *4 oz*
SHELLED WALNUTS *10*
GRATED PECORINO *2 tablespoons*
EXTRA VIRGIN OLIVE OIL *5 tablespoons*
SALT *to taste*

1 Rinse and dry the basil. Chop the basil and the walnuts together (can be done very rapidly in a food processor). Set aside a few basil leaves and some nuts for decoration.

2 In a bowl, mix the chopped basil and nuts with the grated pecorino and the extra virgin olive oil (this can also be done in a food processor). Mix with a wooden spoon until the sauce is well blended and creamy.

3 Cook the spaghetti in abundant boiling salted water until al dente. Drain and transfer to a serving bowl. Pour the sauce over and toss well. Top with the basil leaves and the nuts set aside for decoration and serve immediately.

Spaghetti in aluminum foil

Difficulty **medium** • *Time needed* **over an hour** • *Calories per serving* **560**

INGREDIENTS
serves 4

SPAGHETTI *12 oz*
COCKLES *14 oz*
BABY OCTOPUS *11 oz*
MUSSELS *14 oz*
TOMATOES *7 oz, ripe and firm*
PARSLEY *1 bunch*
GARLIC *1 clove*
HOT CHILI PEPPER *1 small piece*
EXTRA VIRGIN OLIVE OIL *6 tablespoons*
SALT *to taste*

1 Brush and clean all the shellfish under running water. Immerse all in a large bowl of cold water and set aside for 1 hour to eliminate excess sand. Drain.

2 Scald the tomatoes in boiling water, drain and peel; squeeze delicately to remove all seeds and water, then mince. Peel the garlic and crush lightly. Rinse, dry and chop the parsley.

3 Put all the shellfish in a large skillet and cook, shaking the pan, until all the shells are open. Remove from heat. Separate the meat from the shells and put in a bowl, throwing out the shells and the closed shellfish.

4 In a pan, heat the oil over low heat; add the shellfish, the garlic and the chili pepper. Sauté for 3 minutes. Add the tomatoes, a pinch of salt and cook another 5 minutes on high heat. Add the chopped parsley and remove from heat. Preheat the oven to 450°F.

5 Cook the spaghetti in abundant boiling salted water until al dente (even a little hard). Drain and transfer to the pan. Toss well. Prepare 4 large squares of aluminum paper. Divide the cooked pasta among the 4 squares. Close the aluminum wrap tightly and place on a cookie sheet. Put in the oven for 5-7 minutes. Serve in the aluminum paper, to be opened just before eating.

71

Spaghetti with vegetarian sauce

Difficulty **easy** • *Time needed* **over an hour** • *Calories per serving* **510**

INGREDIENTS
serves 4

SPAGHETTI *14 oz*
TOMATOES *1 1/4 lbs*
CELERY *4 leaves*
ONION *1*
GARLIC *3 cloves*
PARSLEY *1 bunch*
MINT *a few leaves*
HOT CHILI PEPPER *1*
GRATED PECORINO *4 tablespoons*
EXTRA VIRGIN OLIVE OIL *5 tablespoons*
SALT *to taste*

1 Rinse the tomatoes. Pass in a food mill and put in a saucepan. Peel and thinly slice the onion. Peel the garlic. Rinse, dry and chop the parsley, the mint and the celery leaves. Add all to the saucepan with salt, the whole chili pepper and the extra virgin olive oil.

2 Cover and cook on medium heat for 30 minutes, stirring from time to time. If the sauce tends to become thick, add a few tablespoons of hot water.

3 During this time, cook the spaghetti in abundant boiling salted water until al dente. Drain and transfer to a serving bowl.

4 Remove sauce from heat. Discard the garlic and the chili pepper. Add sauce to the spaghetti and toss well. Sprinkle with grated pecorino and serve immediately.

Spaghetti with anchovies

Difficulty **easy** • *Time needed* **less than 30 minutes** • *Calories per serving* **610**

INGREDIENTS
serves 4

SPAGHETTI *14 oz*
ANCHOVY FILLETS *2 oz, de-salted*
GARLIC *1/2 clove*
WHITE WINE VINEGAR *a few drops*
EXTRA VIRGIN OLIVE OIL *6 tablespoons*
SALT & PEPPER *to taste*

1 In a food processor, mix the extra virgin olive oil, the anchovies, the garlic, teaspoon of black pepper, the vinegar on low speed for 30 seconds. Mix on high speed for another 30 seconds or until the mixture is smooth.

2 Cook the spaghetti in abundant boiling salted water until al dente. Drain and transfer to a serving bowl. Add the anchovy sauce and toss well. Serve.

> ### SUGGESTION
> *Rinse salted anchovies well and pat dry before using. Anchovies in oil can be put directly in the food processor.*

Spaghetti with lobster and capers

Difficulty **medium** • *Time needed* **under an hour** • *Calories per serving* **510**

INGREDIENTS
serves 4

SPAGHETTI *14 oz*
LOBSTER *1, about 1 1/2 lbs*
CAPERS PRESERVED IN SALT *2 oz*
TOMATOES *4, ripe and firm*
BASIL *5 leaves*
PARSLEY *1 oz*
GARLIC *1 clove*
EXTRA VIRGIN OLIVE OIL *4 tablespoons*
SALT & PEPPER *to taste*

1 In abundant boiling salted water, immerse the lobster (head first) and cook for 15 to 20 minutes (depending on size). Remove the lobster and set aside for a couple of minutes. Cut in half and, using a small sharp knife, remove the meat from the shell. Remove and discard the intestines.

2 Extract all the meat from the legs and the claws and set aside. Scald the tomatoes, peel and squeeze to remove the seeds and the juice, then mince.

3 Rinse and dry the basil and the parsley. Peel the garlic and chop finely with the basil and the parsley. Transfer to a large bowl and add the capers and the diced tomatoes. Season with salt and pepper and mix gently, adding the extra virgin olive oil. Slice the lobster meat and add to the herbs and tomatoes.

4 Cook the spaghetti in abundant boiling salted water until al dente. Drain and transfer to the bowl with the lobster and herbs. Toss well and serve.

SUGGESTION
To get a more flavorful sauce, parboil the lobster for a few minutes, then cut it into pieces and boil with the tomato, eliminating the carcass half way though the cooking.

Spaghetti carbonara

Difficulty **easy** • *Time needed* **less than 30 minutes** • *Calories per serving* **760**

INGREDIENTS
serves 4

SPAGHETTI *11 oz*
PANCETTA *7 oz*
EGGS *4*
GRATED PECORINO *4 tablespoons*
EXTRA VIRGIN OLIVE OIL
1/2 tablespoon
SALT & PEPPER *to taste*

1 Slice the pancetta in long strips and cook it in a saucepan with the extra virgin olive oil over medium heat until it loses some of its fat.

2 In a small bowl, beat the eggs with the grated pecorino and as much pepper as you like.

3 Cook the spaghetti in abundant salted water until al dente. Reserving half a cup of cooking water, drain the pasta. Transfer the spaghetti to a large serving bowl. Add the pancetta, the beaten eggs and, little by little, the reserved cooking water. Mix until well blended. Serve immediately.

SUGGESTION
To make the sauce creamier, try using egg yolks and 1 cup of heavy cream instead of the 4 whole eggs.

Spaghetti with mushrooms and tuna 'ventresca'

Difficulty **easy** • *Time needed* **less than 30 minutes** • *Calories per serving* **440**

INGREDIENTS
serves 4

SPAGHETTI *11 oz*
PORCINI MUSHROOMS *5 oz*
TUNA "VENTRESCA" *2 oz, in oil*
PANCETTA *2 oz*
GARLIC *1 clove*
EXTRA VIRGIN OLIVE OIL *2 tablespoons*
SALT & PEPPER *to taste*

Note: 'Ventresca' is a special part of the tuna, preserved in oil. It is a gastronomic specialty of Sardinia and Sicily. If you cannot get it, use canned tuna in olive oil, even though the taste is very different.

1 Brush the mushrooms and slice them. Dice the pancetta. Peel and crush the garlic. In a large pan, heat the oil and cook the pancetta and the garlic. After two minutes remove the garlic and discard. Add the sliced mushrooms. Season with salt and pepper and mix. Cook for 5 minutes. Drain the tuna, break apart and add to the mixture. Cook for 8-10 minutes on low heat, stirring from time to time.

2 Cook the spaghetti in abundant boiling salted water until al dente. Drain and transfer to a large bowl. Add the tuna sauce and toss well. Serve at once.

Spaghetti marinara

Difficulty **medium** • *Time needed* **under an hour** • *Calories per serving* **560**

INGREDIENTS
serves 4

SPAGHETTI *12 oz*
SEAFOOD *2 lbs*
(cockles, mussels, razor shells, clams)
PARSLEY *1 bunch*
GARLIC *3 cloves*
EXTRA VIRGIN OLIVE OIL *8 tablespoons*
SALT & PEPPER *to taste*

1 Clean all the shellfish. Brush clams and mussels and soak them in cold water for an hour so they lose any excess sand they might have. Rinse all seafood and set aside.

2 Rinse, dry and chop the parsley finely. Peel and crush the garlic (leave whole if you do not wish a strong taste of garlic). In a large pan, lightly oiled, put all the drained shellfish. Cover and cook on low heat until all clams and mussels are open.

3 Remove shellfish from pan (discard any shells that are not open). Remove the meat from the shells. Set aside a few for garnishing. Filter the liquid and set aside.

4 In a pan, heat the oil. Add the remaining raw seafood and the garlic. Cook for 2 minutes. Discard the garlic. Add the shellfish and the filtered liquid. Pepper to taste. Cook on medium heat for 5 minutes.

5 During this time, cook the spaghetti in abundant boiling salted water until al dente. Drain and transfer to the pan with seafood. Add the parsley and toss well. Garnish with the cooked shellfish set aside. Serve at once.

Spaghetti alla puttanesca

Difficulty **easy** • *Time needed* **under an hour** • *Calories per serving* **480**

INGREDIENTS
serves 4

SPAGHETTI *12 oz*
TOMATOES *1 lb, ripe and firm*
ANCHOVY FILLETS *2*
BLACK OLIVES *3 oz*
CAPERS *1 teaspoon*
PARSLEY *1 bunch*
GARLIC *1 clove*
EXTRA VIRGIN OLIVE OIL *5 tablespoons*
SALT & PEPPER *to taste*

1 Scald the tomatoes, drain and peel. Gently squeeze to remove seeds and water. Chop coarsely. Peel the garlic and crush lightly. Rinse, dry and finely chop the parsley.

2 Pit the olives and chop coarsely. In a large saucepan, heat the extra virgin olive oil; add the anchovy fillets and the garlic. Cook for 2 minutes.

3 Add the chopped olives, the capers, the diced tomatoes, a pinch of salt and a little pepper. On medium heat, cook the sauce for 20 minutes, stirring from time to time. Add half the chopped parsley.

4 Cook the spaghetti in abundant boiling salted water until al dente. Drain and transfer to a large serving bowl. Pour the sauce over and toss well. Sprinkle with the remaining chopped parsley and serve.

Spaghetti alla trapanese

Difficulty **easy** • *Time needed* **less than 30 minutes** • *Calories per serving* **540**

INGREDIENTS
serves 4

SPAGHETTI *12 oz*
TOMATOES *11 oz, ripe and firm*
TUNA IN OLIVE OIL *3 oz*
BLACK OLIVES *2 oz*
SHALLOT *1*
PARSLEY *1 bunch*
BASIL *1 bunch*
GARLIC *1 clove*
OREGANO *to taste*
HOT CHILI PEPPER *1 small piece*
EXTRA VIRGIN OLIVE OIL *6 tablespoons*
SALT *to taste*

1 Scald the tomatoes in boiling water; drain and peel, cut in half and squeeze gently to remove seeds and water. Chop coarsely. Peel the garlic and the shallot. Chop them finely. Rinse, dry and chop the parsley. Rinse, dry and chop the basil.

2 Pit the olives and chop coarsely. Drain the tuna and break apart. In a skillet, heat the oil and add the garlic and the shallot with the chili pepper. Cook for 1 minute. Add the tomatoes and salt. Cook for 10 minutes, stirring with a wooden spoon.

3 Add the chopped olives, the tuna, the oregano, the parsley and basil. Cook on low heat for 5 minutes

4 Cook the spaghetti in abundant boiling salted water until al dente. Drain and transfer to the pan. Toss well and serve.

SUGGESTION

Once prepared with fresh tuna, this dish is also tasty if salted sardines are used in place of tuna in oil: rinse, debone, and dry; cut into small pieces and use as described in the recipe.

Spaghetti with pan fish

Difficulty **medium** • *Time needed* **over an hour** • *Calories per serving* **560**

INGREDIENTS
serves 4

SPAGHETTI *14 oz*
PAN FISH *14 oz*
TOMATO PASTE *2 tablespoons*
LEEKS *1*
ONION *1*
PARSLEY *1 bunch*
GARLIC *2 cloves*
EXTRA VIRGIN OLIVE OIL *1/4 cup*
SALT *to taste*

1 Thoroughly wash the fish, clean, debone and dice. Clean the parsley, peel the garlic and the onion; use only the white part of the leek and chop all together. Heat the oil in a skillet and lightly brown; when the onions are golden, add the fish and cook for 2 minutes, then add the tomato puree.

2 Cover the ingredients with hot water, season with salt, cover and cook over low heat for an hour. When the sauce has thickened, pass all through a food strainer to make a thick sauce.

3 Cook the spaghetti in abundant boiling salted water until al dente. Drain and transfer to a large bowl and mix with the sauce. Serve at once garnished with chopped parsley.

> **SUGGESTION**
> *If you don't have a food strainer,
> use a food processor to blend the ingredients
> into a very thick sauce.*

Spaghetti with olives

Difficulty **easy** • *Time needed* **less than 30 minutes** • *Calories per serving* **410**

INGREDIENTS
serves 4

SPAGHETTI *11 oz*
BLACK OLIVES *3 oz*
TOMATOES *11 oz, ripe and firm*
ONION *1*
PARSLEY *1 bunch*
BASIL *1 bunch*
GARLIC *1 clove*
CHILI PEPPER *1 small piece*
EXTRA VIRGIN OLIVE OIL *4 tablespoons*
SALT & PEPPER *to taste*

1 Peel and slice the onion very thin. Peel the garlic and crush it. Pit the olives and chop coarsely.

2 Scald the tomatoes in boiling water, drain, peel, halve, and press lightly to remove all seeds and water, then mince.

3 In a saucepan, heat the extra virgin olive oil and cook the onions until just transparent. Add the garlic, the chili pepper and the diced tomatoes. Season

with salt and pepper and cook for 10 minutes. Add the olives and cook for another 5 minutes (reserve 1 tablespoon for garnish).

4 Rinse, dry and chop both the basil and the parsley. In abundant salted boiling water, cook the spaghetti until al dente. Drain well and transfer into the saucepan. Add the chopped parsley and basil. Toss well and serve on a platter, garnished with the olives.

Spaghetti with zucchini

Difficulty **easy** • *Time needed* **less than 30 minutes** • *Calories per serving* **440**

INGREDIENTS
serves 4

SPAGHETTI *14 oz*
ZUCCHINI *4*
PARSLEY *1 bunch*
EXTRA VIRGIN OLIVE OIL *4 tablespoons*
SALT *to taste*

1 In a large pot, boil abundant water and add salt. In the meantime, trim, rinse, dry and cut the zucchini in thin slices.

2 In a skillet, heat the extra virgin olive oil and sauté the zucchini, stirring with a wooden spoon. Add a pinch of salt. Cook until zucchini are soft. Set aside.

3 Rinse, dry and finely chop the parsley. In abundant boiling salted water, cook the spaghetti until al dente. Drain and transfer to a serving plate.

4 Add the zucchini and the chopped parsley and toss well. Serve. Traditionally, this dish is served without any grated cheese.

Spaghetti with tuna

Difficulty **easy** • *Time needed* **less than 30 minutes** • *Calories per serving* **570**

INGREDIENTS
serves 4

SPAGHETTI *11 oz*
TUNA IN OLIVE OIL *5 oz*
TOMATO SAUCE *4 tablespoons*
BASIL *a few leaves*
PARSLEY *1 oz*
GARLIC *2 cloves*
EXTRA VIRGIN OLIVE OIL *2 tablespoons*
SALT & PEPPER *to taste*

1 Peel the garlic. Break the tuna apart. In a saucepan, heat the oil, add the tuna and the garlic and cook for 2 minutes; discard the garlic. Add the tomato sauce, mix well. Add a pinch of salt and a little pepper. Cook for 5 minutes on low heat.

2 Cook the spaghetti in abundant boiling salted water until al dente. Drain and transfer to a warm serving bowl.

3 Rinse, dry and finely chop the parsley and the basil. Add to the sauce and cook for 2 minutes. Pour over the spaghetti and toss well. Serve.

SUGGESTION
To make the dish even more flavorful, dissolve 2 desalted anchovy fillets in the oil before adding to the tuna and, immediately after, add a tablespoon of chopped capers.

Spaghetti with asparagus and almonds

Difficulty **easy** • *Time needed* **less than 30 minutes** • *Calories per serving* **570**

INGREDIENTS
serves 4

SPAGHETTI *12 oz*
FROZEN APARAGUS TIPS *11 oz*
SHREDDED ALMONDS *2 oz*
GRATED PARMIGIANO *4 tablespoons*
BUTTER *2 oz*
SALT & PEPPER *to taste*

1 Cook the spaghetti in a pot of boiling salted water. During this time, heat the butter in a saucepan; as soon as it is hot, add the slivered almonds and cook over low heat until golden. Remove with a perforated ladle and transfer to a bowl.

2 Remove any stems from the asparagus tips; put the asparagus tips into the skillet, add 2 or 3 tablespoons of the pasta cooking water, cover and cook over moderate heat.

3 Season with salt and fresh ground pepper; return the almonds to the sauce and, as soon as the spaghetti are al dente, drain, reserving a few tablespoons of the cooking water, and transfer to the saucepan.

4 Finish by adding the grated parmigiano, mix carefully with a spoon and fork, letting the flavors blend well; if necessary, add a spoonful or two of the cooking water. Serve immediately.

Spaghetti with capers and olives

Difficulty **easy** • *Time needed* **less than 30 minutes** • *Calories per serving* **420**

INGREDIENTS
serves 4

SPAGHETTI *12 oz*
CAPERS *1 tablespoon*
BLACK OLIVES *3 oz*
ANCHOVY FILLETS IN OIL *6*
PARSLEY *1 bunch*
GARLIC *1 clove*
EXTRA VIRGIN OLIVE OIL *3 tablespoons*
SALT *to taste*

1 Rinse, dry and chop the parsley. Pit the olives and chop them. Peel and crush the garlic. In a small pan, heat the oil and add the anchovies, the black olives, the garlic, the parsley and the capers. With a wooden spoon, stir to melt the anchovies for 2 minutes.

2 Remove from heat and discard the garlic. In abundant boiling salted water, cook the spaghetti until al dente. Drain and transfer to the saucepan. Toss well and serve.

Spaghetti with artichokes

Difficulty **easy** • *Time needed* **under an hour** • *Calories per serving* **560**

INGREDIENTS
serves 4

SPAGHETTI *14 oz*
ARTICHOKES *8*
LEMON *1*
PARSLEY *1 bunch*
GARLIC *1 clove*
GRATED PECORINO *4 tablespoons*
EXTRA VIRGIN OLIVE OIL *6 tablespoons*
SALT & PEPPER *to taste*

1 Prepare the artichokes. Cut off the stems, tear off all the exterior leaves. Cut in half and take off the artichoke hair. Slice lengthwise and immerse the pieces in a bowl of cold water mixed with the juice of the lemon. Set aside.

2 Peel the garlic and crush it. In a large pan, heat the oil, add the garlic and the sliced artichokes, add a pinch of salt, a little fresh ground pepper and sauté for 5 minutes. Add three tablespoons of water, lower the heat and cover the pan. Cook for 30 minutes or until the artichokes are soft.

3 During this time, cook the spaghetti in abundant salted boiling water. Rinse, dry and finely chop the parsley. Drain the spaghetti. Add the parsley to the artichokes. Transfer the spaghetti to the artichoke preparation and toss well. Add the grated pecorino and toss. Serve immediately.

Spaghetti with tomato sauce

Difficulty **easy** • *Time needed* **less than 30 minutes** • *Calories per serving* **470**

INGREDIENTS
serves 4

SPAGHETTI *12 oz*
TOMATOES *1 lb, ripe*
BASIL *2 leaves, shredded*
GARLIC *1 clove*
GRATED PECORINO *to taste*
EXTRA VIRGIN OLIVE OIL *3 tablespoons*
SALT & PEPPER *to taste*

1 Rinse and dry the tomatoes. Peel and slice the garlic. In abundant boiling salted water, cook the spaghetti until al dente.

2 At the same time, in a large saucepan, heat the extra virgin olive oil. Add the whole tomatoes and the crushed garlic, a pinch of salt and a pinch of pepper. Cook on high heat.

3 When the tomatoes are soft, flatten them gently with a wooden spoon so all tomato pulp will be in direct contact with the heat. Season with salt and pepper again, if needed. Cook gently.

4 When the spaghetti is ready, drain and transfer to a large serving bowl. Tear the basil leaves and add them to the tomato sauce. Pour the tomatoes over the spaghetti. Sprinkle with the grated pecorino and toss well. Serve immediately.

Spaghetti with cuttlefish

Difficulty **medium** • *Time needed* **over an hour** • *Calories per serving* **530**

INGREDIENTS
serves 4

SPAGHETTI *11 oz*
CUTTLEFISH *4*
TOMATOES *1 lb*
PARSLEY *1 oz*
ONION *1*
GARLIC *2 cloves*
FISH STOCK *2 cups*
EXTRA VIRGIN OLIVE OIL *4 tablespoons*
SALT & PEPPER *to taste*

1 Thoroughly clean the cuttlefish, leaving the sacks whole; cut off the tentacles, chop and set aside. Trim and rinse the parsley, peel the garlic, and chop them together; put in a bowl and add the chopped tentacles, the bread crumbs, 2 tablespoons of oil; season with salt and pepper; blend well. Stuff the cuttlefish sacks with this mixture, closing the opening with kitchen string.

2 Rinse the tomatoes, peel and crush. Peel and chop the onion. In a saucepan, heat the remaining oil and sauté the onion until transparent; add the tomatoes, season with salt and pepper. Cook for 15 minutes, then add the filled cuttlefish. Pour on the fish stock, cover and cook over very low heat for 40 minutes.

3 When the cuttlefish are almost cooked, boil the spaghetti in abundant boiling salted water; drain and transfer to a serving dish. Strain the cooking juices from the cuttlefish and pour over the spaghetti; toss carefully. Remove the string from the cuttlefish sacks and place the cuttlefish on top of the spaghetti.

Spaghetti with clams in white sauce

Difficulty **easy** • *Time needed* **under an hour** • *Calories per serving* **380**

INGREDIENTS
serves 4

SPAGHETTI *11 oz*
CLAMS *2 lbs*
PARSLEY *1 oz*
GARLIC *2 cloves*
HOT CHILI PEPPER *1 small piece*
EXTRA VIRGIN OLIVE OIL *3 tablespoons*
SALT *to taste*

1 Clean the clams of any sand by leaving them in abundant salted water, changing the water several times; after 40 minutes, drain and put in a large covered saucepan over high heat and cook until they are all open; remove from heat.

2 Peel the garlic, chop finely and sauté in a casserole with the oil until golden; filter the cooking water from the clams and add with the chili pepper to the garlic, simmering for 2 minutes over low heat. Trim the parsley, rinse and chop.

3 In a large pot, boil abundant water; add salt and cook the spaghetti; drain. Add the clams to the casserole with the sauce; mix in the spaghetti and transfer to a serving plate. Sprinkle with the chopped parsley and serve.

Spaghetti with clams in red sauce

Difficulty **easy** • *Time needed* **under an hour** • *Calories per serving* **430**

INGREDIENTS
serves 4

SPAGHETTI *12 oz*
CLAMS *2 lbs*
ROMA TOMATOES *1 1/4 lbs*
ONION *1*
PARSLEY *2 bunches*
GARLIC *1 clove*
EXTRA VIRGIN OLIVE OIL *to taste*
SALT & PEPPER *to taste*

1 Thoroughly wash the clams under running water, put into a pot and without adding water, cover and cook over high heat until all are open. Remove from heat, separate from the shells (save about twenty in the shells for decoration). Filter the cooking water and set aside.

2 Peel and slice the onion, clean and chop the parsley, clean and crush the garlic. In a skillet, heat the oil and lightly sauté the onion, parsley and garlic. Dice the tomatoes and add to the mixture with the clams.

3 Cook until sufficiently thick, adding the cooking water a little at a time; season with salt and pepper.

4 Meanwhile, cook the spaghetti in abundant boiling salted water until al dente; drain, toss with the sauce and serve immediately.

Spaghetti with pancetta and potatoes

Difficulty **easy** • *Time needed* **less than 30 minutes** • *Calories per serving* **560**

INGREDIENTS
serves 4

SPAGHETTI *14 oz*
PANCETTA *2 oz, in 1 slice*
POTATOES *7 oz*
ONION *1*
ROSEMARY *1 bunch*
WORCESTER SAUCE *2-3 drops*
EXTRA VIRGIN OLIVE OIL *3 tablespoons*
SALT & PEPPER *to taste*

1 Peel the onion and slice thinly. Peel the potatoes, rinse and dice. Rinse the rosemary, remove the stem and chop finely.

2 Cut the pancetta in julienne. In a saucepan, heat the oil and sauté the onion until transparent; add the pancetta and cook until golden, stirring with a wooden spoon.

3 Add the diced potatoes, season with salt and pepper, sprinkle with the chopped rosemary, cover the pan and continue cooking over moderate heat for about 5 minutes, stirring from time to time with a wooden spoon.

4 Add the Worcester sauce and carefully blend the mixture; cook for another 5 minutes. In the meantime, boil abundant water, add salt and cook the spaghetti. When al dente, drain, transfer to a serving bowl, and toss with the pancetta and potato sauce. Serve immediately.

Spaghetti with paprika and yogurt

Difficulty **easy** • *Time needed* **less than 30 minutes** • *Calories per serving* **400**

INGREDIENTS
serves 4

SPAGHETTI *12 oz*
CHILI PEPPER *2 small pieces*
YOGURT *1 cup*
BLACK OLIVES *1 tablespoon, chopped*
GARLIC *1 clove*
EXTRA VIRGIN OLIVE OIL *2 tablespoons*
SEA SALT *to taste*

1 Peel and chop the garlic. In abundant salted boiling water, cook the spaghetti until al dente. During this time, in a skillet, heat the oil and add the garlic. Sauté for a few seconds before adding the chopped olives.

2 Add the yogurt, a pinch of salt and the paprika. Mix well and turn off the heat. Drain the spaghetti and transfer to the skillet. Toss well. Add another dash of paprika and serve.

Spaghetti with turnips and cherry tomatoes

Difficulty **medium** • *Time needed* **under an hour** • *Calories per serving* **390**

INGREDIENTS
serves 4

SPAGHETTI *12 oz*
TURNIPS *11 oz*
CHERRY TOMATOES *3*
SHALLOTS *2*
PARSLEY *1 bunch*
CHILI PEPPER *1, small*
EXTRA VIRGIN OLIVE OIL *3 tablespoons*
SALT & PEPPER *to taste*

1 Peel and cut the turnips in small cubes. Steam until tender and set aside. Scald the tomatoes, drain and peel. Squeeze gently to eliminate all seeds and water. Dice the tomatoes.

2 Peel and finely slice the shallots. In a pan, heat the extra virgin olive oil, add the shallots and the turnips. Cook for a few minutes and add the chili powder, stirring. Add the tomatoes, a pinch of salt and fresh ground pepper to taste. Cook for another 5-6 minutes. Chop the parsley.

3 In abundant salted boiling water, cook the spaghetti until al dente. Drain and transfer to a large serving bowl. Toss with the turnip sauce and the chopped parsley. Serve.

SUGGESTION
To make an elegant version of this dish, use caramelized baby turnips with whole cherry tomatoes.

"Lite" spaghetti

Difficulty **easy** • *Time needed* **less than 30 minutes** • *Calories per serving* **460**

INGREDIENTS
serves 4

WHOLE WHEAT SPAGHETTI *14 oz*
LOW FAT YOGURT *8 oz*
GRATED PECORINO *3 tablespoons*
EXTRA VIRGIN OLIVE OIL *3 tablespoons*
SALT *to taste*

1 In pot, bring abundant water to a boil, add salt and cook the spaghetti until al dente. During this time, in a bowl, mix together the yogurt, the grated pecorino, and a pinch of salt. Slowly whisk in the extra virgin olive oil.

2 Drain the spaghetti. Transfer to a large serving bowl. Add the yogurt sauce and toss well. Serve at once.

SUGGESTION
The yogurt sauce will develop a more delicate taste if you substitute the extra virgin olive oil with sesame seed oil.

Spaghetti with pumpkin

Difficulty **easy** • *Time needed* **under an hour** • *Calories per serving* **490**

INGREDIENTS
serves 4

SPAGHETTI *14 oz*
PUMPKIN *2 lbs*
TOFU CREAM *or* RICOTTA *6 tablespoons*
ONION *1*
SESAME SEED OIL *3 tablespoons*
SALT *to taste*

1 Dice the pumpkin. Peel and cut the onion in very thin slices. In a large skillet, heat the sesame oil. Add the onion and the diced pumpkin. Stirring constantly to prevent scorching, cook until the pumpkin is soft. Turn off the heat and, using a fork, crush the pumpkin.

2 In abundant boiling salted water, cook the spaghetti until al dente. Drain and transfer to a serving bowl.

3 Add the tofu cream (or ricotta) to the pumpkin puree and mix well. Pour over the spaghetti and toss. Serve at once.

SUGGESTION
To prepare the tofu cream: in boiling salted water, cook 7 oz of tofu for two to three minutes. With a slotted spoon, transfer the tofu to the bowl of a mixer. Add 2 tablespoons of the cooking water and mix until very creamy. If you use ricotta, mix it with 3 tablespoons of milk before adding to the sauce.

Spaghetti with almonds

Difficulty **easy** • *Time needed* **under an hour** • *Calories per serving* **500**

INGREDIENTS
serves 4

SPAGHETTI *12 oz*
ALMONDS *2 oz*
AVOCADO *1*
LEMON *1/2, juice*
PINE NUTS *1 tablespoon*
BUTTER *2 tablespoons*
SALT *to taste*

1 Peel the avocado, cut in two and remove the pit; dice, sprinkle with the lemon juice to prevent blackening and transfer to a mixing bowl.

2 In a skillet, boil a little water, add the almonds and briefly scald. Remove the skin by squeezing between thumb and index finger; dry the almonds well, then mince with the pine nuts.

3 In abundant boiling salted water, cook the spaghetti until al dente.

4 During this time, heat the butter in a small saucepan, add the almond and pine nut mixture and simmer over moderate heat; add a little pasta cooking water, mix well and remove from heat.

5 Drain the pasta, transfer to a serving bowl, toss with the sauce. Dry the avocado on paper towels and mix with the pasta. Serve at once.

Vegetarian spaghetti

Difficulty **easy** • *Time needed* **over an hour** • *Calories per serving* **470**

INGREDIENTS
serves 4

SPAGHETTI *14 oz*
GREEN PEPPER *1, large*
CARROT *1*
CELERY HEART *1*
BASIL *8 leaves*
PARSLEY *1 bunch*
GARLIC *1 clove*
EXTRA VIRGIN OLIVE OIL *4 tablespoons*
SALT & PEPPER *to taste*

1 Rinse and dry the vegetables and the herbs. Slice the pepper, the carrot and the celery in very thin julienne. In a large bowl, mix all the julienned vegetables, extra virgin olive oil, a pinch of salt, a pinch of fresh ground pepper. Peel, crush and chop the garlic; add to the vegetables. Cover with plastic wrap and set aside for at least one hour.

2 In abundant boiling salted water, cook the spaghetti al dente. Drain and toss with the vegetables. Serve at once.

> **SUGGESTION**
> *Other vegetables can be used for this recipe, like fennel, onions, and baby artichokes. Just remember to slice all vegetables very thinly.*

Spaghetti, quick and tasty

Difficulty **easy** • *Time needed* **less than 30 minutes** • *Calories per serving* **440**

INGREDIENTS
serves 4

SPAGHETTI *12 oz*
CRUSHED TOMATOES *6 tablespoons*
OLIVE PASTE *1 tablespoon*
PARSLEY *1 bunch*
GARLIC *1 clove*
GRATED PARMIGIANO *to taste*
EXTRA VIRGIN OLIVE OIL *2 tablespoons*
SALT *to taste*

1 Cook the spaghetti in abundant boiling salted water. During this time, prepare the sauce. In a large saucepan, mix together the crushed tomatoes, the garlic, and the olive paste. Chop the parsley and add to the sauce with 2 tablespoons of the cooking water from the pasta. Cook on medium heat, stirring for 8-10 minutes. Remove the garlic clove and discard.

2 Add the olive oil to the sauce and mix. Taste for salt and add if necessary. Drain the pasta and add to the sauce. Toss very well. Serve the spaghetti with grated parmigiano.

SUGGESTION
The dish will have a more Middle-Eastern flavor if you substitute the olive paste with 1 tablespoon of tahini.

Spaghettini with chives

Difficulty **easy** • *Time needed* **less than 30 minutes** • *Calories per serving* **400**

INGREDIENTS
serves 4

SPAGHETTINI *12 oz*
CHIVES *1 bunch*
PARSLEY *1 bunch*
BUTTER *1 tablespoons*
EXTRA VIRGIN OLIVE OIL *3 tablespoons*
SALT & PEPPER *to taste*

1 In abundant boiling salted water, cook the spaghettini. During this time, rinse, dry and finely chop the parsley and all chives. In a large pan, gently heat the olive oil and the chopped herbs.

2 When al dente, drain the spaghettini. Transfer to the pan with the herbs, add 3 tablespoons of pasta cooking water and mix well with a wooden spoon.

3 Turn off the heat. Add the butter (if desired) and a pinch of fresh ground pepper. Serve immediately.

SUGGESTION
If you have no fresh chives, you can use dried chives: in this case, remember that 1 tablespoon of fresh herbs equals about 1 teaspoon of dried herbs.

Spaghettini with walnuts and gorgonzola

Difficulty **easy** • *Time needed* **less than 30 minutes** • *Calories per serving* **570**

INGREDIENTS
serves 4

SPAGHETTINI *12 oz*
SHELLED WALNUTS *8*
GORGONZOLA *4 oz*
VODKA *1 tablespoon*
PARSLEY *1 bunch, chopped*
BUTTER *2 oz*
SALT *to taste*

1 In abundant boiling salted water, cook the spaghettini al dente.

2 Pass the gorgonzola through a sieve into a bowl; then mix in the vodka and the chopped parsley, blending thoroughly with a wooden spoon.

3 Melt the butter in a small saucepan without burning; slowly blend in the gorgonzola until smooth and creamy; chop the walnuts finely and blend into the mixture in the saucepan.

4 Drain the cooked spaghettini, transfer into the bowl with the sauce, mix gently to blend the ingredients, then transfer to a heated serving dish and serve immediately.

SUGGESTION
If you don't care for the aroma of vodka, which is very subtle anyway, you can replace it with rum. But if you want to have a dish with lighter flavor, add a tablespoon of the pasta cooking water.

Spaghettoni with tofu

Difficulty **medium** • *Time needed* **under an hour** • *Calories per serving* **490**

INGREDIENTS
serves 4

SPAGHETTONI *14 oz*
TOFU *7 oz*
TOMATO SAUCE *14 oz*
CARROT *1*
CELERY *1 stalk*
ONIONS *2*
GARLIC *1 clove*
BASIL *5-6 leaves*
VEGETABLE BROTH *1/2 cup*
GRATED CACIOCAVALLO CHEESE
5 tablespoons
EXTRA VIRGIN OLIVE OIL *3 tablespoons*
SALT & PEPPER *to taste*

1 Peel the onions and the garlic. Peel the carrot. Chop the celery, the carrot, the onions and the garlic. In a saucepan, heat the oil and cook all vegetables, stirring, for 5 minutes. Dice the tofu finely and add to the vegetables. Sauté for a few minutes. Cover the pan and, on low heat, cook for 5-6 minutes.

2 Add the vegetable broth, a pinch of salt, a pinch of fresh ground pepper and the tomato sauce. Cook for 20 minutes at medium heat to reduce the sauce a little. Add the basil leaves. Taste for salt and add if necessary.

3 In abundant boiling salted water, cook the spaghettoni cut in 3 pieces, until al dente. Drain and add to the sauce. Toss well. Add the grated caciocavallo. Toss again and serve.

Spaghettoni with rose petals

Difficulty **easy** • *Time needed* **less than 30 minutes** • *Calories per serving* **530**

INGREDIENTS
serves 4

SPAGHETTONI *11 oz*
FRESH ROSE PETALS *2 oz*
LEAN COOKED HAM *4 oz,*
in 1 slice
HEAVY CREAM *3/4 cup*
BUTTER *1 tablespoon*
SALT *to taste*

1 In a large pot, boil abundant water, add salt and cook the spaghettoni al dente.

2 Meanwhile, separate the petals from freshly cut roses, preferably rose colored, and delicately wipe them with a light and damp cloth, then cut into small pieces, saving about a dozen whole. Dice the cooked ham.

3 In a large pan, melt the butter, fry the ham and add the cream; as soon as it starts to boil, add the cut rose petals and reduce over moderate heat.

4 Drain the spaghettoni, transfer into the pan and mix well with the sauce tossing and turning with a large fork. Transfer to a hot serving dish, decorate with the whole rose petals, and serve.

Stracci with turnip tops

Difficulty **medium** • *Time needed* **under an hour** • *Calories per serving* **310**

INGREDIENTS
serves 4

For the pasta
UNBLEACHED FLOUR *2 cups*
EGGS *2*
SALT *a pinch*

For the sauce
TURNIP TOPS *5 oz*
GARLIC *1 clove*
HOT CHILI PEPPER *1/2*
EXTRA VIRGIN OLIVE OIL *4 tablespoons*
SALT *to taste*

1 Prepare the pasta. Sift the flour and make a mound; form a well in the center and mix in the eggs and the salt. Work the ingredients until the dough becomes smooth and elastic. Cover with a kitchen towel and let rest for about 30 minutes in a cool place.

2 Prepare the turnip tops. Discard the largest leaves and the flowers; cut off the tops and chop into pieces with the more tender leaves, and rinse in abundant cold water. Roll out the pasta into thin

sheets and cut into rectangles of 2 inches by 4.

3 In abundant boiling salted water, cook the pasta rectangles with the turnip tops. During this time, peel and crush the garlic. Rinse and dry the hot pepper.

4 In a skillet, heat the olive oil and sauté the garlic and the pepper. Set aside. Drain the pasta and the turnip tops and transfer to a serving bowl. Toss in the oil. Serve at once.

Tagliatelle with gorgonzola

Difficulty **easy** • *Time needed* **less than 30 minutes** • *Calories per serving* **520**

INGREDIENTS
serves 4

TAGLIATELLE *11 oz*
MILD GORGONZOLA *5 oz*
MILK *1/2 cup*
BASIL *1 bunch*
NUTMEG *a pinch*
GRATED PARMIGIANO *2 tablespoons*
BUTTER *2 tablespoons*
SALT *to taste*

1 Cut off and discard any crust around the gorgonzola. Dice the gorgonzola in large pieces. In abundant boiling salted water, cook the tagliatelle until al dente.

2 In the meantime, prepare the sauce. In a saucepan, heat the milk with the gorgonzola, the parmigiano, the nutmeg, and a pinch of salt (taste for the salt, since both cheeses are already salted).

Chop the basil and set aside.

3 On medium heat, cook the sauce, mixing with a wooden spoon, until all cheese is melted and the mixture becomes very creamy. Never let the mixture boil (lower the heat, if necessary). Add the basil. Drain the pasta. Transfer to a serving bowl, add the sauce and toss carefully. Serve very hot.

Tagliatelle with red peppers

Difficulty **difficult** • *Time needed* **over an hour** • *Calories per serving* **590**

INGREDIENTS
serves 4

For the pasta
UNBLEACHED FLOUR *4 cups*
SEMOLINA *2 tablespoons*
RED PEPPERS *2*
EGGS *1*
EXTRA VIRGIN OLIVE OIL *1 tablespoon*
SALT *to taste*

For the sauce
WATERCRESS *11 oz*
LEEK *1*
SHALLOT *1*
HEAVY CREAM *1/2 cup*
DRY WHITE WINE *1/4 cup*
BUTTER *2 oz*
SALT & PEPPER *to taste*

1 Prepare the pasta. Rinse and dry the peppers. Cut in half and discard the seeds and any white parts. Transfer the peppers to the bowl of a mixer and purée. Pour the pepper mixture into a small saucepan and, mixing, reduce slightly. Sift the flour and make a mound on the working surface; form a well in the center and mix in the egg, a tablespoon of water, the oil, the pepper mixture, the semolina and a pinch of salt; mix the ingredients thoroughly and work the dough until it becomes smooth and elastic. Cover the pasta dough with plastic wrap and set aside for at least 30 minutes.

2 With a rolling pin, roll the dough to about 1/16 in thickness. Dust the sheet of pasta lightly with flour. Roll the pasta on to itself and, with a sharp knife, slice into thin, 1/2 inch wide strips. Separate the strips and set aside.

3 Prepare the sauce. Carefully rinse the watercress. Blanch in boiling salted water for 1 minute. Drain and press the watercress to eliminate as much water as possible.

4 In a mixer, purée the watercress with the butter. Set aside. Clean and slice the leek. Peel and slice the shallot. In a pan, pour the white wine, add the leek and the shallots. Bring to a boil and let cook until the liquid has reduced to 2 tablespoons. Add the cream and reduce by half. Turn off the heat.

5 To the cream, whisk in the butter-watercress preparation a little at a time until all is well blended. Taste and add salt and pepper as needed. In the meantime, cook the tagliatelle in abundant boiling salted water until al dente. Drain. Transfer to a large serving dish. Pour the sauce onto the pasta. Serve at once.

Tagliatelle with prosciutto

Difficulty **medium** • *Time needed* **under an hour** • *Calories per serving* **600**

INGREDIENTS
serves 4

For the pasta
UNBLEACHED FLOUR *3 1/2 cups*
EGGS *2*
SALT *to taste*

For the sauce
PROSCIUTTO *4 oz, in 1 slice*
TOMATOES *4, large, ripe*
ONION *1 small, chopped*
DRY WHITE WINE *1/4 cup*
GRATED PARMIGIANO *3 tablespoons*
BUTTER *2 oz*
SALT & PEPPER *to taste*

1 Sift the flour and make a mound on the working surface; form a well in the center and mix in the egg, a tablespoon of water, the oil, the pepper mixture, the semolina and a pinch of salt; mix the ingredients thoroughly and work the dough until it becomes smooth and elastic. Wrap the dough in a wet towel and set aside for 30 minutes.

2 Roll the dough into a fine sheet. Dust with flour. Roll the dough onto itself. With a sharp knife, cut into long wide strips. Separate the strips and set aside to dry.

3 Prepare the sauce. Rinse and dice the tomatoes. Let them drain to remove most liquid. Slice off the fat from the prosciutto and set aside; dice the leant part. In a large skillet over low heat, melt the butter with the prosciutto fat. Chop the onion finely and add to the pan. Cook until transparent. Add the diced prosciutto and the dry white wine. On high heat, let the wine evaporate. Add the drained tomatoes, salt and pepper, and cook for 10 minutes.

4 During this time, cook the tagliatelle in abundant boiling salted water until al dente. Transfer the pasta to a large serving bowl. Pour the sauce over the pasta and toss well. Add the grated parmigiano cheese and fresh ground pepper to taste. Serve at once.

Tagliatelle with tuna

Difficulty **easy** • *Time needed* **less than 30 minutes** • *Calories per serving* **620**

INGREDIENTS
serves 4

TAGLIATELLE *14 oz*
TUNA IN OLIVE OIL *5 oz*
TOMATO SAUCE *5 tablespoons*
SALTED ANCHOVIES *3*
CHOPPED PARSLEY *to taste*
GARLIC *1 clove*
EXTRA VIRGIN OLIVE OIL *6 tablespoons*
SALT & PEPPER *to taste*

1 Peel and crush the garlic. Rinse and debone the anchovies. In a large pan, heat the olive oil. Add the garlic and the anchovies over low heat; using a wooden spoon, press the anchovies until they melt. Add the tomato sauce and 2 tablespoons of warm water. Cook for 1 minute. Add the tuna. Cook on low heat for 12 minutes.

2 During this time, cook the tagliatelle in abundant boiling salted water until al dente. Drain and add to the pan. Sprinkle with the chopped parsley. Toss well and serve in deep warm bowls.

Genoa style tagliatelle

Difficulty **medium** • *Time needed* **over an hour** • *Calories per serving* **450**

INGREDIENTS
serves 4

TAGLIATELLE *11 oz*
SMALL PEELED SHRIMPS *8 oz*
MONKFISH *8 oz*
LETTUCE *8 oz*
EGG YOLK *1*
MILK *1/2 cup*
ONION *1/2*
SAGE *2 leaves*
PARSLEY *1 bunch*
BRANDY *1 tablespoon*
NUTMEG *to taste*
EXTRA VIRGIN OLIVE OIL *3 tablespoons*
SALT & PEPPER *to taste*

1 Clean and wash the fish. Transfer to a large pot, cover with cold water, 2 tablespoons of salt and the sage leaves. Cook for 20 minutes. Drain the fish. Take out all fish bones and flake the fish meat.

2 Peel and chop the onion finely. Rinse, dry and chop the lettuce. In a large pan, heat the olive oil, add the onion and cook until transparent. Add the shrimp, the lettuce, a pinch of salt and a dash of pepper. Add a cup of water, cover and cook over low heat for 8 minutes. Take off the cover and let the cooking water evaporate almost completely.

3 Add the flaked fish and the brandy. Cook for one minute. With a long match, flambé, shaking the pan until all flames are gone. In a small bowl, mix the egg yolk and the milk. Add this mixture to the pan and mix well. Sprinkle with chopped parsley.

4 During this time, cook the tagliatelle in abundant boiling salted water until al dente. Drain and transfer the pasta to 4 warm serving bowls. Distribute the fish preparation over the pasta. Serve immediately.

Roman style tagliatelle

Difficulty **easy** • *Time needed* **less than 30 minutes** • *Calories per serving* **510**

INGREDIENTS
serves 4

TAGLIATELLE *12 oz*
RICOTTA *7 oz*
SHELLED WALNUTS *2 oz*
PARSLEY *1 bunch*
MARJORAM *a pinch*
GRATED PECORINO *2 tablespoons*
SALT & PEPPER *to taste*

1 Remove the stems from the parsley, trim, rinse, dry and chop finely; chop the walnuts and mix in a bowl with the parsley, the marjoram, the ricotta and the grated pecorino.

2 Work the mixture vigorously with a wooden spoon so it becomes foamy and smooth. Cook the tagliatelle in a pot with abundant boiling salted water.

3 Just before draining the pasta, reserve a few tablespoons of the cooking water and blend into the ricotta preparation; season with salt and pepper and mix again. Drain the tagliatelle when al dente, transfer to a deep bowl with the ricotta mixture, toss well and serve immediately.

Umbrian style tagliatelle

Difficulty **medium** • *Time needed* **over an hour** • *Calories per serving* **590**

INGREDIENTS
serves 4

For the pasta
UNBLEACHED FLOUR *3 cups*
EGGS *2*

For the sauce
BLACK TRUFFLE *1, small*
FRESH MUSHROOMS *14 oz*
PANCETTA *4 oz*
GARLIC *3 cloves*
CHILI PEPPER *1*
GRATED PECORINO *2 tablespoons*
BUTTER *2 oz*
SALT & PEPPER *to taste*

1 Arrange the flour in a mound on the working surface. Lightly beat the eggs and incorporate into the flour with a little water, working the mixture until it becomes smooth, and elastic. Continue to knead carefully turning it several times on the working surface.

2 Wrap in a wet towel and set aside for 20 minutes. With a rolling pin, roll the dough until thin. Dust with flour. With a sharp knife, cut the dough into long equal trips. Set aside to dry.

3 Chop the pancetta, the garlic and the pepper. During this time, in a saucepan, melt the butter and sauté the pancetta, the garlic and the pepper. Rinse, dry and cut the mushrooms into large pieces and add them to the saucepan. Salt and cook on low heat until the mushrooms are tender.

4 In abundant boiling salted water, cook the tagliatelle al dente. Transfer to a large serving bowl. Add the sauce, the grated pecorino and fresh ground pepper to taste. Toss well. Shave the truffle over the preparation and serve immediately.

Tagliatelle with mussels and clams

Difficulty **medium** • *Time needed* **under an hour** • *Calories per serving* **430**

INGREDIENTS
serves 4

TAGLIATELLE *8 oz*
MUSSELS *1 1/2 lbs*
CLAMS *2 lbs*
YELLOW PEPPER *1/2*
PARSLEY *1 bunch*
GARLIC *1 clove*
EXTRA VIRGIN OLIVE OIL *5 tablespoons*
SALT & PEPPER *to taste*

1 Brush the mussels under running water, dry and set aside. Place the clams in a large bowl and cover with cold water. Set aside for 2 hours so they lose some of the sand in their shells. Drain them and set aside. Rinse the yellow pepper, remove all seeds and white parts from the inside and dice.

2 Transfer the mussels and the clams in a large skillet. Crush the garlic and add to the shells. Pour 2 tablespoons of olive oil on top and cover the skillet. Cook on moderate heat, shaking the pan from time to time, until all shells are open. Discard any shells that remain closed.

3 Turn off the heat. Remove all meat from the shells and transfer to a bowl. Filter the cooking liquid through a fine mesh colander. Set aside.

4 In a pan, heat 3 tablespoons of olive oil. Add the diced yellow pepper and sauté for 2 minutes. Add the shellfish and the filtered liquid. Season with salt and pepper.

5 During this time, in abundant boiling salted water, cook the tagliatelle al dente. Drain and transfer to the pan. Toss well. Sprinkle with chopped parsley and serve.

Tagliatelle with herbs and tomatoes

Difficulty **medium** • *Time needed* **under an hour** • *Calories per serving* **380**

INGREDIENTS
serves 4

For the pasta
UNBLEACHED FLOUR *2 1/2 cups*
EGGS *2*
PARSLEY *1 bunch*
MARJORAM *1 bunch*
THYME *1 bunch*
EXTRA VIRGIN OLIVE OIL *1 tablespoon*
SALT *to taste*

For the sauce
TOMATOES *11 oz, ripe and firm*
SAGE *1 leaf*
MARJORAM *1 bunch*
BASIL *1 bunch*
GRATED PARMIGIANO *3 tablespoons*
EXTRA VIRGIN OLIVE OIL *2 tablespoons*
SALT & PEPPER *to taste*

1 Prepare the pasta dough. Remove the stalks and trim the parsley, the marjoram and the thyme; rinse and dry with a dish towel; chop finely. Sift the flour into a mound on the working surface; beat the eggs lightly with a fork and place in the center of the mound. Mix in the extra virgin olive oil, the chopped herbs, a pinch of salt and work the ingredients until the dough is uniform and smooth and elastic. If the dough is too hard, add a little water.

2 Roll out the pasta about 1/16 inch thick. Dust the surface with flour, roll the sheet onto itself and, with a sharp knife (or an indented rotary cutter) cut into strips about 1/2 inch wide. Lay out the tagliatelle on the lightly floured working surface to dry.

3 Prepare the sauce. Scald the tomatoes in boiling water, drain, peel, squeeze gently to remove the seeds and the water and dice the rest. Heat the oil in a pot with the sage, the marjoram and a few leaves of basil; add the diced tomato and a pinch of salt and pepper. Cook over high heat for 7-8 minutes. Rinse and chop the remaining basil, and add to the sauce at the end of cooking.

4 During this time cook the tagliatelle in abundant boiling salted water; drain, mix with the prepared sauce and serve, accompanied by the grated parmigiano.

Tagliatelle with butter, sage and walnuts

Difficulty **easy** • *Time needed* **less than 30 minutes** • *Calories per serving* **710**

INGREDIENTS
serves 6

TAGLIATELLE *1 1/4 lbs*
SAGE *2 branches*
SHELLED WALNUTS *7 oz*
GRATED PARMIGIANO *6 tablespoons*
BUTTER *2 oz*
SALT *to taste*

1 Cook the tagliatelle in abundant boiling salted water until al dente.

2 In the meantime, chop the walnuts in a small food processor. In a small pan, heat the butter and cook the sage. Drain the pasta and toss with the butter and sage, the grated parmigiano and the chopped nuts. Serve at once, while hot.

Tagliatelle with tofu tidbits

Difficulty **medium** • *Time needed* **under an hour** • *Calories per serving* **410**

INGREDIENTS
serves 4

EGG TAGLIATELLE *11 oz*
TOFU *8 oz*
TOMATOES *11 oz*
PARSLEY *1 bunch*
GARLIC *1 clove*
HOT CHILI PEPPER *1*
DRY WHITE WINE *1/2 cup*
SESAME SEED OIL *3 tablespoons*
SALT & PEPPER *to taste*

1 Scald the tomatoes in boiling water. Drain and peel. Press them gently to remove the seeds and chop into large pieces. In a skillet, heat the extra virgin olive oil with the sliced garlic. Dice the tofu and add to the oil. Sauté over high heat for a few minutes. Season with salt and pepper. Add the white wine and let evaporate.

2 Add the tomatoes and the chili pepper. Cover the skillet and cook on moderate heat for 25 minutes. Add the parsley to the tofu ragù and cook another 5 minutes.

3 Cook the tagliatelle al dente in abundant salted boiling water. Drain and transfer to a serving bowl. Toss in the ragù and serve very hot.

> **SUGGESTION**
> *You can replace the parsley with basil or, in winter, with a few leaves of sage to add to the chopped tomatoes.*

Tagliatelle with potatoes and kale

Difficulty **medium** • *Time needed* **over an hour** • *Calories per serving* **510**

INGREDIENTS
serves 4

For the pasta
UNBLEACHED FLOUR *3 cups*
EGGS *3*
SALT *to taste*

For the sauce
POTATOES *8 oz*
KALE *14 oz*
GRATED PARMIGIANO *2 tablespoons*
EXTRA VIRGIN OLIVE OIL *4 tablespoons*
SALT *to taste*

1 Sift the flour and form a mound on the working surface. Break the eggs into the center, add the salt and work the ingredients until the dough becomes smooth and elastic. Wrap in a moist kitchen towel and let rest in a cool place for about 30 minutes.

2 When rested, take the dough and roll it out into a very thin sheet; dust with flour, roll onto itself and, with a very sharp knife, cut into 3/8 inch slices; roll out onto the flour dusted working surface and let dry.

3 Clean the kale, remove the hard stalks, rinse thoroughly and cut into strips. Peel the potatoes, rinse and cut into small pieces.

4 In a large pot, boil abundant water, add salt, potatoes and the kale; cook for 10 minutes, then add the tagliatelle. When cooked al dente, drain together with the vegetables, transfer to a serving dish, drizzle with the extra virgin olive oil and sprinkle with the grated parmigiano. Serve immediately.

> **SUGGESTION**
> *If you want to skip making the pasta yourself, this dish will be just as satisfying if you use 1 lb of fresh egg pasta instead.*

Tagliatelle with herbs and anchovies

Difficulty **easy** • *Time needed* **less than 30 minutes** • *Calories per serving* **560**

INGREDIENTS
serves 4

TAGLIATELLE *14 oz*
ANCHOVY FILLETS *2, desalted*
HARD BOILED EGGS *2*
ONION *1 slice*
SAGE *2 leaves*
ROSEMARY *1/2 branch*
THYME *a pinch*
GRATED PARMIGIANO *to taste*
BUTTER *3 tablespoons*
SALT & PEPPER *to taste*

1 Rinse, dry and chop all herbs and the onion together very finely. Chop the anchovy fillets and mix with the herbs. Peel the eggs and dice.

2 In abundant boiling salted water, cook the tagliatelle al dente.

3 In the top saucepan of a double boiler, melt the butter. Add the herbs and the anchovy mixture and the chopped eggs. Season with salt and pepper. Transfer to a serving bowl that you can keep warm over the double boiler.

4 When the tagliatelle are cooked, add them to the bowl. Add 2 tablespoons of the pasta cooking water and the thyme. Toss. Serve accompanied with the grated parmigiano.

Tagliatelle with basil and tomato

Difficulty **easy** • *Time needed* **less than 30 minutes** • *Calories per serving* **450**

INGREDIENTS
serves 4

TAGLIATELLE *14 oz*
TOMATO SAUCE *14 oz*
ONION *1*
BASIL *1 bunch*
GARLIC *1 clove*
GRATED PARMIGIANO *3 tablespoons*
EXTRA VIRGIN OLIVE OIL *1 tablespoon*
SALT & PEPPER *to taste*

1 Cook the tagliatelle al dente in abundant boiling salted water. During this time, chop the onion, garlic and basil very finely and transfer to a small pan.

2 In the same pan, pour the tomato sauce, add 1 tablespoon of extra virgin olive oil, a pinch of salt and as much fresh ground pepper as you like. Mix well and cook on medium heat for 5 minutes.

3 When the pasta is ready, drain and transfer to a large serving bowl. Add the tomato sauce and the grated parmigiano. Toss well and serve immediately.

SUGGESTION
If you don't have ready made tomato sauce, you can use fresh tomatoes, peeled and passed through a food mill. Simply cook the sauce an extra 10 minutes.

Tagliatelle with poppy seeds

Difficulty **easy** • *Time needed* **less than 30 minutes** • *Calories per serving* **480**

INGREDIENTS
serves 4

TAGLIATELLE *11 oz*
POPPY SEEDS *2 tablespoons*
SHELLED ALMONDS *2 oz*
SESAME SEED OIL *3 tablespoons*
COARSE SEA SALT *to taste*

1 Peel the almonds and cut into thin strips. Cook the tagliatelle in abundant boiling salted water. In a large pan, heat the oil, add the almonds and the poppy seeds and cook briefly.

2 Drain the pasta and transfer to the pan, add a pinch of salt and gently stir while cooking for another 2 minutes. Transfer to a warm serving plate and serve immediately.

Tagliatelle with zucchini and eggs

Difficulty **easy** • *Time needed* **under an hour** • *Calories per serving* **480**

INGREDIENTS
serves 4

FRESHLY MADE TAGLIATELLE *14 oz*
ZUCCHINI *4*
EGGS *2*
MILK *2 tablespoons*
PARSLEY *1 bunch, chopped*
GARLIC *1 clove*
NUTMEG *a pinch*
GRATED PARMIGIANO *2 oz*
EXTRA VIRGIN OLIVE OIL *3 tablespoons*
SALT & PEPPER *to taste*

1 Clean, dry and cut the zucchini in thick slices. In a large skillet, heat the oil, add the garlic clove. Cook for 1 minute and remove the garlic. Add the zucchini.

2 On high heat, brown the zucchini. Lower the heat and, stirring, let the zucchini cook until tender. Add salt and fresh ground pepper.

3 In a bowl, beat the eggs with the milk, a pinch of salt and the nutmeg. Stirring, add the eggs to the zucchini and cook until the eggs are just settled but not dry. Set aside.

4 In abundant boiling salted water, cook the tagliatelle until al dente. Drain well and add to the zucchini and egg mix. Toss well; sprinkle with chopped parsley. Serve with the grated parmigiano.

Tagliatelle with borage

Difficulty **medium** • *Time needed* **over an hour** • *Calories per serving* **720**

INGREDIENTS
serves 4

For the pasta
UNBLEACHED FLOUR *3 1/2 cups*
BORAGE *5 oz, only leaves*
EGGS *3*
SALT *to taste*

For the sauce
GROUND BEEF *11 oz*
PANCETTA *2 oz*
TOMATO PASTE *2 tablespoons*
CARROT *1*
CELERY *1 stalk*
ONION *1*
DRY WHITE WINE *1/2 cup*
EXTRA VIRGIN OLIVE OIL *4 tablespoons*
SALT & PEPPER *to taste*

1 Prepare the paste: clean and trim the borage; cook it for 10 minutes in boiling salted water. Drain well and pass it through a food mill.

2 Sift the flour onto a work surface. Add the eggs and the borage. Work the ingredients until you obtain a smooth and elastic dough. Roll the dough until you have a very thin sheet. Set aside to dry for a few minutes on the flour dusted work surface. Fold the dough in 3 layers and slice into strips about 3/8 inch wide. Set aside to dry on a kitchen towel.

3 Prepare the sauce: chop the onion, carrot, celery and pancetta coarsely. In a large saucepan, heat the oil on low heat. Add the pancetta and let it melt slowly. Add the ground beef and mix well. Add the white wine and, on high heat, let it evaporate.

4 Dilute the tomato paste in a spoonful of warm water and add it to the meat. Season with salt and pepper. Turn down the heat, cover the saucepan and cook for 2 hours.

5 In abundant boiling salted water, cook the tagliatelle until al dente. Drain and pour into a large serving bowl. Add the sauce and toss well. Serve.

Chestnut tagliatelle

Difficulty **medium** • *Time needed* **over an hour** • *Calories per serving* **450**

INGREDIENTS
serves 4

For the pasta
CHESTNUT FLOUR *2 cups*
UNBLEACHED FLOUR *1 cup*
EGGS *3*
SALT & PEPPER *to taste*

For the sauce
RICOTTA *5 oz*
HEAVY CREAM *4 tablespoons*
BUTTER *1 tablespoon*
SALT & PEPPER *to taste*

1 Sift both flours on the work surface adding a pinch of salt and pepper; form a mound and, in the center, break the eggs. Work the ingredients until the dough becomes smooth and elastic. Make a ball and let it rest in a cool place, not in the fridge, covered with a cloth for about 30 minutes.

2 Divide the dough into 3 parts; pass them through a pasta machine, one at a time, until the sheet is not too thin; then pass though the tagliatelle cutter. Set the cut paste on a kitchen towel and let dry for about 15 minutes.

3 In a large pot, boil abundant water, add salt, and cook the tagliatelle al dente. During this time, in a mixing bowl, work the ricotta with a wooden spoon, add the butter, the heavy cream, a pinch of pepper and heat the mixture in a "bain-marie," stirring frequently.

4 When done, drain the tagliatelle, transfer to a heated serving bowl and toss with the ricotta and cream sauce. Serve immediately.

Buckwheat tagliatelle with basil

Difficulty **medium** • *Time needed* **over an hour** • *Calories per serving* **360**

INGREDIENTS
serves 4

For the pasta
BUCKWHEAT FLOUR *1 1/2 cups*
UNBLEACHED FLOUR *1 1/2 cups*
SALT *a pinch*

For the sauce
BASIL *2 oz*
TOMATOES *7 oz*
CIDER VINEGAR *2 tablespoons*
EXTRA VIRGIN OLIVE OIL *4 tablespoons*
SALT & PEPPER *to taste*

1 Sift both flours onto the work surface; make a mound and in the center add a pinch of salt and enough water to make a dough of proper consistency. Knead the ingredients until smooth and elastic. Cover with a slightly humid kitchen towel and let rest for 30 minutes in a cool place. At the end of this time, roll out the paste to a thickness of about 1/16 inch.

2 Dust the dough sheet with flour, roll onto itself and, with a very sharp knife, cut the tagliatelle to a width of about 1/8 inch. Scald the tomatoes in boiling water, drain, peel, squeeze to eliminate the seeds and the water, and dice coarsely.

3 Place the diced tomatoes in a colander and let rest for 20 minutes to lose the vegetal juice. Rinse the basil and gently pat dry with a kitchen towel. Put into the bowl of a mixer, add a dash of salt and blend, adding the olive oil little by little. When well blended, transfer to a bowl.

4 Blend the tomatoes in a food processor and add to the basil sauce, add the cider vinegar and a pinch of salt and fresh ground pepper; mix with a whisk until well blended. Cook the tagliatelle in abundant boiling salted water; when al dente, drain and toss with the tomato and basil sauce. Serve immediately.

Whole wheat tagliatelle with herbs

Difficulty **medium** • *Time needed* **under an hour** • *Calories per serving* **400**

INGREDIENTS
serves 4

For the pasta
WHOLE WHEAT FLOUR *5 cups*
EGGS *2*
BASIL *1 small bunch*
PARSLEY *1 bunch*
SAGE *a few leaves*
ROSEMARY *1 branch*
LUKEWARM WATER *1/2 cup*
EXTRA VIRGIN OLIVE OIL *1 teaspoon*
SALT & PEPPER *to taste*

For the sauce
TOMATO & BASIL SAUCE *(p. 107)*

1 Sift the flour onto a work surface in a mound. Make a well and pour in the eggs, the oil, the water, the salt and the pepper. Mix well until you obtain a firm dough. Rinse, dry and chop all herbs and add to the pasta dough.

2 Work the dough vigorously keeping the work surface well floured. When the dough is smooth and elastic, form a ball, cover with a kitchen towel, and let rest for 15-20 minutes, preferably in the refrigerator.

3 Divide the dough into 3 equal parts, then roll in a pasta machine to the de-sired thickness and then cut with the appropriate tagliatelle cutter. Cook the tagliatelle in abundant boiling salted water until al dente. Drain, transfer to a tureen and toss with the tomato and basil sauce. Serve in individual bowls.

SUGGESTION
The tagliatelle prepared in this way can be served with butter, vegetable sauce, olive paste, tofu ragù, squash and ricotta, etc.

Trentino style tagliatelle

Difficulty **medium** • *Time needed* **over an hour** • *Calories per serving* **680**

INGREDIENTS
serves 4

For the pasta
UNBLEACHED FLOUR *3 cups*
EGGS *3*

For the sauce
VEAL ROAST *2 lbs, in one piece*
ONION *1*
UNBLEACHED FLOUR *as needed*
HEAVY CREAM *1/3 cup*
BEEF BROTH *1 cup*
DRY WHITE WINE *1/2 cup*
BUTTER *3 tablespoons*
SALT & PEPPER *to taste*

1 Prepare the sauce: roll the meat in some flour. Peel and slice the onion. In a large pan, melt the butter, add the onion and the meat. Brown on all sides. Add the wine and let it evaporate over high heat. Season with salt and pepper. Add half the broth and cover the pan. Let cook on low heat, adding the rest of the broth as needed. After 1 1/2 hours, the sauce should be nicely dense.

2 Sift the flour into a mound on the work surface. Break the eggs in the center and work the flour, first slowly, then vigorously for about 15 minutes until the dough becomes smooth and elastic.

With a rolling pin, roll out the dough until thin. Dust with flour and roll onto itself. With a very sharp knife, slice into wide strips. Set the strips aside to dry.

3 In abundant boiling salted water, cook the pasta until al dente. Take the piece of meat out of its pan. Set aside and cut into thick slices. Leave in a warm oven. In the pot, add the cream and mix well on low heat.

4 Drain the pasta and transfer to the sauce. Toss well and serve with the sliced meat. This is served without grated cheese.

Hungarian style tagliatelle

Difficulty **medium** • *Time needed* **over an hour** • *Calories per serving* **470**

INGREDIENTS
serves 4

For the pasta
UNBLEACHED FLOUR *11 oz*
EGGS *3*
SALT *to taste*

For the sauce
WHITE CABBAGE *7 oz*
VEGETABLE BROTH *1 cup*
GRATED PARMIGIANO *4 tablespoons*
BUTTER *3 tablespoons*
FRESH GROUND PEPPER *a pinch*
SALT *to taste*

1 Prepare the pasta: sift the flour in a mound, make a well in the middle; add eggs and salt. Work the ingredients until you obtain a smooth and elastic dough; dust the dough with flour and roll it onto itself. With a very sharp knife, slice the dough into wide strips. Set aside to dry. In a large pan, melt the butter, add the cabbage, sliced in long strips, the salt and the pepper. Cover the pan and cook on low heat for 20 minutes. Add the vegetable broth and cook another 20 minutes.

2 In abundant salted boiling water, cook the tagliatelle until al dente. Drain well and pour into a large serving bowl. Pour the cooked cabbage over; add the grated cheese and toss well. Serve.

Green tagliatelle with peas and mint

Difficulty **medium** • *Time needed* **under an hour** • *Calories per serving* **340**

INGREDIENTS
serves 4

For the pasta
UNBLEACHED FLOUR *2 cups*
EGGS *2*
CHARD *4 oz*
SALT *to taste*

For the sauce
SHELLED PEAS *7 oz*
MINT *1 bunch*
ONION *1*
GRATED PARMIGIANO *2 tablespoons*
SESAME SEED OIL *2 tablespoons*
SALT *to taste*

1 Clean the chard; cook for 1 minute in salted water. Drain well in a towel and chop finely. Sift the flour in a mound, make a well in the center, add the eggs, salt, chopped chard and work all ingredients until you obtain a smooth and elastic dough.

2 Roll the dough until thin. Dust with flour and roll it onto itself. With a very sharp knife, slice into wide strips. Set aside to dry. Peel and slice the onion; rinse, dry and chop the mint.

3 In a skillet, heat the oil, add the onions and cook just until transparent. Add the fresh peas; salt, and cook for 13 minutes, mixing with a wooden spoon. Add half the chopped mint and cook another 2 minutes.

4 During this time, cook the tagliatelle in abundant salted boiling water until al dente. Drain and transfer to a serving plate. Pour the sauce over and toss well. Add the rest of the mint and the grated cheese. Serve very hot.

Green tagliatelle with carrots and rosemary

Difficulty **easy** • *Time needed* **under an hour** • *Calories per serving* **440**

INGREDIENTS
serves 4

GREEN TAGLIATELLE *12 oz*
CARROTS *8 oz*
ROSEMARY *1 bunch*
SOY SAUCE *1 tablespoon (optional)*
GRATED PARMIGIANO *2 tablespoons*
EXTRA VIRGIN OLIVE OIL *3 tablespoons*
SALT *to taste*

1 Clean the rosemary and take off all needles. Discard the stem. Chop the rosemary finely. Clean, peel, and cut the carrot in julienne.

2 In a skillet, heat the oil. Add the carrots and the rosemary. Add a pinch of salt and cook on low heat, mixing delicately. When the carrots are tender, add the soy sauce and mix well. Set aside.

3 In abundant boiling salted water, cook the green tagliatelle until al dente. Drain and pour into the skillet. Toss with the carrots and serve immediately with grated parmigiano.

Green tagliatelle with cured tongue

Difficulty **easy** • *Time needed* **under h alf an hour** • *Calories per serving* **660**

INGREDIENTS
serves 4

GREEN TAGLIATELLE *12 oz*
SALT CURED TONGUE *4 oz*
PARSLEY *1 bunch*
HEAVY CREAM *1 cup*
VEGETABLE EXTRACT *as needed*
GRATED PARMIGIANO *4 tablespoons*
BUTTER *4 tablespoons*
SALT & PEPPER *to taste*

1 In abundant boiling salted water, cook the tagliatelle until al dente. During this time, in a saucepan, mix the cream, the butter, the cheese, the tongue (cut in thin slices), the cube of vegetable extract and a little salt and pepper.

2 Heat the ingredients. Drain the pasta and add it to the sauce. Toss well to cover all pasta with the sauce. Before serving, sprinkle with the chopped parsley.

SUGGESTION
You can substitute the parsley with chives finely chopped and you can use the kind of pasta you prefer, preferably long.

Buckwheat taglierini

Difficulty **medium** • *Time needed* **under an hour** • *Calories per serving* **290**

INGREDIENTS
serves 4

For the pasta
BUCKWHEAT FLOUR *1 cup*
UNBLEACHED FLOUR *1 cup*
EGGS *2*
SALT *a pinch*

For the sauce
BASIL *1 bunch*
SHALLOT *1*
GRATED PARMIGIANO *2 tablespoons*
SESAME SEED OIL *3 tablespoons*
SALT & PEPPER *to taste*

1 Sift both flours onto a work surface in a mound. Make a well in the middle and add the eggs and the salt. Work the ingredients until you obtain a smooth and elastic dough. Wrap in a humid towel and set aside for 30 minutes. With a rolling pin, roll the dough until thin. Dust the dough with flour, roll it onto itself and, with a very sharp knife, slice into thin taglierini. Set aside to dry a few minutes.

2 In abundant boiling salted water, cook the taglierini until al dente. During this time, chop the shallot. Rinse, dry and chop the basil. In a large skillet, heat the oil on low heat, add the shallot and half the basil and cook until the shallot is transparent. Season with salt and pep-

per. Set aside.

3 Drain the taglierini. Pour them into the skillet and toss with the sauce. Add the rest of the basil and the parmigiano. Toss again and serve immediately.

Taglierini with caviar and smoked salmon

Difficulty **easy** • *Time needed* **less than 30 minutes** • *Calories per serving* **520**

INGREDIENTS
serves 4

TAGLIERINI *12 oz*
CAVIAR *2 oz*
SMOKED SALMON *5 oz*
PARSLEY *1 bunch*
EXTRA VIRGIN OLIVE OIL *4 tablespoons*
SALT *to taste*

1 In abundant boiling salted water, cook the taglierini. Clean, dry; and chop the parsley finely. Slice the smoked salmon into thin strips.

2 Drain the taglierini. Pour them into a large serving bowl. Add the caviar, the smoked salmon and the parsley. Toss. Add the extra virgin olive oil and mix well. Serve.

Tagliolini with fennel

Difficulty **easy** • *Time needed* **under an hour** • *Calories per serving* **440**

INGREDIENTS

serves 4

EGG TAGLIOLINI *11 oz*
FENNEL *2, small*
ONION *1*
HEAVY CREAM *2 tablespoons*
GRATED PARMIGIANO *to taste*
EXTRA VIRGIN OLIVE OIL *3 tablespoons*
SALT & PEPPER *to taste*

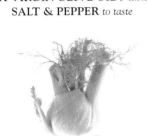

1 Clean the fennel. Discard the exterior branches but keep the little green sprigs. Slice in small pieces and cook in abundant salted water. Drain when soft. Blend the fennel in a food processor to obtain a creamy texture.

2 Dice the onion. Heat the oil in a pan; add the onion, season with salt and pepper; when the onion is transparent, add the fennel cream and cook for 10 minutes. Add the heavy cream and mix well.

3 In a large pot bring abundant water to a boil, add salt and cook the tagliolini

until al dente (this should take only a few minutes). Drain the tagliolini and pour them into a serving dish. Add the parmigiano and the hot cream of fennel. Toss well and serve.

Tagliolini with gorgonzola and ricotta

Difficulty **medium** • *Time needed* **under an hour** • *Calories per serving* **510**

INGREDIENTS

serves 4

For the pasta
UNBLEACHED FLOUR *3 cups*
EGGS *3*
SALT *to taste*

For the sauce
GORGONZOLA *3 oz*
RICOTTA *5 oz*
MILK *1 cup*
BASIL *1 bunch*
CHIVES *1 bunch*
GRATED PARMIGIANO *3 tablespoons*
SALT & PEPPER *to taste*

1 Prepare the pasta: sift the flour on a work surface and make a mound. Make a well in the middle and add the eggs and a large pinch of salt. Work all ingredients until the dough is smooth and elastic. Wrap the dough in plastic wrap and set aside for at least 30 minutes.

2 Prepare the sauce: rinse, drain and chop the basil and the chives. Discard the crust from the gorgonzola and dice. In the bowl of a food processor, add the gorgonzola, the ricotta, half the milk and blend until creamy; pour into a saucepan with the leftover milk. Add a little salt and pepper, the chopped basil, and the chives. Mix all ingredients thoroughly.

3 Prepare the tagliolini: roll the pasta dough until very thin. Dust with flour and roll the dough onto itself. With a sharp knife, slice into thin strips. Leave the strips of pasta to dry for a few minutes. Heat the gorgonzola sauce lightly, stirring constantly.

4 In abundant boiling salted water, cook the tagliolini until al dente. Add 2 tablespoons of the pasta cooking water to the sauce. Drain the tagliolini and pour them into a warm serving bowl. Add the sauce and toss well. Serve immediately with the grated parmigiano.

Black tagliolini with cuttlefish

Difficulty **medium** • *Time needed* **under an hour** • *Calories per serving* **310**

INGREDIENTS
serves 4

For the pasta
UNBLEACHED FLOUR *2 cups*
EGGS *1*
SQUID INK *1 ready made portion*
SALT *to taste*

For the sauce
BABY CUTTLEFISH *11 oz*
TOMATOES *7 oz, ripe and firm*
PARSLEY *1 bunch*
GARLIC *1 clove*
EXTRA VIRGIN OLIVE OIL *3 tablespoons*
SALT & PEPPER *to taste*

1 Prepare the pasta dough. Pass the black ink though a fine mesh colander and dilute with one tablespoon of water. Sift the flour over a work surface into a small mound. Make a well in the middle; add the egg, a pinch of salt and the ink. Work all ingredients into a smooth and elastic ball of dough. Cover the dough with plastic wrap and set aside for 30 minutes in a cool place.

2 Clean the baby cuttlefish, wash and drain; pat dry with a clean towel. Slice into thin strips.

3 In a pot of boiling water, drop in the tomatoes for one minute. Drain them, peel and squeeze out the seeds. Dice the tomatoes and set aside. Peel the garlic and chop finely.

4 In a skillet, heat the oil on low heat. Add the garlic; cook for 1 minute. Slice the cuttlefish and add to the skillet. Cook, mixing with a wooden spoon for minute. Add the tomatoes and continue cooking for 5-6 minutes. Add the parsley and mix well. Set aside.

5 With a rolling pin, roll the dough; into a thin long sheet. Dust with flour. Roll the pasta sheet onto itself. Using a sharp knife, slice the roll of pasta into thin strips.

6 In abundant salted water, cook the tagliolini until al dente. Drain them and pour them into a warm serving bowl. Pour the sauce over and toss gently. Serve immediately.

Tagliolini with radicchio

Difficulty **easy** • *Time needed* **under an hour** • *Calories per serving* **380**

INGREDIENTS
serves 4

For the pasta
UNBLEACHED FLOUR *2 1/2 cups*
EGGS *2*
SALT *a pinch*

For the sauce
RADICCHIO *11 oz*
FRESH SAUSAGE *4 oz*
TOMATOES *2*
ONION *1, small*
EXTRA VIRGIN OLIVE OIL *2 tablespoons*
SALT & PEPPER *to taste*

1 Prepare the pasta. Sift the flour into a mound on the work surface. In the center, break the eggs, add the salt and work the ingredients until the dough is smooth and elastic. With a rolling pin roll out the dough to a thickness of about 1/16 inch. Dust the sheet with flour, roll onto itself and, with a very sharp knife, cut the tagliolini about 1/16 in wide. Lay out on a floured work surface and let dry.

2 Trim the radicchio, rinse it, carefully pat dry, separate the leaves and tear them lengthways, then cut crossways. Rinse the tomatoes, cut in half, squeeze out the seeds and the water, then dice.

3 Peel the onion, slice thinly, put in a pan with the oil and sauté over low heat until transparent. Crumble the sausage and add to the onion and cook for a few minutes stirring with a wooden spoon.

4 Add the radicchio strips, cook for about 2 minutes, season with a pinch of salt and a dash of pepper and remove from heat; add the diced tomatoes and mix well. In the meantime, cook the tagliolini in abundant boiling salted water until al dente. Drain, transfer to a serving bowl and mix with the hot radicchio sauce. Serve at once.

Tagliolini with roast meat sauce

Difficulty **easy** • *Time needed* **over an hour** • *Calories per serving* **560**

INGREDIENTS
serves 4

EGG TAGLIOLINI *14 oz*
VEAL ROAST *2 lbs*
TOMATO SAUCE *2 tablespoons*
PANCETTA *2 oz*
CARROT *1*
CELERY *1 stalk*
ROSEMARY *1 branch*
GARLIC *1 clove*
BEEF STOCK *1 cup*
GRATED PARMIGIANO *4 tablespoons*
BUTTER *2 tablespoons*
SALT & PEPPER *to taste*

1 Peel the garlic. Rinse and dry the rosemary. Slice the garlic and the rosemary. With a little knife, make fine incisions into the meat. Fill the cuts with rosemary and garlic pieces.

2 Chop the pancetta and cook it with the butter in a saucepan on medium heat. When the pancetta has melted slightly, add the veal and brown it on all sides.

3 Season the meat with salt and pepper. Slice the carrot and the celery and add to the pan. Mix the tomato sauce with the bouillon and add to the saucepan.

4 Cover the pan and cook on low heat for about 45 minutes. Add a little bouillon, if necessary. When cooked there should be abundant meat juice.

5 Set the meat aside (you can serve it as a main dish). Filter the meat juices left in the pan. Cook the tagliolini in abundant boiling salted water until al dente. Return the filtered meat juices to the pan. Pour in the tagliolini and toss well. Serve with grated parmigiano.

Tagliolini with truffles

Difficulty **medium** • *Time needed* **under an hour** • *Calories per serving* **450**

INGREDIENTS
serves 4

For the pasta
CHESTNUT FLOUR *1 cup*
UNBLEACHED FLOUR *2 cups*
EGGS *2*
EGG WHITES *1*
SALT *to taste*

For the sauce
TRUFFLE *1, small*
BUTTER *6 tablespoons*

1 Prepare the pasta. Sift the chestnut flour and the unbleached flour on a work surface in a mound. Make a well in the middle. In the well, add the eggs, the egg white and a pinch of salt. Work all ingredients until the dough is elastic and smooth. Cover in plastic wrap and set aside for at least 30 minutes.

2 Prepare the tagliolini. Roll out the pasta into a thin sheet; dust with a little flour, roll the sheet onto itself, and with a very sharp knife, cut into thin strips.

Roll out on the flour dusted work surface and let dry.

3 Prepare the sauce. Brush the truffle, rinse, dry and cut into thin slices. Melt the butter in a skillet.

4 In the meantime, cook the tagliolini in abundant boiling salted water. When al dente, drain, transfer to a serving dish; pour the melted butter over, place the truffle slices on top and serve hot.

Tagliolini with aromatic herbs

Difficulty **easy** • *Time needed* **under an hour** • *Calories per serving* **430**

INGREDIENTS
serves 4

TAGLIOLINI *14 oz*
PARSLEY *1 bunch*
BASIL *1 bunch*
SAGE *3 leaves*
ROSEMARY *1 bunch*
MARJORAM *1 bunch*
THYME *1 bunch*
OREGANO *a pinch*
PEELED TOMATOES *11 oz*
GARLIC *1 clove*
EXTRA VIRGIN OLIVE OIL *3 tablespoons*
SALT & PEPPER *to taste*

1 In a skillet, heat the extra virgin olive oil and add the peeled garlic. Cook until lightly browned and discard the garlic. Add the diced tomatoes and cook on low heat for 20 minutes, stirring with a wooden spoon. Rinse, dry and chop the parsley, basil, sage and rosemary.

2 In a large pot, boil abundant salted water. Throw in the pasta and cook until al dente. Season the tomato sauce with salt and pepper. Add the chopped herbs, the marjoram, the thyme, a large pinch of oregano and mix well. Drain the pasta. Pour it into a large serving bowl and add the sauce. Toss well and serve.

Tagliolini with chicken and leeks

Difficulty **easy** • *Time needed* **under an hour** • *Calories per serving* **320**

INGREDIENTS
serves 4

FRESH TAGLIOLINI *8 oz*
CHICKEN BREAST *4 oz*
LEEKS *3*
GREEN ONIONS *2*
DRY WHITE WINE *3 tablespoons*
GRATED PARMIGIANO *3 tablespoons*
EXTRA VIRGIN OLIVE OIL *2 tablespoons*
SALT & PEPPER *to taste*

1 Rinse the green onions and the leeks. Take off all surface leaves and slice them separately. Rinse and dry the chicken breast. In a skillet, heat the extra virgin olive oil. Salt and pepper the chicken breast and fry in the oil on both sides. Let cook for about 8 minutes. Set aside between two plates to keep the chicken warm.

2 In the same skillet, cook the leeks until transparent. Add the wine and 3 tablespoons of water and cook for 10 minutes. Add the green onions and continue cooking for another 10 minutes. Add 1/2 cup of water and cook for 10 minutes, mixing with a wooden spoon. Season with salt and pepper.

3 Pour the mixture in a blender and mix until you obtain an homogenous sauce. In the meantime, cook the tagliolini in abundant boiling salted water until al dente.

4 Drain the tagliolini and pour them into a large warm serving dish. Toss with the grated parmigiano and a dash of extra virgin olive oil. Slice the chicken breast into strips and add to the pasta with the sauce. Serve immediately.

Tagliolini from Campobasso

Difficulty **easy** • *Time needed* **less than 30 minutes** • *Calories per serving* **370**

INGREDIENTS
serves 4

FRESH TAGLIOLINI *11 oz*
PROSCIUTTO *3 oz, in 1 slice*
ONION *1, small*
PARSLEY *1 bunch*
CHILI PEPPER *1/2*
EXTRA VIRGIN OLIVE OIL *3 tablespoons*
SALT & PEPPER *to taste*

1 In a large pot, bring water to boil. Add salt and the tagliolini. During this cooking time, heat the oil in a large skillet. Add the sliced onion and the crushed pepper. Sauté until the onion is transparent.

2 Cut the prosciutto into very thin slices and add to the onion mixture. Add 2-3 tablespoons of the pasta water, the chopped parsley and salt and fresh ground pepper to taste.

3 Drain the tagliolini. Add to the skillet and mix well with the onion-prosciutto preparation. Serve immediately.

Three colored tagliolini

Difficulty **medium** • *Time needed* **over an hour** • *Calories per serving* **490**

INGREDIENTS
serves 6

For the pasta
UNBLEACHED FLOUR *6 cups*
EGGS *5*
SPINACH *11 oz*
TOMATO PASTE *2 tablespoons*
SAFFRON *1 sachet*
SALT *to taste*

For the sauce
BUTTER *2 oz*
SAGE *3 leaves*

1 Clean the spinach and drain well. In a non-stick pan, cook the spinach for 3 minutes to dry them. Press well to remove excess water. Chop the spinach finely (or pass in a food processor). Return the chopped spinach to the pan and cook a few minutes to dry again, stirring with a spoon. Set aside to cool.

2 On a work surface, sift the flour into three equal mounds. Make a well in the middle of each. In the first, add the spinach and one egg with a dash of salt. Work the ingredients until the dough is homogenous, smooth, and elastic.

3 In the second mound, add 2 eggs and the tomato paste. To the third, add 2 eggs, a dash of salt and the saffron, diluted in one tablespoon of cold water. Work each preparation until homogenous and elastic.

4 Each type of dough needs to be wrapped in a humid towel and set aside for at least 30 minutes (never in the refrigerator where it becomes hard). After 30 minutes, take each ball of pasta and roll out separately on a floured work surface until very thin.

5 Dust each sheet of pasta with flour and roll them tightly. With a very sharp knife, slice the pasta into thin tagliolini. Bring abundant salted water to a boil. Add the colored tagliolini and cook al dente.

6 During the cooking time, in a small saucepan, melt the butter and heat the sage. Drain the tagliolini, put them in a large serving bowl and toss with the melted butter. Serve immediately with grated parmigiano.

Green tagliolini with salmon

Difficulty **medium** • *Time needed* **under an hour** • *Calories per serving* **630**

INGREDIENTS
serves 4

For the pasta
UNBLEACHED FLOUR *3 cups*
EGGS *2*
SPINACH *8 oz*
SALT *to taste*

For the sauce
FRESH SALMON FILLET *14 oz*
ZUCCHINI *2*
SHALLOT *1*
DILL *1 bunch*
GARLIC *1 clove*
DRY WHITE WINE *1/4 cup*
EXTRA VIRGIN OLIVE OIL *5 tablespoons*
SALT & PEPPER *to taste*

1 Prepare the pasta dough. Clean the spinach under running water and drain. In a non-stick pan, wilt the spinach. This should take 2-3 minutes. Chop the spinach very finely. Replace in the non-stick pan and sauté until very dry. Remove from heat and set aside to cool.

2 Sift the flour on the work surface, form a mound, put the cold spinach in the middle, add the eggs and a pinch of salt; work the ingredients until the dough becomes smooth and elastic. Cover with plastic wrap and let rest for 30 minutes. Roll the dough in thin layer and slice into thin strips. Flour the tagliolini delicately and let them dry.

3 Prepare the sauce. Rinse and pat dry the salmon and cut into small cubes. Peel, rinse and dry the shallot and chop finely. Rinse, dry and chop the dill. Peel, rinse and crush the garlic. Rinse, dry and slice the zucchini in julienne (matchsticks).

4 In a skillet, heat 3 tablespoons of extra virgin olive oil. Add the shallot and cook until just transparent. Add the pieces of salmon and sauté 2 minutes or until all pieces are golden. Add a pinch of salt and some fresh ground pepper. Add the white wine and let it evaporate on high heat. Add the dill. Set aside.

5 In a second skillet, heat the rest of the olive oil on low heat. Add the crushed garlic and let it perfume the oil without browning the garlic. Discard the garlic and add the zucchini. Sauté 3-4 minutes. Season with salt and pepper. Drain and add to the salmon.

6 In a large pot, bring a large amount of water to a boil. Add salt and delicately add the tagliolini. Cook until al dente and drain well. Add them to the salmon-zucchini preparation. Mix well. Add abundant fresh ground pepper. Serve very hot.

Green tagliolini with fontina and white truffles

Difficulty **medium** • *Time needed* **over an hour** • *Calories per serving* **600**

INGREDIENTS
serves 4

For the pasta
UNBLEACHED FLOUR *2 1/4 cups*
SPINACH *11 oz*
EGGS *2*
SALT *a pinch*

For the sauce
WHITE TRUFFLE *1*
FONTINA CHEESE *11 oz*
MILK *1 cup*
EGG YOLKS *3*
SALT & WHITE PEPPER *to taste*

1 Cut the fontina into thin slices, put in a bowl high and narrow enough for all slices, cover with the milk and let it sit for one hour. Clean the white truffle with a light brush, rinse well and pat dry. Set aside. Clean the spinach, dry it and wilt in a non-stick pan for 3 minutes. Pass the spinach in a mixer. Return the spinach to the pan and cook until all water is evaporated.

2 On a work surface, make mound with the flour and make a well in the center. Add salt, the eggs, and the spinach in the well and start mixing. Work all ingredients until you have a homogenous and elastic dough. Cover with a clean kitchen towel and set aside for 30 minutes. Unwrap the pasta and roll it until it is about 1/16 inch thick. Delicately dust the pasta with flour, roll it on itself and with a very sharp knife, slice into strips about 3/8 inch wide.

3 In a double boiler, place the fontina, 3 tablespoons of milk and the egg yolks. Stir until the cheese is melted: first the cheese will make long strands, then it will become almost liquid before finally becoming dense. When the sauce is creamy, take it off the heat, add the white pepper and mix well.

4 In abundant salted water, cook the pasta until al dente. Drain the tagliolini and put in a large warm serving bowl. Mix in the fontina sauce. Shave the white truffle directly over the pasta. Serve immediately.

> ### SUGGESTION
> *To make the "fonduta" sauce successfully, the cheese must not be stringy but have the consistency of cream. Generally, no salt is added but it is best to try the sauce and add a dash of salt only if necessary.*

Trenette with pesto

Difficulty **easy** • *Time needed* **less than 30 minutes** • *Calories per serving* **790**

INGREDIENTS
serves 4

TRENETTE *12 oz*
STRING BEANS *5 oz*
POTATO *1*
BASIL *4 oz*
PINE NUTS *2 oz*
SHELLED WALNUTS *3*
GARLIC *1 clove*
GRATED PARMIGIANO *2 tablespoons*
GRATED PECORINO *2 tablespoons*
EXTRA VIRGIN OLIVE OIL *1/4 cup*
SALT *to taste*

1 Prepare the pesto. Delicately rinse and dry the basil leaves. In a mixer, blend the garlic, the pine nuts, and the walnuts. Add the basil leaves and a pinch of salt. With the machine running, slowly add the extra virgin olive oil until the sauce becomes thick and homogenous. Add the parmigiano and the pecorino cheeses. Pour the pesto in a bowl, cover and set aside.

2 Clean the string beans and slice them into 1 inch lengths. Peel, rinse and slice the potato into thick strips and cover with cold water to prevent them turning black.

3 During this time, bring a large pot of water to boil, add salt and cook the trenette. After 3 minutes, add the string beans and the potato strips. Cook for another 7-8 minutes until the pasta is al dente. Add 3 tablespoons of pasta cooking water to the pesto and mix well. Drain the trenette and the vegetables. In a large serving bowl, delicately mix the pesto with the trenette and the vegetables. Serve immediately.

Troccoli with shrimps

Difficulty **medium** • *Time needed* **under an hour** • *Calories per serving* **500**

INGREDIENTS
serves 4

For the pasta
UNBLEACHED FLOUR *2 1/2 cups*
EGGS *2*
EXTRA VIRGIN OLIVE OIL *1 tablespoon*
SALT *to taste*

For the sauce
SHRIMPS *11 oz*
TOMATOES *2, ripe and firm*
RED PEPPERS *3, sweet*
ONION *1*
PARSLEY *1 bunch*
HEAVY CREAM *2 tablespoons*
EXTRA VIRGIN OLIVE OIL *6 tablespoons*
SALT & WHITE PEPPER *to taste*

1 Prepare the pasta. Sift the flour on a clean work surface and make a deep well in the center. Break the eggs in the well, add the extra virgin olive oil and a dash of salt. Start incorporating all the ingredients. Add enough warm water and knead until you get a uniform ball of dough. Cover with plastic wrap and let rest for 30 minutes.

2 During this time, drop the tomatoes into boiling water for a few seconds, drain, peel and dice. Peel the shrimps, rinse and dry. Set aside on paper towels. Slice the red peppers in long strips. Rinse, dry and chop the parsley. Peel the onion and chop it finely.

3 In a skillet, heat 4 tablespoons of extra virgin olive oil. Add the onion and cook until transparent. Add half the pepper strips and sauté; add the tomatoes, a little salt and pepper and 2 tablespoons of water. Cover the skillet and cook on low heat for 30 minutes, stirring every five minutes.

4 Turn off the heat and let the mixture cool a few minutes before passing it through a food mill. Cut the dough into quarters and roll it until you get a long strip about 1/8 inch thick. Divide this pasta dough into short strips; flour them well and, holding one end with one hand, twist the other end to get slightly curved strips of pasta. Dry these strips of pasta for a few minutes.

5 In a non-stick pan, heat 2 tablespoons of extra virgin olive oil. Add the leftover red pepper strips and cook for 3-4 minutes, stirring delicately with a wooden spoon. Add the shrimps, a dash of salt and pepper and sauté for 3 minutes.

6 In abundant boiling salted water, cook the pasta. During this time, heat the first sauce on low heat, add the heavy cream and mix well. Drain the pasta and mix it with the sauce. Turn it into a large serving plate and top it with the shrimps and red pepper strips. Sprinkle with parsley and serve immediately.

SUGGESTION
In the province of Foggia, where this recipe is very popular, the traditional way is to prepare the pasta with a small roller called "materello" made of wood or bronze. We suggest you use a pasta machine or a traditional "chitarra" pasta cutter from Abruzzo.

Vermicelli with bacon, garlic and hot pepper

Difficulty **easy** • *Time needed* **less than 30 minutes** • *Calories per serving* **570**

INGREDIENTS

serves 4

VERMICELLI *14 oz*
BACON *3 oz*
PARSLEY *1 bunch*
GARLIC *3 cloves*
CHILI PEPPERS *2*
EXTRA VIRGIN OLIVE OIL *2 tablespoons*
SALT *to taste*

1 Cook the vermicelli in a large pot of boiling salted water. While the pasta is cooking, dice the bacon, chop the garlic and grind the chili peppers separately.

2 In a large skillet, heat the extra virgin olive oil. Add the garlic, the bacon and the chili peppers. Cook for 2 minutes or until golden. Drain the pasta and put it in a large mixing bowl. Mix the pasta and the sauce. You can also sprinkle the pasta with chopped parsley, if desired.

> **SUGGESTION**
> *You can substitute the bacon with a few tablespoons of extra virgin olive oil.*

Vermicelli with almonds and raisins

Difficulty **easy** • *Time needed* **less than 30 minutes** • *Calories per serving* **610**

INGREDIENTS

serves 4

VERMICELLI *11 oz*
SHELLED ALMONDS *2 oz*
RAISINS *2 oz*
DAY OLD BREAD *4 oz*
EXTRA VIRGIN OLIVE OIL *8 tablespoons*
SALT *to taste*

1 Soak the raisins for 15 minutes in a bowl of lukewarm water. In abundant boiling salted water, cook the vermicelli al dente. During this time, cook the almonds in a small saucepan filled with boiling water for 1 minute. Drain the almonds, peel and dry well; chop the almonds coarsely.

2 In a small pan, heat the extra virgin olive oil and add the bread crumbs; let cook for a few minutes, add the drained raisins and the almonds. Cook 2-3 minutes. Remove from the heat.

3 When the vermicelli are cooked, drain and turn into a warm bowl. Add the sauce and toss gently. Serve at once.

> **SUGGESTION**
> *For a different flavor, add sliced roasted peppers to the oil before adding the bread crumbs.*

Vermicelli with chicken giblets

*Difficulty **easy*** • *Time needed **under an hour*** • *Calories per serving **530***

INGREDIENTS
serves 4

VERMICELLI *11 oz*
CHICKEN GIBLETS *7 oz*
ONION *1/2*
CHOPPED PARSLEY *1/2 tablespoon*
BEEF BROTH *1/2 cup*
RED WINE *1/2 cup*
GRATED PARMIGIANO *2 oz*
BUTTER *2 oz*
SALT *to taste*

1 Prepare the giblets, rinse and slice in small pieces. Finely chop the onion. Heat the butter in a large skillet and add the onion. Cook until transparent. Add the giblets and cook for 5 minutes. Salt to taste. Add the wine and let it evaporate.

2 Add the chopped parsley; add the beef broth and cook on low heat for 20 minutes. In a large pot of salted water, cook the vermicelli al dente. Drain and place in a large serving bowl. Pour the sauce over the pasta and mix delicately. Add the grated parmigiano and serve immediately.

SUGGESTION
The original recipe calls for "bigoli,"
a dark pasta, similar to spaghetti
like that shown in the photo below.

Vermicelli with zucchini flowers

Difficulty **easy** • *Time needed* **under an hour** • *Calories per serving* **450**

INGREDIENTS
serves 4

VERMICELLI *12 oz*
ZUCCHINI FLOWERS *10*
PARSLEY *1 bunch*
ONION *1*
GARLIC *1 clove*
SAFFRON *1 sachet*
GRATED PECORINO *2 tablespoons*
EXTRA VIRGIN OLIVE OIL *4 tablespoons*
SALT & PEPPER *to taste*

1 Peel the garlic and the onion, rinse, dry and dice them finely; rinse the parsley, dry and chop. Delicately clean the zucchini flowers. Keep one aside for decoration. Slice the others into strips.

2 In a large skillet, heat the extra virgin olive oil. Add the onion and the garlic. Fry them over low heat for 1-2 minutes. Add the sliced zucchini flowers, half the parsley and let them cook a few more minutes, stirring with a wooden spoon.

3 Add salt and pepper to taste and the saffron dissolved in 3 tablespoons of hot water. Keep on low heat for another 4-5 minutes. Pass this mixture in a blender and return to the skillet.

4 Cook the vermicelli in abundant boiling salted water. When cooked al dente, drain, reserving 4 tablespoons of the cooking water. Add the vermicelli to the skillet with the reserved pasta water. Add the grated pecorino and mix well. Serve in warm bowls, sprinkled with chopped parsley.

Short pasta

Cavatelli with arugula

Difficulty **medium** • *Time needed* **under an hour** • *Calories per serving* **410**

INGREDIENTS
serves 4

FRESH CAVATELLI *12 oz*
ARUGULA *a small bunch*
TOMATOES *14 oz, ripe*
GARLIC *1 clove*
GRATED PECORINO CHEESE
2 tablespoons
EXTRA VIRGIN OLIVE OIL *4 tablespoons*
SALT & PEPPER *to taste*

1 Scald tomatoes in boiling water; drain, peel, press to remove seeds and dice. Peel and crush garlic clove. In a saucepan, heat olive oil with garlic clove. Add tomatoes, salt and fresh ground pepper. Cook on high heat for about 10-15 minutes. Remove the garlic.

2 In the meantime, in abundant boiling salted water, cook the Cavatelli al dente. Rinse arugula, dry on a kitchen towel and cut in small pieces.

3 Drain pasta, place in a serving dish and toss with the tomato sauce; add arugula and sprinkle with grated pecorino cheese. Serve immediately.

Cavatieddi with anchovies

Difficulty **medium** • *Time needed* **under an hour** • *Calories per serving* **510**

INGREDIENTS
serves 4

For the pasta
UNBLEACHED FLOUR *2 cups*
SEMOLINA *1 cup*
SALT *to taste*

For the sauce
ANCHOVIES PRESERVED IN SALT *3*
GARLIC *2 cloves*
EXTRA VIRGIN OLIVE OIL *2 tablespoons*

1 Sift flour, semolina and a pinch of salt on pastry board into a mound. Mix with a fork and add lukewarm water little by little, until dough is smooth and elastic.

2 With your hands, cut a few cylinders 1/2 inch in diameter and 8-12 inches long. Cover the dough with a dish towel and set aside. Slice each cylinder in small pieces 1/2 inch long and press each with your thumb. Shape like little shells and lay on work surface to dry for 30 minutes.

3 Rinse anchovies in running water, dry,

remove bones and cut in small pieces; peel the garlic cloves and crush. In a pan, heat olive oil; add garlic and anchovies; crush using a fork.

4 In abundant boiling salted water, cook the cavatieddi al dente; transfer to pan with anchovies, stirring well. Cook for 2 minutes, remove garlic cloves and serve immediately.

SUGGESTION

The cavatieddi can also be mixed with tomato sauce, meat sauce, small broccoli and olive oil.

Conchiglie with milk

Difficulty **easy** • *Time needed* **less than 30 minutes** • *Calories per serving* **500**

INGREDIENTS
serves 4

CONCHIGLIE *12 oz*
MILK *4 tablespoons*
EGGS *3*
PARSLEY *1 bunch*
GRATED GRANA CHEESE *2 tablespoons*
BUTTER *3 tablespoons*
SALT & PEPPER *to taste*

1 Clean parsley, rinse, dry and finely chop. In abundant boiling salted water, cook the pasta al dente.

2 In the meantime, in an bowl, break the eggs, add the milk and beat with a fork. Add a pinch of salt, fresh ground pepper and half grated grana cheese; mix well.

3 Drain pasta. In a saucepan, heat butter. Add pasta, stirring with a wooden spoon. Remove from heat and add egg-cheese mixture

4 Sauté the pasta for a minute, then sprinkle with remaining grated grana and chopped parsley. Transfer to a serving dish and serve immediately.

SUGGESTION
*The roots of this dish go back to ancient traditions of the region of Molise where pasta and meat dishes were flavored with eggs and caciocavallo cheese.
If you like strong flavors, you can replace the grated grana cheese by aged pecorino or caciocavallo.*

Ancona style conchiglie

Difficulty **easy** • *Time needed* **under an hour** • *Calories per serving* **650**

INGREDIENTS
serves 4

CONCHIGLIE *12 oz*
TOMATOES *11 oz, ripe, firm*
PANCETTA *4 oz, in one slice*
CARROT *1*
CELERY *1 stalk*
ONION *1*
SHALLOTS *2*
ROSEMARY *1 sprig*
PARSLEY *1 bunch*
DRY WHITE WINE *1/4 cup*
GRATED PARMIGIANO *4 tablespoons*
EXTRA VIRGIN OLIVE OIL *4 tablespoons*
SALT & PEPPER *to taste*

1 Scald tomatoes in boiling water; drain, peel, press to remove seeds and dice. Peel onion and shallots. Trim carrot and peel. Remove large filaments from celery.

2 Rinse vegetables, dry and chop. Rinse rosemary, dry and chop. Rinse parsley, dry and finely chop. Dice pancetta and set aside.

3 In a saucepan, heat olive oil and cook onion, shallots, carrot, celery and rosemary. Add diced pancetta and cook; pour white wine and let evaporate on high heat.

4 Add tomatoes, a pinch of salt and pepper. Cook for approximately 15 minutes, stirring from time to time. In the meantime, in abundant boiling salted water, cook the pasta al dente and drain. Transfer to pan with sauce, toss well and sprinkle with parsley and grated grana cheese. Serve hot.

Conchiglie with lettuce

Difficulty **medium** • *Time needed* **under an hour** • *Calories per serving* **380**

INGREDIENTS
serves 4

CONCHIGLIE *11 oz*
LETTUCE *1*
RED PEPPER *1*
ONION *1*
DRY WHITE WINE *1/4 cup*
EXTRA VIRGIN OLIVE OIL *4 tablespoons*
SALT & PEPPER *to taste*

1 Peel onion and slice thinly; remove seeds of red pepper, rinse, dry and cut in strips. Carefully rinse the lettuce, drain, dry and cut in strips.

2 In a pan, heat olive oil and cook the onion until transparent; add red pepper and cook for a minute, stirring with a wooden spoon. Pour white wine (or same quantity of water) and let evaporate on high heat. Season with salt and pepper

and cook covered over a low heat for 15 minutes adding, if needed, a little water. A minute before the cooking ends, add lettuce and stir well.

3 In the meantime, in abundant boiling salted water, cook the conchiglie al dente and drain. Transfer on a serving dish and add sauce. Toss well. Serve very hot.

Conchiglie with vegetables

Difficulty **easy** • *Time needed* **under an hour** • *Calories per serving* **530**

INGREDIENTS
serves 4

CONCHIGLIE *12 oz*
EGGPLANT *1*
YELLOW PEPPER *1*
PANCETTA *3 oz, in one slice*
ONION *1*
PARSLEY *1 bunch*
GARLIC *1 clove*
EXTRA VIRGIN OLIVE OIL *3 tablespoons*
SALT & PEPPER *to taste*

1 Cut off the ends of eggplant, rinse, cut in strips, salt and drain in a colander for 30 minutes to remove water. Rinse and dry carefully. Remove seeds from pepper, rinse, dry and cut in strips.

2 Peel onion and garlic; chop coarsely. Dice pancetta. Rinse parsley, dry and chop. In a saucepan, heat olive oil; cook garlic and onion until transparent. Add diced pancetta and pepper strips; cook for 2 minutes, stirring with a wooden spoon.

3 Add eggplant strips and cook for 7-8 minutes on moderate heat; generously season with salt and pepper. In the meantime, in abundant boiling salted water, cook the conchiglie al dente. Drain well. Transfer on a serving dish and toss with sauce. Sprinkle the conchiglie with chopped parsley. Serve hot.

Conchiglie with cauliflower

Difficulty **medium** • *Time needed* **less than 30 minutes** • *Calories per serving* **410**

INGREDIENTS
serves 4

CONCHIGLIE *12 oz*
CAULIFLOWER *1 1/4 lbs*
ANCHOVIES PRESERVED IN SALT *2*
GARLIC *1 clove*
HOT PEPPER *1/2*
EXTRA VIRGIN OLIVE OIL *3 tablespoons*
SALT *to taste*

1 Separate florets from cauliflower, discard stems, cut florets in big pieces and tender leaves into strips. Rinse in cold water. Carefully rinse anchovies under running water; debone, remove tail and cut in small pieces.

2 In abundant boiling salted water, cook the conchiglie. Five minutes before the end of cooking, add cauliflower florets and leaf strips.

3 Peel garlic. In a skillet, heat olive oil with garlic and hot pepper. Add anchovies and 2 tablespoons of pasta cooking water. Stir with a wooden spoon until anchovies are melted.

4 Drain pasta and cauliflower heads; transfer to saucepan and toss well. Remove garlic. Transfer pasta and sauce to a serving plate and serve immediately.

Conchiglie with rapini

Difficulty **easy** • *Time needed* **less than 30 minutes** • *Calories per serving* **420**

INGREDIENTS
serves 4

CONCHIGLIE *12 oz*
RAPINI *2 lbs*
ANCHOVY FILLETS IN OLIVE OIL *3*
GARLIC *1 clove*
CHILI POWDER *a pinch*
EXTRA VIRGIN OLIVE OIL *4 tablespoons*
SALE *to taste*

1 Clean rapini, discard stems and hard leaves. Rinse in cold water, drain and set aside. Peel the garlic and slice thinly. In a saucepan, heat 2 tablespoons of olive oil and fry the garlic until lightly golden.

2 Cut anchovy fillets in small pieces and add to saucepan; stir with a wooden spoon until melted. In abundant boiling salted water, cook the conchiglie al dente. Add 3 tablespoons of pasta cooking water to saucepan and stir.

3 Five minutes before pasta is cooked, add rapini and finish cooking together.

Drain conchiglie and vegetables. Transfer to a mixing bowl and add anchovy sauce. Toss well and sprinkle with a pinch of chili powder. Serve at once.

Conchiglie with walnuts

Difficulty **easy** • *Time needed* **less than 30 minutes** • *Calories per serving* **700**

INGREDIENTS
serves 4

CONCHIGLIE *14 oz*
SHELLED WALNUTS *5 oz*
ORGANIC LEMON *1*
SUGAR *1 teaspoon*
CINNAMON *a pinch*
EXTRA VIRGIN OLIVE OIL *3 tablespoons*
SALE *to taste*

1 In abundant boiling salted water, cook pasta al dente. In the meantime, rinse lemon carefully and grate the peel. Chop walnuts.

2 In a large mixing bowl; add lemon peel, walnuts, sugar and cinnamon. Drain pasta and transfer to mixing bowl. Add olive oil and toss well. Serve immediately in small portions.

Conchiglie with cannellini bean purée

*Difficulty **medium*** • *Time needed **over an hour*** • *Calories per serving **560***

INGREDIENTS
serves 4

CONCHIGLIE *11 oz*
DRIED CANNELLINI BEANS *8 oz*
BEET TOPS *11 oz*
CELERY *2 stalks*
ONION *1/2*
GARLIC *1 clove*
BAY LEAF *1*
EXTRA VIRGIN OLIVE OIL *4 tablespoons*
SALT & PEPPER *to taste*

1 In a bowl, soak beans in abundant water for approximately 12 hours; drain. Peel onion, and chop finely. Remove large filaments from celery, (set aside the more tender leaves) and cut in small pieces.

2 In a saucepan, place beans and celery. Peel and crush garlic. Add bay leaf and garlic to saucepan. Cover with water, boil and cook for approximately 40 minutes; add a pinch of salt; cook for another 40 minutes.

3 In the meantime, wash the beet tops in cold water and the celery leaves you set aside; drain and cut in small strips. Drain beans; keep a few whole beans aside. Remove garlic clove and bay leaf. Pass beans in a food mill, setting aside one tablespoon; blend until mixture is creamy and homogeneous. Add 2 tablespoons of water and blend well.

4 Transfer purée to a skillet and stir constantly with a wooden spoon.. At the end, add olive oil and fresh ground pepper. In abundant boiling salted water, cook the conchiglie. Two minutes before the cooking ends, add beet and celery leaves. Drain vegetables and pasta. Transfer to a serving bowl with bean purée and mix well. Garnish with the whole beans you set aside earlier. Serve immediately.

Conchiglie with pumpkin and black olives

Difficulty **medium** • *Time needed* **over an hour** • *Calories per serving* **420**

INGREDIENTS
serves 4

CONCHIGLIE *12 oz*
PUMPKIN *14 oz*
PITTED BLACK OLIVES *2 oz*
CAPERS *1 tablespoon*
ONION *1/2*
GARLIC *1 clove*
ROSEMARY *1 branch*
BASIL *a few leaves, chopped*
PARSLEY *a bunch, chopped*
VEGETABLE BROTH *3 tablespoons*
SESAME SEED OIL *3 tablespoons*
SALT & PEPPER *to taste*

1 Dice pumpkin and set aside. Peel and finely chop the garlic and th4e onion with the rosemary. In a large pan, heat the olive oil and cook on medium heat until onions are transparent. Add the diced pumpkin and cook until all pieces are golden, stirring with a wooden spoon.

2 Add hot broth to saucepan, cover and continue cooking on low heat. Rinse and drain capers. After 20 minutes, add salt, fresh ground pepper, capers and olives. Stir well and cook on low heat for 10 minutes. Keep cooking water.

3 In the meantime, in abundant boiling salted water, cook the conchiglie al dente; drain and transfer to saucepan, stirring well. If needed, add 1-2 tablespoons of cooking water. Sprinkle with chopped parsley and basil. Transfer pasta to a serving dish and serve at once.

Vegetarian style conchiglie

Difficulty **medium** • *Time needed* **over an hour** • *Calories per serving* **500**

INGREDIENTS
serves 4

CONCHIGLIE *14 oz.*
STRING BEANS *5 oz*
PEELED TOMATOES *7 oz*
SHELLED PEAS *7 oz*
ZUCCHINI *2*
CARROT *2*
ONION *1*
GARLIC *1 clove*
BASIL *1 bunch*
EXTRA VIRGIN OLIVE OIL *3 tablespoons*
SALT & PEPPER *to taste*

1 Trim string beans, remove filaments and rinse. In abundant boiling salted water, scald for 2 minutes; drain and set aside.

2 Chop tomatoes in small pieces. Rinse peas. Peel and rinse zucchini and carrots, then cut in julienne. In abundant boiling salted water, scald carrots for 4 minutes; drain and set aside.

3 Peel and thinly slice onion; peel garlic clove. In a saucepan, heat olive oil; on low heat, cook onion and garlic clove, until onion is transparent. Add zucchini, carrot, peas, beans, salt and pepper; cook, stirring from time to time, for 2 minutes. Add tomatoes and cook for 15-20 minutes.

4 Before removing from heat, rinse basil, dry and chop; add half of it to sauce; mix well. In the meantime, in abundant boiling salted water, cook the conchiglie al dente. Transfer to serving plates and toss well with the sauce. Sprinkle with remaining basil. Serve hot.

Conchiglie with sea snails

Difficulty **medium** • *Time needed* **under an hour** • *Calories per serving* **430**

INGREDIENTS
serves 4

CONCHIGLIE RIGATE *12 oz*
SEA SNAILS *1 lb*
ANCHOVIES PRESERVED IN SALT *2*
PARSLEY *1 bunch*
GARLIC *1 clove*
EXTRA VIRGIN OLIVE OIL *4 tablespoons*
SALT & PEPPER *to taste*

1 Brush sea snails and soak in salted water. Rinse anchovies, debone and cut in small pieces. Rinse parsley, dry and chop with peeled garlic clove.

2 In a saucepan, heat 2 tablespoons of olive oil and heat half mixture. Add snails and sauté on high heat for 10 minutes. Remove snails from shells and add to saucepan with remaining oil, anchovies, garlic and parsley.

3 In the meantime, in abundant boiling salted water, cook pasta al dente, drain and transfer to saucepan; Toss well and sauté for 2 minutes. Serve at once.

Conchiglie with herbs

Difficulty **medium** • *Time needed* **under an hour** • *Calories per serving* **460**

INGREDIENTS
serves 4

CONCHIGLIE RIGATE *12 oz*
BASIL *a bunch*
PARSLEY *a bunch*
ROSEMARY *1 branch*
CAPERS IN BRINE *2 tablespoons*
RICOTTA *4 oz*
GRATED PECORINO *3 tablespoons*
EXTRA VIRGIN OLIVE OIL *3 tablespoons*
SALT *to taste*

1 Rinse basil, parsley and rosemary. Rinse capers, dry on a kitchen towel. Chop all ingredients and mix together. In abundant boiling salted water, cook the pasta al dente.

2 In the meantime, in a large saucepan, heat olive oil; cook herbs and capers on low heat. Crumble ricotta in a serving bowl and dilute with a little cooking water from the pasta.

3 Drain pasta, transfer to saucepan and sauté with herbs. Transfer to the serving bowl with the ricotta, sprinkle with pecorino cheese and serve immediately.

> **SUGGESTION**
> *If the mixed herbs become too dry, add a teaspoon of pasta cooking water.*

Corzetti with pine nuts

Difficulty **medium** • *Time needed* **over an hour** • *Calories per serving* **560**

INGREDIENTS
serves 4

For the pasta
UNBLEACHED FLOUR *4 cups*
EGGS *1*
EGG YOLKS *1*
SALT *a pinch*

For the sauce
PINE NUTS *2 oz*
MARJORAM *1 branch*
GRATED PARMIGIANO *4 tablespoons*
BUTTER *4 tablespoons*

1 Sift the flour on work surface into a mound. Make a well in the middle; add salt, egg and egg yolk. Work ingredients well, adding some lukewarm water, if necessary, until dough is smooth. Knead vigorously for 10 minutes until dough is smooth and elastic.

2 Form dough into a ball. Roll small pieces of the dough into little balls the size of chickpeas. Press each ball with your fingers, making a cup-shaped pasta. Set aside on work surface.

3 In abundant boiling salted water, cook the corzetti until they rise to the top. Drain with a slotted spoon.

4 In the meantime, rinse marjoram and chop coarsely. In a pan, place the butter, marjoram and pine nuts, sauté until butter has completely melted. Transfer corzetti in a serving dish; sprinkle with grana cheese. Toss with pine nut butter and serve immediately.

Ditalini with green peppers

Difficulty **medium** • *Time needed* **less than 30 minutes** • *Calories per serving* **390**

INGREDIENTS
serves 4

DITALINI RIGATI *12 oz*
GREEN PEPPER *1*
ANCHOVIES PRESERVED IN SALT *2*
CHOPPED PARSLEY *1 tablespoon*
GARLIC *1 clove*
EXTRA VIRGIN OLIVE OIL *3 tablespoons*
SALT *to taste*

1 Rinse anchovies several times in cold water, debone and cut in pieces. Rinse pepper, remove seeds and white parts; dice. In abundant boiling salted water, cook the ditalini al dente.

2 In the meantime, peel and crush garlic. In a small saucepan, heat olive oil and brown garlic lightly. Remove from heat, add anchovies and with a fork, crush to a paste. Add green peppers and cook for approximately 10 minutes over moderate heat.

3 Drain pasta. Transfer to a warm serving dish, add sauce and toss well. Sprinkle with parsley and serve immediately.

SUGGESTION

To make this dish more digestible, grill the green pepper in a very hot oven or hold it directly on the gas flame with a fork. Cool in a paper bag for a few minutes, remove the skin and fklproceed with recipe.

Milan style ditalini

Difficulty **easy** • *Time needed* **less than 30 minutes** • *Calories per serving* **460**

INGREDIENTS
serves 4

DITALINI RIGATI *12 oz*
SAFFRON *2 sachets*
ONION *1/2*
VEGETABLE BROTH *4 cups*
GRATED PARMIGIANO *4 tablespoons*
BUTTER *3 tablespoons*

1 Boil the broth. Peel onion, rinse and chop. In a saucepan, heat 2 tablespoons of butter and cook onion. Add pasta and cook, stirring with a wooden spoon. Add 1/2 cup of boiling broth. In a bowl, mix saffron with 1/2 cup of broth; add to saucepan. Cook on low heat until broth is absorbed.

2 Add remaining broth 1/2 cup at a time and cook on low heat until pasta is al dente. Remove from heat, add remaining butter and grated grana cheese. Serve immediately.

Ditaloni with beans and ground beef

Difficulty **medium** • *Time needed* **over an hour** • *Calories per serving* **470**

INGREDIENTS
serves 4

DITALONI *9 oz*
GROUND BEEF *5 oz*
BOILED BORLOTTI BEANS *7 oz*
PEELED TOMATOES *8 oz*
ONION *1*
PARSLEY *a bunch*
DRY WHITE WINE *1/4 cup*
GRATED PARMIGIANO *2 tablespoons*
BUTTER *3 tablespoons*
SALT & PEPPER *to taste*

1 Finely chop the onion; in a saucepan heat butter and cook onion until transparent. Add ground beef; stir and separate in small pieces with a wooden spoon. Add peeled tomatoes, a pinch of salt and pepper. Cover and cook on low heat for about 40 minutes, stirring from time to time.

2 While it is cooking, add a few tablespoons of hot water so that the bottom of saucepan does not burn. When cooking is almost done, add white wine, the beans and the finely chopped parsley. Cook a few more minutes, then turn heat off

3 In abundant boiling salted water, cook the pasta al dente, drain and transfer to saucepan. Stir well. Season with fresh ground pepper and serve with grated cheese.

Eliche with anchovies and lettuce

Difficulty **easy** • *Time needed* **under an hour** • *Calories per serving* **460**

INGREDIENTS
serves 4

ELICHE *12 oz*
ESCAROLE *2 heads*
TOMATOES *4, ripe, firm*
ANCHOVIES PRESERVED IN SALT *2*
GARLIC *1 clove*
RED CHILI PEPPER *a pinch*
EXTRA VIRGIN OLIVE OIL *5 tablespoons*
SALT *to taste*

1 Clean the escarole lettuce, discard outside leaves and the core, cut in little pieces and rinse in cold water. Scald in boiling salted water for 2-3 minutes and drain.

2 In abundant boiling salted water, scald tomatoes, drain, peel, press gently to remove seeds and water, and chop coarsely. Rinse anchovies under running water, debone and cut in small pieces. Peel and crush garlic clove.

3 In a skillet, heat olive oil and cook the garlic clove and chili pepper. Add anchovy pieces; cook briefly, stirring with a wooden spoon. Add tomatoes and a pinch of salt; cook on low heat for approximately 10 minutes, stirring from time to time. Add the escarole and cook for approximately 10 minutes.

4 In the meantime, in abundant boiling salted water, cook the eliche al dente. Drain; toss with anchovy and lettuce sauce and serve.

Farfalle with tomatoes and black olive sauce

Difficulty **easy** • *Time needed* **under an hour** • *Calories per serving* **450**

INGREDIENTS
serves 4

FARFALLE *12 oz*
TOMATOES *11 oz*
BLACK OLIVES *5 oz*
CAPERS IN BRINE *1 oz*
GARLIC *1 clove*
EXTRA VIRGIN OLIVE OIL *3 tablespoons*
SALT & PEPPER *to taste*

1 Scald tomatoes in boiling water; drain, peel, press gently to remove seeds and water, chop coarsely. Pit the olives and chop coarsely. Rinse capers under cold water, drain and dry on a kitchen towel.

2 In a food processor, mix olives, capers and garlic clove; add oil and a pinch of salt. Blend the sauce well. Transfer to a skillet and bring to a boil; add tomatoes and cook a few minutes on low heat.

3 In the meantime, in abundant boiling salted water, cook the farfalle al dente. Drain. Mix with olive and tomato sauce, adding, if needed, 2-3 tablespoons of pasta cooking water. Serve hot.

Farfalle with chicken and pesto

Difficulty **medium** • *Time needed* **under an hour** • *Calories per serving* **500**

INGREDIENTS

serves 4

FARFALLE *12 oz*
CHICKEN BREAST *7 oz*
PESTO *4 oz*
BAY LEAF *1*
BASIL *1 branch*
PARSLEY *a bunch*
DRY WHITE WINE *1/4 cup*
EXTRA VIRGIN OLIVE OIL *2 tablespoons*
SALT & PEPPER *to taste*

1 Remove skin from the chicken breast, rinse, dry, salt and pepper. In a pan, heat olive oil with bay leaf, chopped basil and parsley. Add chicken breast and cook on high heat until completely browned on both sides. Remove from the pan and keep it warm.

2 Pour off the cooking fat from pan. Add white wine and let evaporate on high heat. Return chicken breast to pan with a few tablespoons of water. Cover and cook for 15 minutes over moderate heat, basting it from time to time in cooking juices.

3 In abundant boiling salted water, cook the farfalle al dente. In the meantime remove chicken breast from pan, slice in strips and place it in the serving plate with the pesto sauce. Drain pasta, transfer to serving plate, toss well and serve immediately.

SUGGESTION
By increasing the ingredients,
this recipe is an excellent one-dish meal.

Fresh farfalle with provolone and zucchini

Difficulty **easy** • *Time needed* **under an hour** • *Calories per serving* **510**

INGREDIENTS
serves 4

For the pasta
UNBLEACHED FLOUR *3 cups*
EGGS *3*
SALT *to taste*

For the sauce
ZUCCHINI *11 oz*
MILD PROVOLONE *3 oz*
SHALLOT *1*
PARSLEY *1 bunch*
EXTRA VIRGIN OLIVE OIL *5 tablespoons*
SALT & PEPPER *to taste*

1 Prepare the pasta. Sift the flour on pastry board into a mound. Make a well in the middle; add eggs and a pinch of salt. Work until dough is smooth and elastic. Cover with plastic wrap and set aside for 30 minutes in a cool place.

2 Thinly roll pasta dough and, with pastry wheel, cut into 2 inch wide strips. With a knife, divide the strips into rectangles about 1 inch wide. Pinch each rectangle in the middle forming a butterfly. Place on a floured pastry board to dry.

3 Prepare the sauce. Trim zucchini, rinse and slice. Rinse parsley, dry delicately with a kitchen towel and chop. Peel shallot and chop finely. In a skillet, heat olive oil and cook shallot until transparent. Add zucchini and cook for

7-8 minutes, stirring from time to time with a wooden spoon; season with a pinch of salt and pepper and add parsley.

4 In abundant boiling salted water, cook the pasta al dente; drain and transfer to saucepan. Add 2-3 tablespoons pasta cooking water and stir well. Place farfalle in each individual plate. Grate provolone cheese over pasta and serve immediately.

SUGGESTION
This dish is also prepared in the Molise region where the provolone cheese is replaced by aged caciocavallo cheese, which is grated directly on the farfalle before serving.

Farfalle with olives

Difficulty **easy** • *Time needed* **less than 30 minutes** • *Calories per serving* **610**

INGREDIENTS
serves 4

FARFALLE *12 oz*
PITTED BLACK OLIVES *7 oz*
SAFFRON *1 teaspoon*
ONION *1/2*
PARSLEY *a bunch*
HEAVY CREAM *1/4 cup*
DRY WHITE WINE *1/4 cup*
GRATED PARMIGIANO *6 tablespoons*
EXTRA VIRGIN OLIVE OIL *2 tablespoons*
SALT & PEPPER *to taste*

1 Peel and dry onion. Rinse parsley and dry well. Finely chop both and place in a bowl. Coarsely chop olives.

2 In a saucepan, heat olive oil; cook onion and parsley until onion is transparent. Add olives, sauté for a few minutes, add the wine and let evaporate.

3 In a small bowl, dissolve the saffron with a tablespoon of lukewarm water and a pinch of salt. When wine is evaporated, add cream and saffron; stir with a wooden spoon and blend well.

4 In abundant boiling salted water, cook the farfalle al dente. Drain and place on a serving dish. Add saffron sauce, grated parmigiano cheese and a pinch of fresh ground pepper. Toss well and serve immediately.

SUGGESTION
In this recipe, the heavy cream can be substituted by yogurt.

Farfalle with sardines and zucchini

Difficulty **medium** • *Time needed* **under an hour** • *Calories per serving* **490**

INGREDIENTS
serves 4

FARFALLE *14 oz*
FRESH SARDINES *8 oz*
ZUCCHINI *4*
TOMATOES *3*
ONION *1*
PARSLEY *1 bunch*
GARLIC *1 clove*
EXTRA VIRGIN OLIVE OIL *3 tablespoons*
SALT & PEPPER *to taste*

1 Remove head and bones of sardines, rinse well in running water, dry on a kitchen towel and cut in small pieces. Trim zucchini, rinse and cut in julienne. Rinse tomatoes, press to remove seeds and cut in small pieces.

2 Peel onion and garlic; slice thinly. In a pan, heat olive oil; cook onion and garlic on low heat until just transparent. Add zucchini, salt and pepper, stirring well.

3 Add sardines, tomatoes, a pinch of salt, pepper and chopped parsley. Cook for approximately 6-7 minutes. In abundant boiling salted water, cook the farfalle al dente, drain al dente and add to saucepan with sardine sauce; toss well. Serve hot.

Green farfalle with asparagus and ricotta

Difficulty **medium** • *Time needed* **under an hour** • *Calories per serving* **460**

INGREDIENTS
serves 4

GREEN FARFALLE *14 oz*
ASPARAGUS *11 oz*
RICOTTA *4 oz*
ONION *a small piece*
BUTTER *3 tablespoons*
SALT & PEPPER *to taste*

1 Remove the hard stem of the asparagus, peel and rinse. Cut in small pieces. Slice the tips in strips.

2 Peel onion and chop. In a saucepan, melt butter; cook onion until just transparent. Add asparagus and cook a few minutes. Add 3 tablespoons of hot water and cook for some 10 minutes.

3 Transfer to a food processor and mix. Filter and return mixture to the saucepan, adding salt; boil a few minutes. In abundant boiling salted water, cook the pasta al dente.

4 Pass ricotta through a fine mesh sieve. Drain pasta and transfer to a serving dish. Remove saucepan from heat; add ricotta, fresh ground pepper and asparagus tips. Cook a few minutes, then turn heat off. Transfer sauce to serving dish and serve immediately.

Farfalle with smoked salmon

Difficulty **easy** • *Time needed* **less than 30 minutes** • *Calories per serving* **480**

INGREDIENTS
serves 4

FARFALLE *12 oz*
SMOKED SALMON *3 oz, sliced*
HEAVY CREAM *4 oz*
NUTMEG *to taste*
VODKA *2 oz*
SWEET PAPRIKA *1 teaspoon*
BUTTER *3 tablespoons*
SALT *to taste*

1 In abundant boiling salted water, cook the pasta al dente. In the meantime, cut smoked salmon in small pieces.

2 In a skillet, heat heavy cream; add butter and melt, stirring with a wooden spoon. Add salmon pieces, a pinch of nutmeg and paprika.

3 Before sauce boils, add vodka and a pinch of salt. Drain the farfalle, transfer to skillet, stir well and cook for 2-3. Serve hot.

SUGGESTION
When using smoked salmon, be sure not to buy it too salted, otherwise it will alter the sauce.

Green and yellow farfalline with lamb kidneys

Difficulty **medium** • *Time needed* **over an hour** • *Calories per serving* **760**

INGREDIENTS
serves 4

For the spinach pasta
UNBLEACHED FLOUR *1 cup*
SEMOLINA *1 cup*
SPINACH *5 oz*
EGGS *1*
GRATED PARMIGIANO *2 tablespoons*
SALT *to taste*

For the egg pasta
UNBLEACHED FLOUR *1 cup*
SEMOLINA *1 cup*
EGGS *2*
SALT *to taste*

For the sauce
LAMB KIDNEYS *12 oz*
PANCETTA *2 oz, in one slice*
TOMATOES *11 oz, ripe, firm*
CARROT *1*
CELERY *1 stalk*
LEEK *1*
MARSALA *3 tablespoons*
BEEF STOCK *1/4 cup*
EXTRA VIRGIN OLIVE OIL *4 tablespoons*
SALT & PEPPER *to taste*

1 Clean spinach, rinse in cold water and drain. In a non-stick pan, cook for a few minutes, stirring from time to time. Drain, return to pan and cook again until dry. Remove from heat and let cool completely.

2 Prepare the spinach pasta. Sift the flour and semolina on a pastry board into a mound. Make a well in the middle; add egg, chopped spinach, grated grana cheese and a pinch of salt. Work the ingredients until dough is smooth and elastic. cover with plastic wrap and set aside for 30 minutes.

3 Prepare the egg pasta. On the pastry board sift the flour and semolina into a mound. Make a well in the middle; add eggs and a pinch of salt. Work the ingredients until dough is smooth and elastic. Cover with plastic wrap and set aside for 30 minutes in a cool place.

4 Roll both pasta doughs in thin sheets and cut into 1 1/2 by 1 inch rectangles; pinch in the middle to form butterfly-shaped pasta. Place on floured pastry board to dry.

5 In the meantime, prepare the sauce. Clean lamb kidneys, rinse, dry and cut in small pieces. Chop pancetta and set aside. Peel the carrot; rinse and dry the celery; rinse leek and cut off the green part; chop finely. Scald tomatoes, drain, peel and press to remove seeds; chop coarsely.

6 In a saucepan, heat olive oil; add pancetta, chopped carrot, celery and leek. Cook a few minutes. Add lamb kidneys and cook on all sides. Add marsala and let evaporate on high heat. Add tomatoes, broth, a pinch of salt and pepper. Cook for approximately 15 minutes on low heat.

7 In abundant boiling salted water, cook pasta al dente. Drain and transfer to saucepan. Serve with with grated grana cheese.

Fusilli with spinach and pine nuts

Difficulty **medium** • *Time needed* **under an hour** • *Calories per serving* **540**

INGREDIENTS
serves 4

SHORT FUSILLI *12 oz*
FROZEN SPINACH *1 lb*
PINE NUTS *4 tablespoons*
PEPPERS IN OIL *2 pieces*
RICOTTA *7 oz*
CHOPPED PARSLEY *a bunch*
GARLIC *1 clove*
MILK *3 tablespoons*
GRATED GRANA CHEESE *to taste*
BUTTER *3 tablespoons*
SALT & PEPPER *to taste*

1 In a saucepan with boiling salted water, thaw spinach; drain well, coarsely chop and set aside. Drain pepper from oil and dice.

2 In a bowl, mix the diced pepper, parsley and ricotta. Blend in 3 tablespoons of milk, until it becomes a soft cream. In abundant boiling salted water, cook the pasta al dente.

3 In the meantime, melt the butter in a saucepan; lightly brown peeled garlic clove. Discard the garlic; add spinach, pine nuts and a pinch of fresh ground pepper. Cook for a few minutes, then remove from heat.

4 Drain pasta and transfer to saucepan, mixing well with ricotta cream. Transfer to a baking dish. Place layers of pasta, alternating with the spinach; finish with the pasta and sprinkle with grated grana. Serve immediately.

> **SUGGESTION**
> *Herbs or nettles can be substituted for the spinach. The pepper in oil can also be replaced by a fresh pepper grilled over a gas flame or in the oven, placed in a paper bag for 10 minutes and then peeled.*

Fusilli alla carrettiera

Difficulty **easy** • *Time needed* **less than 30 minutes** • *Calories per serving* **570**

INGREDIENTS
serves 4

FUSILLI *12 oz*
PORCINI MUSHROOMS *11 oz*
PANCETTA *3 oz, in one slice*
TUNA IN OLIVE OIL *3 oz*
GARLIC *1 clove*
PARSLEY *1 bunch*
EXTRA VIRGIN OLIVE OIL *4 tablespoons*
SALT & PEPPER *to taste*

1 Clean the porcini mushrooms, rapidly rinse in cold water, drain, dry delicately with a kitchen towel and slice. Dice the pancetta and set aside. Drain tuna from oil and crumble.

2 Peel garlic and crush. Rinse parsley, dry delicately with a kitchen towel and chop. In a saucepan, heat olive oil; lightly brown garlic and pancetta.

3 Add mushrooms, cook for 2-3 minutes on high heat. Season with a pinch of salt and pepper. Add tuna and cook for 2 minutes. Add parsley.

4 In abundant boiling salted water, cook the pasta al dente; drain and transfer to saucepan, mixing well. Serve hot..

Fusilli with porcini mushrooms and prosciutto

*Difficulty **easy*** • *Time needed **less than 30 minutes*** • *Calories per serving **570***

INGREDIENTS
serves 4

FUSILLI *12 oz*
PORCINI MUSHROOMS *11 oz*
TOMATOES *14 oz, ripe, firm*
PROSCIUTTO *3 oz, in one slice*
PARSLEY *1 bunch*
BASIL *1 bunch*
GARLIC *2 cloves*
HOT PEPPER *1*
GRATED PECORINO *4 tablespoons*
EXTRA VIRGIN OLIVE OIL *5 tablespoons*
SALT & PEPPER *to taste*

1 In boiling water, scald tomatoes, drain, peel, press to remove seeds and coarsely chop. Dice prosciutto and set aside. Peel garlic cloves and dry. Rinse parsley and basil, delicately dry with a kitchen towel; separately chop.

2 Clean porcini mushrooms, rapidly rinse in cold water, drain, delicately dry with a kitchen towel and slice thinly. In a saucepan, heat 3 tablespoons of oil with one garlic clove, chili pepper and prosciutto, stirring with a wooden spoon.

3 Add tomatoes, a little parsley, basil and a pinch of salt. Cook on low heat for 15 minutes, stirring with a wooden spoon.

4 Crush remaining garlic clove. In the meantime, in a saucepan heat remaining olive oil. Cook garlic clove; add mushrooms, season with a pinch of salt and pepper and cook for approximately 2-3 minutes on high heat. Sprinkle with remaining parsley, add to tomato sauce and cook for a minute.

5 In abundant boiling salted water, cook the pasta al dente; drain. Toss well with sauce and sprinkle with remaining basil. Serve hot with grated pecorino cheese.

Fusilli with zucchini

Difficulty **medium** • *Time needed* **under an hour** • *Calories per serving* **430**

INGREDIENTS
serves 4

FUSILLI *12 oz*
ZUCCHINI *1 lb*
CHOPPED PARSLEY *1 tablespoon*
GARLIC *1 clove*
POWDERED HOT PEPPER *a pinch*
GRATED PARMIGIANO *1 tablespoon*
GRATED PECORINO *1 tablespoon*
SESAME SEED OIL *3 tablespoons*
SALT *to taste*

1 Peel zucchini, rinse and boil for about 10 minutes in boiling salted water. Drain, dry and cut in small sticks. Peel garlic clove and crush. In a large pan, heat the oil with garlic clove; add zucchini and sauté for a few minutes. Add a pinch of salt.

2 In abundant boiling salted water, cook the fusilli al dente; drain well and transfer to pan; stir and cook for a few minutes.

3 Remove garlic clove; add grated parmigiano and pecorino. Stirring well, add parsley and a pinch of chili pepper. Stir again a few minutes, mixing all ingredients well. Serve immediately.

SUGGESTION
Instead of boiling them, you can steam the zucchini for about10 minutes. The grated cheeses are optional and can be substituted by crumbled tofu, cooked with the zucchini.

Fusilli with rabbit stew

Difficulty **medium** • *Time needed* **over an hour** • *Calories per serving* **640**

INGREDIENTS
serves 4

FUSILLI *12 oz*
RABBIT *1 1/4 lbs*
PANCETTA *2 oz*
DRIED MUSHROOMS *1 oz*
TOMATOES *11 oz*
CARROT *1*
CELERY *1 stalk*
ONION *1*
PARSLEY *1 bunch*
BAY LEAF *1*
DRY WHITE WINE *1/4 cup*
EXTRA VIRGIN OLIVE OIL *3 tablespoons*
SALT & PEPPER *to taste*

1 In abundant boiling salted water, scald tomatoes, drain, peel, cut in half, press to remove seeds and finely chop. Peel and rinse onion, carrot, celery and parsley, and chop them. Finely chop pancetta and cut the rabbit in small pieces

2 Rinse and dry rabbit pieces. Soak mushrooms in lukewarm water, then chop. In a saucepan, heat olive oil. Add pancetta and vegetables, stirring with a wooden spoon. Cook on low heat for a few minutes. Add rabbit, salt and pepper, stirring well. Add wine and let evaporate on high heat. Reduce heat and add mushrooms, bay leaf and tomatoes. Cook for 30 minutes.

3 Drain rabbit pieces, debone and cut meat in strips. Remove bay leaf and return rabbit strips to the saucepan. Cook on low heat, stirring, for 5 minutes.

4 In the meantime, in abundant boiling salted water, cook the fusilli al dente. Drain, transfer to another saucepan and add the sauce, mixing well. Transfer to a serving dish and serve immediately.

SUGGESTION
To make the rabbit meat tastier, you can marinate it in two parts of water and 1 part of vinegar with rosemary and thyme for 3 to 5 hours; then rinse the meat and proceed with the recipe..

Fusilli with mushrooms and tomatoes

Difficulty **medium** • *Time needed* **under an hour** • *Calories per serving* **430**

INGREDIENTS
serves 4

FUSILLI *12 oz*
FRESH MUSHROOMS *14 oz*
TOMATOES *8 oz*
PARSLEY *3 bunches*
BASIL *1 bunch*
GARLIC *1 clove*
HOT PEPPER *a pinch*
EXTRA VIRGIN OLIVE OIL *4 tablespoons*
SALT & PEPPER *to taste*

1 Clean mushrooms, rapidly rinse in cold water, drain, delicately dry and slice. Peel garlic cloves and crush. In boiling water, scald tomatoes, drain, peel, press to remove seeds and cut in strips.

2 Separately rinse parsley and basil. Dry and cut basil in strips. In a saucepan, heat 2 tablespoons of olive oil with one garlic clove and parsley. Add mushrooms and cook on low heat for approximately 3 minutes, stirring well.

3 In another saucepan, heat remaining olive oil with remaining garlic clove and chili pepper. Add tomatoes, a pinch of salt and pepper. Cook on low heat for 5 minutes. Add mushrooms and cook for 5 minutes, stirring from time to time.

4 In the meantime, in abundant boiling salted water, cook the fusilli al dente. Drain, toss with mushroom sauce, transfer to a serving dish and sprinkle with basil strips. Serve immediately with grated grana cheese.

SUGGESTION
If you prefer a stronger mushroom flavor, replace the mushrooms with 4 oz. of dried porcini mushrooms. Soak in warm water for 30 minutes and drain before using.

Garganelli with porcini mushrooms

Difficulty **easy** • *Time needed* **less than 30 minutes** • *Calories per serving* **380**

INGREDIENTS
serves 4

GARGANELLI *11 oz*
PORCINI MUSHROOMS *8 oz*
ZUCCHINI *7 oz*
PARSLEY *1 bunch*
BASIL *1 bunch*
GARLIC *1 clove*
EXTRA VIRGIN OLIVE OIL *4 tablespoons*
SALT & PEPPER *to taste*

1 Rinse parsley and basil, dry delicately and chop. Clean mushrooms, rapidly rinse in cold water, drain, dry with a kitchen towel and slice. Trim zucchini, rinse and slice into strips.

2 Peel and crush garlic. In a skillet, heat olive oil with the crushed garlic. Add zucchini and cook for 2-3 minutes, stirring from time to time. Add mushrooms and cook for 3-4 minutes on high heat, stirring with a wooden spoon; add salt and pepper. At the end of cooking, remove garlic, add chopped parsley and basil.

3 In the meantime, in abundant boiling salted water, cook the garganelli al dente; drain, toss with sauce and serve immediately.

SUGGESTION
Fresh mushrooms can be substituted with dry mushrooms. Because drying the mushrooms concentrates the taste, it is necessary to pay attention to the quantity used. For this recipe, 8 oz of fresh porcini mushrooms equal 1 oz of dried ones. These should be soaked in lukewarm water for 30 minutes; then drain and pat dry with a clean towel.

Garganelli with clams

Difficulty **medium** • *Time needed* **under an hour** • *Calories per serving* **440**

INGREDIENTS
serves 4

GARGANELLI *12 oz*
CLAMS *1 lb*
RED PEPPER *1*
BASIL *1 bunch*
PARSLEY *1 bunch*
GARLIC *1 clove*
DRY WHITE WINE *1/4 cup*
EXTRA VIRGIN OLIVE OIL *4 tablespoons*
SALT & PEPPER *to taste*

1 Wash clams and soak in cold water for a few hours. Drain. In a saucepan, heat 1 tablespoon of olive oil; add clams, peeled garlic and wine. Cover. Shake pan from time to time until the clams open.

2 Remove saucepan from heat. Remove clams from shells, discarding the closed shells. Keep clam cooking water. Remove seeds from red pepper, rinse and cut in pieces.

3 In a pan, heat remaining olive oil with pepper; season with a pinch of salt and fresh ground pepper. Add clams with 3-4 tablespoons of cooking water. Cook for 2-3 minutes.

4 In abundant boiling salted water, cook the garganelli al dente. Drain and toss with sauce. Transfer to a serving dish, sprinkle with basil and parsley. Serve hot.

Garganelli with peas

Difficulty **easy** • *Time needed* **under an hour** • *Calories per serving* **490**

INGREDIENTS
serves 4

GARGANELLI *12 oz*
SHELLED PEAS *1 lb*
ONIONS *3*
CHOPPED PARSLEY *3 tablespoons*
EXTRA VIRGIN OLIVE OIL *3 tablespoons*
SALT & PEPPER *to taste*

1 Peel onion, rinse and slice thinly. In a saucepan, heat olive oil and cook onion; add peas, cook for a minute, then cover with boiling water.

2 Add a pinch of salt and fresh ground pepper. Cover and cook on low heat until almost all water is completely absorbed and the peas are cooked. Add salt and pepper.

3 In the meantime, in abundant boiling salted water, cook the pasta al dente, drain and transfer to saucepan, mixing well. Transfer to a serving dish, sprinkle with parsley and serve immediately.

> **SUGGESTION**
> *To add more taste to this dish,*
> *add a teaspoon of coriander.*

Gemelli with fish ragù

Difficulty **medium** • *Time needed* **under an hour** • *Calories per serving* **580**

INGREDIENTS
serves 4

GEMELLI *12 oz*
MIXED SHELLFISH
(mussels, clams, etc) 2 1/2 lbs
BABY CUTTLEFISH *8 oz*
SHRIMP *7 oz*
TOMATOES *11 oz, ripe, firm*
PARSLEY *1 bunch*
OREGANO *to taste*
RED CHILI PEPPER *a small piece*
GARLIC *2 cloves*
DRY WHITE WINE *1/4 cup*
EXTRA VIRGIN OLIVE OIL *5 tablespoons*
SALT & PEPPER *to taste*

1 Peel garlic. Clean and scrub all shellfish, rinse several times under running water and drain. In a very large pan, heat 2 tablespoons of olive oil and add shellfish. Add white wine, one garlic clove and chili pepper; cook on low heat. Cover and, shaking from time to time, cook until all shells are open.

2 Remove pan from heat. Discard any shells that remained closed. Remove meat from shells and set aside in a few tablespoons of the cooking liquid. Reserve all cooking liquids. Clean baby cuttlefish, dry and slice. Peel and devein shrimps, rinse and dry well.

3 In boiling water, scald tomatoes, drain, peel, press to remove seeds and chop.

Rinse parsley and chop 1/2 together with remaining garlic clove.

4 In a pan, heat remaining oil with chopped parsley and garlic. Add cuttlefish and cook, stirring with a wooden spoon. Add tomatoes, season with a pinch of salt and fresh ground pepper. Add cooking liquid from shellfish and cook for 12 minutes on medium heat.

5 Add shrimps and cook for 3 minutes. Add shellfish and cook for 2 minutes or until just heated through. In the meantime, cook the gemelli al dente in abundant boiling salted water; drain and transfer to a large serving bowl. Add oregano and parsley. Pour fish sauce over. Serve hot.

Gemelli with zucchini flowers

Difficulty **easy** • *Time needed* **under an hour** • *Calories per serving* **410**

INGREDIENTS
serves 4

GEMELLI *12 oz*
ZUCCHINI WITH FLOWERS *11 oz*
SHALLOT *1*
ONION *1*
SAFFRON *1 teaspoon*
EXTRA VIRGIN OLIVE OIL *4 tablespoons*
SALT & PEPPER *to taste*

1 Separate flowers from zucchini. Clean flowers, rinse, delicately dry with a kitchen towel and cut in strips. Trim zucchini, rinse, dry and cut in julienne. Peel shallot and onion, rinse and finely chop.

2 In a saucepan, heat olive oil; cook shallot and onion until transparent. Add zucchini and cook for a few minutes, stirring from time to time.

3 In a small bowl, mix saffron with a tablespoon of water. Add 2 tablespoons of water to saucepan; cover and cook for approximately 6-7 minutes on low heat. Add zucchini flowers and cook for a minute. Add saffron and cook for 5 minutes on low heat. Add a pinch of salt and fresh ground pepper.

4 In the meantime, in abundant boiling salted water, cook pasta al dente. Drain and toss with sauce in a warm serving bowl. Serve immediately.

Gnocchetti Sardi with five cheeses

Difficulty **easy** • *Time needed* **less than 30 minutes** • *Calories per serving* **480**

INGREDIENTS
serves 4

GNOCCHETTI SARDI *12 oz*
GORGONZOLA *1 oz*
TOMA CHEESE *1 oz*
FRESH RICOTTA *1 oz*
FONTINA CHEESE *1 oz*
GRATED PARMIGIANO *1 oz*
BUTTER *3 tablespoons*
SALT *to taste*

1 Boil 16 cups of water (the gnocchetti sardi are made of semolina and require much water to cook well), add a handful of salt and cook the gnocchetti, for at least 20 minutes.

2 In the meantime, dice gorgonzola cheese, toma cheese and fontina cheese, removing any crust. Place in a mixing bowl and add the crumbled ricotta.

3 Drain pasta and return to cooking pot. Add the various cheeses, butter and grated parmigiano. Toss well and serve immediately in a heated serving dish.

Gnocchetti Sardi alla marinara

Difficulty **medium** • *Time needed* **under an hour** • *Calories per serving* **600**

INGREDIENTS
serves 4

GNOCCHETTI *14 oz*
TUNA IN OLIVE OIL *4 oz*
ANCHOVIES PRESERVED IN SALT *2*
TOMATO *1*
HARD BOILED EGGS *2*
LEMON JUICE *3 tablespoons*
PARSLEY *1 bunch*
BASIL *12 leaves*
GARLIC *1 clove*
EXTRA VIRGIN OLIVE OIL *5 tablespoons*
SALT *to taste*

1 In abundant boiling salted water cook the pasta al dente. Drain and toss with 1 tablespoon of olive oil. Spread on waxed paper to cool.

2 Rinse the anchovies, remove bones and cut in small pieces. Rinse tomatoes, dice, peel, squeeze gently to remove seeds and add salt. In a food processor, mix one hard boiled egg and a hard boiled yolk, 4 tablespoons of olive oil, lemon, parsley, basil and garlic. Blend until mixture is smooth and creamy.

3 Transfer the cold pasta to a tureen. Toss with sauce, crumbled tuna and anchovies. Toss well, add tomatoes and serve immediately.

> **SUGGESTION**
> *To add a unique touch to this dish, add 1 tablespoon of soy sauce to the ingredients.*

Gramigna with pesto and peppers

Difficulty **medium** • *Time needed* **less than 30 minutes** • *Calories per serving* **610**

INGREDIENTS
serves 4

GRAMIGNA *12 oz*
RED PEPPER *4 oz*
BASIL *4 oz*
GARLIC *1 clove*
PINE NUTS *2 oz*
SHELLED WALNUTS *5*
GRATED PARMIGIANO *2 tablespoons*
GRATED PECORINO *2 tablespoons*
EXTRA VIRGIN OLIVE OIL *5 tablespoons*
COARSE SALT *to taste*

1 In boiling salted water, scald red pepper; drain, pass under running cold water, peel, remove seeds and dice. Rinse basil leaves, lay on clean kitchen towel and dry.

2 In a food processor, place garlic clove, pine nuts and walnuts; blend well. Add basil and salt. Mix well until all ingredients are incorporated. Transfer sauce to a bowl and add grated cheeses. Stir with a wooden spoon. Add oil, little by little and mix well. Add diced pepper.

3 In the meantime, in abundant boiling salted water, cook the pasta al dente; drain and toss with sauce. At the last moment, add 2 or 3 tablespoons of pasta cooking water. Serve hot.

Pasta salad with fresh vegetables

Difficulty **easy** • *Time needed* **under an hour** • *Calories per serving* **420**

INGREDIENTS
serves 4

ELICHE *11 oz*
ARUGULA *1 bunch*
BASIL *1 bunch*
CARROT *2, small*
ZUCCHINI *2, small*
CUCUMBER *1, small*
CELERY *1 stalk*
YELLOW PEPPER *1/2*
RED PEPPER *1/2*
BIG GREEN ONION *1*
WHITE WINE VINEGAR *2 tablespoons*
WORCESTER SAUCE *1/2 teaspoon*
EXTRA VIRGIN OLIVE OIL *1/4 cup*
SALT *to taste*

1 In boiling salted water, cook the pasta al dente. Drain, add 1 tablespoon of olive oil, mix well, lay on a plate and let cool. Rinse arugula, dry with a kitchen towel and cut in small pieces. Rinse basil and tear in small pieces.

2 Trim carrot and peel. Trim zucchini. Peel cucumber. Remove large filaments from celery stalk. Remove seeds from red and yellow peppers. Discard green part of the onion.

3 Rinse vegetables and dry. Thinly slice carrots, cucumber, zucchini and onion. Cut peppers in strips. Cut celery in small pieces. Transfer all vegetables to a bowl. In a mixing bowl, mix white wine vinegar, a pinch of salt and Worcester sauce.

4 Add remaining oil to mixing bowl. Beat lightly with a fork until ingredients are well blended. Add vegetables, arugula and basil. Toss well. Add pasta, mixing well. Serve cold.

Summer pasta salad

Difficulty **medium** • *Time needed* **less than 30 minutes** • *Calories per serving* **610**

INGREDIENTS
serves 4

SHORT PASTA *14 oz*
TOMATOES *4*
TUNA IN OLIVE OIL *5 oz*
YELLOW PEPPERS *2*
EGGS *3*
PITTED OLIVES *12*
BASIL *a few leaves*
CHIVES *to taste*
GARLIC *2 cloves*
EXTRA VIRGIN OLIVE OIL *2 tablespoons*
SALT & PEPPER *to taste*

1 In boiling water, scald tomatoes; drain, peel, press to remove seeds and excess water. Blend in a food processor and transfer to a mixing bowl; add olive oil, peeled garlic cloves, salt, pepper and basil leaves.

2 Set aside. In the meantime, dice peppers. Boil eggs and cut in segments. Drain tuna from oil and cut in pieces.

3 In abundant boiling salted water, cook pasta al dente. Drain, rinse under cold water, drain well and place in salad bowl. Remove garlic from mixing bowl.

4 Pour tomato sauce into salad bowl, add peppers, hard-boiled eggs, tuna, pitted olives and pasta. Toss well. If necessary, add olive oil. Sprinkle with chives and serve immediately.

Fresh maccheroncelli from Bobbio

Difficulty **medium** • *Time needed* **over an hour** • *Calories per serving* **680**

INGREDIENTS
serves 4

For the pasta
UNBLEACHED FLOUR *3 cups*
EGGS *2*
SALT *to taste*

For the sauce
BEEF ROAST *2 lbs*
PANCETTA *3 oz, in 1 piece*
TOMATO PASTE *1 tablespoon*
ONION *1*
BAY LEAF *2*
ROSEMARY *1 branch*
GARLIC *2 cloves*
CLOVES *4*
NUTMEG *to taste*
RED WINE *1 cup*
BUTTER *3 tablespoons*
EXTRA VIRGIN OLIVE OIL *3 tablespoons*
SALT *to taste*
BLACK PEPPERCORNS *5*

1 Prepare the pasta. Sift flour on work surface into a mound. Make a well in the middle; add eggs and a pinch of salt. Mix ingredients together, adding one or two tablespoons of water if needed. Work until dough is smooth and elastic. Cover with plastic wrap and set aside for 30 minutes. Separate the dough into several little pieces. Form every piece into a cylinder and cut into pieces 1/2 inch long.

2 Use a thick knitting needle to shape the pasta. Flatten the dough with the palm of your hand and roll it around the needle. Let the maccheroncelli fall onto a floured surface and let dry for 30 minutes.

3 Prepare the sauce. Peel garlic and onion; rinse and finely chop. Slice pancetta in long strips. Salt and pepper the roast and transfer to a deep dish. Add bay leaves, garlic, onions, rosemary, cloves, peppercorns and red wine. Marinate for 1 hour, turning the meat twice.

4 Drain the meat and dry it. In a pan, heat olive oil and butter. Add meat and roast on all sides on high heat. Add marinade and nutmeg. Cook for 8 minutes. Add tomato paste and 1/2 cup of water. Stir the sauce, cover and cook for 30 minutes.

5 Remove roast from pan. Cut one thick slice and chop meat in strips. Pass the sauce in a food mill and return to the pan. Add the strips of meat. Cook to reduce the sauce a little. In abundant boiling salted water, cook the maccheroncelli al dente. Drain and transfer to a serving dish. Pour sauce over and toss well. Serve immediately.

SUGGESTION
In the region of Bobbio, the tradition is to serve the roast meat as the main dish after the pasta. You can also use that meat to make fillings for ravioli.

Maccheroncini with ratatouille

Difficulty **medium** • *Time needed* **over an hour** • *Calories per serving* **410**

INGREDIENTS
serves 4

MACCHERONCINI *11 oz*
EGGPLANT *1*
RED PEPPER *1/2*
YELLOW PEPPER *1/2*
ZUCCHINI *3*
TOMATOES *2*
ONION *1*
BASIL *1 bunch*
PARSLEY *1 bunch*
GARLIC *1 clove*
GRATED PARMIGIANO *2 tablespoons*
EXTRA VIRGIN OLIVE OIL *3 tablespoons*
SALT & PEPPER *to taste*

1 Trim eggplants; dice, salt and drain in a colander for approximately 20 minutes. Pass under running water, drain well and dry.

2 Remove seeds from red and yellow peppers. Trim the zucchini. Separately rinse peppers and zucchini; dice. In abundant water, scald tomatoes; drain, peel, press to remove seeds and dice. Rinse basil and tear in pieces.

3 Peel onion and garlic, rinse and finely chop. In a skillet, heat olive oil; cook onion and garlic until transparent. Add diced pepper and cook for 2 minutes. Add eggplants and zucchinis; cook on high heat for a few minutes, stirring well with a wooden spoon.

4 Add tomatoes, mix well, season with salt and fresh ground pepper. Cover and cook for approximately 15 minutes on moderate heat. Two minutes before the end of cooking, add basil.

5 In the meantime, in abundant boiling salted water, cook the maccheroncini al dente; drain and transfer to a serving dish. Add sauce to dish. Sprinkle with chopped parsley and grated grana. Serve hot.

SUGGESTION
This dish is just as good if you substitute the maccheroncini with ditalini rigati (as shown in the photo below).

Maccheroncini with lentils and celery

Difficulty **medium** • *Time needed* **over an hour** • *Calories per serving* **370**

INGREDIENTS
serves 4

MACCHERONCINI *or* **SEDANINI RIGATI**
7 oz
DRIED LENTILS *5 oz*
CELERY *1 stalk*
ONION *1*
GARLIC *1 clove*
BAY LEAF *1*
EXTRA VIRGIN OLIVE OIL *3 tablespoons*
SALT & PEPPER *to taste*

1 Place lentils in a bowl, cover with abundant cold water and soak for 12 hours. Peel onion and finely chop. Remove large filaments from celery stalk and cut in small pieces.

2 Drain lentils, dry and place in a pan. Cover with cold water, add onion, garlic, bay leaf and celery. Slowly bring to boil and add salt. Cook on low heat for approximately one hour. If lentils absorb too much, add hot water.

3 Remove from heat. Place lentils in a saucepan, adding boiling water. Bring to boil, add maccheroncini and cook for approximately 10 minutes. The water should be completely absorbed.

4 Remove from heat, add olive oil and fresh ground pepper. Transfer pasta to a tureen and serve hot.

Maccheroncini with tomatoes and lentils

Difficulty **medium** • *Time needed* **over an hour** • *Calories per serving* **460**

INGREDIENTS
serves 4

MACCHERONCINI *11 oz*
TOMATOES *4*
LENTILS *4 oz*
ONION *1*
GARLIC *1 clove*
BAY LEAF *1*
CELERY *1 stalk*
EXTRA VIRGIN OLIVE OIL *3 tablespoons*
SALT & PEPPER *to taste*

1 Place lentils in a bowl, cover with abundant cold water and soak for 12 hours. Drain, rinse, place in a skillet and cover with cold water. Cut celery in small pieces. Add finely chopped onion, garlic, bay leaf and celery to skillet. Bring to boil and add salt. Cook on low heat for approximately one hour, adding cold water if the lentils absorb too much.

2 In the meantime, in abundant boiling salted water, cook the maccheroncini al dente. Drain and pass under cold water. Rinse tomatoes, scald in boiling water, peel, press to remove seeds and dice. Add tomatoes to lentils 15 minutes before cooking is done.

3 Five minutes before the end of cooking, add maccheroncini, delicately stirring with a wooden spoon. Remove from heat. Add olive oil and fresh ground pepper. Toss well and serve hot, adding chopped parsley.

Maccheroncini with cold sauce

Difficulty **medium** • *Time needed* **less than 30 minutes** • *Calories per serving* **470**

INGREDIENTS
serves 4

MACCHERONCINI *11 oz*
ARUGULA *a small bunch*
TUNA IN OLIVE OIL *5 oz*
ANCHOVY FILLETS *3*
TOMATO PUREE *2 teaspoons*
PICKLED PEPPERS *4*
CHIVES *2 shoots*
MUSTARD *1 tablespoon*
EXTRA VIRGIN OLIVE OIL *3 tablespoons*
SALT *to taste*

1 Chop chives, pickled peppers and anchovies. Place them in a food processor. Add tuna, mustard, tomato purée and olive oil. Blend until mixture is smooth. Rinse arugula, dry and cut in strips.

2 In the meantime, in abundant boiling salted water, cook the maccheroncini al dente; drain in a bowl and add sauce.

3 Transfer to a serving dish and add arugula strips. Set aside for 10 minutes before serving.

SUGGESTION
If you do not like the taste of arugula, you can use parsley, instead.

Maccheroncini with broccoli

Difficulty **medium** • *Time needed* **less than 30 minutes** • *Calories per serving* **410**

INGREDIENTS
serves 4

MACCHERONCINI *11 oz*
BROCCOLI *1 lb*
BLACK OLIVES *2 oz*
ANCHOVIES PRESERVED IN SALT *2*
ONION *1*
GARLIC *1 clove*
EXTRA VIRGIN OLIVE OIL *4 tablespoons*
SALT *to taste*

1 Rinse anchovies under running water, remove bones and cut in fillets. Peel onion, rinse, dry and finely chop. Peel garlic clove and chop finely.

2 Separate the florets from broccoli and discard the stem; rinse in abundant cold water. In a skillet, heat olive oil; cook garlic and onion until transparent. Add anchovy fillets. Stir well with a wooden spoon, then add olives.

3 In abundant boiling salted water, cook maccheroncini al dente. Five minutes before the end of cooking, add broccoli. Drain pasta and broccoli. Toss with anchovy sauce and serve hot.

Maccheroncini with herbs

Difficulty **easy** • *Time needed* **less than 30 minutes** • *Calories per serving* **470**

INGREDIENTS
serves 4

MACCHERONCINI *12 oz*
PARSLEY *a bunch*
BASIL *a bunch*
TARRAGON *1 branch*
THYME *1 branch*
HEAVY CREAM *3/4 cup*
GRATED PARMIGIANO *4 tablespoons*
SALT & PEPPER *to taste*

1 In a large pot, bring abundant salted water to a boil and cook the pasta al dente. In the meantime, trim and rinse the herbs thoroughly under running water; with a sharp knife chop them finely.

2 In a saucepan, heat heavy cream, add herbs and 2 tablespoons of pasta cooking water. Drain pasta to a mixing bowl. Add grated grana cheese, heavy cream and fresh ground pepper. Toss well. Serve hot.

Pasta salad with baby cuttlefish

Difficulty **medium** • *Time needed* **less than 30 minutes** • *Calories per serving* **460**

INGREDIENTS
serves 4

MACCHERONCINI *or* **SEDANI** *12 oz*
BABY CUTTLEFISH *11 oz*
TOMATOES *11 oz*
YELLOW PEPPER *1*
CORNICHONS *2 oz*
LEMON JUICE *3 tablespoons*
CIDER VINEGAR *2 tablespoons*
EXTRA VIRGIN OLIVE OIL *4 tablespoons*
SALT & PEPPER *to taste*

1 Rinse tomatoes, dry, press to remove seeds, drain in colander for approximately 10 minutes and dice. Place in a bowl; add 1 tablespoon of olive oil, salt and fresh ground pepper.

2 In abundant boiling salted water, cook pasta al dente. Drain, pass under water and transfer to a salad bowl. Add 2 tablespoons of olive oil, lemon juice, salt and fresh ground pepper. Set aside.

3 In a pot, boil abundant boiling salted water and add 2 tablespoons of cider vinegar. In the meantime, clean the ba-by cuttlefish and discard eyes and insides; rinse under running water and cook for approximately 5 minutes in a pot.

4 Drain and let cool; cut in small pieces and mix with olive oil, a pinch of salt and fresh ground pepper. Set aside.

5 Remove seeds from yellow pepper, rinse, dry and dice. Drain cornichons and thinly slices length-wise. Add cuttlefish, pepper, tomatoes and cornichons to salad bowl. Toss delicately and serve immediately.

Maccheroni with porcini mushrooms

Difficulty **medium** • *Time needed* **under an hour** • *Calories per serving* **530**

INGREDIENTS
serves 4

MACCHERONI *14 oz*
PORCINI MUSHROOMS *2*
TOMATO SAUCE *2*
ONION *1*
PARSLEY *a bunch*
VEGETABLE BROTH *1 cup*
GRATED PARMIGIANO *4 tablespoons*
BUTTER *1 tablespoon*
EXTRA VIRGIN OLIVE OIL *3 tablespoons*
SALT & PEPPER *to taste*

1 Peel onion and slice thinly. In a saucepan, heat olive oil and butter; add onion and cook until transparent. Rapidly rinse mushrooms, peel, slice thinly and add to saucepan. Add salt and cook for 10 minutes.

2 In boiling water, scald tomatoes, drain, peel, press to remove seeds and chop. Add to saucepan, cover and cook for 30 minutes on low heat, adding the broth,

little by little. At the end of cooking, season with pepper.

3 In the meantime, in abundant boiling salted water, cook pasta al dente. Rinse parsley, chop and add to saucepan. Cook for 5 minutes. Remove from heat. Drain pasta, transfer to a serving dish and toss well with sauce and grated cheese. Serve hot.

Maccheroni alla bergamasca

Difficulty **medium** • *Time needed* **under an hour** • *Calories per serving* **680**

INGREDIENTS
serves 4

MACCHERONI *12 oz*
FRESH MUSHROOMS *11 oz*
ARTICHOKES *3*
PANCETTA *3 oz*
EGGS *2*
MILK *4 tablespoons*
LEMON *1, the juice of*
SHALLOTS *2*
PARSLEY *1 bunch*
GRATED PARMIGIANO *3 tablespoons*
EXTRA VIRGIN OLIVE OIL *5 tablespoons*
SALT & PEPPER *to taste*

1 Clean mushrooms, rapidly rinse in cold water, drain, dry and slice thinly. Clean artichokes, discard stems and the outer, hard leaves; cut in half, remove hairs, thinly slice length-wise and transfer to a bowl with cold water, mixed with 1 tablespoon of lemon juice.

2 Rinse parsley, delicately dry with kitchen towel and chop. Peel shallots, rinse, dry and finely chop. Dice pancetta and set aside. In a saucepan, heat 3 tablespoons of olive oil and cook shallots until transparent. Add artichokes and cook for 3 minutes on high heat. Season with salt and pepper. Cover and cook on moderate heat for 3-4 minutes.

3 In the meantime, in a skillet, heat remaining olive oil and cook mushrooms on high heat for 2-3 minutes; add salt and pepper. Transfer to saucepan and cook for 2 minutes. Add parsley.

4 In a non-stick pan, brown pancetta on all sides. In abundant boiling salted water, cook pasta al dente. In a mixing bowl, place eggs, 2 tablespoons of grated grana cheese, milk, a pinch of salt and pepper. Lightly beat with a fork.

5 Drain pasta. Transfer to non-stick pan. Add a few tablespoons of pasta cooking water, the artichoke mixture and mix well with a wooden spoon. Remove from heat, add egg mixture, season with salt and fresh ground pepper. Replace saucepan on moderate heat, mixing all ingredients well. The sauce should be creamy. Serve with remaining grated grana.

Maccheroni with mint

Difficulty **easy** • *Time needed* **less than 30 minutes** • *Calories per serving* **500**

INGREDIENTS
serves 4

MACCHERONI *14 oz*
FRESH MINT *a small bunch*
TOMATO SAUCE *11 oz*
GRATED PECORINO *4 tablespoons*
EXTRA VIRGIN OLIVE OIL *3 tablespoons*
SALT *to taste*

1 Peel tomatoes, press to remove seeds and chop. In a saucepan, heat olive oil and add tomatoes. Cover and cook on low heat for 20 minutes.

2 In the meantime, in abundant boiling salted water, cook maccheroni al dente, drain and transfer to a serving dish. Add chopped mint leaves, mix well and sprinkle with grated pecorino. Add tomato sauce and toss well. Before serving, let cool for a few minutes

Maccheroni with chickpeas

Difficulty **medium** • *Time needed* **over an hour** • *Calories per serving* **570**

INGREDIENTS
serves 4

MACCHERONI *12 oz*
CHICKPEAS *5 oz*
BASIL *1 tablespoon, chopped*
BAKING POWDER *a pinch*
GARLIC *2 cloves*
GRATED PARMIGIANO *2 tablespoons*
EXTRA VIRGIN OLIVE OIL *to taste*
SALT *to taste*

1 Soak chickpeas in lukewarm water and baking powder for 12 hours. Drain and transfer to a pot with cold water, bring to boil and cook on high heat for about 10 minutes. Lower heat and boil covered until chickpeas are soft.

2 In the meantime, in abundant boiling salted water, cook maccheroni al dente. Peel garlic and crush. In a saucepan, heat 4 tablespoons of olive oil with the garlic. Drain pasta and remove garlic from saucepan. Transfer pasta to saucepan.

3 Add chopped basil and cook a few minutes on low heat. Season with salt and pepper. Add olive oil and serve hot with grated parmigiano.

Maccheroni in salsa

Difficulty **easy** • *Time needed* **less than 30 minutes** • *Calories per serving* **630**

INGREDIENTS
serves 4

MACCHERONI *14 oz*
LEMON *1, the juice of*
SAFFRON *1 sachet*
GRATED PECORINO *6 tablespoons*
EXTRA VIRGIN OLIVE OIL *4 tablespoons*
SALT *to taste*

1 In abundant boiling salted water, cook the maccheroni al dente. In the meantime, in a saucepan, heat olive oil.

2 Add lemon juice, saffron and grated pecorino. Mix well. Drain pasta and add to saucepan. Toss well and cook for 2-3 minutes. Serve immediately.

Maccheroni with ricotta

Difficulty **easy** • *Time needed* **less than 30 minutes** • *Calories per serving* **460**

INGREDIENTS
serves 4

MACCHERONI *12 oz*
RICOTTA *7 oz*
GRATED PARMIGIANO *3 tablespoons*
MILK *1/4 cup*
CINNAMON *a pinch*
SALT & PEPPER *to taste*

1 In abundant boiling salted water, cook the maccheroni al dente. In the meantime, in a bowl, mix ricotta and grated grana cheese.

2 In a saucepan, heat milk. Add to bowl. Add 2 tablespoons of pasta cooking water, cinnamon, salt and pepper. Mix well until mixture is creamy.

3 Drain pasta and toss well with the ricotta preparation. Serve hot, sprinkled with a little cinnamon.

SUGGESTION
The cinnamon can be substituted with nutmeg or paprika.

166

Malloreddus with tofu

Difficulty **medium** • *Time needed* **under an hour** • *Calories per serving* **390**

INGREDIENTS
serves 4

MALLOREDDUS *11 oz*
TOFU *7 oz*
TOMATO SAUCE *11 oz*
ONION *1*
BASIL *4*
SAFFRON *1 teaspoon*
EXTRA VIRGIN OLIVE OIL *3 tablespoons*
SALT & PEPPER *to taste*

1 Crumble tofu in small pieces. Peel onion, rinse and chop. In boiling water, scald tomatoes, drain, peel, press to remove seeds and pass through a sieve over a bowl.

2 In a saucepan, heat 2 tablespoons of olive oil; cook tofu until lightly golden; drain and set aside. In the same pan, heat remaining olive oil; cook onion until transparent. Add tomato juice, saffron and basil. Stir with a wooden spoon and cook for approximately 10 minutes.

3 Add tofu, salt and fresh ground pepper. Cook for approximately 15 minutes, on moderate heat. In the meantime, in abundant boiling salted water, cook the malloreddus al dente. Transfer to individual serving plates and toss well with the sauce. Serve immediately.

Malloreddus with bottarga

Difficulty **easy** • *Time needed* **less than 30 minutes** • *Calories per serving* **490**

INGREDIENTS
serves 4

MALLOREDDUS *12 oz*
BOTTARGA *4 oz*
LEMON JUICE *to taste*
PARSLEY *a bunch, chopped*
EXTRA VIRGIN OLIVE OIL *5 tablespoons*
SALT *to taste*

1 In abundant boiling salted water, cook the malloreddus al dente.

2 In the meantime, grate the bottarga. Drain pasta, transfer to a tureen and add olive oil, bottarga and lemon juice. Sprinkle with chopped parsley and serve immediately.

> **SUGGESTION**
> *The parsley can be substituted with chives and a diced tomato can be added to the ingredients.*

Malloreddus with tomato and pancetta sauce

Difficulty **medium** • *Time needed* **under an hour** • *Calories per serving* **650**

INGREDIENTS
serves 4

MALLOREDDUS *12 oz*
TOMATOES *1 lb, ripe, firm*
PANCETTA *4 oz*
ONION *1*
SAFFRON *a pinch*
BASIL *1 bunch*
GRATED PECORINO SARDO *3 tablespoons*
EXTRA VIRGIN OLIVE OIL *4 tablespoons*
SALT & PEPPER *to taste*

1 In boiling water, scald tomatoes, drain, peel, press to remove seeds and chop. Dice pancetta; in a non-stick pan, heat olive oil and brown pancetta; remove from pan and discard fat from pan.

2 Peel onion, rinse and slice finely. In a saucepan, heat olive oil; cook onion until transparent. Add saffron and cook, stirring well with a wooden spoon; add pancetta and cook a few minutes. Tear basil in small pieces.

3 Add tomatoes, salt and fresh ground pepper; cook on moderate heat for approximately 20-25 minutes, stirring with a wooden spoon. At the end of cooking, add basil.

4 In the meantime, in abundant boiling salted water, cook malloreddus al dente. Drain, toss with sauce and serve with grated pecorino.

Maltagliati with goose ragù

Difficulty **easy** • *Time needed* **over an hour** • *Calories per serving* **870**

INGREDIENTS
serves 4

For the pasta
UNBLEACHED FLOUR *3 cups*
WHOLE WHEAT FLOUR *1 cup*
EGGS *4*
SALT *to taste*

For the sauce
PRESERVED GOOSE BREAST *4 oz*
SHELLED WALNUTS *5 oz*
MILK *3 tablespoons*
PARSLEY *1 oz*
GRATED PARMIGIANO *4 tablespoons*
SALT *to taste*

1 Prepare the pasta. Sift flour on work surface into a mound. Make a well in the middle; add eggs and salt. Work ingredients for 10 minutes, adding lukewarm water, if needed. Thinly roll pasta dough and dry for 15 minutes. Divide in 3 sheets.

2 Roll each sheet onto itself. With a sharp knife, slice dough into unequal strips. Slice each strip diagonally in several pieces. Separate each piece and set aside on work surface. In abundant boiling salted water, cook pasta al dente and drain.

3 Coarsely chop walnuts. Chop goose breast (meat and fat) in small pieces. In a skillet, cook the diced goose on low heat; cover and cook for 5-6 minutes. Add walnuts. Cook for 3-4 minutes.

4 Finely chop parsley and add to skillet. Cook a few minutes; add milk, stirring well. Add salt and cook for 3 minutes. Turn heat off. In a serving dish, place pasta with grated grana; toss with sauce and serve immediately.

SUGGESTION
Preserved goose breast is cooked and preserved in its own fat. Fresh goose can also be used with longer cooking time.

Maltagliati with fresh anchovies and string beans

Difficulty **medium** • *Time needed* **under an hour** • *Calories per serving* **460**

INGREDIENTS
serves 4

For the pasta
UNBLEACHED FLOUR *3 cups*
EGGS *3*
SALT *to taste*

For the sauce
FRESH ANCHOVIES *7 oz*
STRING BEANS *11 oz*
ONION *1*
GARLIC *1 clove*
EXTRA VIRGIN OLIVE OIL *4 tablespoons*
SALT & PEPPER *to taste*

1 Prepare the pasta. Sift flour on work surface into a mound. Make a well in the middle; add eggs and a pinch of salt. Work ingredients until dough is smooth and elastic. Cover with plastic wrap and set aside for 30 minutes.

2 In the meantime, prepare the sauce. Clean anchovies, discard head and remove bones and fillet; rinse fillets, dry and cut in small pieces. Peel garlic and onion, rinse, delicately dry and chop finely.

3 Trim the green beans; blanch for 3-4 minutes in boiling water. Drain and set aside. In a skillet, heat olive oil; cook garlic and onion until transparent. Add green beans and cook for 2-3 minutes.

4 Add anchovies and cook for 2 minutes, stirring with a wooden spoon. Season with salt and generous fresh ground pepper. Thinly roll pasta dough. With a pastry wheel or a sharp knife, slice dough into unequal strips. Slice each strip diagonally in several pieces. Separate each piece and set aside on floured work surface. In abundant boiling salted water, cook pasta al dente and toss well with sauce. Serve immediately.

Corn pasta with asiago cheese

Difficulty **medium** • *Time needed* **under an hour** • *Calories per serving* **800**

INGREDIENTS
serves 4

CORN FLOUR 3 *cups*
UNBLEACHED FLOUR 2 *cups*
EGGS 5
ASIAGO CHEESE 6 *oz*
BUTTER 4 *tablespoons*
SALT *to taste*

1 Sift both corn and all-purpose flours on work surface into a mound. Make a well in the middle; add eggs, a pinch of salt and 1-2 tablespoons of lukewarm water. Work ingredients until dough is smooth and elastic.

2 Cover with plastic wrap and set aside for 30 minutes in a cool place. Thinly roll pasta dough with a rolling pin.

3 With a pastry wheel, cut 1 x 2 inch rectangles of pasta. In abundant boiling salted water, cook the rectangles al dente.

4 In the meantime, remove crust from asiago cheese and chop coarsely. In a skillet, heat butter with asiago cheese on moderate heat, stirring with a wooden spoon until melted.

5 Drain pasta. Toss with cheese sauce and a tablespoon of pasta cooking water. Serve immediately.

Mezze maniche with olive sauce

Difficulty **easy** • *Time needed* **less than 30 minutes** • *Calories per serving* **450**

INGREDIENTS
serves 4

MEZZE MANICHE 12 *oz*
PITTED BLACK OLIVES 4 *oz*
FRESH RICOTTA 5 *oz*
ONION 1/2, *chopped*
SALT & PEPPER *to taste*

1 In abundant boiling salted water, cook the pasta al dente. Finely chop olives and transfer to a mixing bowl with ricotta and chopped onion.

2 Mix ingredients well; add 4-5 tablespoons of pasta cooking water and fresh ground pepper. Drain pasta and toss with sauce. Serve immediately.

Mezze maniche with onions

Difficulty **medium** • *Time needed* **under an hour** • *Calories per serving* **430**

INGREDIENTS

serves 4

MEZZE MANICHE *or* **CHIFFERI** *11 oz*
ONIONS *14 oz*
ANCHOVIES IN OIL *12 fillets*
GRATED PARMIGIANO *2 tablespoons*
EXTRA VIRGIN OLIVE OIL *4 tablespoons*
SALT & PEPPER *to taste*

1 Peel onions, slice thinly and cover with abundant cold water. Drain and dry well on a kitchen towel. Drain anchovies from oil.

2 In a skillet, heat olive oil; cook onions until transparent. Add 4 tablespoons of water, cover and cook on moderate heat for approximately 30 minutes. Add salt and fresh ground pepper. Stir well with a wooden spoon. Five minutes before removing from heat, add anchovies and mix well.

3 In the meantime, in abundant boiling salted water, cook the mezze maniche al dente.

4 Drain pasta, transfer to saucepan and toss well. Transfer pasta and sauce to a serving dish and serve immediately with grated grana cheese.

Pasta with cauliflower

Difficulty **medium** • *Time needed* **under an hour** • *Calories per serving* **440**

INGREDIENTS
serves 4

SEMOLINA *3 cups*
CAULIFLOWER *14 oz*
TOMATO SAUCE *1 lb*
GRATED PECORINO *4 tablespoons*
EXTRA VIRGIN OLIVE OIL *3 tablespoons*
SALT *to taste*

1 Sift semolina on pastry board into a mound. Make a well in the middle and add lukewarm water. Work well until dough is smooth. Knead for about 15 minutes. Roll dough into long cylinders, the size of a pencil. Cut cylinders into 1 1/2 inch long pieces.

2 Flatten each piece of dough and wrap around a clean pencil, pressing with the palm of your hand. Drop the pieces of pasta on the floured work surface. Transfer to a kitchen towel and set aside to dry for one hour.

3 In the meantime, rinse cauliflower and separate florets. In boiling salted water, boil flowers for approximately 10 minutes. Drain, set aside in a covered bowl, keeping it warm..

4 In abundant boiling salted water, cook pasta for 5-6 minutes; drain and toss with preheated tomato sauce, cauliflower, olive oil and grated pecorino. Serve immediately.

SUGGESTION
The cauliflower can be substituted with broccoli.

Chestnut pasta with porcini mushrooms

Difficulty **medium** • *Time needed* **under an hour** • *Calories per serving* **400**

INGREDIENTS
serves 4

For the pasta
UNBLEACHED FLOUR *1 1/2 cups*
CHESTNUT FLOUR *1 1/2 cups*
EGGS *2*
EGG WHITES *1*
SALT *to taste*

For the sauce
PORCINI MUSHROOMS *11 oz*
SHALLOT *1*
PARSLEY *1 bunch*
EXTRA VIRGIN OLIVE OIL *4 tablespoons*
SALT & PEPPER *to taste*

1 Prepare the pasta. Sift both chestnut and white flour on work surface into a mound. Make a well in the middle; add eggs, the egg white and a pinch of salt. Work ingredients until dough is smooth and elastic. Cover with plastic wrap (or kitchen towel) and set aside for 30 minutes in a cool place.

2 Roll the pasta into thin sheets. With a sharp knife, cut 1/2 by 1 1/4 inch strips. Press lightly in the middle of each piece of pasta, twisting each side in opposite directions to form the "nodini," a sort of bow.

3 Prepare the sauce. Peel shallot and finely chop. Clean mushrooms, rapidly rinse under running water, dry with a clean kitchen towel and slice thinly.

4 In a skillet, heat olive oil; cook shallot until transparent. Add mushrooms and cook a few minutes, stirring with a wooden spoon. Add salt, fresh ground pepper and chopped parsley.

5 In the meantime, in abundant boiling salted water, cook pasta al dente. Drain, toss with mushroom sauce and serve hot.

Orecchiette with porcini

Difficulty **medium** • *Time needed* **under an hour** • *Calories per serving* **430**

INGREDIENTS
serves 4

ORECCHIETTE *12 oz*
PORCINI MUSHROOMS *8 oz*
GRATED LEMON PEEL *a pinch*
LEEKS *1*
PARSLEY *1 bunch*
BASIL *a few leaves, chopped*
GARLIC *1 clove*
GRATED PARMIGIANO *2 tablespoons*
EXTRA VIRGIN OLIVE OIL *3 tablespoons*
SALT & PEPPER *to taste*

1 Remove leaves from leek and discard root; rinse and slice thinly. Rapidly rinse mushrooms, dry well and slice thinly.

2 In a saucepan, heat olive oil; cook leek with crushed garlic, until transparent. Add sliced mushrooms and cook on high heat for 2-3 minutes. Season with salt and fresh ground pepper. Add grated lemon peel. Set aside.

3 In abundant boiling salted water, cook the orecchiette al dente. Drain and mix with mushrooms. Sprinkle with chopped parsley and basil. Toss well and serve hot, with grated grana cheese.

Orecchiette with basil

Difficulty **medium** • *Time needed* **less than 30 minutes** • *Calories per serving* **520**

INGREDIENTS
serves 4

ORECCHIETTE *14 oz*
BASIL *a bunch*
SHELLED WALNUTS *1 oz*
GARLIC *2 cloves*
GRATED PARMIGIANO *3 tablespoons*
EXTRA VIRGIN OLIVE OIL *4 tablespoons*
SALT & PEPPER *to taste*

1 In abundant boiling salted water, cook the orecchiette al dente. Finely chop garlic. In a saucepan, heat olive oil; add garlic and cook for a few minutes. Add chopped walnuts.

2 Cook another minute; add chopped basil, salt and fresh ground pepper. Mix well. Drain pasta and transfer to saucepan. Toss well, remove from heat, sprinkle with grated grana cheese and serve immediately.

SUGGESTION
If you can not get basil, use parsley, instead.

Orecchiette with tomato and aged ricotta

Difficulty **easy** • *Time needed* **under an hour** • *Calories per serving* **470**

INGREDIENTS
serves 4

ORECCHIETTE *14 oz*
TOMATO SAUCE *11 oz*
GRATED RICOTTA *4 tablespoons*
SALT *to taste*

1 In abundant boiling salted water, cook the orecchiette al dente. Drain and place in a serving dish.

2 Preheat tomato sauce. Add ricotta and mix well. Transfer to serving dish, tossing well with pasta. Serve hot.

SUGGESTION
If you can not find aged ricotta, you can use grated parmigiano or grated pecorino.

Orecchiette with beef sauce

Difficulty **medium** • *Time needed* **over an hour** • *Calories per serving* **440**

INGREDIENTS
serves 4

ORECCHIETTE *11 oz*
SLICES OF BEEF *12*
PANCETTA *4 oz, sliced*
TOMATOES *12 oz*
ONION *1*
PARSLEY *1 oz*
GARLIC *3 cloves*
PECORINO *4 oz*
DRY WHITE WINE *1/4 cup*
EXTRA VIRGIN OLIVE OIL *2 tablespoons*
SALT & PEPPER *to taste*

1 Flatten the beef slices with a mallet; crumble the pecorino; trim and rinse the parsley; peel the garlic cloves and quarter.

2 On each slice of beef put a slice of pancetta, a little pecorino, a few leaves of parsley, a piece of garlic, salt and pepper. Roll up and tie with butcher's twine so they stay closed during cooking..

3 Peel and slice the onion; rinse and pass the tomatoes through a food mill. Heat the oil in a saucepan and cook the onion; when transparent, raise the heat and brown the beef rolls evenly.

4 Add the wine and let evaporate; add the tomato purée and 4 tablespoons of water. Cook over low heat to reduce the sauce. Cook the orecchiette in abundant boiling salted water; when al dente, drain and toss with the cooking juices of the beef rolls which can be used as another dish.

SUGGESTION
You can also serve the orechiette in the middle of the serving plates, surrounded by the beef rolls.

Orecchiette with mussels

Difficulty **medium** • *Time needed* **under an hour** • *Calories per serving* **420**

INGREDIENTS
serves 4

ORECCHIETTE *11 oz*
MUSSELS *2 lbs*
VERY RIPE TOMATOES *12 oz*
(*or* CANNED TOMATOES)
PARSLEY *1 bunch*
GARLIC *2 cloves*
EXTRA VIRGIN OLIVE OIL *4 tablespoons*
SALT & PEPPER *to taste*

1 Scrape the mussels and rinse well. In a skillet, heat 1 tablespoon of olive oil with 1 peeled garlic clove; add mussels and parsley, cover and cook on high heat until mussels open.

2 Drain mussels, discard closed ones and remove mussels from shells. Keep a few shells with mussels to decorate plates.

Transfer mussels to a bowl. Filter liquid and set aside. In boiling water, scald tomatoes, peel and coarsely chop.

3 In a skillet, heat remaining olive oil with remaining garlic clove; add tomatoes, salt and fresh ground pepper. Cook on high heat for 10 minutes. Add mussel liquid, mussels and cook another 2 minutes.

4 In abundant boiling salted water, cook pasta al dente and drain. Toss with sauce and sprinkle with chopped parsley. Serve hot.

Orecchiette with rapini

Difficulty **easy** • *Time needed* **less than 30 minutes** • *Calories per serving* **480**

INGREDIENTS
serves 4

ORECCHIETTE *12 oz*
RAPINI *12 oz*
GARLIC *2 cloves*
GRATED PARMIGIANO *to taste*
EXTRA VIRGIN OLIVE OIL *5 tablespoons*
SALT & PEPPER NERO *to taste*

1 Rinse rapini, dry on a kitchen towel and cut at the base of each flower. In abundant boiling salted water, cook the orecchiette and rapini together.

2 In the meantime, peel garlic and crush. In a saucepan, heat olive oil; cook garlic for a few minutes.

3 Drain pasta and rapini; transfer to the saucepan. Add grated grana cheese and fresh ground pepper. Sauté a few minutes to mix well and serve immediately.

Orecchiette with potatoes

Difficulty **medium** • *Time needed* **under an hour** • *Calories per serving* **530**

INGREDIENTS
serves 4

ORECCHIETTE *14 oz*
POTATOES *14 oz*
TOMATOES *11 oz*
SAGE *1 leaf*
BASIL *1 branch*
MARJORAM *1 branch*
THYME *1 branch*
PARSLEY *1 branch*
GRATED AGED RICOTTA *2 tablespoons*
EXTRA VIRGIN OLIVE OIL *2 tablespoons*
SALT & PEPPER *to taste*

1 In boiling water, scald tomatoes; drain, peel, press to remove seeds and chop coarsely.

2 In a skillet, heat olive oil with sage, basil leaves, marjoram, thyme and parsley; add tomatoes and cook for approximately 10 minutes on high heat. Season with salt and pepper.

3 In the meantime, peel potatoes, rinse and slice in julienne. In abundant boiling salted water, cook potatoes and the orecchiette.

4 Remove herbs from skillet. Drain pasta and potatoes. Transfer to a serving dish and toss with tomato sauce. Serve hot with grated ricotta.

SUGGESTION
If you can not find aged ricotta, you can use grated parmigiano or grated pecoriono.

Orecchiette all'antica

Difficulty **medium** • *Time needed* **over an hour** • *Calories per serving* **340**

INGREDIENTS
serves 4

UNBLEACHED FLOUR *3 cups*
SEMOLINA *1 cup*
SALT *to taste*

1 Sift the two flours into a mound on the work surface, add a pinch of salt and gradually add enough lukewarm water to make a firm dough; knead for about 15 minutes. Roll pieces of the dough on the floured work surface into 1/2 inch diameter sticks.

2 One at a time, cut the sticks into thin slices, covering the rest with a towel. With the round point of a table knife, press the disks lightly, leaving marks as on a seashell.

3 Press each disk with your thumb to form a tiny cap, pushing the rough part to the outside. When all the orecchiette are made, dry them on the flour-dusted work surface. In a large pot, boil abundant water, add salt and cook the orecchiette for about 15 minutes. Drain and serve with a sauce of your choice.

> **SUGGESTION**
> *This traditional recipe for orechiette is often modified by adding eggs. One of the traditional sauces served with orechiette is prepared with sun dried tomatoes cooked with extra virgin olive oil, hot chili peppers and oregano to which is added grated ricotta which is made with the milk of goats or sheep and then salted and dried. Orecchiette are the most common type of pasta in southern central Italy, especially in Puglia, and in Lucania and its neighboring regions. Besides the name of orecchiette, the same pasta is also called, depending on the region: strascinati, chiancarelle, pociacche ecc.*

Pastasciutta with tuna

Difficulty **easy** • *Time needed* **less than 30 minutes** • *Calories per serving* **540**

INGREDIENTS
serves 4

SHORT PASTA *12 oz*
TUNA IN OLIVE OIL *5 oz*
OLIVE PASTE *2 tablespoons*
HEAVY CREAM *4 oz*
RED CHILI PEPPER *or* **NUTMEG**
a pinch
EXTRA VIRGIN OLIVE OIL *2 tablespoons*
SALT *to taste*

1 In abundant boiling salted water, cook pasta al dente. In the meantime, drain tuna and place in a saucepan with olive oil and olive paste. Cook for a few minutes. Add heavy cream.

2 Cook for a few more minutes, adding a red hot pepper or nutmeg (optional). Drain pasta and transfer to saucepan. Toss well and serve immediately.

Sicilian casserole

Difficulty **medium** • *Time needed* **over an hour** • *Calories per serving* **650**

INGREDIENTS
serves 4

GNOCCHETTI *12 oz*
EGGPLANTS *2*
TOMATOES *1 1/4 lbs*
SHALLOTS *2*
BASIL *a few leaves*
GRATED CACIOCAVALLO CHEESE *4 oz*
EXTRA VIRGIN OLIVE OIL *to taste*
SALT & PEPPER *to taste*

1 Trim eggplants, rinse, slice thinly and place in a colander for approximately 20 minutes; add salt. In the meantime, in boiling water, scald tomatoes, drain, peel, press to remove seeds and coarsely chop.

2 Peel shallots, rinse, dry and finely chop. Rinse basil, delicately dry with a kitchen towel and tear in small pieces. In a saucepan, heat 4 tablespoons of olive oil; cook shallots until transparent.

3 Add tomatoes, basil, salt and pepper; cook on moderate heat for 20 minutes, stirring from time to time. Rinse egg-plants and dry carefully on kitchen towel. Brush oil on a non-stick pan, brown eggplants on both sides; drain on paper towel.

4 In a cast-iron pot, place one layer of uncooked pasta, top with tomato sauce, grated caciocavallo cheese and cover with eggplants. Repeat until all ingredients are used. Finish with eggplants and caciocavallo. Cover with water up to the top and cook on low heat for 40 minutes. Serve hot.

Penne with wild fennel

Difficulty **medium** • *Time needed* **under an hour** • *Calories per serving* **520**

INGREDIENTS
serves 4

PENNE LISCE *12 oz*
WILD FENNEL *2 bunches*
ANCHOVIES IN OLIVE OIL *4*
TOMATOES *14 oz, very ripe*
ONION *1, small*
GARLIC *1 clove*
BREAD CRUMBS *3 oz*
EXTRA VIRGIN OLIVE OIL *5 tablespoons*
SALT & PEPPER *to taste*

1 Trim wild fennel, removing the hard parts; rinse and cook in a large pot of salted water for 5 minutes. Drain and set aside cooking liquid.

2 In boiling water, scald tomatoes for approximately 1 minute; peel, press to remove seeds and coarsely chop. In a saucepan, heat 4 tablespoons of olive oil; lightly brown chopped onion and crushed garlic clove. Add chopped anchovies and stir well. Add tomatoes, salt and pepper. Cook for 10 minutes. After 5 minutes of cooking, add wild fennel and blend with sauce.

3 In the meantime, in a non-stick pan, toast bread crumbs, stirring often with a wooden spoon; transfer to a plate. Add remaining olive oil to pan, return to heat with the bread crumbs and cook for 1 minute, stirring constantly.

4 Bring the fennel cooking water to a boil and cook the penne al dente. Drain and transfer to a bowl with fennel sauce and toss. Sprinkle with toasted bread crumbs. Serve immediately.

SUGGESTION
If you can not get wild fennel, use the feathery leaves of common fennel which has a lighter flavor or use dried fennel seeds.

Penne with pepper purée

Difficulty **medium** • *Time needed* **under an hour** • *Calories per serving* **590**

INGREDIENTS
serves 4

PENNE RIGATE *12 oz*
PEPPERS *2*
SMOKED BACON *2 oz*
GARLIC *2 cloves*
GRATED PARMIGIANO *3 tablespoons*
EXTRA VIRGIN OLIVE OIL *4 tablespoons*
SALT *to taste*

1 Peel garlic and crush. Remove seeds and stalk from peppers, rinse, dry, cut in strips then chop. In a saucepan, heat 3 tablespoons of olive oil with garlic clove brown lightly. Remove garlic; add chopped peppers and cook on moderate heat for a few minutes. Remove from heat and press through a sieve, over a mixing bowl.

2 Dice pancetta. In a skillet, heat remaining olive oil and brown pancetta. Add pepper purée and cook on low heat.

3 In the meantime, in abundant boiling salted water, cook penne al dente; drain and toss with sauce. Serve hot with grated grana cheese.

Penne with parsley and basil

Difficulty **easy** • *Time needed* **less than 30 minutes** • *Calories per serving* **450**

INGREDIENTS
serves 4

PENNE *12 oz*
PARSLEY *1 bunch*
BASIL *1 bunch*
ANCHOVIES PRESERVED IN SALT *2*
CAPERS IN BRINE *1 tablespoon*
GARLIC *1 clove*
EXTRA VIRGIN OLIVE OIL *6 tablespoons*
SALT & PEPPER *to taste*

1 Trim and rinse parsley and basil; dry with a kitchen towel. Rinse capers to remove salt. Rinse anchovies under running water; remove heads and bones; slice in small fillets and cut in small pieces.

2 Place all these ingredients in the food processor; add garlic clove, olive oil, salt and fresh ground pepper. Blend well and pour mixture in a sauce boat.

3 In abundant boiling salted water, cook pasta al dente. Drain and place in individual plates, adding a little sauce. Serve immediately, with remaining sauce on the side.

Penne with tuna and vegetables

Difficulty **medium** • *Time needed* **under an hour** • *Calories per serving* **470**

INGREDIENTS
serves 6

PENNE *1 lb*
STRING BEANS *8 oz*
SPINACH *11 oz, cleaned*
BEET TOPS *11 oz, cleaned*
TUNA IN WATER *5 oz*
CHERRY TOMATOES *6, sliced*
ONION *1*
GARLIC *1 clove*
HEAVY CREAM *2 tablespoons*
GRATED PARMIGIANO *2 tablespoons*
EXTRA VIRGIN OLIVE OIL *5 tablespoons*
SALT & PEPPER *to taste*

1 Trim green beans, rinse and cut in small pieces. In salted water, boil green beans for 10 minutes and drain. Rinse spinach and beets, drain and cut in wide strips.

2 In a saucepan, heat olive oil with chopped onion and garlic. Add beets and spinach, mixing well; cook for a few minutes and season with salt and pepper.

3 Drain tuna from water, crumble and set aside. Add green beans and tomatoes to saucepan. Mix well and cook for 20 minutes on low heat. Add tuna; mix well and cook for 10 minutes.

4 In abundant boiling salted water, cook penne al dente. Drain and transfer to a serving dish, toss well with sauce and heavy cream. Sprinkle with grated parmigiano. Serve immediately.

> **SUGGESTION**
> *You can replace the canned tuna with fresh tuna. In this case, dice the tuna and sauté in a non-stick pan for 4 minutes before adding to the recipe.*

Penne all'arrabbiata

Difficulty **easy** • *Time needed* **under an hour** • *Calories per serving* **630**

INGREDIENTS
serves 4

PENNE *12 oz*
TOMATOES *1 lb, ripe, firm*
GARLIC *1 clove*
ONION *1*
PANCETTA *3 oz*
HOT PEPPER *a small piece*
GRATED PECORINO *3 tablespoons*
EXTRA VIRGIN OLIVE OIL *5 tablespoons*
SALT *to taste*

1 In boiling water, scald tomatoes, drain, peel, press to remove seeds and coarsely chop. Peel garlic and onion; rinse and finely chop. Dice pancetta. In a skillet, heat 1 tablespoon of olive oil and brown pancetta on all sides; drain and set aside.

2 Discard cooking fat from pan. Heat remaining olive oil, add onion, garlic and chili pepper; cook until onion is transparent. Add pancetta, tomatoes and salt. Cook for approximately 20 minutes on moderate heat, stirring from time to time.

3 In the meantime, in abundant boiling salted water, cook pasta al dente. Drain, toss with sauce and sprinkle with grated pecorino. Serve hot.

SUGGESTION
The term "all'arrabbiata" identifies a dish that is particularly spicy, usually with chili peppers in the preparation. Recipes that are "all'arrabbiata" usually call for meat or pasta, such as the one herein. The sauce should always contain tomatoes, pancetta, and, obviously, hot peppers, which is the signature ingredient. Among the types of pasta used most often "all'arrabbiata", besides the smooth penne, is ziti, which complements the sauce perfectly.

Penne alla carbonara with artichokes

Difficulty **medium** • *Time needed* **under an hour** • *Calories per serving* **700**

INGREDIENTS
serves 4

PENNE *12 oz*
ARTICHOKES *3*
PANCETTA *4 oz,*
LEMON *1, the juice of*
PARSLEY *1 bunch*
GARLIC *1 clove*
EGGS *3*
MILK *4 tablespoons*
GRATED PARMIGIANO *2 tablespoons*
GRATED PECORINO *2 tablespoons*
EXTRA VIRGIN OLIVE OIL *4 tablespoons*
SALT & PEPPER *to taste*

1 Dice pancetta. Clean artichokes, discard hard leaves and tips; cut in half, remove chokes, slice thinly. Soak the artichokes pieces in a bowl of cold water and lemon juice. Clean parsley, rinse, delicately dry and chop. Peel garlic and chop finely.

2 Drain artichokes. In a saucepan, heat olive oil; cook garlic for 1 minute and add artichokes. Cook for 3 minutes on high heat; add salt and fresh ground pepper. Cover and cook on moderate heat for approximately 3-4 minutes. Add parsley.

3 In a non-stick pan, brown pancetta on all sides. In a mixing bowl, place eggs, grated grana cheese, grated pecorino, milk and salt; lightly beat with a fork.

4 In abundant boiling salted water, cook pasta al dente. Drain, keeping some cooking water; transfer to a non-stick pan; add 2-3 tablespoons of pasta cooking water and artichokes. Mix well with a wooden spoon.

5 Remove from heat, add egg-cheese mixture and fresh ground black pepper. Return pan to heat and sauté for a few seconds; remove and sprinkle with remaining parsley. Serve immediately.

Penne alla lucana

Difficulty **medium** • *Time needed* **over an hour** • *Calories per serving* **620**

INGREDIENTS
serves 4

PENNE RIGATE *12 oz*
DRIED LIMA BEANS *5 oz*
PANCETTA *2 oz, in one slice*
TOMATOES *11 oz, ripe, firm*
CARROT *1*
ONION *1*
CELERY *1 stalk*
SAGE *3 leaves*
PARSLEY *1 bunch*
ROSEMARY *1 branch*
GARLIC *1 clove*
EXTRA VIRGIN OLIVE OIL *4 tablespoons*
SALT & PEPPER *to taste*

1 Soak beans in cold water for 12 hours. In boiling water, scald tomatoes, drain, peel, press to remove seeds and coarsely chop. Trim carrot and peel. Remove large filaments from celery. Rinse vegetables separately.

2 Drain beans and place in a saucepan. Add half onion, carrot, celery, garlic and 1 sage leaf. Cover with cold water, slowly bring to boil and cook beans on low heat for approximately 1 hour. Add salt at the end of cooking time.

3 Dice pancetta. Rinse parsley, rosemary and remaining sage; dry and chop finely. In a skillet, heat olive oil and cook remaining onion until transparent. Add parsley, rosemary and sage. Add diced pancetta and brown on all sides, stirring with a wooden spoon.

4 Add tomatoes, salt and pepper; cook on high heat for approximately 5 minutes. Add beans and cook for 2 minutes. In the meantime, in abundant boiling salted water, cook pasta al dente. Drain. Transfer to serving bowl and mix well with bean sauce. Serve hot.

Penne alla marchigiana

Difficulty **medium** • *Time needed* **under an hour** • *Calories per serving* **490**

INGREDIENTS
serves 4

PENNE *12 oz*
EGGPLANT *1*
YELLOW PEPPER *1*
TOMATOES *11 oz, ripe, firm*
ANCHOVIES PRESERVED IN SALT *2*
CAPERS IN BRINE *1 tablespoon*
BLACK OLIVES *8*
BASIL *1 bunch*
GARLIC *1 clove*
GRATED PECORINO *2 tablespoons*
EXTRA VIRGIN OLIVE OIL *4 tablespoons*
SALT & PEPPER *to taste*

1 Trim eggplant, rinse, dry, slice in julienne. Place in a colander, add salt and let drain for 30 minutes. In the meantime, rinse yellow pepper and dry. Grill in the oven until charred. Remove to a brown paper bag for 10 minutes.

2 Remove pepper from paper bag, peel, remove seeds, rinse, dry and slice. In boiling water, scald tomatoes, drain, peel, press to remove seeds and slice. Rinse anchovies in cold running water, remove bones and cut fillets in pieces.

3 Slice olives. Rinse capers, dry and chop coarsely. Rinse basil, dry and tear. Peel garlic, rinse, dry and crush. In a skillet, heat olive oil; lightly brown garlic; add anchovies and peppers. Cook for 2 minutes, stirring with a wooden spoon.

4 Add eggplants and brown for 2 minutes. Add tomatoes, salt and fresh ground pepper; cook for 10-15 minutes on moderate heat. Approximately 5 minutes before cooking ends, add capers, olives and basil.

5 In abundant boiling salted water, cook penne al dente. Drain and toss with sauce. Sprinkle with grated pecorino and serve hot.

Penne with ricotta

Difficulty **medium** • *Time needed* **under an hour** • *Calories per serving* **510**

INGREDIENTS
serves 4

PENNE *14 oz*
RICOTTA *7 oz*
BEET GREENS *3 bunches*
NUTMEG *a pinch*
GRATED PARMIGIANO *to taste*
BUTTER *to taste*
SALT & PEPPER *to taste*

1 Clean beets and cut in small pieces; transfer to boiling water, add salt and cook on low heat for 10 minutes.

2 Pass ricotta through a sieve, over a mixing bowl. Add 1 tablespoon of butter at room temperature, parmigiano and nutmeg; mix well.

3 In abundant boiling salted water, cook penne al dente. Drain pasta and beet greens; transfer to mixing bowl, add ricotta and toss well. Add fresh ground pepper and serve immediately.

Penne alla napoletana

Difficulty **medium** • *Time needed* **over an hour** • *Calories per serving* **530**

INGREDIENTS
serves 4

PENNE *14 oz*
TOMATOES *11 oz*
EGGPLANTS *11 oz*
ANCHOVIES PRESERVED IN SALT *3*
MOZZARELLA *5 oz*
SHALLOT *1*
BASIL *1 bunch*
EXTRA VIRGIN OLIVE OIL *3 tablespoons*
SALT & PEPPER *to taste*

1 In boiling water, scald tomatoes; drain, peel, press to remove seeds and dice. Trim eggplants, rinse and dice; add salt and set aside to drain in a colander for 20 minutes.

2 Rinse anchovies under running water, remove bones and cut in small pieces. Dice the mozzarella. Peel shallot and finely chop. Rinse basil, dry and tear in pieces. In a skillet, heat olive oil; cook shallot and basil until shallot is transparent. Rinse and dry eggplants.

3 Add eggplants to skillet. Cook for 3 minutes on high heat, stirring well. Add tomatoes, salt and fresh ground pepper. Cook for approximately 20 minutes on moderate heat. Add anchovies and remaining basil; mix well. Remove from heat after a few minutes.

4 In the meantime, cook pasta al dente. Drain and transfer to eggplant mixture; add mozzarella and toss well. Transfer to a serving dish and serve immediately.

Penne alla milanese

Difficulty **easy** • *Time needed* **less than 30 minutes** • *Calories per serving* **520**

INGREDIENTS
serves 4

PENNE *12 oz*
FRESH SAUSAGE *4 oz*
SAFFRON *1 teaspoon*
HEAVY CREAM *4 oz*
GRATED PARMIGIANO *3 tablespoons*
SALT & PEPPER *to taste*

1 Remove the sausage skin, crumble, place in a non-stick pan and briefly cook on all sides. Drain, discard fat from pan and return sausage to pan.

2 Add heavy cream and saffron; stir well and cook for approximately 3 minutes on moderate heat. Add salt and fresh ground pepper.

3 In the meantime, in abundant boiling salted water, cook penne al dente. Drain and transfer to a serving dish. Add sauce and toss well. Sprinkle with grated grana cheese and serve hot.

Penne with vegetables

Difficulty **medium** • *Time needed* **under an hour** • *Calories per serving* **560**

INGREDIENTS
serves 4

PENNE *12 oz*
PEELED TOMATOES *1 lb*
TALEGGIO CHEESE *2 oz*
PEPPERS *2*
PANCETTA *2 oz*
ONION *1*
BUTTER *1 tablespoon*
EXTRA VIRGIN OLIVE OIL *2 tablespoons*
SALT & PEPPER *to taste*

1 Peel onion, rinse and chop. In a saucepan, heat olive oil and butter over moderate heat. Cook onion on low heat until transparent. Dice bacon, add to saucepan and cook slowly.

2 Crush tomatoes with a fork. Rinse peppers, remove seeds, dice and add to saucepan. Stir well and cook on low heat for 5 minutes. Add crushed tomatoes; stir well, add salt and pepper; cook for 20 minutes on moderate heat.

3 In the meantime, in abundant boiling salted water, cook penne al dente. Dice taleggio cheese and add to sauce. Mix well until sauce is creamy. Drain pasta and toss with sauce. Serve hot.

Penne with broccoli

Difficulty **medium** • *Time needed* **under an hour** • *Calories per serving* **480**

INGREDIENTS
serves 4

PENNE *12 oz*
BROCCOLI *2 lbs*
ANCHOVIES PRESERVED IN SALT *2 oz*
GARLIC *2 cloves*
RED CHILI PEPPER *to taste*
EXTRA VIRGIN OLIVE OIL *5 tablespoons*
SALT *to taste*

1 Rinse broccoli and cook in abundant boiling salted water for approximately 15 minutes. Drain with a slotted spoon, leaving cooking water; transfer broccoli to a serving dish and set aside.

2 Bring the broccoli cooking water to a boil and cook penne al dente. In the meantime, rinse anchovies and remove bones. Peel garlic. In a pan, heat olive oil with garlic and chili pepper.

3 Add anchovies and crush with a fork to melt completely. Drain pasta and transfer to serving dish with broccoli. Add anchovy sauce and serve hot.

> **SUGGESTION**
> *This is the traditional recipe. It can be modified to your taste, reducing or eliminating the garlic. Without anchovies, it becomes a vegetarian dish.*

Penne with asparagus, carrot and celery

Difficulty **medium** • *Time needed* **under an hour** • *Calories per serving* **420**

INGREDIENTS
serves 4

PENNE *12 oz*
ASPARAGUS *1 bunch*
CARROT *2*
CELERY *1 stalk*
ONION *1*
BUTTER *1 tablespoon*
EXTRA VIRGIN OLIVE OIL *2 tablespoons*
SALT & PEPPER *to taste*

1 Remove hard stems of asparagus, rinse and slice. Peel carrots, rinse and dice. In boiling salted water, cook carrots for 3-4 minutes. Drain and set aside.

2 Rinse celery stalk, slice thinly and scald for one minute in boiling salted water. Finely chop onion. In a saucepan, heat olive oil and butter; cook onion until transparent.

3 Add carrots, celery, asparagus, salt and pepper; cover and cook for 7-8 minutes. In the meantime, in abundant boiling salted water, cook penne al dente. Drain and toss with vegetables. Serve immediately.

Penne with cauliflower and tomatoes

Difficulty **medium** • *Time needed* **under an hour** • *Calories per serving* **490**

INGREDIENTS
serves 4

PENNE *12 oz*
CAULIFLOWER *1 1/2 lbs*
PEELED TOMATOES *1 lb*
GARLIC *1 clove*
HOT PEPPER *1*
GRATED PECORINO *4 tablespoons*
EXTRA VIRGIN OLIVE OIL *3 tablespoons*
SALT *to taste*

1 Separate cauliflower in florets and rinse. In abundant boiling salted water, cook cauliflower. After 4 minutes, add penne.

2 Pass tomatoes through a sieve over a bowl. In the meantime, in a skillet, heat olive oil with peeled garlic and chili pepper. Add tomato juice and salt; cook for approximately 15 minutes. Drain pasta and cauliflower. Toss with sauce and grated cheese. Serve immediately.

> **SUGGESTION**
> *Other types of short pasta can be used for this recipe, The pecorino can be substituted by grana or even parmigiano cheeses.*
> *Discard the garlic and hot pepper before adding tomatoes if you wish the dish to be less spicy.*

Penne with peppers

Difficulty **medium** • *Time needed* **under an hour** • *Calories per serving* **490**

INGREDIENTS
serves 4

PENNE RIGATE *14 oz*
YELLOW PEPPER *1*
RED PEPPER *1*
ANCHOVIES IN OLIVE OIL *2 fillets*
CHERRY TOMATOES *6*
ONION *1*
PARSLEY *a bunch, chopped*
BASIL *4 leaves, chopped*
GARLIC *1 clove*
DRY WHITE WINE *2 tablespoons*
GRATED PARMIGIANO *3 tablespoons*
EXTRA VIRGIN OLIVE OIL *3 tablespoons*
SALT & PEPPER *to taste*

1 Remove seeds from peppers, divide in slices and cut using a heart-shaped cookie cutter. Finely chop onion and garlic. In a saucepan, heat olive oil; lightly brown garlic and onion on low heat. Cut anchovies in small pieces.

2 Add anchovy pieces to saucepan and stir to dissolved. Add the sliced peppers. Sauté for a few minutes on high heat; lower heat and add salt and fresh ground pepper. Peel tomatoes, press to remove seeds and slice thinly.

3 Add the dry white wine and let evaporate on high heat. Add tomato slices and season with salt; cook for 15 minutes on low heat. Chop parsley and basil.

4 In the meantime, in abundant boiling salted water, cook penne al dente. Drain and transfer to saucepan. Mix well; add parsley, basil and grated parmigiano. Serve immediately.

Penne with eggplant and sausage

Difficulty **medium** • *Time needed* **over an hour** • *Calories per serving* **500**

INGREDIENTS
serves 4

PENNE *11 oz*
EGGPLANT *1*
SAUSAGE *4 oz*
TOMATOES *14 oz*
RED PEPPER *1*
ONION *1, chopped*
HOT PEPPER *a small piece*
PARSLEY *1 bunch*
GARLIC *1 clove*
OREGANO *a pinch*
DRY WHITE WINE *1/4 cup*
GRATED PARMIGIANO *4 tablespoons*
EXTRA VIRGIN OLIVE OIL *2 tablespoons*
SALT & PEPPER *to taste*

1 Rinse eggplants, dice, add salt and drain in colander for 30 minutes. Rinse under running water and dry with a kitchen towel.

2 In a saucepan, heat olive oil; cook onion until transparent. Add peeled crumbled sausage and cook for 2-3 minutes. Add wine and let evaporate on high heat. Add eggplants, diced red pepper and chili pepper. Cook for 5 minutes. Add peeled chopped tomatoes, oregano, salt and pepper. Cover and cook for 20 minutes on moderate heat.

3 Add chopped parsley and garlic. Cook for 7-8 minutes. In the meantime, in abundant boiling salted water, cook penne al dente. Drain, remove chili pepper from sauce and toss. Sprinkle with grated parmigiano and serve hot.

SUGGESTION
This recipe can be prepared without the sausage; substitute it with pitted olives.

Penne with zucchini and fried onions

Difficulty **medium** • *Time needed* **under an hour** • *Calories per serving* **600**

INGREDIENTS
serves 4

PENNE *12 oz*
ZUCCHINI *12 oz*
ONIONS *2*
BASIL *8 leaves*
EGGS *2*
CORN STARCH *2 tablespoons*
BEER *1/4 cup*
GRATED PECORINO *3 tablespoons*
PEANUT OIL
enough for frying
EXTRA VIRGIN OLIVE OIL *2 tablespoons*
SALT & PEPPER *to taste*

1 In abundant boiling salted water, cook penne al dente. In the meantime, rinse zucchini, dry and slice. Peel onion, cut into thick slices and rinse under running water.

2 Mix egg yolks in a bowl. In another bowl, beat egg whites to stiff peaks. Place cornstarch in mixing bowl; gradually add beer, milk, a pinch of salt and egg whites.

3 Dip slices of zucchini and onion in batter one at a time and deep fry in abundant oil. Remove with slotted spoon, drain on absorbent paper towels and immediately sprinkle with salt. Set aside.

4 Drain penne, transfer to a warm serving dish; mix with olive oil, grated pecorino cheese, chopped basil leaves and fresh ground pepper. Add zucchini and onion slices, toss and serve immediately.

SUGGESTION
With any leftover pasta, you can make delicious fritters by adding to the batter bits of cheese: italico, fontina, emmental, or even shards of parmigiano or grana.

Penne with zucchini and cheese fondue

Difficulty **medium** • *Time needed* **under an hour** • *Calories per serving* **790**

INGREDIENTS
serves 4

PENNE *1 lb*
ZUCCHINI *12 oz*
ONION *1*
PARSLEY *a handful*
GARLIC *1 clove*
EGG YOLKS *1*
EMMENTAL *7 oz*
MILK *1/4 cup*
THYME *a pinch*
NUTMEG *a pinch*
VEGETABLE EXTRACT *1/2 teaspoon*
BUTTER *1 tablespoon*
EXTRA VIRGIN OLIVE OIL *3 tablespoons*
SALT *to taste*

1 Chop zucchini in small pieces. In a skillet, heat olive oil; cook chopped garlic, onion, parsley and zucchini.

2 Add vegetable extract dissolved in a quarter cup of hot water, a pinch of thyme and grated nutmeg. Cover and cook on low heat until zucchini are tender and liquid evaporates.

3 In abundant boiling salted water, cook the penne al dente. In the meantime, prepare the fondue. In a small saucepan, melt the butter; add emmental cheese and cook over low heat with warm milk, stirring constantly.

4 When is creamy, remove from heat and blend in egg yolk, with a pinch of salt. Drain pasta; transfer to a bowl with zucchini and fondue sauce. Serve hot.

Penne with mushrooms and prosciuttto

Difficulty **medium** • *Time needed* **under an hour** • *Calories per serving* **550**

INGREDIENTS
serves 4

PENNE *14 oz*
DRIED MUSHROOMS *2 oz*
TOMATOES *14 oz*
ONION *1*
PROSCIUTTO *2 oz*
PARSLEY *1 bunch*
GRATED PARMIGIANO *3 tablespoons*
EXTRA VIRGIN OLIVE OIL *3 tablespoons*
SALT & PEPPER *to taste*

1 Soak mushrooms in lukewarm water. In boiling water, scald tomatoes; drain, peel, press to remove seeds and press through a strainer. Peel onion, rinse and finely chop. Chop prosciutto. Rinse, dry, and chop parsley.

2 In a large skillet, heat olive oil; cook onion until transparent. Add prosciutto and cook a few minutes, stirring with a wooden spoon. Add drained mushrooms and cook for one minute. Add tomatoes, a pinch of salt and pepper; cook for approximately 15 minutes, stirring.

3 In the meantime, in abundant boiling salted water, cook the penne al dente. Drain and transfer to skillet. Ad 2 tablespoons of pasta cooking water. Cook for one minute.

4 Remove saucepan from heat; add grated grana cheese and toss well. Place pasta on a serving dish, sprinkle with chopped parsley and serve immediately.

SUGGESTION
This dish can be even more flavorful if you replace the dried mushrooms with fresh porcini: brush away any dirt and slice them thinly..

Penne with trevise lettuce

Difficulty **easy** • *Time needed* **less than 30 minutes** • *Calories per serving* **580**

INGREDIENTS
serves 4

PENNE *12 oz*
TREVISE LETTUCE *7 oz*
ONION *1/2*
WALNUTS *4 oz*
RICOTTA *7 oz*
GRATED PARMIGIANO *2 tablespoons*
EXTRA VIRGIN OLIVE OIL *4 tablespoons*
SALT & PEPPER *to taste*

1 Rinse lettuce carefully, drain and cut in small pieces. Finely chop onion. Chop walnuts. In a saucepan, heat olive oil; lightly brown onion; add lettuce and sauté for a few minutes. Add walnuts, salt, pepper, ricotta and parmigiano cheese. Mix well and remove from heat.

2 In abundant boiling salted water, cook the penne al dente. Drain, transfer to saucepan with 1/2 cup of pasta cooking water. Toss well and serve immediately.

Penne with arugula

Difficulty **easy** • *Time needed* **under an hour** • *Calories per serving* **450**

INGREDIENTS
serves 4

PENNE *14 oz*
ARUGULA *5 oz*
TOMATOES *14 oz*
GARLIC *1 clove*
RED CHILI PEPPER *a small piece*
GRATED PARMIGIANO *3 tablespoons*
EXTRA VIRGIN OLIVE OIL *2 tablespoons*
SALT *to taste*

1 Rinse arugula and drain well. Crush tomatoes with a fork. In a saucepan, heat olive oil with garlic and chili pepper. Remove garlic and chili from pan and add tomatoes.

2 Add salt and cook on moderate heat for approximately 15 minutes. In abundant boiling salted water, cook arugula together with penne until pasta is al dente.

3 Drain and transfer pasta to saucepan; toss well and serve immediately with grated parmigiano cheese.

SUGGESTION
You can use whole or shredded arugula leaves. If leaves are small, it will be simpler to eat them.

Pennette with squash

Difficulty **medium** • *Time needed* **under an hour** • *Calories per serving* **510**

INGREDIENTS
serves 4

PENNETTE LISCE *11 oz*
SQUASH *1 1/4 lbs*
ONION *1*
AMARETTI *2*
HEAVY CREAM *3 tablespoons*
GRATED PARMIGIANO *2 tablespoons*
BUTTER *4 tablespoons*
SALT & PEPPER *to taste*

1 Peel the squash, remove seeds, rinse, dry and cut in big pieces, then slice thinly. Peel onion, rinse and slice thinly.

2 Crumble the amaretti. In a skillet, melt half the butter and cook onion until transparent. Add squash slices and cook a few minutes, stirring carefully with a wooden spoon.

3 Season with salt and pepper; cover and cook for 10-15 minutes on moderate heat, adding from time to time a tablespoon of hot water. Add heavy cream and the amaretti. Mix well.

4 In the meantime, in abundant boiling salted water, cook pennette al dente. Drain and toss with squash sauce. Add remaining butter and grated grana; toss well. Serve immediately.

Pennette with string bean purée

Difficulty **medium** • *Time needed* **under an hour** • *Calories per serving* **530**

INGREDIENTS
serves 4

PENNETTE RIGATE *12 oz*
STRING BEANS *11 oz*
EGG YOLKS *2*
HEAVY CREAM *1/4 cup*
GRATED PARMIGIANO *4 tablespoons*
BUTTER *3 tablespoons*
SALT & PEPPER *to taste*

1 Trim string beans, rinse and add to a large pot of boiling salted water. Cook uncovered. In a bowl, beat egg yolks, cream, grated grana cheese, a generous pinch of salt and fresh ground pepper. Mix well and set aside.

2 Drain string beans using a slotted spoon and pass through food mill; transfer to a bowl. Keep cooking water and use to cook pennette al dente.

3 In the meantime, in a large saucepan, melt butter; add string bean purée, stirring for a few minutes. Add the egg mixture, mix again and add pasta. Toss quickly and sprinkle with fresh ground pepper. Serve immediately.

Pennette alla Siciliana

Difficulty **medium** • *Time needed* **under an hour** • *Calories per serving* **490**

INGREDIENTS
serves 4

PENNETTE *12 oz*
EGGPLANTS *2, small*
MUSHROOMS *7 oz*
TOMATOES *11 oz*
PARSLEY *1 bunch*
GARLIC *1 clove*
GRATED PECORINO *2 tablespoons*
EXTRA VIRGIN OLIVE OIL *5 tablespoons*
SALT & PEPPER *to taste*

1 Trim eggplants, rinse and chop. Rapidly rinse mushrooms and slice thinly. In boiling water, scald tomatoes; drain, press to remove seeds and chop. Set aside.

2 In a saucepan, heat olive oil with crushed garlic; add eggplants and cook until golden on all sides. Add mushrooms and cook for 2-3 minutes. Drain eggplants and mushrooms. Set aside.

3 Chop parsley and set aside. In the same saucepan, place tomatoes, salt and fresh ground pepper. Cook on high heat for 15 minutes. Add eggplants and mushrooms; cook for another 5 minutes. Add parsley and mix well. Remove from heat.

4 In abundant boiling salted water, cook pennette al dente. Drain. Toss with sauce and sprinkle with grated pecorino cheese. Serve immediately.

> **SUGGESTION**
> *If you want to garnish the dish with thin slices of eggplant, fry them in a skillet with extra virgin olive oil and place on absorbent towels to eliminate excess oil.*

Pennette with lemon rind

Difficulty **easy** • *Time needed* **less than 30 minutes** • *Calories per serving* **540**

INGREDIENTS
serves 4

PENNETTE *14 oz*
ORGANIC LEMONS *3*
HEAVY CREAM *4 oz*
GRATED PARMIGIANO *to taste*
BUTTER *3 tablespoons*
SALT *to taste*

1 Grate lemon peel and place in a bowl. Add heavy cream and softened butter. Using a wooden spoon, mix well until sauce is smooth.

2 In the meantime, in abundant boiling salted water, cook pennette al dente. Drain and toss with sauce. Add abundant grated parmigiano cheese. Transfer to a serving dish and serve hot.

> **SUGGESTION**
> *For this recipe it is best to use organic, untreated lemons. If you want to add a bit of color to the presentation of the dish, garnish with a sprinkling of chopped parsley and a few very thin slices of lemon.*

Pennette with fresh tomatoes

Difficulty **easy** • *Time needed* **over an hour** • *Calories per serving* **420**

INGREDIENTS
serves 4

PENNETTE *12 oz*
TOMATOES *6-7, ripe, firm*
BASIL *1 bunch*
GARLIC *1 clove*
OREGANO *a pinch*
EXTRA VIRGIN OLIVE OIL *3 tablespoons*
SALT & PEPPER *to taste*

1 Rinse tomatoes, dry with a kitchen towel, dice and place in a bowl. Add chopped basil, crushed garlic, oregano, a pinch of salt, fresh ground pepper and olive oil. Mix and set aside for 2 hours.

2 In abundant boiling salted water, cook pennette al dente.

3 Drain pasta, transfer to a serving bowl and add sauce. Toss and serve at once.

Pipe with green pepper

Difficulty **medium** • *Time needed* **under an hour** • *Calories per serving* **480**

INGREDIENTS
serves 4

PIPE *12 oz*
GREEN PEPPER *1*
PANCETTA *3 oz, in one piece*
ONION *1*
MARJORAM *a few sprigs*
BASIL *1 bunch*
EXTRA VIRGIN OLIVE OIL *2 tablespoons*
SALT & PEPPER *to taste*

1 Cut green pepper in half, remove seeds and white parts; rinse and slice. Rinse marjoram and basil; dry and chop. Peel the onion and chop finely. Slice pancetta thinly.

2 In a saucepan, heat olive oil; cook onion until transparent with some basil and marjoram. Add pancetta and sauté a few minutes until lightly golden.

3 Add pepper slices and cook on high heat, stirring with a wooden spoon. Add 3-4 tablespoons of water, salt and fresh ground pepper. Cover and cook on moderate heat for 15 minutes.

4 In the meantime, in abundant boiling salted water, cook pipe al dente. Drain and mix with sauce. Add remaining marjoram and basil. Serve immediately, with grated cheese.

Pipe with cauliflower

Difficulty **medium** • *Time needed* **under an hour** • *Calories per serving* **530**

INGREDIENTS
serves 4

PIPE *14 oz*
CAULIFLOWER *1, about 1 lb*
TOMATOES *1 lb*
PARSLEY *2 bunches*
GARLIC *2 cloves*
GRATED PECORINO *4 tablespoons*
EXTRA VIRGIN OLIVE OIL *4 tablespoons*
SALT & PEPPER *to taste*

1 Separate cauliflower into florets and rinse. In abundant boiling salted water, cook cauliflower for approximately 15 minutes.

2 In the meantime, rinse tomatoes and pass through a food mill. Rinse parsley and chop finely. Peel garlic and crush. Place these ingredients in a serving bowl; add salt, fresh ground pepper and olive oil. Mix well and set aside.

3 After 15 minutes of boiling cauliflower, add the pipe and cook al dente. Drain pasta and cauliflower together and transfer to serving bowl. Toss well and add grated pecorino cheese. Serve immediately.

Pipe alla Sangiovanniello

Difficulty **easy** • *Time needed* **less than 30 minutes** • *Calories per serving* **410**

INGREDIENTS
serves 4

PIPE *12 oz*
TOMATOES *1 lb, ripe, firm*
ANCHOVIES PRESERVED IN SALT *2*
CAPERS *1 tablespoon*
PARSLEY *a bunch*
GARLIC *2 cloves*
HOT PEPPER *a small piece*
EXTRA VIRGIN OLIVE OIL *3 tablespoons*
SALT *to taste*

1 Rinse tomatoes, peel, press to remove seeds and chop. Peel garlic. Rinse anchovies and remove bones. Rinse parsley and chop finely.

2 In a saucepan, heat olive oil with garlic and anchovies, crushing with a fork to melt. Add tomatoes, chili pepper, capers and parsley. Cook for about 15 min-

utes, adding a little water if the sauce becomes too dense.

3 In abundant boiling salted water, cook pasta al dente. Drain, transfer to a serving bowl and add sauce. Toss well and serve hot.

Pipette with potatoes and capers

Difficulty **medium** • *Time needed* **under an hour** • *Calories per serving* **490**

INGREDIENTS
serves 4

PIPETTE *11 oz*
POTATOES *(Yukon gold) 14 oz*
CAPERS *1 tablespoon*
PARSLEY *1 bunch*
GARLIC *1 clove*
GRATED PARMIGIANO *4 tablespoons*
EXTRA VIRGIN OLIVE OIL *4 tablespoons*
SALT & PEPPER *to taste*

1 Peel potatoes, rinse and finely chop. Rinse, dry and chop parsley. Rinse capers, dry and chop. In a skillet, heat olive oil; lightly brown crushed garlic. Remove garlic; add potatoes and cook until golden, stirring with a wooden spoon. Add salt and fresh ground pepper; cook a few minutes. Add parsley and capers.

2 In the meantime, in abundant boiling salted water, cook pipette al dente.

Drain and transfer to a mixing bowl and mix in sauce. Transfer to individual plates and serve immediately with grated parmigiano on the side.

SUGGESTION
*For a variation of this dish, use
11 oz of potatoes and 4 oz of diced tofu,
and follow the recipe as usual.*

Pasta with borlotti beans

Difficulty **medium** • *Time needed* **over an hour** • *Calories per serving* **680**

INGREDIENTS
serves 4

For the pasta
UNBLEACHED FLOUR *2 cups*
BREAD CRUMBS *7 oz*
BOILING WATER *2 1/2 cups*

For the sauce
DRIED BORLOTTI BEANS *5 oz*
PANCETTA *2 oz, in one slice*
TOMATOES *11 oz, ripe, firm*
CARROT *1/2*
CELERY *1/2 stalk*
ONION *1*
PARSLEY *1 bunch*
BASIL *1 bunch*
GARLIC *1 clove*
GRATED PARMIGIANO *3 tablespoons*
EXTRA VIRGIN OLIVE OIL *3 tablespoons*
SALT & PEPPER *to taste*

1 Soak beans in abundant cold water for 12 hours. Drain and place in a saucepan. Cover with cold water, add 1/2 onion; cover and cook on low heat for approximately one hour. Add salt at the end of cooking period. In the meantime, in a large bowl, mix flour and bread crumbs; add little by little some boiling water, stirring until dough is firm.

2 Knead dough for approximately 10 minutes. Pull a piece off and roll in a chalk-size cylinder; divide it in 1/2 inch pieces and, pressing it with the thumb, roll it on itself forming the bean-size "pisarei." Repeat until all dough is used.

3 In boiling water, scald tomatoes; drain, peel, press to remove seeds and coarsely chop. Trim carrot and peel. Remove large filaments from celery. Peel garlic.

Chop parsley and basil. Rinse vegetables, dry and chop. Chop remaining half onion. Chop pancetta. In a skillet, heat olive oil; add carrot, celery, garlic, onion, parsley and basil; cook until onion is transparent.

4 Drain beans and set aside. Add pancetta to the skillet cook for 2 minutes. Add tomatoes, 1/2 cup of bean cooking water, beans and pepper. Mix, cover and cook on low heat for approximately 30 minutes. If needed, add more bean cooking water.

5 In the meantime, in abundant boiling salted water, cook "pisarei" al dente. Drain with a slotted spoon; toss with sauce and sprinkle with grated grana cheese. Serve immediately.

Pizzoccheri

Difficulty **medium** • *Time needed* **over an hour** • *Calories per serving* **860**

INGREDIENTS
serves 4

For the pasta
UNBLEACHED FLOUR *2 1/2 cups*
BUCKWHEAT FLOUR *2 1/2 cups*
EGGS *3*
SALT *to taste*

For the sauce
POTATOES *8 oz, peeled and diced*
SAVOY CABBAGE *8 oz, cleaned and sliced*
FONTINA CHEESE *7 oz*
SAGE *4-5 leaves*
ONION *1*
GARLIC *1 clove*
GRATED PARMIGIANO *4 tablespoons*
BUTTER *6 tablespoons*
SALT *to taste*

1 Sift both flours on work surface into a mound. Make a well in the middle; add eggs, a pinch of salt and a tablespoon of water. Knead vigorously for 10 minutes until the dough is smooth and soft. Form dough in a ball. Cover with kitchen towel and set aside in a cool place for 30 minutes.

2 With a rolling pin, roll the dough into a thin sheet; cut in long and wide strips. In abundant boiling salted water, cook potatoes and cabbage for 20 minutes.

3 Add pasta and cook al dente for 6-7 minutes. In a skillet, melt half the butter; peel and chop the onion and cook until transparent. Drain pasta and vegetables, and toss with the onions.

4 In remaining butter, sauté garlic and sage rapidly. Put 1/3 of the pasta mixture in a large serving bowl, drizzle with 1/2 of melted butter and cover with 1/2 the diced fontina. Repeat and finish with a layer of pasta mixture. Sprinkle with parmigiano and serve.

SUGGESTION
Normally, pizzoccheri are home made and cooked immediately; they are not very common in supermarkets, but may be found, dried, in some specialty shops.

Rigatoni with curry

Difficulty **easy** • *Time needed* **less than 30 minutes** • *Calories per serving* **500**

INGREDIENTS
serves 4

RIGATONI *12 oz*
CURRY *1 teaspoon*
TOMATO SAUCE *5 oz*
COOKED HAM *4 oz*
ONION *a small piece*
PARSLEY *to taste*
EXTRA VIRGIN OLIVE OIL *3 tablespoons*
SALT *to taste*

1 Slice onion. Slice the ham in strips. Rinse, dry and chop parsley. In abundant boiling salted water, cook rigatoni al dente.

2 In a saucepan, heat olive oil; cook onion and prosciutto on low heat. Add tomato sauce. When it starts to boil, add curry and salt. Cook for a few minutes.

3 Drain pasta, transfer to saucepan and mix well with sauce. Add parsley and toss. Serve hot.

> **SUGGESTION**
> *If you with to use curry the Indian way, toast it in a non-stick pan to enhance the flavor and cook it with onions before adding ham and tomato sauce. The taste will be much stronger. Curry is an important element of the cuisines of India, Thailand, and Indonesia. In the Mediterranean cuisine, it is used in small quantities because all spices are used sparingly.*

Rigatoni with potatoes

Difficulty **easy** • *Time needed* **under an hour** • *Calories per serving* **540**

INGREDIENTS
serves 4

RIGATONI *11 oz*
POTATOES *(Yukon gold) 14 oz*
COOKED HAM *2 oz, in one slice*
ONION *1*
ROSEMARY *1 branch*
GARLIC *1 clove*
GRATED PARMIGIANO *4 tablespoons*
BUTTER *1 tablespoon*
EXTRA VIRGIN OLIVE OIL *3 tablespoons*
SALT & PEPPER *to taste*

1 Peel potatoes, rinse and dice; cover with cold water and set aside. Peel onion, rinse and slice finely. Peel garlic and crush.

2 Slice hams in strips. Finely chop rosemary leaves. Drain potatoes and dry. In a skillet, heat butter and olive oil; cook garlic and onion until transparent. Add potatoes and cook for a few minutes, stirring well with a wooden spoon.

3 Cover and cook on moderate heat for approximately 15 minutes. Add salt and pepper. In abundant boiling salted water, cook rigatoni al dente.

4 Five minutes before the end of cooking for the potatoes, add rosemary, ham and a few tablespoons of pasta cooking water. Stir well. Drain rigatoni and add to potato preparation. Sprinkle with grated grana cheese and serve.

Rigatoni with cauliflower and raisins

Difficulty **easy** • *Time needed* **less than 30 minutes** • *Calories per serving* **420**

INGREDIENTS
serves 4

RIGATONI *12 oz*
CAULIFLOWER *11 oz, cooked*
ANCHOVY FILLETS *4*
ONION *1/2*
PINE NUTS *1 tablespoon*
RAISINS *1 tablespoon, pre-soaked*
SAFFRON *1/2 teaspoon*
EXTRA VIRGIN OLIVE OIL *3 tablespoons*
SALT & PEPPER *to taste*

1 Chop cauliflower in small pieces. Chop onion and anchovies. In a saucepan, heat olive oil with onion and anchovies. Add pine nuts, raisins and cauliflower. Add salt and pepper. If needed, add lukewarm water.

2 In a bowl, soak saffron with lukewarm water; transfer to saucepan. In the meantime, in abundant boiling salted water, cook pasta al dente. Drain and transfer to saucepan. Toss well and serve immediately.

> **SUGGESTION**
> *The pine nuts can also be substituted with chopped peanuts or cashews.*

Rigatoni with veal tripe

Difficulty **medium** • *Time needed* **over an hour** • *Calories per serving* **630**

INGREDIENTS
serves 4

RIGATONI *12 oz*
VEAL TRIPE *2 lbs*
(cleaned, ready for cooking)
TOMATO PASTE *2 tablespoons*
CELERY *1 stalk*
ONION *1*
PARSLEY *1 oz*
GARLIC *1 clove*
DRY WHITE WINE *3/4 cup*
GRATED PECORINO *4 tablespoons*
EXTRA VIRGIN OLIVE OIL *4 tablespoons*
SALT & PEPPER *to taste*

1 Cut the tripe into 3/4 inch lengths and join the ends of each piece with butcher's twine, forming a series of rings. Peel the onion and slice thinly; peel the garlic; remove the coarse filaments from the celery and rinse; trim and rinse the parsley.

2 Chop the vegetables and fry in a saucepan with the oil; when lightly browned, add the tripe, season with salt and pepper and cook; add the wine and let it evaporate over high heat.

3 Dilute the tomato paste in 1 cup of hot water, season with salt and pepper; cover and cook on very low heat for about 3 hours, adding water from time to time, if needed.

4 Cook the rigatoni in abundant boiling salted water. Remove the tripe from the saucepan, and set aside. Drain the rigatoni and pour into the saucepan, add the pecorino, mix thoroughly. Remove the twine and add the tripe to the pasta. Transfer the mixture to a serving bowl and serve immediately.

Rigatoni with meat sauce

Difficulty **medium** • *Time needed* **over an hour** • *Calories per serving* **540**

INGREDIENTS
serves 4

RIGATONI *12 oz*
GROUND BEEF *5 oz*
GROUND PORK LOIN *2 oz*
GROUND VEAL *2 oz*
SAUSAGE *1 oz*
TOMATOES *8 oz, ripe, firm*
ONION *1*
BASIL *1 bunch*
ROSEMARY *1 branch*
SAGE *2 leaves*
PARSLEY *1 bunch*
BAY LEAF *1*
GARLIC *1/2 clove*
RED WINE *1/4 cup*
GRATED PARMIGIANO *2 tablespoons*
BUTTER *1 tablespoon*
EXTRA VIRGIN OLIVE OIL *2 tablespoons*
SALT & PEPPER *to taste*

1 In boiling water, scald tomatoes; drain, peel, press to remove seeds and coarsely chop.

2 In a saucepan, heat olive oil. Rinse and dry onion, garlic, basil, rosemary, sage and parsley; chop together and cook with oil in saucepan until onion is transparent.

3 Peel sausage and crumble. In a large bowl, mix beef, pork, veal and sausage. Transfer to saucepan and add bay leaf.

Brown meat on high heat and add wine; let evaporate on high heat.

4 Coarsely chop tomatoes and add to sauce. Add salt and fresh ground pepper; cover and cook on moderate heat for approximately 1 hour. In abundant boiling salted water, cook pasta al dente.

5 Transfer sauce to a large bowl, add pasta and toss well, adding butter and grated grana cheese. Transfer to a serving dish and serve hot.

Rombi with meat ragù

Difficulty **medium** • *Time needed* **over an hour** • *Calories per serving* **640**

INGREDIENTS
serves 4

ROMBI *12 oz*
PROSCIUTTO *2 oz, in one piece*
GROUND BEEF *7 oz*
GROUND PORK *4 oz*
SAUSAGE *4 oz*
TOMATOES *11 oz, ripe, firm*
CARROT *1/2*
CELERY *1/2 stalk*
ONION *1/2*
MARJORAM *a few branches*
CLOVE *1*
CINNAMON *to taste*
RED WINE *1/4 cup*
BEEF STOCK *1/4 cup*
GRATED PARMIGIANO *to taste*
EXTRA VIRGIN OLIVE OIL *3 tablespoons*
SALT & PEPPER *to taste*

1 Trim carrot and peel. Remove large filaments from celery. Peel onion. Rinse vegetables, dry and chop. Peel sausage and crumble. Chop the prosciutto. Rinse marjoram, delicately dry and chop finely.

2 In boiling water, scald tomatoes; drain, peel, press to remove seeds and chop. In a saucepan, heat olive oil; add prosciutto and cook on low heat. Add chopped onion, celery and carrot; brown until onion is transparent.

3 Add beef, pork and sausage, cook until brown. Add wine and let evaporate. Add tomatoes, clove, cinnamon and marjoram.

4 Season with salt and pepper; add stock, cover and cook on moderate heat for approximately 1 hour, stirring well with a wooden spoon. Add more broth, if needed. In abundant boiling salted water, cook pasta al dente. Drain and toss with sauce. Serve immediately, with grated parmigiano cheese.

> **SUGGESTION**
> *In the cuisine of Modena, the meat ragù in this recipe is also used as a sauce with fresh tagliatelle or as a filling for tortellini, which are slightly larger than the classic tortellini of Bologna.*

Rotelle with hot pepper and vodka

Difficulty **easy** • *Time needed* **over an hour** • *Calories per serving* **400**

INGREDIENTS
serves 4

ROTELLE *12 oz*
VODKA *3 tablespoons*
RED CHILI PEPPER *1*
TOMATOES *11 oz*
MILK *5 tablespoons*
PARSLEY *1 bunch*
BUTTER *3 tablespoons*
SALT *to taste*

1 Cut chili pepper in half and soak 24 hours with vodka and 1 tablespoon of water. Remove pepper. In boiling water, scald tomatoes for a minute; peel, press to remove seeds and chop coarsely.

2 In a skillet, place tomatoes, milk and butter. Cook for 10 minutes, stirring with a wooden spoon. In the meantime, in abundant boiling salted water, cook pasta al dente.

3 Drain pasta, transfer to skillet, add vodka and mix well for a few minutes. Add parsley and serve hot.

SUGGESTION
The vodka can be substituted with mirin or saké; the milk can be substituted with soy milk or water and butter with extra virgin olive oil.

Pasta vegetable salad

Difficulty **easy** • *Time needed* **under an hour** • *Calories per serving* **440**

INGREDIENTS
serves 4

ROTELLE *11 oz*
TOMATOES *3, ripe, firm*
YELLOW PEPPER *1*
SHELLED PEAS *7 oz*
THYME *a few sprigs*
MARJORAM *a few sprigs*
BAY LEAF *1*
CAPERS *1 oz*
WHITE WINE VINEGAR *3 tablespoons*
EXTRA VIRGIN OLIVE OIL *5 tablespoons*
SALT & PEPPER *to taste*

1 In boiling water, scald tomatoes; drain, peel, press to remove seeds and dice; drain in a colander for 15 minutes. In abundant boiling salted water, cook pasta al dente. Drain, pass under running water and transfer to a salad bowl. Season with 2 tablespoons of olive oil, a pinch of salt and pepper. Toss well and set aside.

2 Cut pepper, emove seeds, rinse, dry and dice. In boiling salted water, cook peas for 4-5 minutes and drain. Rinse thyme, marjoram and bay leaf; dry and

chop together. Add diced peppers, tomatoes, capers and peas to pasta; mix well.

3 In a bowl, beat salt and white wine vinegar with a fork; add remaining olive oil and chopped herbs; transfer to pasta and toss well. Serve immediately.

Rotelle with two-cheese sauce

Difficulty **easy** • *Time needed* **less than 30 minutes** • *Calories per serving* **510**

INGREDIENTS
serves 4

RUOTE *12 oz*
RICOTTA *5 oz*
MILD GORGONZOLA *4 oz*
CELERY HEARTS *2 stalks with leaves*
POWDERED HOT PEPPER *to taste*
BUTTER *3 tablespoons*
SALT *to taste*

1 Rinse celery, dry and chop. In a tureen, mix ricotta and gorgonzola with a wooden spoon until mixture is creamy.

2 Add celery and pepper (or chili pepper powder). In abundant boiling salted water, cook pasta al dente. Drain pasta. Add 2 tablespoons of pasta cooking water to tureen. Transfer pasta to tureen and toss with butter. Serve immediately.

> **SUGGESTION**
> *To shorted the preparation time, you can make the cheese cream by blending the ingredients in a food processor.*

Macaroni with meat sauce

Difficulty **easy** • *Time needed* **over an hour** • *Calories per serving* **530**

INGREDIENTS
serves 4

SHORT MACARONI *12 oz*
GROUND PORK *7 oz*
TOMATO SAUCE *5, ripe*
GRATED PECORINO *4 tablespoons*
BUTTER *3 tablespoons*
SALT & PEPPER *to taste*

1 Rinse tomatoes, scald a few seconds in salted water, drain, peel, press to remove seeds and chop coarsely.

2 In a saucepan, heat butter; brown pork and brown on all sides, stirring with a wooden spoon. Add chopped tomatoes, salt and pepper. Cook for approximately 45 minutes, adding a little hot water or broth if sauce is too dense..

3 In abundant boiling salted water, cook pasta al dente. Drain and transfer to a serving bowl with sauce. Sprinkle with grated pecorino and serve hot.

> **SUGGESTION**
> *To give a different taste to this dish, you can substitute the ground pork with chopped salami.*

Sedani with herbs

Difficulty **easy** • *Time needed* **less than 30 minutes** • *Calories per serving* **550**

INGREDIENTS
serves 4

SEDANI *14 oz*
ONION *1*
PARSLEY *a bunch*
GARLIC *2 cloves*
BAY LEAF *2*
ROSEMARY *1 branch*
GRATED PECORINO *5 tablespoons*
EXTRA VIRGIN OLIVE OIL *5 tablespoons*
SALT & PEPPER *to taste*

1 Peel onion and slice thinly. Peel garlic and crush. Rinse parsley, bay leaves and rosemary; chop. In a saucepan, heat olive oil with onion, garlic and chopped herbs. Add salt and pepper; cook on low heat for approximately 15 minutes.

2 In the meantime, in abundant boiling salted water, cook sedani al dente. Drain, transfer to a bowl, add sauce and pecorino. Toss well and serve hot.

Sedani with turkey and pine nuts

Difficulty **medium** • *Time needed* **under an hour** • *Calories per serving* **570**

INGREDIENTS
serves 4

SEDANI *12 oz*
TURKEY BREAST *7 oz*
PINE NUTS *2 oz*
WHITE FLOUR *1 or 2 tablespoons*
CHOPPED PARSLEY *1 tablespoon*
VEGETABLE BROTH *as needed*
DRY WHITE WINE *1/4 cup*
GRATED PARMIGIANO *4 tablespoons*
BUTTER *4 tablespoons*
SALT & PEPPER *to taste*

1 Coarsely chop turkey breast or dice in small pieces. In a skillet, melt 2 tablespoons of butter; sauté turkey on high heat. Add pine nuts and, stirring with a wooden spoon, add flour, salt and pepper.

2 Add wine and let evaporate. Add 1/2 cup of broth and cook slowly for about 15 minutes, adding more broth if needed. Add remaining butter and chopped parsley.

3 In abundant boiling salted water, cook pasta al dente. Drain well, transfer to a serving bowl. Add sauce and sprinkle with grated parmigiano. Serve at once.

Sedani with cream and arugula

Difficulty **easy** • *Time needed* **less than 30 minutes** • *Calories per serving* **530**

INGREDIENTS
serves 4

SEDANI *12 oz*
HEAVY CREAM *1/2 cup*
ARUGULA *1 bunch*
KETCHUP *2 tablespoons*
GRATED PARMIGIANO *2 tablespoons*
EXTRA VIRGIN OLIVE OIL *3 tablespoons*
SALT *to taste*

1 Discard wilted leaves from arugula, rinse and chop. In a skillet, heat olive oil with arugula and salt. Add heavy cream, stirring well with a wooden spoon. Add ketchup and cook a few minutes. Set aside.

2 In abundant boiling salted water, cook pasta al dente. Drain and toss with sauce. Serve immediately with grated parmigiano.

SUGGESTION
The ketchup can be substituted with 1 tablespoon of soy sauce, diluted with 2 tablespoons of vegetable broth.

Spätzli with speck

Difficulty **medium** • *Time needed* **under an hour** • *Calories per serving* **510**

INGREDIENTS
serves 4

For the pasta
UNBLEACHED FLOUR *3 cups*
EGGS *3*
MILK *3 tablespoons*
EXTRA VIRGIN OLIVE OIL *1 tablespoon*
SALT *to taste*

For the sauce
SPECK *4 oz, in one piece*
ONION *1, small*
CHIVES *1 bunch*
GRATED GRANA CHEESE *2 tablespoons*
EXTRA VIRGIN OLIVE OIL *4 tablespoons*
SALT & PEPPER *to taste*

1 Prepare the pasta. In a bowl, place flour, eggs, milk and salt. Mix and knead until dough is smooth. In a large pot, boil abundant water, add salt. Push the dough through a slotted spoon, letting the spätzli drop into the water.

2 When the spätzli rise to the top, drain them and transfer to a bowl of ice water to cool off. When all are cooked and cooled, drain again with a slotted spoon. Transfer to an oiled cookie sheet to prevent them from sticking to each other.

3 Prepare the sauce. Slice the speck into strips. Rinse onion and chop finely. In a saucepan, heat olive oil and cook onion until transparent; add speck and cook a few minutes; add salt and pepper.
4 Add chives and spätzli, stirring with a wooden spoon. Add 2-3 tablespoons of pasta cooking water, if needed. Transfer to a serving dish and serve immediately with grated grana cheese.

SUGGESTION
Originating in Germany, these "gnochetti" are found all over Europe. There is a special tool to make the spätzli, but you can use a spoon to drop the pasta into the boiling water; or push the dough through a slotted spoon; or push the dough through the large holes of a grater.

Green spätzli with peppers

*Difficulty **medium** • Time needed **over an hour** • Calories per serving **550***

INGREDIENTS
serves 4

For the pasta
UNBLEACHED FLOUR *3 cups*
SPINACH *1 lb*
EGGS *3*
MILK *1/2 cup*
EXTRA VIRGIN OLIVE OIL *1 tablespoon*
SALT & PEPPER *to taste*

For the sauce
YELLOW PEPPERS *1 lb*
TOMATOES *2, ripe & firm*
ONION *1*
HEAVY CREAM *3 tablespoons*
EXTRA VIRGIN OLIVE OIL *4 tablespoons*
SALT & WHITE PEPPER *to taste*

1 Prepare the spätzli. Clean spinach, rinse in abundant cold water, drain and steam (or scald for 2 minutes in boiling salted water). Drain well, transfer to food processor, add an egg and mix well.

2 Pour mixture in a large bowl; add flour, remaining eggs, milk, salt and fresh ground pepper. Knead vigorously until dough is smooth.

3 In a large pot, bring abundant salted water to boil. If you have the special tool to make spätzli, use it to push the pasta into the water. You can also use a grater with large holes or a teaspoon to transfer the dough into the water. When the spätzli return to the top of the water, drain them. Transfer immediately to a bowl of ice water to cool off. Drain again, transfer to a bowl and add olive

oil so the spätzli do not stick together.

4 Prepare the sauce. Remove seeds from pepper, rinse, dry and cut in small pieces. In boiling water, scald tomatoes, drain, peel, press to remove seeds and coarsely chop.

5 Peel onion, rinse, dry and finely chop. In a saucepan, heat olive oil; cook onion until transparent. Add peppers, tomatoes, salt and fresh ground pepper; cover and cook on moderate heat for approximately 30 minutes.

6 Remove from heat; mix sauce in food processor; transfer to a skillet and add heavy cream; stir and warm up the mixture. In abundant boiling salted water, reheat pasta for several seconds; drain, mix with pepper sauce and serve at once.

215

Testaroli from Lunigiana

Difficulty **medium** • *Time needed* **over an hour** • *Calories per serving* **480**

INGREDIENTS
serves 4

For the pasta
UNBLEACHED FLOUR *1 1/2 cups*
WHOLE WHEAT FLOUR *1 1/2 cups*
WATER *2 cups*
SALT *to taste*

For the sauce
DRIED BORLOTTI BEANS *5 oz*
SAVOY CABBAGE *14 oz*
CELERY *1 stalk*
ONION *1*
SHALLOT *1*
PARSLEY *1 bunch*
GARLIC *1 clove*
BAY LEAF *1*
WHITE WINE VINEGAR *1 tablespoon*
DRY WHITE WINE *3 tablespoons*
EXTRA VIRGIN OLIVE OIL *4 tablespoons*
SALT & PEPPER *to taste*

1 Soak beans in cold water for 12 hours. Drain and rinse. Peel onion and garlic. Remove large filaments from celery stalk. In a pot, place garlic, onion, celery, beans and bay leaf. Cover with water, boil and cook for approximately 1 hour.

2 Prepare the testaroli. Sift both flours in a bowl, add salt and water, little by little. Mix well until batter is smooth and liquid (of a crepe batter consistency).

3 Heat the base and cover of the "testo" (or cast iron pan) until burning hot. Remove from heat source. Pour a small quantity of the batter on the pan and distribute it equally all over (use enough batter to make a thick crepe). Cover and cook for 7-8 minutes, without returning the pan to heat source. Remove cooked sheet of pasta from the pan and set aside.

4 Return the pan to the heat and remove it when burning hot. Repeat the same operation with the batter until all batter is used. On a work surface, slice all cooked pasta sheets in diamond shapes. Clean cabbage, remove all outer leaves and heart; slice in strips and blanch in boiling water. Drain and set aside.

5 Peel shallot and chop. In a saucepan, heat olive oil and cook shallot until transparent. Add cabbage and cook for a few minutes, stirring. Add white wine vinegar and white wine; let evaporate on high heat.

6 Add 1/2 cup of water, salt and fresh ground pepper. Cook for approximately 20 minutes. Add drained beans and cook for a few minutes. Add chopped parsley.

7 In abundant boiling salted water, cook the "testaroli." In a large pot, bring abundant salted water to a boil. Add the testaroli and immediately turn off the heat. Leave pasta in water for 4 minutes, then drain, transfer to a heated serving dish and toss well with bean sauce. Serve immediately.

SUGGESTION
The name of this recipe comes from the traditional pan used in Lunigiana to cook this dish, called "testo". It is basically a plate of terracotta (on which one places the batter) with a rounded cover. When closed, it has the effect of a small oven. To do this recipe well, it is important that both the base and the cover remain hot at all times. You can also use a heated cast iron pan, very effectively.

Trofie with pesto

Difficulty **medium** • *Time needed* **less than 30 minutes** • *Calories per serving* **540**

INGREDIENTS
serves 4

For the pasta
UNBLEACHED FLOUR *4 cups*
SALT *to taste*

For the sauce
PESTO *7 oz, prepared*

1 Prepare the pasta. Sift the flour on pastry board into a mound. Make a well in the middle; add salt and, if needed, water. Mix well and knead vigorously for a few minutes until dough becomes smooth.

2 Make nut-size balls with the dough and roll them into a tiny sausage shape 1 to 1 1/2 inches long.

3 In abundant boiling salted water, cook the pasta al dente, drain, transfer to a serving dish and toss with pesto sauce. Serve immediately.

SUGGESTION

"Trofie" is a traditional pasta from the region of Liguria. The name is given in Liguria to gnocchi, prepared either with dough made with flour and water, as it has been made for ages, or with the use of potatoes as was popular in the 18th century.

Zite with clams and zucchini

Difficulty **medium** • *Time needed* **less than 30 minutes** • *Calories per serving* **460**

INGREDIENTS
serves 4

ZITE *12 oz, already broken*
CLAMS *2 lbs*
TOMATOES *3, ripe, firm*
ZUCCHINI *11 oz*
SHALLOTS *2*
PARSLEY *1 bunch*
EXTRA VIRGIN OLIVE OIL *4 tablespoons*
SALT & PEPPER *to taste*

1 Brush clams and place in a bowl with cold water for a few hours. Rinse parsley, dry and chop. Drain clams. In a saucepan, heat 1 tablespoon of olive oil; add clams and parsley.

2 Cover and cook on high heat, shaking the saucepan from time to time. Remove clams from shells, discarding closed shells; keep aside some whole shells (with clams) for decoration.

3 In boiling water, scald tomatoes, drain, peel, press to remove seeds and dice.

Trim zucchini, rinse, dry and cut in julienne. Peel shallots, rinse, dry and finely chop. In a skillet, heat remaining olive oil and half the parsley; cook shallots until transparent. Add zucchini and cook for 3-4 minutes. Add salt and pepper.

4 Add clams, tomatoes and remaining parsley; cook for 2-3 minutes. In abundant boiling salted water, cook pasta al dente. Drain, transfer to a serving plate and add sauce, tossing well. Garnish with whole clams. Serve immediately.

Zite with tomatoes and escarole

Difficulty **medium** • *Time needed* **under an hour** • *Calories per serving* **420**

INGREDIENTS
serves 4

ZITE *12 oz, already broken*
ESCAROLE *2 lbs*
TOMATOES *1 lb, ripe, firm*
GARLIC *4 cloves*
EXTRA VIRGIN OLIVE OIL *3 tablespoons*
SALT & PEPPER *to taste*

1 Clean the lettuce. Remove leaves and slice hearts. Put in a saucepan and cover with cold water. Bring to a boil and cook for 6 minutes. Drain and set aside.

2 In another pot, bring abundant salted water to boil, cook lettuce heart and leaves again for 5 more minutes. This double operation will remove the bitterness.

3 In the meantime, peel garlic and chop. Rinse tomatoes, peel, press to remove seeds and chop. In a skillet, heat olive oil with garlic. Add tomatoes, salt and fresh ground pepper; cover and cook on medium heat for approximately 15 minutes.

4 When the lettuce is almost cooked, add the pasta and cook al dente. Drain and transfer to a serving plate. Add sauce, toss well and serve hot with grated pecorino..

SUGGESTION
*Zite or ziti are long tubular pasta popular
in Campania and in all southern Italy.
Before cooking, it has to be broken up.
If no fresh tomatoes are available,
use tomato sauce.*

Zite alla napoletana

Difficulty **medium** • *Time needed* **under an hour** • *Calories per serving* **460**

INGREDIENTS
serves 4

ZITE *11 oz, broken*
PORK LOIN *5 oz*
TOMATOES *11 oz, ripe, firm*
ONION *1*
BASIL *1 bunch*
GRATED PARMIGIANO *2 tablespoons*
BUTTER *1 tablespoon*
EXTRA VIRGIN OLIVE OIL *2 tablespoons*
SALT & PEPPER *to taste*

1 Peel onion, rinse and finely chop. Rinse pork loin, dry and chop. Rinse basil, delicately dry and tear in small pieces. In boiling water, scald tomatoes, drain, peel, press to remove seeds and drain for 15 minutes; pass in a food mill, over a bowl.

2 In a saucepan, heat olive oil and butter. Cook onion and 1/2 the basil until onion is transparent. Add meat and brown on all sides, stirring well with a wooden spoon. Add tomato purée, salt and fresh ground pepper. Cover and cook on moderate heat for approximately 30 minutes, adding water if needed.

3 In abundant boiling salted water, cook zite al dente. Drain and transfer to a serving plate. Add sauce and remaining basil; toss well. Serve immediately.

Zite with broccoli and prosciutto

Difficulty **medium** • *Time needed* **under an hour** • *Calories per serving* **550**

INGREDIENTS
serves 4

ZITE *12 oz*
BROCCOLI *14 oz*
ONION *1*
PROSCIUTTO *2 oz, in one piece*
CAPERS IN BRINE *1 tablespoon*
PITTED BLACK OLIVES *2 oz*
GARLIC *1 clove*
GRATED PARMIGIANO *2 tablespoons*
EXTRA VIRGIN OLIVE OIL *5 tablespoons*
SALT & PEPPER *to taste*

1 Break zite into 2 inch long pieces and set aside. Separate florets of broccoli, discard stem and rinse florets in cold water. Peel garlic and crush. Peel onion and chop finely. Cut prosciutto in strips. Carefully rinse capers. Coarsely chop olives.

2 In boiling salted water, blanch broccoli for 3 minutes. Drain and cool under cold running water. In a saucepan, heat 3 tablespoons of olive oil with garlic.

Add onion and prosciutto; sauté for a few minutes. Remove garlic. Drain broccoli well and add to the saucepan. Add capers, olives, salt and fresh ground pepper. Cook for a minute, stirring well.

3 In the meantime, in abundant boiling salted water, cook pasta al dente. Drain. Toss with remaining olive oil. Transfer to saucepan and mix well. Sprinkle with grated grana cheese and serve hot.

Zite with black olives and anchovies

Difficulty **easy** • *Time needed* **less than 30 minutes** • *Calories per serving* **460**

INGREDIENTS
serves 4

ZITE *12 oz*
GREEN PEPPER *1*
CHERRY TOMATOES *1 lb*
ANCHOVIES IN OLIVE OIL *2 fillets*
BLACK OLIVES *4 oz*
CAPERS *1 tablespoon*
PARSLEY *1 bunch*
GARLIC *1 clove*
EXTRA VIRGIN OLIVE OIL *3 tablespoons*
SALT & PEPPER *to taste*

1 Cut zite in small pieces. Trim green pepper and remove seeds; rinse and cut in strips. In boiling water, scald tomatoes, peel, cut in half, remove seeds, coarsely chop and drain in a colander for approximately 10 minutes.

2 In a saucepan, heat olive oil with garlic; add anchovies, melt slightly and add pepper strips. Cook for a few minutes. Add olives, coarsely chopped capers, and tomatoes; season with salt and pepper.

Cook 15 minutes and add chopped parsley.

3 In abundant boiling salted water, cook zite al dente. Drain and transfer to saucepan. Toss well and serve immediately.

Zite with mussels

Difficulty **medium** • *Time needed* **under an hour** • *Calories per serving* **510**

INGREDIENTS
serves 4

ZITE *12 oz*
MUSSELS *2 lbs*
CHERRY TOMATOES *8 oz*
PARSLEY *a bunch*
GARLIC *1 clove*
DRY WHITE WINE *3 tablespoons*
GRATED AGED PROVOLONE
2 tablespoons
EXTRA VIRGIN OLIVE OIL *4 tablespoons*
SALT & PEPPER *to taste*

1 Break zite in small pieces and set aside. Scrape mussels and rinse under running water. Rinse parsley, dry and chop. Scald tomatoes in boiling water, drain, peel, cut in half, remove seeds and coarsely chop; then drain in a colander for approximately 10 minutes.

2 In a large saucepan, heat 1 tablespoon of olive oil. Add mussels and wine. Sprinkle with parsley, cover and cook on high heat until mussel open. Remove from heat. Separate meat from shells and discard the closed mussels. Reserve 3 ta-

blespoons of the cooking water.

3 Peel garlic and crush. In a skillet, heat remaining olive oil with garlic. Add tomatoes, salt and pepper. Cook on high heat for approximately 5 minutes. Add mussels and 3 tablespoons of mussel cooking water. Cook for 2 minutes.

4 In the meantime, in abundant boiling salted water, cook zite al dente. Drain and transfer to skillet. Sprinkle with grated provolone. Toss well. Serve immediately.

Zite with pork hocks

Difficulty **medium** • *Time needed* **over an hour** • *Calories per serving* **790**

INGREDIENTS
serves 4

ZITE *12 oz, broken*
PORK HOCKS *1*
TOMATOES *1 lb, ripe, firm*
PANCETTA *3 oz, in one slice*
CELERY *1 stalk*
ONION *1*
DRY WHITE WINE *1/4 cup*
CACIORICOTTA CHEESE *4 tablespoons*
EXTRA VIRGIN OLIVE OIL *3 tablespoons*
SALT & PEPPER *to taste*

1 Peel onion, rinse, dry and chop. Remove large filaments from celery, rinse, dry and chop. Chop pancetta. In boiling water, scald tomatoes; drain, peel, press to remove seeds and coarsely chop.

2 In a saucepan, heat olive oil; add pork hock and brown on high heat on all sides. Add wine and let evaporate on high heat. Remove hocks from saucepan and set aside. Remove fat from saucepan; add onion and celery. Cook a few minutes.

3 Add chopped pancetta and brown, stirring with a wooden spoon; add tomatoes, hocks, salt and fresh ground pepper. Cook on moderate heat for approximately 2 hours. Remove hocks; cut in strips with a sharp knife.

4 In abundant boiling salted water, cook pasta al dente. Drain and toss with sauce and meat strips. Sprinkle with grated cacioricotta cheese. Serve immediately.

SUGGESTION
The cacioricotta is a traditional cheese, found in southern Italy, made of aged salted ricotta, and used to flavor pasta dishes. The flavor being particularly strong, a small quantity is sufficient. To grate the cacioricotta, you should press the cheese against the grater and slowly push it down to obtain long strings of cheese. These will melt very well on the warm pasta.

Filled pasta

Three-flavor agnolotti

Difficulty **medium** • *Time needed* **over an hour** • *Calories per serving* **830**

INGREDIENTS
serves 6

For the pasta
UNBLEACHED FLOUR *4 cups*
EGGS *4*
EXTRA VIRGIN OLIVE OIL *1 tablespoon*
SALT *a pinch*

For the first filling
SPINACH *11 oz*
RICOTTA *7 oz*
EGGS *1*
GRATED PARMIGIANO *3 tablespoons*
SALT & PEPPER *to taste*

For the second filling
VEAL ROAST *5 oz*
BOILED SPINACH *4 oz*
BOILED POTATOES *1, mashed*
PARSLEY *a bunch*
EGGS *1*
BREAD *1 oz*
MILK *to taste*
NUTMEG *a pinch*
GRATED PARMIGIANO *1 tablespoon*
SALT & PEPPER *to taste*

For the third filling
MUSHROOMS *11 oz*
COOKED HAM *4 oz*
HEAVY CREAM *1/4 cup*
SAGE *a few leaves*
EXTRA VIRGIN OLIVE OIL *2 tablespoons*

For the sauce
SAGE *8-10 leaves*
GRATED PARMIGIANO *6 tablespoons*
BUTTER *6 tablespoons*

1 Prepare the pasta dough. Sift the flour onto the work surface and form a mound; make a well in the mound and lightly beat the eggs in it; add the oil, a dash of salt and work the ingredients until the dough becomes smooth and elastic; cover the dough with plastic wrap and let it rest in a cool place for at least half an hour.

2 Prepare the fillings. Boil the spinach, drain and chop, and put it in a bowl to cool; when cool, blend in the ricotta, the egg, the parmigiano, the salt and the pepper; mix well. The first filling is done.

3 Finely chop the roast, the spinach and the parsley, mixing well. In a separate bowl, mix the egg, the mashed potato, the milk soaked bread, the parmigiano, the salt, the pepper and the nutmeg. Mix all the ingredients together with a wooden spoon to finish the second filling.

4 For the third filling: clean the mushrooms and cut off the stem ends; finely chop the mushrooms and the cooked ham. Heat the oil in a skillet and sauté the mushrooms with the sage and the ham for 10 minutes; at this point, add the cream and let it thicken for a few minutes.

5 Roll out the pasta dough into thin sheets about 4 in. wide. Place small heaps of the first filling equally spaced on a sheet of pasta; cover with another sheet of pasta, press the pasta well around the fillings and cut into squares to make the agnolotti. Repeat with the other two fillings until used up. Boil the agnolotti for about 10 minutes in abundant salted water. Melt the butter with the sage. Drain the agnolotti; sprinkle with grated parmigiano and drizzle with the melted butter.

Agnolotti with truffles

Difficulty **medium** • *Time needed* **over an hour** • *Calories per serving* **610**

INGREDIENTS
serves 4

For the pasta
UNBLEACHED FLOUR *3 cups*
EGGS *4*
SALT *to taste*

For the filling
BLACK TRUFFLES *2 oz (fresh or preserved)*
LETTUCE *14 oz*
SHALLOTS *1*
PARSLEY *a bunch*
EGGS *1*
GRATED GRANA CHEESE *3 tablespoons*
BUTTER *1 tablespoon*
SALT & PEPPER *to taste*

For the sauce
BLACK TRUFFLES *1 oz*
SAGE *2-3 leaves*
BUTTER *6 tablespoons*
SALT & PEPPER *to taste*

1 Make the pasta dough. Sift the flour into a mound on the work surface; make a well in the flour and lightly beat the eggs in it; add a dash of salt and work the ingredients until the dough becomes smooth and elastic; cover the dough with in plastic wrap and let it rest in a cool place for at least 30 minutes.

2 Prepare the filling. Brush the truffles, was, dry and chop finely; rinse the lettuce, drain, dry gently with a towel and cut into fine strips. Clean, rinse and chop the shallot and the parsley.

3 Melt the butter in a skillet; add the scallion and heat until transparent; mix in the truffles; add the lettuce and brown for about 2 minutes, stirring with a wooden spoon. Flavor with salt and pepper and continue cooking on high heat for another 2-3 minutes stirring continually until the liquid is evaporated. Remove from the heat, pour into a bowl and let cool completely. Add the chopped parsley, the egg, the grated parmigiano, a dash of salt and pepper and mix until well blended.

4 Roll the pasta dough into thin sheets, a little at a time; beat the remaining egg with a fork and brush on one half of the pasta sheet; with a teaspoon, distribute the filling equally spaced on half of the pasta sheet and fold over the other half; press the dough around the heaps of filling to seal the dough, and cut into agnolotti squares with an indented cutting wheel. Cook the agnolotti in abundant salted water until al dente.

5 On the side, prepare the sauce. Brush the truffle, rinse it, dry it and shave into thin slices. In a pan, melt the butter with the sage, add the truffle, 2 tablespoons of the agnolotti cooking water, and a dash of salt and pepper; mix and cook for one minute. Drain the agnolotti, toss with the truffle sauce and serve immediately.

Agnolotti with oranges

Difficulty **medium** • *Time needed* **over an hour** • *Calories per serving* **840**

INGREDIENTS
serves 4

For the pasta
UNBLEACHED FLOUR *3 1/2 cups*
EGGS *2*
SALT *to taste*

For the filling
ORANGES *1, grated peel*
SPINACH *12 oz*
ONIONS *1, small*
GRATED FRESH PECORINO SARDO *12 oz*
EGGS *1*
NUTMEG *a pinch*
LIGHT BROWN SUGAR
1 level tablespoon
EXTRA VIRGIN OLIVE OIL *1 tablespoon*

For the sauce
TOMATO SAUCE *1 cup*
GRATED AGED PECORINO
4 tablespoons

1 Form a mound with the flour on the working surface; make a well in the middle, lightly beat the eggs in it and add a dash of salt; work the ingredients using just enough lukewarm water to get a smooth and elastic dough. Let it rest while preparing the filling.

2 Prepare the spinach, rinse and boil in little water for 15 minutes; drain well and fry it in a skillet with the oil and the chopped onion.

3 In a bowl, mix the fresh pecorino with the spinach, the egg, the grated orange peel, a dash of nutmeg and the light brown sugar. Roll the pasta dough in-to thin sheets; distribute the filling equally spaced on one pasta sheet and cover with another sheet.

4 With the end of your finger, press the dough around the heaps of filling to seal the dough; cut into agnolotti squares with an indented cutting wheel. Cook the agnolotti in abundant salted water until al dente, about 10 minutes.

5 Drain the agnolotti and transfer into an oven dish, cover with the tomato sauce and sprinkle with the aged pecorino; mix well and bake at 350°F for a few minutes. Serve immediately.

Agnolotti, Piedmont style

Difficulty **medium** • *Time needed* **over an hour** • *Calories per serving* **720**

INGREDIENTS
serves 4

FRESH EGG PASTA *12 oz*
EGGS *1*
SALT *to taste*

For the filling
GROUND RABBIT *4 oz*
GROUND PORK *5 oz*
GROUND VEAL *4 oz (or beef)*
SPINACH *7 oz, cooked*
CARROTS *1*
ONIONS *1/2*
ROSEMARY *a branch*
EGGS *2*
GRATED GRANA CHEESE *4 tablespoons*
BUTTER *1 tablespoon*
EXTRA VIRGIN OLIVE OIL *2 tablespoons*
SALT & PEPPER *to taste*

For the sauce
GROUND BEEF *7 oz*
TOMATOES *3, ripe and firm*
ONIONS *1/2*
PARSLEY *a bunch*
GARLIC *1/2 clove*
NUTMEG *to taste*
RED WINE *1/4 cup*
BEEF STOCK *1/4 cup*
EXTRA VIRGIN OLIVE OIL *2 tablespoons*
SALT & PEPPER *to taste*

1 Prepare the sauce. Scald the tomatoes in boiling water, peel, remove the seeds and the juice; mince the pulp. Peel the onion and the garlic, rinse, dry and chop finely; rinse, dry and finely chop the parsley. Heat the oil in a skillet; cook the onion and garlic lightly without browning the garlic; add the ground beef and cook until uniformly brown; add the wine and evaporate it over high heat.

2 Mix the tomatoes and the chopped parsley, flavor with the nutmeg, a dash of salt and fresh ground pepper.; cover and continue cooking for about an hour, from time to time adding a little hot beef stock.

3 In the meantime, prepare the filling. Peel, rinse and dice the carrot; peel the onion, rinse and dry, and chop finely. Heat the oil in a skillet and cook the onion and the carrot with the rosemary without browning; add the ground rabbit, the ground pork and the ground veal, cooking them on high heat until uniformly brown; season with salt and

pepper to taste, cover and cook on mod-

erate heat for another 30 minutes. In a skillet, melt the butter and wilt the spinach for 2 minutes, sprinkle with a dash of salt and pepper and chop finely.

4 Allow the meat to cool in a mixing bowl; add the chopped spinach, eggs, the grated parmigiano, a dash of salt and pepper and blend all the ingredients with a wooden spoon until the mixture is uniform.

5 Prepare the agnolotti. Roll out the fresh pasta dough, a little at a time, into thin sheets; brush one half with the remaining egg, beaten with a fork; with a teaspoon, distribute the filling equally spaced on half of the pasta sheet and fold over the other half; with your fingers, press the dough around the heaps of filling to seal the dough and cut into agnolotti squares with an indented cutting wheel. Cook the agnolotti in abundant salted water until al dente; drain. Pour the sauce over the agnolotti, toss lightly and serve while hot.

Agnolotti with herbs

Difficulty **medium** • *Time needed* **over an hour** • *Calories per serving* **670**

INGREDIENTS
serves 4

For the pasta
UNBLEACHED FLOUR *3 1/2 cups*
HOT WATER *to taste*

For the filling
LEMON BALM, MINT, PARSLEY
1 bunch or each type of herb
POTATOES *1 1/4 lbs*
CABBAGE *1*
ONIONS *1*
RAISINS *1 tablespoon*
ORGANIC LEMONS *1*
DRIED FIGS *a few, chopped*
CINNAMON *a pinch*
CLOVES *1*
BREAD CRUMBS *1 tablespoon*
GRATED GRANA CHEESE *1 tablespoon*
BUTTER *1 tablespoon*

For the sauce
GRATED SMOKED RICOTTA
2 tablespoons
CINNAMON *a pinch*
BUTTER *3 tablespoons*
SALT & PEPPER *to taste*

1 Rinse the potatoes and cook them in abundant salted water for about 40 minutes. Clean the cabbage. In another saucepan, bring abundant water to boil, salt and add the cabbage; cook for 30 minutes. Rinse and dry the herbs and chop finely. Peel and chop the onions. In a pan, melt the butter and cook the onions until transparent.

2 Peel the potatoes and, in a large bowl, mix with cabbage and herbs. Mash with a fork; add the grana, bread crumbs, raisins, grated lemon peel, dried figs, cinnamon, cloves and cooked onion. Mix with hands until all ingredients are well blended.

3 Prepare the pasta. Sift the flour on a working surface and mix it with hot water until dough is smooth and elastic. With a rolling pin, roll out the dough and cut circles with a cookie cutter. In the center of each disk, place a little ball of filling and fold back the dough. Press the sides with fingers to close the agnolotti carefully.

4 In abundant salted boiling water, cook the agnolotti. Drain and transfer to a serving dish. In a small saucepan, melt the remaining butter; pour it over the agnolotti. Sprinkle with cinnamon, pepper and grated smoked ricotta. Toss and serve immediately.

Agnolotti with swiss chard cream

Difficulty **medium** • *Time needed* **over an hour** • *Calories per serving* **700**

INGREDIENTS
serves 4

AGNOLOTTI *1 lb*
SWISS CHARD *2 lbs*
FONTINA CHEESE *7 oz*
LEMONS *1, the juice*
SHALLOTS *1*
MILK *1 cup*
GRATED PARMIGIANO *to taste*
BUTTER *1 tablespoon*
EXTRA VIRGIN OLIVE OIL *3 tablespoons*
SALT & PEPPER *to taste*

1 Prepare the swiss chard and use the most tender parts. Cut into small pieces and rinse in water mixed with the lemon juice to avoid blackening, then cook in salted water for 30 minutes; drain well and pass through a food mill, catching the purée in a bowl.

2 Heat the extra virgin olive oil and brown the cleaned and chopped shallot with the butter and a dash of salt and fresh ground pepper. After a few minutes, add the chard purée, mix well and simmer for 10 minutes. Then add the preheated milk and the diced fontina. Continue to stir with a wooden spoon until the mixture becomes creamy.

3 In a large pot, boil abundant water, add salt and drop in the agnolotti. Cook until al dente. When cooked, drain well and transfer the agnolotti into the pan with the creamed chard, add the grated parmigiano and mix well; toss the agnolotti until well covered with the sauce, then transfer into a heated serving dish and serve immediately.

Agnolotti toscani

Difficulty **medium** • *Time needed* **over an hour** • *Calories per serving* **620**

INGREDIENTS
serves 4

For the pasta
UNBLEACHED FLOUR *3 cups*
EGGS *3*
SALT *to taste*

For the filling
GROUND VEAL *5 oz*
VEAL BRAINS *4 oz*
MORTADELLA *3 oz*
NUTMEG *a pinch*
BEEF STOCK *1/2 cup*
EGGS *1*
BREAD CRUMBS *1 oz*
GRATED GRANA CHEESE *5 tablespoons*
EXTRA VIRGIN OLIVE OIL *2 tablespoons*
SALT *to taste*

1 Prepare the filling. In a skillet, heat the olive oil and cook the ground veal for 25 minutes adding the beef stock. Dice the mortadella; scald the brains in lightly salted water, remove the membrane and cut into small pieces. Put the ground veal, the mortadella, the brains, the bread crumbs, the parmigiano, the egg, a dash of nutmeg, a little salt and mix well until all the ingredients are uniformly mixed.

2 Prepare the pasta dough. On the work table, form a mound with the flour and make a well in the center; break the eggs into the well, salt to taste and mix with a fork; work the dough until it becomes smooth and elastic. Roll the dough into thin sheets.

3 On one half of a sheet of dough, spread out the filling in small balls, spacing them about one inch from the edges and from each other. Cover with the other half of the sheet and press together around the filling to seal the dough; cut the squares around the filling in the center with the appropriate cutting wheel.

4 Let the agnolotti dry for about ten minutes, then cook them in a large pot with abundant salted water for 10-12 minutes. Serve in a broth or drained and tossed with butter and sage, with meat or other sauce you choose.

Anolini with parmigiano

Difficulty **medium** • *Time needed* **over an hour** • *Calories per serving* **890**

INGREDIENTS
serves 4

For the pasta
UNBLEACHED FLOUR *4 cups*
EGGS *4*
SALT *to taste*

For the filling
BEEF *1 1/4 lbs*
TOMATO CONCENTRATE *1 tablespoon*
PANCETTA *2 oz, in 1 piece*
CELERY *1 stalk*
CARROTS *1*
ONIONS *1*
GARLIC *1 clove*
CINNAMON *1 stick*
CLOVES *3*
NUTMEG *a pinch*
EGGS *2*
BREAD CRUMBS *4 oz*
GRATED PARMIGIANO *4 tablespoons*
RED WINE *1/2 cup*
BEEF STOCK *2 cups*
BUTTER *3 tablespoons*
EXTRA VIRGIN OLIVE OIL *4 tablespoons*
SALT & PEPPER *to taste*

For the sauce
GRATED PARMIGIANO *6 tablespoons*
BUTTER *4 tablespoons*

1 Prepare the filling: bring the beef stock to a boil and add the tomato concentrate; cut incisions into the beef and stuff with pieces of garlic; cut the pancetta in julienne; peel and chop the onion; prepare the celery stalk and the carrot; rinse and cut into pieces. Heat the oil in a casserole; add the meat, the butter and the chopped onion; brown all sides of the meat.

2 When the beef is well browned, add the stock, the wine, the cinnamon, the carrot, the celery stalk and the cloves; season with salt and pepper; cover and cook on very low heat for at least 3 hours. Toast the bread crumbs in a non-stick pan; remove from the heat and set apart.

3 Once cooked, take out the meat, which can be served as a separate dish; pass the pan juices through a sieve into a bowl; add the toasted bread crumbs, the grated parmigiano and the nutmeg; mix and salt to taste; beat the eggs and blend into the mixture.

4 Prepare the pasta dough: form a mound with the flour on the work surface; in the center of the mound make a well and mix in salt and the eggs; knead the dough vigorously for at least 15 minutes, adding lukewarm water, as necessary, to obtain a smooth dough; when the dough is firm, make a ball and flatten it lightly by hand; using a rolling pin on a lightly floured work surface, stretch the dough into thin sheets.

5 Make small walnut-sized balls of the prepared filling and spread them about 2 inches from the edges and apart from each other on one half of a sheet of pasta; cover with the other half sheet; cut little disks with a circular stamp, pressing the edges together to avoid separation during cooking.

6 In a large pot, bring abundant salted water to a boil and drop in the anolini; when cooked, drain and put in a heated bowl, pour the melted butter over and sprinkle with the grated parmigiano. Serve immediately.

Cappellacci with pumpkin in ragù

Difficulty **medium** • *Time needed* **over an hour** • *Calories per serving* **840**

INGREDIENTS
serves 4

FRESH EGG PASTA DOUGH *12 oz*

For the filling
PUMPKIN *1 lb*
EGGS *2*
NUTMEG *to taste*
GRATED GRANA CHEESE *5 oz*
SALT & PEPPER *to taste*

For the sauce
GROUND BEEF *7 oz*
GROUND PORK *5 oz*
PROSCIUTTO *2 oz, in 1 piece*
TOMATOES *1 lb, ripe and firm*
DRIED MUSHROOMS *1 oz*
CARROTS *1/2*
CELERY *1/2 stalk*
ONIONS *1*
PARSLEY *a bunch*
GARLIC *1 clove*
MARJORAM *2 sprigs*
RED WINE *1/4 cup*
BEEF STOCK *1/4 cup*
EXTRA VIRGIN OLIVE OIL *3 tablespoons*
SALT & PEPPER *to taste*

1 Prepare the filling. Slice the pumpkin into one inch thick slices, place in a baking dish and bake for 30 minutes in a preheated oven at 400°F. Pass the baked pumpkin through a potato masher into a bowl, add the grated parmigiano, one egg, a dash of salt, some pepper and some nutmeg; mix well with a wooden spoon.

2 Roll out the dough into thin sheets; beat the remaining egg with a fork and brush on half of the sheet; with a teaspoon, place dabs of the filling equally spaced on the prepared pasta sheet. Fold over the other half of the sheet, pressing around the little mounds with your fingers to seal the dough; cut into squares with an indented cutting wheel.

3 Prepare the ragù. Soak the dried mushrooms in a little lukewarm water. Peel and trim the carrot; strip off the large outer fibers from the celery; peel the onion and the garlic. Rinse the vegetables, dry them and chop finely; prepare the parsley and the marjoram: rinse, dry and chop; dice the cooked ham. Scald the tomatoes in boiling water; remove the skins, the seeds and the juice; finely chop the pulp.

4 Heat the oil in a casserole and quickly brown the diced ham. Add the chopped vegetables: the onion, the celery, the garlic and the carrot; cook without browning. Mix in the soaked and chopped mushrooms, the ground beef and the ground pork; cook while stirring until brown on all sides. Pour in the wine and let evaporate over high heat. Mix in the chopped tomatoes, a dash of salt, some fresh ground pepper., a bit of chopped parsley and marjoram as well as the beef stock.

5 Cook the ragù on moderate heat for about an hour, adding beef stock if needed; finally, add the remaining chopped parsley and marjoram. Cook the cappellacci in abundant salted water, drain when al dente, toss with the ragù and serve while hot, accompanied by grated parmigiano to taste.

Cappelletti with mixed meat sauce

Difficulty **difficult** • *Time needed* **over an hour** • *Calories per serving* 800

INGREDIENTS
serves 4

For the pasta
UNBLEACHED FLOUR *3 cups*
EGGS *3*
SALT *to taste*

For the filling
VEAL *5 oz*
PORK *5 oz*
CHICKEN BREAST *1*
NUTMEG *a pinch*
EGGS *1*
GRATED GRANA CHEESE *5 oz*
BUTTER *3 tablespoons*
SALT *to taste*

For the sauce
TOMATO SAUCE *as needed*

1 Chop all the meat finely and cook on low heat in a covered sauce pan for 10 minutes; season with salt and cook another 10 minutes. Cool the meat and grind it very finely. Place into a bowl, add the parmigiano, the nutmeg and the egg; mix until well blended.

2 Make the pasta dough. Sift the flour into a mound on the work surface; make a well in the flour and lightly beat the eggs in it; add a dash of salt and mix it all little by little.

3 Work the dough with your hands for 15 minutes. Form a dough ball, flatten it, and roll it into a thin sheet. Cut into 2 inch squares. Put a walnut-sized dab of filling on each square and fold into a triangle. Press the dough around the filling to seal. Take each triangle between the index finger and the thumb; wrap the outer points of the triangle around the index finger and squeeze together rolling the ravioli off the finger.

4 Let the ravioli rest for an hour before cooking them for 12-15 minutes in a pot full of boiling, salted water. Drain and toss with the tomato sauce. Serve while hot, sprinkling with grated parmigiano to taste.

Cappelletti stuffed with meat

*Difficulty **difficult*** • *Time needed **over an hour*** • *Calories per serving **580***

INGREDIENTS
serves 4

For the pasta
UNBLEACHED FLOUR *3 cups*
EGGS *3*
SALT *to taste*

For the filling
TURKEY BREAST *7 oz*
LEAN PORK *1*
SAGE *a few leaves*
ROSEMARY *a branch*
NUTMEG *a pinch*
ORGANIC LEMON *1*
EGGS *2*
RICOTTA *1 oz*
GRATED PARMIGIANO *1 tablespoon*
BUTTER *3 tablespoons*
SALT & PEPPER *to taste*

1 Cut the chicken breast and the pork into small pieces. Rinse and dry the sage and the rosemary; put in a casserole with the butter and the chopped meat. Season with salt and pepper and cook for about 20 minutes until well browned, adding a little beef stock if needed.

2 Chop or grind the meat very finely, put into a bowl, and mix with the ricotta, the grated parmigiano, the eggs and a dash of nutmeg. Rinse and dry the lemon and grate a little of the peel into the bowl. Season with salt and pepper, mixing all the ingredients until they are well blended.

3 On the work space, make a mound with the flour. Form a well into which you break the eggs. Add a little salt and work the mixture from the middle of the mound for about 15 minutes.

4 When the dough is firm, form a ball and flatten it with your hands. Roll the dough into a thin sheet. Cut it into 2 inch squares, using a rotary cutter. In the center of each square, put a dollop of filling and fold it over into a triangle.

5 Press the dough around the filling with your fingers; wrap the outer points of the triangle around the index finger; press between the thumb and roll off the finger turning it over. Set apart for half an hour before boiling in salted water for 10-15 minutes.

SUGGESTION
*These ravioli can be served with
a ragù or tomato sauce.
They are also excellent in a broth,
in which case the serving should be reduced.*

Caramelle with lettuce and truffles

Difficulty **difficult** • *Time needed* **over an hour** • *Calories per serving* **600**

INGREDIENTS
serves 4

For the pasta
UNBLEACHED FLOUR *3 cups*
EGGS *4*
EXTRA VIRGIN OLIVE OIL *1 tablespoon*
SALT *to taste*

For the filling
LETTUCE *1 1/4 lbs*
BLACK TRUFFLES *2 oz (or preserved)*
SHALLOTS *1*
PARSLEY *a bunch*
EGGS *1*
GRATED GRANA CHEESE *4 tablespoons*
BUTTER *1 tablespoon*
EXTRA VIRGIN OLIVE OIL *2 tablespoons*
SALT & PEPPER *to taste*

For the sauce
BLACK TRUFFLES *1 oz*
PARSLEY *a bunch*
GRATED GRANA CHEESE *4 tablespoons*
BUTTER *3 tablespoons*
SALT & PEPPER *to taste*

1 Make the pasta dough. Sift the flour into a mound on the work surface; make a well in the flour and lightly beat the eggs in it; add a dash of salt and the extra virgin olive oil; work the ingredients until the dough becomes smooth and elastic; cover the dough with in plastic wrap and let it rest in a cool place for at least 30 minutes.

2 Prepare the filling. Peel the truffle and chop finely. Clean the salad: rinse, drain and dry with a salad spinner, then cut in julienne. Add the chopped truffle and mix. Peel, rinse, dry and chop the shallot.

3 In a skillet, simmer the shallot in the butter and oil without letting it brown. Mix in the chopped truffle. Add the lettuce and let it wilt for 2 minutes, mixing it up with a wooden spoon. Continue to cook on high heat for another 2-3 minutes, stirring often until the liquid is evaporated.

4 Place the mixture in a bowl and let it cool. Add the rinsed and chopped parsley, the egg, the parmigiano and a dash of salt and pepper; mix the ingredients well. Roll out dough gradually into thin sheets. With an indented circular cutter, divide the sheet into 2 x 3 inch rectangles.

5 Beat the remaining egg with a fork and brush on the edges of the rectangles. Put half a teaspoon of the filling in the middle of the rectangles, fold over the narrow width and twist like a candy wrapper. Cook the caramelle in a pot of boiling salted water.

6 Prepare the sauce. Melt the butter in a skillet; add the peeled and sliced or grated truffle, a dash of salt and pepper and 2 tablespoon of the cooking water; mix and cook for 1 minute. When al dente, drain the caramelle and toss with the truffle sauce. Serve hot, sprinkled with cleaned and chopped parsley and grated parmigiano.

Seafood caramelloni

Difficulty **difficult** • *Time needed* **over an hour** • *Calories per serving* **650**

INGREDIENTS
serves 4

For the pasta
UNBLEACHED FLOUR *3 cups*
SPINACH *7 oz*
EGGS *2*
EXTRA VIRGIN OLIVE OIL *1 tablespoon*
SALT *to taste*

For the filling
MIXED SEAFOOD *14 oz*
(shrimp, fillet of sole, whitefish, your choice)
PARSLEY *a bunch*
GARLIC *1 clove*
DRY WHITE WINE *1/4 cup*
EXTRA VIRGIN OLIVE OIL *3 tablespoons*
SALT & PEPPER *to taste*

For the sauce
CLAMS *14 oz*
MUSSELS *14 oz*
SHRIMP *7 oz*
TOMATOES *7 oz, ripe and firm*
SHALLOTS *1*
PARSLEY *a bunch*
GARLIC *1 clove*
DRY WHITE WINE *1/4 cup*
EXTRA VIRGIN OLIVE OIL *5 tablespoons*
SALT *to taste*

1 Make the pasta dough. Clean the spinach, rinse several times in cold water and parboil in a little water for 2 minutes; drain, spin-dry and chop finely. Sift the flour into a mound on the work surface; make a well in the flour and lightly beat the eggs in it; add the chopped spinach, a dash of salt and the extra virgin olive oil; work the ingredients until the dough becomes smooth and elastic; cover the dough with plastic wrap and let rest in a cool place for at least 30 minutes.

2 Prepare the filling. Peel and chop the garlic. Clean the parsley: rinse, dry and chop. Peel the shrimp, devein and rinse; rinse the sole and the whitefish and pat dry. Heat the oil in a skillet and cook the garlic for 30 seconds; add the fish fillets and the shrimp; cook until evenly golden. Add the wine and cook until evaporated; season with salt and fresh ground pepper..

3 Drain the fish on a paper towel, cut into large pieces and place in a bowl, adding the chopped parsley. Roll the pasta dough into very thin sheets; with

a very sharp knife, cut into 3 1/2 by 2 1/2 inch rectangles; brush the edges with water; in the center of each rectangle, place a little of the filling, fold over the narrow side and twist the ends like candy wrappers.

4 Prepare the sauce. Wash the clams thoroughly; scrape the mussels clean and wash; peel the shrimp, remove the vein and rinse. Peel the shallot, rinse and chop finely. Scald the tomatoes, drain, remove the skin, the seeds and the juice; dice the pulp. Rinse and chop the parsley.

5 Put the clams and mussels in a large pan, douse with the white wine, add a spoonful of olive oil, the peeled garlic clove and a little parsley. Cover the pan and cook over high heat; shake from time to time so the shells open. Separate the meat from the shells and discard shells and any clams that remained closed. Strain the cooking liquid and reduce over high heat; set aside.

6 Heat the remaining oil in a skillet and cook the chopped shallot until transparent. Add the seafood, the diced tomato and the cooking liquid set aside. Salt and cook the sauce for a few minutes. Remove from heat and sprinkle with the remaining parsley. Cook the ravioli in abundant salted water until al dente. Drain and toss with the hot seafood sauce.

Casonsei with sausage and turkey

Difficulty **medium** • *Time needed* **over an hour** • *Calories per serving* **990**

INGREDIENTS
serves 4

For the pasta
UNBLEACHED FLOUR *3 cups*
EGGS *4*
SALT *to taste*

For the filling
ROAST TURKEY *11 oz, or chicken*
SAUSAGE *3 oz*
BREAD *1 slice*
MILK *1/2 cup*
EGGS *1*
NUTMEG *a pinch*
POWDERED CINNAMON *a pinch*
GRATED GRANA CHEESE *5 tablespoons*
SALT & PEPPER *to taste*

For the sauce
PANCETTA *3 oz, in 1 piece*
SAGE *a bunch of leaves*
GRATED GRANA CHEESE *to taste*
BUTTER *4 tablespoons*

1 Make the pasta dough. Sift the flour into a mound on the work surface; make a well in the flour and lightly beat 3 eggs in it; add a dash of salt and work the ingredients until the dough becomes smooth and elastic; cover the dough with in plastic wrap and let it rest in a cool place for at least 30 minutes.

2 Prepare the filling. Peel the skin from the sausage, break it apart into small pieces and brown until evenly golden in a non-stick pan; put in a bowl and set apart. Soak the bread in the milk. Cut the roast turkey into small pieces and chop finely. In a bowl, mix the chopped turkey, an egg, the sausage, the grated parmigiano, the bread (well drained and separated into small pieces), a dash of nutmeg and a dash of powdered cinnamon; season with salt and pepper. Mix well with a wooden spoon until well blended.

3 Roll the pasta dough gradually into thin sheets and cut into 3 inch diameter disks with a round stamp. Beat the remaining egg and brush on one side of the disks. Put a small amount of filling in the center of the disk; fold over into a half-moon and press the edges well together to seal the dough.

4 Cook the ravioli in a large pot in abundant salted water for about 10 minutes, checking often. In the meantime, prepare the sauce: dice the pancetta and cook in a non-stick pan all by themselves; drain on paper towels. Rinse and dry the sage; heat the butter in another skillet and briefly cook the sage. When the ravioli are ready, drain, toss with the butter, the sage and the pancetta; sprinkle with grated parmigiano to taste and serve immediately.

Casunzei with smoked ricotta

Difficulty **medium** • *Time needed* **over an hour** • *Calories per serving* **770**

INGREDIENTS
serves 4

For the pasta
UNBLEACHED FLOUR *4 cups*
EGGS *2*
SALT *to taste*

For the filling
GRATED SMOKED RICOTTA *5 tablespoons*
POTATOES *1 lb*
ONIONS *1*
CINNAMON *a pinch*
CLOVES *3, finely ground*
BUTTER *1 tablespoon*
SALT & PEPPER *to taste*

For the sauce
GRATED SMOKED RICOTTA
4 tablespoons
BUTTER *3 tablespoons*

1 Make the pasta dough. Sift the flour into a mound on the work surface; make a well in the flour and lightly beat the eggs in it; add a dash of salt and work the ingredients using a little water to get a smooth and homogenous dough; cover with a towel and let it rest for at least 1 hour.

2 In the meantime, prepare the filling: boil the potatoes for about a half hour in a pot with abundant water; drain and let cool till lukewarm, then peel and pass through a potato masher into a bowl.

3 Peel the onion, chop finely and fry in a skillet with the butter until slightly golden; add the potatoes, the smoked ricotta, the cinnamon, the cloves, the salt

and the pepper; simmer for about 15 minutes over low heat, stirring continually with a wooden spoon.

4 When the dough has rested enough, transfer it to the work surface and roll it out into thin sheets; using a hollow pasta cutter, press out 2 1/2 inch disks. Put a little of the filling in the middle of each disk, fold in half and press the edges firmly together.

5 Boil abundant water in a large pot, add salt, drop in the ravioli and boil for a few minutes; drain and transfer to a serving dish; toss with the grated smoked ricotta and put on a few dabs of butter or drizzle with melted butter. Serve while hot.

Cialzons

Difficulty **medium** • *Time needed* **over an hour** • *Calories per serving* **850**

INGREDIENTS
serves 4

For the pasta
UNBLEACHED FLOUR *4 cups*
EGGS *4*
BUTTER *1 tablespoon*
SALT *to taste*

For the filling
SPINACH *1 lb*
RAISINS *2 oz*
CANDIED CITRON *2 oz*
BAKING CHOCOLATE *2 oz*
DAY-OLD DARK BREAD *3 oz*
POWDERED CINNAMON *1/2 teaspoon*
EGGS *1*
SUGAR *to taste*

For the sauce
GRATED SMOKED RICOTTA
6 tablespoons
SUGAR *1 tablespoon*
POWDERED CINNAMON *to taste*
BUTTER *5 tablespoons*

1 Carefully rinse the spinach and boil in the rinse water; let the raisins soften in a little lukewarm water. In a mixing bowl, finely crumble the dark bread, grate the chocolate, add the well dried and finely cut spinach, the soaked raisins (well drained and towel dried), the candied citron (finely chopped) and the cinnamon; mix well until well blended. Beat an egg yolk with a tablespoon of sugar and blend into the mixture.

2 Make the pasta dough. Sift the flour into a mound on the work surface; make a well in the flour and lightly beat the eggs in it; add a dash of salt and the butter (room temperature soft); knead the ingredients until the dough becomes homogenous. Roll the dough into a thin sheet and cut into 2 1/2 inch disks.

3 Fill the disks with a teaspoonful of the filling, fold over and press the edges so they do not open during cooking. Boil the ravioli in salted water for about 10 minutes; drain and transfer to a serving dish, alternating layers sprinkled with grated smoked ricotta, or with sugar and cinnamon; top off with dabs of butter.

Ciaroncè with lettuce and potatoes

Difficulty **medium** • *Time needed* **over an hour** • *Calories per serving* **630**

INGREDIENTS
serves 4

For the pasta
UNBLEACHED FLOUR *3 cups*
EGGS *2*
SALT *to taste*

For the filling
POTATOES *14 oz*
LETTUCE *1 lb*
GRATED GRANA CHEESE *6 tablespoons*
BUTTER *1 tablespoon*
SESAME SEED OIL
enough for frying
SALT & PEPPER *to taste*

1 Make the pasta dough. Sift the flour into a mound on the work surface; make a well in the flour and lightly beat the eggs in it; add a dash of salt and just enough water to make a smooth and elastic dough. Cover the dough with in plastic wrap and let it rest in a cool place for at least 30 minutes.

2 In the meantime prepare the filling. Rinse the potatoes and put them in a deep pot. Cover with cold water and boil for about 30 minutes until they become soft. Drain, peel, pass through a potato masher into a mixing bowl.

3 Clean the lettuce, rinse it, dry it well, cut it into thin strips; melt the butter in a skillet, add the lettuce, season with salt and pepper and cook for 3-4 minutes, stirring with a wooden spoon. Drain on a paper towel, chop finely; add to the mashed potatoes. Add 5 tablespoons of grated parmigiano, a dash of salt and pepper and mix thoroughly.

4 Roll the pasta dough into a thin sheet and cut into 2 1/2 inch squares. Put a teaspoonful of the filling in the center of each square, fold over to form a rectangle and press the sides of the dough firmly to seal in the filling.

5 In a skillet, heat enough peanut oil to fry the ravioli, a few at a time; remove with a perforated ladle and let drain over paper towels. Transfer onto a serving dish, sprinkle with the remaining parmigiano and serve immediately.

Culingionis

Difficulty **medium** • *Time needed* **over an hour** • *Calories per serving* **990**

INGREDIENTS
serves 4

For the pasta
UNBLEACHED FLOUR *4 cups*
EGGS *4*
UNBLEACHED FLOUR
as needed to dust the work surface
SALT *a pinch*

For the filling
BEETS *14 oz*
GRATED FRESH PECORINO *14 oz*
UNBLEACHED FLOUR *1 tablespoon*
SAFFRON *1 sachet*
NUTMEG *a pinch*
EGGS *4*
SALT & PEPPER *to taste*

For the sauce
TOMATO SAUCE *14 oz*
GRATED PECORINO *4 tablespoons*

1 Sift the flour into a mound on the work surface; make a well in the flour and lightly beat the eggs in it; add a dash of salt and knead the ingredients until the dough becomes smooth and firm, using a little lukewarm water, if needed. Transfer the dough into a bowl sprinkled with flour, cover with a towel and let rest.

2 In the meantime, prepare the filling. Prepare the beets, rinse thoroughly and boil in a pot with little water for about 15 minutes. When cooked, drain thoroughly and chop finely.

3 Transfer the chopped beets into a mixing bowl; add the grated fresh pecorino, the flour, the saffron (soaked in a small amount of water), and a dash of nutmeg; mix well, season with a dash of salt and fresh ground pepper; finally, blend in the eggs.

4 Roll the dough into a thin sheet and separate into two strips of equal dimensions; on one strip, space small amounts of the filling about 2 inches apart; cover with the remaining strip, pressing well around the filling to seal the edges. Cut into squares using an indented rotary cutter.

5 In a large pot, bring abundant water to a boil. Drop in the ravioli and cook for 10-15 minutes. When ready, drain with a perforated ladle, transfer to a serving dish and toss with the heated tomato sauce; sprinkle with the grated pecorino and serve while hot.

Tortellini with wild herbs in walnut sauce

Difficulty **medium** • *Time needed* **over an hour** • *Calories per serving* **970**

INGREDIENTS
serves 4

For the pasta
UNBLEACHED FLOUR *4 cups*
EGGS *4*
SALT *to taste*

For the filling
WILD HERBS *1 1/2 lbs (mint, wild beet, etc.)*
(including 11 oz of borage)
RICOTTA *5 oz*
GARLIC *1/2 clove, chopped*
EGGS *2*
GRATED PARMIGIANO *4 tablespoons*
SALT *to taste*

For the sauce
WALNUTS *1 lb*
GARLIC *1/2 clove*
BREAD *2 slices, soaked in a little milk*
EXTRA VIRGIN OLIVE OIL *a few tablespoons*
SALT *to taste*

1 Sift the flour into a mound on the work surface; make a well in the flour and lightly beat the eggs in it; add a dash of salt and knead the ingredients until the dough becomes smooth and firm. Roll the dough into a thin sheet.

2 Clean and rinse the herbs thoroughly, then drain and wilt in a pot with the water remaining on the herbs, adding a dash of salt; when cooked, drain, cut thinly and chop finely. Transfer the herbs to a mixing bowl and add the beaten eggs, the ricotta, a dash of salt, if needed, and the chopped garlic. Mix well with a wooden spoon and add the grated parmigiano, mixing again.

3 Cut the dough into 2 1/2 inch squares; put a small ball of filling in the center of each, fold into a triangle and press the sides together. Dry the ravioli on a towel.

4 Prepare the sauce: shell the nuts, boil the kernels in water for a few minutes, take them out with a perforated ladle and peel. In a sufficiently large mortar, grind the kernels together with the half clove of garlic, the soaked shredded bread, and the salt; when the mixture becomes creamy, slowly add the olive oil until the sauce is not too fluid. Cook the tortellini in abundant boiling salted water until al dente; drain and toss with the hazelnut sauce.

Ravioli with meat

Difficulty **medium** • *Time needed* **over an hour** • *Calories per serving* **660**

INGREDIENTS
serves 4

For the pasta
UNBLEACHED FLOUR *3 cups*
EGGS *3*
SALT *to taste*

For the filling
BEEF *5 oz*
CHOPPED PANCETTA *2 oz*
ONIONS *1*
MARJORAM *a teaspoon, chopped*
NUTMEG *a pinch*
CINNAMON *a pinch*
EGGS *1*
BUTTER *1 tablespoon*
SALT & PEPPER *to taste*

For the sauce
BUTTER *4 tablespoons*

1 Make a mound with the flour, break an egg in the center; add a pinch of salt and mix the dough for about 10 minutes until it is smooth and firm; roll the dough into a thin sheet. Cover the sheet with a kitchen towel and let rest.

2 Grind the meat and the onion; cook in a pan with the butter for about 20 minutes, stirring frequently. Transfer the cooked meat and onion into a bowl, add the chopped pancetta, a dash of salt and fresh ground pepper.; season with the marjoram, the nutmeg and the cinnamon; mix well and, finally, blend in the egg to hold the ingredients together.

3 Remove the kitchen towel from the sheet of dough and cut into 1 1/2 inch disks. Place a small dab of filling on each disk and cover with another disk; press the edges together to seal the dough.

4 Bring a large pot of water to a boil, salt the water, drop in the ravioli, stir and let cook for a few minutes, then drain. Melt the butter in a large pan, put in the ravioli and toss in the pan, cooking for 2 minutes. Serve while still hot.

SUGGESTION
To save time, the filling can be prepared the day before, keeping it in the refrigerator. A leftover roast can be used instead of the meat.

Abruzzo style ravioli

Difficulty **medium** • *Time needed* **over an hour** • *Calories per serving* **880**

INGREDIENTS
serves 4

For the pasta
UNBLEACHED FLOUR *3 1/2 cups*
EGGS *3*
SALT *to taste*

For the filling
RICOTTA *1 lb*
SUGAR *1/2 tablespoon*
POWDERED CINNAMON *a pinch*
EGGS *2*

For the sauce
ROAST BEEF *1 1/4 lbs, in one piece*
CRUSHED TOMATOES *1 1/4 lbs*
ONIONS *1, small*
GARLIC *1 clove*
CLOVES *1*
BEEF STOCK *1 1/2 cups*
DRY WHITE WINE *1/4 cup*
GRATED PECORINO *to taste*
BACON *2 oz*
BUTTER *1 tablespoon*
SALT & PEPPER *to taste*

1 Prepare the filling: in a mixing bowl, carefully mix the ricotta, the sugar, the cinnamon and the beaten eggs.

2 Prepare the pasta: sift the flour in a mound on the work surface, sprinkle with a dash of salt, break the eggs into the center and carefully knead until the dough is smooth and firm; roll out the dough on a work surface sprinkled with flour into 2 thin sheets of equal dimensions.

3 On one of the sheets, place small quantities of the filling no larger than a walnut at regular intervals; cover with the other sheet of dough. Press the dough around the filling mounds to seal; cut the ravioli with an indented rotary cutter; sprinkle with flour and leave to dry on the work surface for about 30 minutes.

4 Prepare the sauce: peel the garlic and chop it along with the bacon. Make incisions into the piece of beef about 2 inches deep and stuff with a bit of the bacon-garlic mixture. Bind it with butcher's twine to keep a compact shape during the cooking. Melt the butter in a casserole (terracotta, if possible), introduce the meat, brown it for a few minutes, then take it out and lower the heat.

5 Peel the onion, chop finely and put in the casserole with the clove; let it simmer adding the wine, the salt and the pepper. Let the liquid evaporate, add the beef stock and, when boiling, season with salt and introduce the meat; cover and let it cook on low heat for about 2 1/2 hours adding a little water or beef stock, if necessary. Cook the ravioli and abundant salted water, drain, toss with the meat sauce, sprinkle with the grated pecorino and serve while hot. The meat cooked for the sauce can be reused in another recipe.

SUGGESTION

The sugar used in the filling can be substituted with 3-4 tablespoons of grated pecorino.

Ravioli with mushrooms

Difficulty **medium** • *Time needed* **over an hour** • *Calories per serving* **480**

INGREDIENTS
serves 4

For the pasta
UNBLEACHED FLOUR *3 cups*
EGGS *2*
EGG WHITES *1*
SALT *to taste*

For the filling
FRESH MUSHROOMS *14 oz*
ONIONS *1/2*
PARSLEY *a bunch*
GARLIC *1/2 clove*
GRATED GRANA CHEESE *2 tablespoons*
EGGS *1*
EXTRA VIRGIN OLIVE OIL *2 tablespoons*
SALT & PEPPER *to taste*

For the sauce
FRESH MUSHROOMS *5 oz*
ZUCCHINI *2*
PEPPERS *1/2*
EXTRA VIRGIN OLIVE OIL *2 tablespoons*
SALT & PEPPER *to taste*

1 Prepare the pasta. On the work surface, sift the flour in a mound, break the eggs into the center, add a dash of salt and a couple of tablespoons of water. Work and knead until the dough is smooth and firm. Let it rest for about half an hour in a cool place, covered with a lightly floured kitchen towel.

2 In the meantime, prepare the filling. Clean the mushrooms, rinse them rapidly, dry with a kitchen towel and slice thinly. Rinse, dry and chop the parsley. Peel the onion and the garlic and chop finely; put into a skillet with the extra virgin olive oil and cook on moderate heat without browning; add the mushrooms and brown for 2-3 minutes on high heat, stirring with a wooden spoon.

3 Remove the mushrooms, chop coarsely and squeeze out the cooking liquid; replace into the skillet, add the parsley, season with a dash of salt and fresh ground pepper. and simmer until the liquid is completely evaporated, stirring often. Remove from the heat and let cool.

4 Transfer the mixture to a bowl, add the grated parmigiano, the egg and a dash of salt and pepper; mix the ingredients well. Roll the pasta dough into a very thin sheet, dividing it into strips about 2 1/2 inches wide; beat the egg white with a fork and brush on one side of the pasta strips.

5 On one half of the strips, distribute the mushroom filling into small heaps, separated 2 inches from one another; fold over the other half of the pasta, press around the filling to seal. Cut the ravioli with a circular cutter.

6 Prepare the sauce. Trim, rinse and slice the vegetables and the mushrooms. In a skillet, heat the oil, add the sliced pepper and cook for 3-4 minutes stirring often; add the zucchini and cook for 5-6 minutes and add the mushrooms; cook for 2-3 minutes on high heat. Stir often and season with salt and pepper. In a large pot, boil ample salted water and cook the ravioli for 3-4 minutes; drain and toss with the vegetable ragù. Serve at once.

Ravioli with beets

Difficulty **medium** • *Time needed* **under an hour** • *Calories per serving* **540**

INGREDIENTS
serves 4

For the pasta
UNBLEACHED FLOUR *3 cups*
EGGS *2*
SALT *a pinch*

For the filling
COOKED BEETS *8 oz*
POTATO *1*
CARROTS *1*
BREAD CRUMBS *2 tablespoons*
SALT & PEPPER *to taste*

For the sauce
POPPY SEEDS *1 tablespoon*
GRATED GRANA CHEESE *4 tablespoons*
BUTTER *3 tablespoons*
SALT *to taste*

1 Prepare the pasta. Form the flour in a mound on the work surface, break the eggs into the center and add the salt; then knead well until the dough is smooth and firm, adding a little water, if necessary. Wrap in a dish towel and let it rest for about 30 minutes in a cool place.

2 In the meantime, prepare the filling. Trim and peel the carrot; boil in abundant salted water for about 30 minutes. When cooked, crush and pass it through a vegetable mill; do the same with the cooked beets and set the mixture obtained apart.

3 In a small casserole filled with cold water, boil the potato for about 40 minutes, then drain, peel and pass it through a potato masher. In a bowl, add all the mashed ingredients and the bread crumbs, season with a dash of salt and fresh ground pepper. and mix well with a wooden spoon.

4 Take the pasta dough and roll it into a thin sheet; cut into 2 1/2 to 3 inch squares. In the center of each square, place a little filling and fold over to make rectangles; press well all around the edges to get a good seal.

5 In a pot, boil abundant water and add salt; drop in the prepared ravioli and cook for about 10 minutes.

6 In a skillet, melt the butter; when the ravioli are ready, drain with a perforated ladle, transfer to a serving dish, drizzle with the melted butter and sprinkle with the poppy seeds and the grana. Serve while still hot.

Ravioli with eggplant and chicken

Difficulty **medium** • *Time needed* **over an hour** • *Calories per serving* **680**

INGREDIENTS
serves 4

For the pasta
UNBLEACHED FLOUR *3 cups*
EGGS *2*
SALT *to taste*

For the filling
EGGPLANTS *1 lb*
CHICKEN BREAST *7 oz*
PARSLEY *a bunch*
GARLIC *2 cloves*
FRESH RICOTTA *7 oz*
EGGS *1*
VEGETABLE BROTH *4 cups*
EXTRA VIRGIN OLIVE OIL *3-4 tablespoons*
SALT *to taste*

For the sauce
SAGE *a bunch of leaves*
GRATED PARMIGIANO *3 tablespoons*
BUTTER *3 tablespoons*

1 Peel the egg plants, dice, put in a colander, cover with a weight and leave for about an hour to drain out the excess water; then rinse and thoroughly dry. Transfer to a pan with the olive oil and the peeled garlic cloves; when cooked, sprinkle with the chopped parsley and the salt.

2 In a pot, boil the chicken breast in the vegetable broth; chop into small pieces and transfer to a mixing bowl; add the egg plants, the ricotta, the egg and mix thoroughly.

3 In the meantime, prepare the dough: on the work surface, make a mound with the flour; add the eggs and the salt and mix well. If necessary, add a little lukewarm water if the dough becomes very dense.

4 Roll out the pasta dough into a thin sheet and cut into 2 inch squares; in the center of half of the squares, put a small teaspoonful of the filling and cover with the remaining squares, closing the edges with the pressure of your fingers.

5 In a large pot, bring abundant water to boil, add salt, and cook the ravioli. In the meantime, rinse and dry the sage leaves; melt the butter in a skillet and add the sage leaves; cook until light and sparkling.

6 When the ravioli are ready, drain and transfer to a serving dish; drizzle with the sage butter, sprinkle with the parmigiano and serve while hot.

Ravioli with mushroom sauce

Difficulty **easy** • *Time needed* **under an hour** • *Calories per serving* **640**

INGREDIENTS
serves 4

FRESH RAVIOLI *1 1/4 lbs*
DRIED MUSHROOMS *2 oz*
SHELLED WALNUTS *3 oz*
PARSLEY *a bunch*
GARLIC *1 1/2 cloves*
MILK *1/4 cup*
DAY OLD BREAD *1 slice, without crust*
GRATED GRANA CHEESE *1/2 cup*
EXTRA VIRGIN OLIVE OIL *3 tablespoons*
SALT *to taste*

1 Soak the dry mushrooms in a bowl with a little lukewarm water for about a half hour. In a food processor, blend together the hazelnuts, the bread (torn into small pieces), half a clove of peeled garlic, and the milk. When smooth and homogenous, set aside.

2 Press the water out of the mushrooms and cook in a pan with the oil and the remaining piece of the peeled garlic; dry on paper towels, then add some salt and a small amount of filtered soaking water; cook for about 20 minutes adding more soaking water, if necessary; just before the cooking is done, add the cleaned and finely chopped parsley.

3 In the meantime, boil abundant water in a pot, add salt and cook the ravioli al dente; drain, transfer into the pan with the mushroom sauce and toss for about one minute. Drizzle with the hazelnut sauce prepared earlier and sprinkle generously with the grated parmigiano. Mix all the ingredients well and serve immediately.

> ### SUGGESTION
> *This sauce can also be used to make fillings with meat or vegetables. The dried mushrooms can be substituted with 12 oz of fresh porcini mushrooms, well cleaned and cut into slices. Follow the recipe above.*

Spinach ravioli

Difficulty **medium** • *Time needed* **over an hour** • *Calories per serving* **590**

INGREDIENTS
serves 4

For the pasta
RYE FLOUR *4 cups*
EGGS *1*
MILK *to taste*
BUTTER *a dab*
SALT *to taste*

For the filling
SPINACH *1 1/4 lbs*
POWDERED CUMIN *a pinch*
SALT *a pinch*

EXTRA VIRGIN OLIVE OIL *enough for frying*

1 Clean the spinach, rinse several times under running water and cook for 15 minutes in a pot with little water, lightly salted; drain thoroughly, chop finely, then mix with the cumin.

2 Prepare the pasta dough. Arrange the flour in a mound on the working surface, put a dash of salt in the center, add the butter at room temperature and the egg; work the dough, adding the milk little by little until the consistency is right. Roll out the dough into a thin sheet and cut into 2 inch squares.

3 With a teaspoon, distribute a little filling in the center of half the squares covering each with the remaining squares. Seal the edges well, pressing with the ends of your fingers.

4 Pour enough oil into a pan deep enough for frying or in a deep fryer, and when hot enough, put in the ravioli, a few at a time, letting them turn golden all over; remove with a perforated ladle, dry on paper kitchen towels to remove the excess oil. Continue till done. Serve while hot.

Ravioli with dried salted cod and zucchini

*Difficulty **difficult** • Time needed **over an hour** • Calories per serving **450***

INGREDIENTS
serves 4

FRESH EGG PASTA DOUGH *11 oz*
DRIED SALTED COD *11 oz, pre-soaked*
ZUCCHINI *7 oz*
SHALLOTS *1*
PARSLEY *a bunch*
EGG WHITES *1*
DRY WHITE WINE *1/4 cup*
CORN OIL *4 tablespoons*
SALT & PEPPER *to taste*

For the sauce
ZUCCHINI *12 oz*
SHALLOTS *1*
VEGETABLE BROTH *1/2 cup*
CORN OIL *2 tablespoons*
SALT & PEPPER *to taste*

1 Heat two tablespoons of oil in a skillet and cook the peeled and chopped shallot without browning; add the zucchini, cleaned, rinsed and sliced, and brown briefly, stirring with a wooden spoon. Add a few tablespoons of water, a dash of salt and continue cooking for 10 minutes.

2 Strain the zucchini through a vegetable press and transfer into a pot; dry out over medium heat, stirring often. Heat the remaining oil in a pan and brown the soaked cod cut into small pieces. Add the wine and evaporate it over high heat; cover and continue cooking for another 10 minutes on moderate heat.

3 When the cooked cod has cooled, chop finely or pass in a food processor; transfer to a bowl, add the strained zucchini, half the chopped parsley, a dash of salt and pepper and mix well. Roll out the dough into a very thin sheet and cut into 2 1/2 in diameter disks.

4 Put a little filling on each disk, brush the edges with the egg white, lightly beaten, and fold them over, pressing well together to seal the ravioli: bend the ends together and close by pressing together. Prepare the sauce in a pan, by heating the shallot in the oil. Add the zucchini, cut into small pieces and brown for two minutes.

5 Add the remaining parsley, the vegetable broth, season with salt and pepper. Continue cooking for 10 minutes. Pass the mixture in a food processor and return to the pan, heating until slightly thickened. Pour the sauce over the ravioli, cooked al dente.

Genoa style ravioli

Difficulty **medium** • *Time needed* **over an hour** • *Calories per serving* **490**

INGREDIENTS
serves 4

For the pasta
UNBLEACHED FLOUR *4 cups*
SALT *to taste*

For the filling
CALVES BRAINS *5 oz, cleaned*
VEAL SWEETBREADS *5 oz, cleaned*
GROUND VEAL *7 oz*
BORAGE *6 oz*
ESCAROLE *6 oz*
MARJORAM *1 teaspoon*
POWDERED CINNAMON *1 pinch*
NUTMEG *a pinch*
EGGS *2*
EGG YOLKS *1*
DAY-OLD BREAD *3 slices, without crust*
BEEF STOCK *a few tablespoons*
GRATED GRANA CHEESE *4 tablespoons*
BUTTER *1 tablespoon*
SALT *to taste*

For the sauce
RAGÙ SAUCE *7 oz*

1 To prepare the filling, clean the borage and the escarole, rinse carefully and boil in abundant salted water for 5 minutes, then shred. Cook the brains and the sweetbreads in abundant salted water for 10 minutes, then drain. Melt the butter in a pot, brown the veal and cook until done.

2 Grind the vegetables, the brains, the sweetbreads, and the veal in a meat grinder; transfer the mixture into a bowl and add the eggs and the egg yolk; mix in the grana cheese, a little of the day-old bread (soaked in the beef stock), the spices and the chopped marjoram; season with a dash of salt and mix well.

3 To prepare the pasta, form a mound with the flour; pour about 2 tablespoons of lukewarm water into the center with a pinch of salt. Mix well and work the dough carefully until smooth and elastic. Roll out the pasta into a thin sheet.

4 Make little mounds of the filling and carefully lay them out on half of the sheet of pasta separated by about 2 inches from one another; cover with the remaining sheet and cut with an indented cutting wheel so the filling is in the center of each square; press the edges with your fingers. Place the prepared ravioli on a surface covered with a dry dish towel dusted with flour and let dry for an hour.

5 Cook the ravioli in abundant salted water, then drain in a sieve and transfer to a bowl. Sauce the ravioli with the ragù and serve hot.

SUGGESTION
These ravioli can also be served in a broth or with melted butter and sage.

Vegetable ravioli with ricotta, bacon, and sage

Difficulty **easy** • *Time needed* **over an hour** • *Calories per serving* **890**

INGREDIENTS
serves 4

FRESH SPINACH PASTA DOUGH *7 oz*
FRESH EGG PASTA DOUGH *7 oz*
EGGS *1*
UNBLEACHED FLOUR *to taste*
SALT *to taste*

For the filling
RICOTTA *7 oz*
PINE NUTS *1 oz*
SHELLED WALNUTS *2 oz*
EGGS *1*
EGG YOLKS *2, hardboiled*
LEMON JUICE *2 tablespoons*
LEMONS *1/2, grated peel*
NUTMEG *to taste*
GRATED GRANA CHEESE *5 tablespoons*
SALT & PEPPER *to taste*

For the sauce
PANCETTA *4 oz, in 1 piece*
SHELLED WALNUTS *3*
SAGE *3-4 leaves*
BUTTER *3 tablespoons*

1 Prepare the filling. In a small non-stick pan, lightly toast the pine nuts, stirring often with a wooden spoon; remove from heat, let cool and chop finely with the walnuts.

2 Strain the hard boiled egg yolks through a sieve, transfer into a bowl, and mix with the ricotta; add the grated grana cheese, the egg, the chopped pine nuts and hazelnuts, the grated lemon peel and season with a dash of salt, fresh ground pepper and the nutmeg. Mix the ingredients well with a wooden spoon.

3 Prepare the ravioli. Gradually roll out the pasta dough, both the spinach and the egg pasta, into thin sheets; beat the egg lightly with a fork and brush on the spinach pasta sheet; with a teaspoon, place the prepared filling on the sheet in small, regularly spaced mounds; cover

with a sheet of egg pasta, press around the mounds of filling to seal the edges well and cut the ravioli with a 2 inch diameter circular stamp; lay them out on a work surface dusted with flour and let them dry for a little.

4 Prepare the sauce. Dice the bacon and brown evenly in a non-stick frying pan; drain and set apart; coarsely chop the walnuts.

5 In an ample pot, boil abundant water, add salt, and cook the ravioli. In the meantime, heat the butter in a small pan with the rinsed and dried sage leaves. When al dente, drain the ravioli with a perforated ladle, transfer into a serving dish, sprinkle with the diced bacon and the chopped walnuts and serve immediately.

Ravioli with apples

Difficulty **medium** • *Time needed* **over an hour** • *Calories per serving* **620**

INGREDIENTS
serves 4

For the pasta
UNBLEACHED FLOUR *2 cups*
EGGS *2*
EXTRA VIRGIN OLIVE OIL *1 tablespoon*

For the filling
APPLES *1 1/4 lbs*
COOKED HAM *4 oz*
SAGE *3 leaves*
NUTMEG *a pinch*
EGGS *1*
BREAD CRUMBS *to taste*
GRATED PARMIGIANO *4 tablespoons*
BUTTER *4 tablespoons*
SALT & PEPPER *to taste*

1 Arrange the flour in a mound on the work surface; in the middle add the eggs, the oil and a few tablespoons of lukewarm water; work the dough until it is smooth, and elastic. Form into a ball, wrap in a towel and let rest for 20 minutes.

2 In the meantime, peel and grate the apples, then cook in a casserole with a dab of butter and the chopped cooked ham. Cook for 7-8 minutes, stirring often. Remove from heat and mix in one beaten egg, a heaping tablespoon of grated parmigiano, salt, pepper, nutmeg and enough bread crumbs to give the mixture the right consistency. Mix it thoroughly.

3 Roll out the dough into very thin sheets. Regularly space small mounds of the filling on half of the rolled out pasta. Fold over the other half and press the spaces between the mounds of filling to seal. Cut the ravioli into half moons or into squares.

4 When all the ravioli are ready, drop into a pot of abundant boiling salted water and let them cook. As soon as they are cooked, drain and serve in small soup bowls. Heat the remaining butter with the sage and pour over the ravioli; sprinkle with the grated parmigiano and some fresh ground pepper.

Ravioli with chicken and risotto

Difficulty **medium** • *Time needed* **over an hour** • *Calories per serving* **600**

INGREDIENTS
serves 4

For the pasta
UNBLEACHED FLOUR *3 cups*
EGGS *3*
SALT *a pinch*

For the filling
TOMATO RISOTTO *7 oz, pre-cooked*
BOILED CHICKEN *4 oz*
SPINACH *or* YOUNG CHARD *7 oz (boiled)*
EGGS *2*
GRATED PARMIGIANO *4 tablespoons*

For the sauce
MUSHROOMS *7 oz*
SAGE *a few leaves*
BUTTER *3 tablespoons*

1 Finely chop the boiled chicken meat and the spinach. In a bowl, mix the tomato risotto with the eggs, the chicken, and the spinach. Mix well with a wooden spoon, adding the grated parmigiano.

2 Prepare the pasta. On the work surface, form a mound with the flour and mix in the eggs and the salt. Work the dough with your hands until it is smooth and elastic, then let it rest, covered with a cloth in a cool place for about 30 minutes. Divide the dough into two equal parts; roll out into two very thin, large sheets.

3 With a teaspoon, place the filling in small heaps on one of the sheets of dough, space them about 2 1/2 inches apart; cover with the second sheet of dough, pressing with the ends of your fingers around the fillings. Cut the ravioli into squares with a round indented cutter.

4 Clean the mushrooms, slice thinly. In a skillet, melt the butter, add the sage leaves and lightly brown the mushrooms. In a large pot, boil abundant water, add salt and drop in the ravioli; about one minute after they rise to the surface, use a perforated ladle to take them out and transfer them to a serving dish. Toss with the mushroom and sage sauce and serve immediately.

SUGGESTION

To make this a more balanced recipe, prepare the risotto the day before using vegetable broth, a little tomato sauce, rosemary and parmigiano. This is an ancient recipe from Montferrina which was made especially just after Christmas and after Easter using leftover risotto from the holy days and the chicken whose broth was used for the risotto.

Ravioli with chicken and zucchini

Difficulty **medium** • *Time needed* **over an hour** • *Calories per serving* **500**

INGREDIENTS
serves 4

For the pasta
UNBLEACHED FLOUR *3 cups*
EGGS *2*
SALT *a pinch*

For the filling
CHICKEN BREAST *8 oz*
SPINACH *11 oz*
ONIONS *1*
PARSLEY *1*
bunch
THYME *1 sprig*
EGGS *1*
DRY WHITE WINE *1/4 cup*
EXTRA VIRGIN OLIVE OIL *2 tablespoons*
SALT & PEPPER *to taste*

For the sauce
ZUCCHINI *8 oz*
BASIL *1 bunch*
BUTTER *4 tablespoons*
SALT & PEPPER *to taste*

1 Prepare the pasta dough. Sift the flour into a mound on the work surface. Place the eggs and the salt in a well in the center. Work the ingredients until the dough is smooth and elastic. Let rest for half an hour in a cool place, covered with a dish towel. In the meantime, peel the onion, rinse, and chop finely. Rinse and dice the chicken breast. Rinse the spinach several times in cold running water. Heat the oil in a skillet and cook the onion until transparent, add the diced chicken breast and brown evenly, stirring with a wooden spoon. Pour the wine on and let it evaporate over high heat; remove the pan from the heat and let cool.

2 In a frying pan, cook the spinach for a few minutes over high heat evaporating the water that forms. Finely chop the diced chicken, the spinach, the thyme, and the parsley (rinsed and dried). Transfer to a bowl, add the egg, a dash of salt and a pinch of pepper; mix thoroughly with a wooden spoon. Roll out the dough into two very thin sheets of equal dimensions. Distribute the filling in small regularly spaced heaps on one of the sheets. Cover with the other sheet and press with your fingers around the mounds of filling.

3 Cut the ravioli with a pasta stamp or a circular indented wheel. Cut the ends of the zucchini, rinse, dry and cut into thin slices; rinse the basil, dry delicately and cut into thin strips. In a pan, melt the butter, add the zucchini and cook for a few minutes, stirring from time to time; season with salt and pepper, add 3 table-spoons of water and continue to cook on moderate heat for 3-5 minutes; sprinkle with the fine strips of basil. In the mean-time, boil abundant water in a pot, add salt and cook the ravioli; when al dente, drain and add the zucchini sauce. Serve immediately.

Ravioli with ricotta and mint

*Difficulty **medium*** • *Time needed **over an hour*** • *Calories per serving* **510**

INGREDIENTS
serves 4

For the pasta
UNBLEACHED FLOUR *3 cups*
EGGS *2*
EXTRA VIRGIN OLIVE OIL *1 tablespoon*
SALT *to taste*

For the filling
RICOTTA *8 oz*
MINT *1 bunch*
SALT *to taste*

For the sauce
WHOLE MILK YOGURT *4 tablespoons*
BUTTER *3 tablespoons*
SALT & PEPPER *to taste*

1 Prepare the pasta dough. Sift the flour into a mound on the work surface; make a well in the middle and add the eggs, the olive oil and the salt; work the mixture until it becomes a smooth and elastic dough. Cover with a dish towel and let it rest for about 30 minutes.

2 Prepare the filling. Rinse, dry and finely chop the fresh mint, reserving a few sprigs for decoration. In a mixing bowl, add the ricotta, the salt and the chopped mint. Mix the ingredients thoroughly with a wooden spoon.

3 Roll out the pasta into two thin sheets; spread out the filling in small heaps about 1 1/2 inches apart, cover with the other sheet, press around each heap of filling to seal, and cut the ravioli with a pasta stamp into the shape you choose.

4 In a large pot, boil abundant water, add salt and cook the ravioli. In the meantime, melt the butter in a small pan over low heat and add the yogurt.

5 Heat the sauce without letting it boil, stirring continually with a wooden spoon. Season with a dash of salt and a pinch of fresh ground pepper.. When al dente, drain, transfer to a serving dish and pour the sauce on top. Decorate with mint leaves and serve at once.

Ravioli with ricotta and meat sauce

Difficulty **medium** • *Time needed* **over an hour** • *Calories per serving* **750**

INGREDIENTS
serves 4

For the pasta
UNBLEACHED FLOUR *4 cups*
EGGS *2*
SALT *to taste*

For the filling
RICOTTA *14 oz*
PARSLEY *1 oz*
EGGS *2*
GRATED PECORINO *1 tablespoon*
SALT & PEPPER *to taste*

For the sauce
PORK *1 lb, in 1 piece*
PANCETTA *2 oz, sliced thinly*
TOMATO PUREE *1 1/2 cups*
PARSLEY *1 oz*
GARLIC *1 clove*
GRATED NUTMEG *1 pinch*
DRY WHITE WINE *3/4 cup*
PECORiNO *1 tablespoon, in flakes*
GRATED PECORINO *9 tablespoons*
POWDERED CHILI PEPPER *2 pinches*
EXTRA VIRGIN OLIVE OIL *4 tablespoons*
SALT *to taste*

1 To prepare the sauce: peel the garlic, clean and rinse the parsley, then chop all together. Transfer to a mixing bowl, add 4 tablespoons of grated pecorino, the nutmeg and a pinch of chili pepper; mix and season with salt. Cover the meat, first with the chopped mixture, then with the bacon strips; form into a roll and tie with butcher's twine. Heat the olive oil in a casserole, insert the meat and brown all over. Add the wine, let it evaporate, season with salt, add the tomato purée; cover and cook on low heat for about an hour and a half, adding a little water, if needed. Transfer the meat to another plate and add the flaked pecorino to the cooking juice.

2 To prepare the pasta dough: on the work surface, form a mound with the flour; make a well and place in it a pinch of salt; break the eggs into it and work the dough for about 15 minutes, adding lukewarm water, if needed, until the dough is smooth and elastic. Roll the dough into a thin sheet.

3 To prepare the filling: clean the parsley, rinse it and chop finely. Strain the ricotta through a sieve into a mixing bowl; add the eggs, the pecorino, the parsley, the salt, the pepper and carefully mix the ingredients. On one half of the sheet of dough, distribute the filling in small heaps equally spaced; cover with the other half; cut the ravioli into round disks with a pasta stamp or a glass, sealing the edges to prevent the ravioli from opening during cooking. In a large pot, boil abundant water, add salt, then cook the ravioli; drain, transfer to a bowl, toss with the sauce, sprinkle with the remaining pecorino and the chili pepper. Serve immediately.

Ravioli with ricotta and saffron

Difficulty **medium** • *Time needed* **over an hour** • *Calories per serving* **720**

INGREDIENTS
serves 4

For the pasta
UNBLEACHED FLOUR *4 cups*
EGGS *4*

For the filling
RICOTTA *12 oz*
SAFFRON *1 sachet*
ORANGE *1, the grated peel*
NUTMEG *to taste*
EGGS *1*
MILK *1 tablespoon*
SALT *to taste*

For the sauce
ROSEMARY *a branch*
GRATED GRANA CHEESE *to taste*
BUTTER *4 tablespoons*

1 Form a mound with the flour on the work surface; in a well in the center, break the eggs, beat a little with a fork and work the dough with your hands until it becomes smooth and elastic. Let rest for at least 20 minutes, wrapped in a clean dish towel. At the end of that time, roll it into a thin sheet.

2 In a small bowl, soak the saffron in the lukewarm milk. In a mixing bowl, work the ricotta with a wooden spoon adding the saffron, the orange peel, a dash of nutmeg, the egg and a pinch of salt; mix until well blended.

3 Distribute the mixture on half of the sheet of dough in small spoonfuls, at equal distance between them; fold over the other half of the dough and cut out the ravioli with a pasta cutter. Pinch the edges together to seal in the filling. Let rest for about 15 minutes on a dish towel dusted with flour.

4 In a large pot, boil abundant water, add salt and drop in the ravioli; as soon as they surface, push them to the bottom with a perforated ladle until cooked al dente. Clean and chop the rosemary; melt the butter in a pan, and cook the rosemary for a few minutes. When cooked, drain the ravioli, sprinkle with the grated parmigiano and drizzle with the melted rosemary flavored butter. Serve at once.

SUGGESTION
*To reduce the calories in this recipe
and at the same time make a single dish serving,
the ravioli can be served with julienned vegetables
and a splash of olive oil.*

Ravioli with ricotta and chives

Difficulty **medium** • *Time needed* **over an hour** • *Calories per serving* **420**

INGREDIENTS
serves 4

For the pasta
UNBLEACHED FLOUR *2 cups*
EGGS *2*
EGG WHITES *1*
SALT *a pinch*

For the filling
RICOTTA *11 oz*
CHIVES *2 oz*
EGG YOLKS *1*
NUTMEG *1 pinch*
SALT & PEPPER *a pinch*

For the sauce
PEPPERS *1*
ONIONS *1, small*
CHIVES *a bunch*
SAGE *3 leaves*
EXTRA VIRGIN OLIVE OIL *3 tablespoons*
SALT & PEPPER *to taste*

1 On the work surface, make a mound with the flour; break the eggs into a well in the center, add the salt and work the ingredients until the dough is smooth and elastic. Let the dough rest in a cool place for about 30 minutes, wrapped in a dish towel.

2 To prepare the filling: clean the chives and chop finely; in a bowl, mix the ricotta with the egg yolk and the nutmeg, add the cleaned chives, and a dash of salt and pepper. Mix the ingredients thoroughly.

3 Roll out the pasta dough into a very thin sheet; on half the sheet, distribute the filling in small heaps about 1 1/2 inches from one another; brush the edges with the egg white, cover with the other half of the sheet and press together between the filling. Cut the ravioli with the appropriate cutter.

4 To prepare the sauce: rinse and clean the pepper, then dice it; rinse, dry and cut the chives into small pieces; peel and cut the onion into thin slices. In a skillet, heat the oil with the sage and the onion without browning; add the pepper, the chives, a pinch of salt and a dash of fresh ground pepper. and cook on low heat for 5 minutes. Cook the ravioli in abundant boiling salted water; drain, toss with the sauce and serve hot.

SUGGESTION
To make this dish more balanced, add an egg yolk to the filling which can also be made with goat's milk ricotta, giving a stronger flavor to the mixture.

Ravioli with turkey and vegetables

Difficulty **medium** • *Time needed* **over an hour** • *Calories per serving* **560**

INGREDIENTS
serves 4

For the pasta
UNBLEACHED FLOUR *3 cups*
EGGS *1*
SALT *a pinch*

For the filling
TURKEY BREAST *8 oz*
SAGE *2 leaves*
EGGS *1*
MILK *1/4 cup (optional)*
DRY WHITE WINE *1/4 cup (optional)*
GRATED GRANA CHEESE *4 tablespoons*
EXTRA VIRGIN OLIVE OIL *2 tablespoons*
SALT & PEPPER *a pinch*

For the sauce
STRING BEANS *4 oz*
ZUCCHINI *4 oz*
CELERY *1 stalk*
CARROTS *4 oz*
EXTRA VIRGIN OLIVE OIL *3 tablespoons*
SALT & PEPPER *to taste*

1 To prepare the pasta dough: On the work surface, make a mound with the flour; break the eggs into a well in the center, add the salt, add a little water and work the ingredients until the dough is smooth and elastic. Cover the dough with in a dish towel and let it rest in a cool place for about 30 minutes.

2 To prepare the filling. Heat the oil in a skillet with the sage; add the turkey breast and brown until golden. Add the white wine and let it evaporate over high heat. Continue cooking over moderate heat for 15 minutes, then cut the turkey breast with a very sharp knife into very thin slices; place in a bowl, add the egg, the grated grana cheese and, if you like, the milk; season with a pinch of salt and a dash of fresh ground pepper. and mix well.

3 Roll the dough into a very thin sheet onto which you place small heaps of filling about 1 inch apart. Fold over the bare sheet, press around each heap of filling and cut the ravioli with a pasta cutter.

4 To prepare the sauce: Clean and rinse the vegetables carefully; cut them into fine julienne strips. In a skillet, heat the oil and add the vegetables; cook for 2 minutes stirring often with a wooden spoon. Add a few tablespoons of water, a dash of salt and pepper and cook another 6 minutes. Boil sufficient water, add salt, and cook the ravioli in it. When al dente, drain and toss with the vegetables. Serve hot.

Vegetable ravioli

Difficulty **medium** • *Time needed* **over an hour** • *Calories per serving* **430**

INGREDIENTS
serves 4

For the pasta
WHOLE WHEAT FLOUR *1 1/4 cups*
UNBLEACHED FLOUR *1 1/4 cups*
EGGS *1*
EGG WHITES *1*
EXTRA VIRGIN OLIVE OIL *1 tablespoon*
SALT *to taste*

For the filling
SHELLED PEAS *12 oz*
LETTUCE *a few leaves*
ONIONS *5 oz*
SALT & PEPPER *to taste*

For the sauce
MARJORAM *a few sprigs*
PARSLEY *1 bunch*
BASIL *1 bunch*
EXTRA VIRGIN OLIVE OIL *4 tablespoons*

1 Sift the whole wheat and the unbleached flours on the work surface to make a mound; break the eggs into a well in the center, add the salt, the oil and a few tablespoons of water. Work the ingredients until the dough is smooth and elastic. Cover the dough with a dish towel and let it rest in a cool place for about 30 minutes.

2 Prepare the filling. Rinse the peas; clean the lettuce, rinse and cut into fine strips. Peel the onions and slice thinly. Place the peas, the onions and the lettuce in a pan; add 1/2 cup of water and bring to a boil. Continue cooking for 15-20 minutes until the peas are tender; season while cooking with a pinch of salt and a dash of fresh ground pepper.

3 Let the mixture cool then strain in a vegetable mill and return to the pan; heat to eliminate the moisture, continually stirring with a wooden spoon. Roll out the pasta into a very thin sheet and brush one half with the lightly beaten egg white; on this half sheet distribute small heaps of the filling about 1 inch apart from one another.

4 Fold the other half of the dough sheet over the filling, pressing well around the heaps; cut the ravioli with an indented circular cutter. Cook the ravioli in abundant boiling salted water. Meanwhile, rinse, dry and finely chop the aromatic herbs. Heat the oil in a skillet, remove from the heat, add the chopped herbs and mix well. Drain the ravioli when al dente, drizzle with the oil and herb mixture and serve at once.

Ravioli with cabbage and peppers

Difficulty **difficult** • *Time needed* **over an hour** • *Calories per serving* **730**

INGREDIENTS
serves 4

For the pasta
UNBLEACHED FLOUR *12 oz*
EGGS *3*
MILK *2 tablespoons*
SALT *a pinch*

For the filling
CABBAGE *2 lbs*
YELLOW PEPPER *1/2*
SHALLOTS *1*
RICOTTA *5 oz*
GRATED GRANA CHEESE *4 tablespoons*
EGGS *1*
BUTTER *1 tablespoon*
SALT & PEPPER *to taste*

For the sauce
SAGE *8-10 leaves*
GRATED GRANA CHEESE *to taste*
BUTTER *3 tablespoons*

1 Prepare the pasta dough: on the work surface, make a mound with the flour; break the eggs into a well in the center, add the salt, and work the ingredients for about 15 minutes, adding the milk. When the dough is smooth and elastic, roll into a thin sheet. Cover with a dish towel and leave to rest.

2 Prepare the filling: clean the cabbage, remove the core and the tougher external leaves and rinse thoroughly. Scald the cabbage in a large pot of boiling water; drain and chop finely. Clean the pepper of seeds and filaments; rinse, dry and chop finely.

3 Peel and chop the shallot; in a skillet, melt the butter and cook the shallot without browning; add the chopped pepper and the cabbage and cook for 3-4 minutes to boil off the water.

4 Remove from heat and let cool; transfer to a bowl and add the ricotta, the grated grana cheese, the egg, the salt and the fresh ground pepper.. Mix thoroughly with a wooden spoon. Cut the pasta dough into 1 1/2 inch diameter circles and put a nut size dab of filling in the middle of each.

5 Fold the disks over into half moons, taking care to leave the top edge slightly smaller than the bottom; press the edges together and roll the bottom edge over the upper. Cook the ravioli in a large pot with abundant boiling salted water for 5-7 minutes; remove with a perforated ladle, transfer into serving plates. In a skillet, melt the butter and briefly cook the sage leaves. Toss the ravioli with the sauce and sprinkle generously with the grated grana cheese. Serve immediately.

Whole wheat ravioli with fennel

Difficulty **medium** • *Time needed* **over an hour** • *Calories per serving* **590**

INGREDIENTS
serves 4

For the pasta
WHOLE WHEAT FLOUR *4 cups*
EGGS *5*
EXTRA VIRGIN OLIVE OIL *1 tablespoon*
SALT *a generous pinch*

For the filling
FENNEL *1/2 lb*
TOMATOES *1/2 lb*
CHOPPED BASIL *2 teaspoons*
GARLIC *1 clove*
EXTRA VIRGIN OLIVE OIL *2 tablespoons*
SALT & PEPPER *to taste*

For the sauce
GRATED PARMIGIANO *4 tablespoons*

1 Prepare the pasta dough for the ravioli by making a mound with the flour on the work surface; make a well in the middle, break the 4 eggs into the center and add the salt and the olive oil. Mix the ingredients well with a fork, then knead by hand for another 5 minutes until the dough is smooth and elastic.

2 Form a ball with the dough, cover with a dish towel and let rest for about 30 minutes before rolling it out into a very thin sheet. Meanwhile, prepare the filling: clean and finely slice the fennel; boil for 5 minutes and drain.

3 Peel and chop the garlic. Heat the oil and stew the fennel with the chopped garlic until soft. Scald the tomatoes, remove the skin and chop. Add the chopped garlic and the fennel and stew until soft. Add the tomatoes and the basil and cook for another 10 minutes until soft enough to pass through a sieve. Season with salt and pepper and let cool.

4 Lay out the filling in small heaps regularly spaced on half the pasta sheet with a teaspoon.

5 Lightly beat the remaining egg and brush it around the filling; cover with the other half of the pasta sheet. Press well around the filling to seal and cut into ravioli with a rotary cutter or a small knife.

6 Fill a large pot with water, bring to a boil, salt and delicately drop in the ravioli; cook uncovered for 12-15 minutes. Drain and serve immediately sprinkled with grated parmigiano.

Raviolini arlecchino

Difficulty **difficult** • *Time needed* **over an hour** • *Calories per serving* **640**

INGREDIENTS
serves 4

For the pasta
UNBLEACHED FLOUR *6 cups*
SPINACH *7 oz*
TOMATO PASTE *1 tablespoon*
SAFFRON *1 sachet*
BOILED BEET *1*
EGGS *5*
SALT *to taste*

For the filling
ROQUEFORT *4 oz*
RICOTTA *8 oz*
ONIONS *1, chopped*
EGGS *1*
BUTTER *a dab*
SALT & PEPPER *to taste*

For the sauce
SAGE *2-3 leaves*
BUTTER *4 tablespoons*

1 Prepare the pasta dough. Clean the spinach, rinse, drain and cook for 2-3 minutes in a non-stick pan; drain, finely chop, return to the pan and cook to evaporate the water. Remove from the heat and set aside to cool. Peel the beet and strain through a vegetable press.

2 On the work surface, separate the flour into 4 mounds; form a well in each and break 1 egg into each well. In one, add the chopped spinach and a pinch of salt; in the second, add the tomato paste and salt; in the third, add the saffron, pre-soaked in a little water, and a dash of salt; in the last, add the strained beet and some salt. Work the four mixtures separately until they are all smooth and elastic; wrap each dough in a sheet of plastic wrap and let rest for about 30 minutes.

3 Prepare the filling. Melt the butter in a skillet and cook the onion until transparent; drain off the butter and let cool in a bowl. Crumble the Roquefort with a fork and add it to the onion; add the ricotta, the egg, the salt and the pepper. Mix thoroughly.

4 Roll out the pasta dough into 4 separate thin sheets; beat the remaining egg and brush half of each sheet. Distribute small heaps of the filling on the brushed parts at regular intervals; fold over the other half of the pasta, press around the filling to seal and cut into ravioli; let dry on the work surface. In a large pot, boil salted water and cook the ravioli al dente. In a small pan, melt the butter and heat with the sage. Drain the ravioli and drizzle with the sage flavored butter. Serve accompanied with grated parmigiano.

Ravioli cooked in sauce

Difficulty **easy** • *Time needed* **under an hour** • *Calories per serving* **480**

INGREDIENTS
serves 4

FRESH RAVIOLI *1 lb*
TOMATO SAUCE *1 lb*
ONIONS *1, peeled*
BASIL *a few leaves*
VEGETABLE BROTH *3 cups*
GRATED PARMIGIANO *4 tablespoons*
BUTTER *3 tablespoons*
SALT & PEPPER *to taste*

1 Finely chop the onion; cook in a casserole with 1 tablespoon of butter; when the onion starts to turn golden, add the tomato paste and simmer for a few minutes. In another pot, bring the vegetable broth to a boil and then transfer to the casserole, adding a dash of salt and fresh ground pepper..

2 Bring to a boil, add the ravioli and the basil (rinsed and dried); partially cover the casserole and continue cooking for about 20 minutes, stirring from time to time with a wooden spoon.

3 Add more hot broth if the sauce becomes too thick; on the other hand, if the sauce is too liquid, reduce it over high heat for the last minutes of cooking. Transfer to a serving plate, mix in the remaining butter and sprinkle with the parmigiano. Serve at once.

SUGGESTION
You can enrich the sauce in this recipe by adding chopped mushrooms, carrots and celery.

Ravioli with fresh beans

Difficulty **medium** • *Time needed* **under an hour** • *Calories per serving* **750**

INGREDIENTS
serves 4

FRESH EGG PASTA DOUGH *12 oz*

For the filling
FRESH SHELLED LIMA BEANS *11 oz*
EGGS *2*
GRATED PECORINO *4 tablespoons*
BUTTER *3 tablespoons*
SALT & PEPPER *to taste*

For the sauce
CARROTS *1*
ZUCCHINI *2*
LEEKS *1*
BUTTER *3 tablespoons*
SALT & PEPPER *to taste*

1 Boil the beans for 1 minute in boiling salted water; drain and remove the skins. Heat the butter in a skillet; beat the eggs lightly and scramble in the pan, leaving them runny; add the beans (save 2 tablespoons), and simmer for 2 minutes, stirring with a wooden spoon.

2 Remove from the heat and let cool. Mix in a food processor; add the pecorino and a dash of salt and pepper. Roll out the pasta dough into a very thin sheet; on one half, lay out the filling in small heaps the size of a walnut spaced about 1 inch apart.

3 Fold the other half sheet over the filling; press around the filling to seal the pasta and cut the ravioli with an indent-ed cutter. Set aside to rest. Prepare the sauce. Cut off the green part and the tougher leaves of the leek, rinse, dry and cut into very thin slices. Cut the ends of the carrot and the zucchini, peel the carrot, rinse the zucchini and cut both julienne .

4 Heat the butter in a skillet and brown the leek for a few seconds; add the carrot, the zucchini and the two saved tablespoons of beans; add a few tablespoons of water, season with a pinch of salt and a little pepper and cook for 6 minutes. Cook the ravioli in abundant salted boiling water for 5-6 minutes, drain when al dente. Place the ravioli in a serving dish and toss with the sauce. Serve at once.

Seafood ravioli

*Difficulty **medium** • Time needed **over an hour** • Calories per serving **540***

INGREDIENTS
serves 4

FRESH EGG PASTA DOUGH *11 oz*

For the filling
FILLETED FRESH WHITEFISH *7 oz*
(sea bass, monkfish, etc.)
BOILED CHARD *3 oz*
PARSLEY *a bunch*
SHALLOTS *1*
GARLIC *1/2 clove*
EGGS *1*
EXTRA VIRGIN OLIVE OIL *4 tablespoons*
SALT & PEPPER *to taste*

For the sauce
CLEANED SHELLFISH *5 oz*
TOMATOES *7 oz, ripe and firm*
PARSLEY *1 bunch, chopped*
GARLIC *1 clove*
CHILI PEPPER *1 small*
EXTRA VIRGIN OLIVE OIL *4 tablespoons*
SALT & PEPPER *to taste*

1 Prepare the filling. Heat the oil in a skillet with the garlic and the pinch of parsley; add the fish and cook about 2 minutes; drain and chop finely. Peel and chop the shallot; cut the chard into fine strips and then chop finely. In the same skillet, add the finely chopped shallot, cook till tender, add the chard; mix with a wooden spoon and cook for a few minutes to eliminate the moisture. Add the chopped fish and mix anew; remove from the heat and transfer to a bowl; when cooled, season with a pinch of salt and a dash of fresh ground pepper.; add the egg and mix thoroughly.

2 Roll out the pasta dough in small quantities at a time; cut into 1 1/2 inch strips and space small mounds of filling on it 1 1/2 inches apart. Brush the edges of the pasta with a little water and cover with another strip of pasta. Press the pasta around the filling to seal and cut the ravioli with an indented rotary cutter.

3 Prepare the sauce. Scald the tomatoes in boiling water, remove the peel, the seeds and the juice; chop the remainder. In a skillet, heat 3 tablespoons of the oil with the garlic (finely chopped) and the chili pepper; add the shellfish and cook briefly. Add the tomatoes, cook on high heat for 3-4 minutes and season with salt and pepper. Remove from the heat, add the remaining olive oil, add the chopped parsley and mix well.

4 Cook the ravioli in abundant boiling salted water, drain when al dente, toss with the sauce and serve while hot.

Ravioli with asparagus

Difficulty **medium** • *Time needed* **over an hour** • *Calories per serving* **600**

INGREDIENTS
serves 4

For the pasta
UNBLEACHED FLOUR *3 cups*
EGGS *3*
EGG WHITES *1*
EXTRA VIRGIN OLIVE OIL *1 teaspoon*
SALT *a pinch*

For the filling
ASPARAGUS *1 1/4 lbs*
EGGS *2*
GRATED GRANA CHEESE *3 tablespoons*
SALT & PEPPER *to taste*

For the sauce
HEAVY CREAM *4 tablespoons*
GRATED GRANA CHEESE *2 tablespoons*
BUTTER *3 tablespoons*
SALT *to taste*

1 Prepare the pasta dough. Sift the flour into a mound on the work surface; make a well in the mound and pour in the olive oil, 2-3 tablespoons of water and the salt. Work the ingredients until the dough becomes smooth and elastic.

2 Prepare the filling. Cut the stems of the asparagus, peel and steam; drain and delicately dry with a dish towel; set apart a few asparagus points for decoration; chop the rest finely.

3 In a mixing bowl, add the chopped asparagus, the grated parmigiano, the eggs, the salt and fresh ground pepper.; mix well with a wooden spoon.

4 Let the mixture cool completely and then keep in the refrigerator for at least 30 minutes to let it set. Prepare the ravioli. Roll out the pasta dough, a little at a time, into strips 3 inches wide. On one half of each strip, place the filling in small heaps 1 1/2 inches apart; lightly beat the egg white and use to brush the edges of the pasta.

5 Fold over the other half of the pasta strip, pressing the edges well to seal in the filling. Cut the ravioli with an indented rotary cutter or with a pasta stamp. Cook the ravioli in abundant boiling salted water for 5 minutes; when al dente, drain, place on a serving dish, distribute dabs of butter over the hot ravioli, sprinkle with the grated grana and delicately drizzle with the heavy cream.

6 Just before serving, bake in a preheated oven 450°F for 5 minutes to brown the surface. Take out of the oven, decorate with the asparagus tips and serve immediately.

Fried ravioli with squash and beans

Difficulty **medium** • *Time needed* **over an hour** • *Calories per serving* **640**

INGREDIENTS
serves 4

For the pasta
UNBLEACHED FLOUR *3 1/2 cups*
SALT *a pinch*

For the filling
SQUASH *1 lb*
CANNED CANNELLINI BEANS *4 oz*
RICE *2 oz*
PARSLEY *2 sprigs*
GARLIC *1 clove*
MARJORAM *2 sprigs*
GRATED GRANA CHEESE *3 tablespoons*
GRATED PECORINO *1 tablespoon*
EGGS *2*
EXTRA VIRGIN OLIVE OIL *2 tablespoons*
SESAME SEED OIL
enough for frying
SALT & PEPPER *to taste*

1 Sift the flour onto the work surface; add a pinch of salt and a little water, then work the dough until it is smooth and elastic; cover with a dish towel and let rest in a cool place for about 30 minutes. Preheat the oven to 400°F.

2 Drop the rice into a pot of boiling salted water, cook al dente and drain. Peel and chop the garlic. Clean and rinse the parsley and the marjoram and chop both. Clean and rinse the squash and cut into thin slices, put into a baking dish and put in the oven for 30 minutes. Let cool and strain through a potato masher into a mixing bowl.

3 Mash the beans and add to the squash; mix in the chopped herbs, the garlic, the parmigiano and the pecorino, the rice, the eggs, the olive oil and a dash of salt and fresh ground pepper., mixing thoroughly with a wooden spoon.

4 Roll out the pasta dough into a thin sheet and cut into 4 inch squares. In the middle of each square, put a small amount of filling, fold into a rectangle and seal the edges well. Fry the ravioli in a deep skillet with abundant hot peanut oil. Drain with a perforated ladle over a paper towel and serve immediately.

SUGGESTION
Dried beans can be used instead of canned beans in the same amount; soak overnight in cold water, then drain and boil for about an hour.

Green ravioloni filled with seafood

Difficulty **difficult** • *Time needed* **over an hour** • *Calories per serving* **660**

INGREDIENTS
serves 4

For the pasta
UNBLEACHED FLOUR *3 cups*
SPINACH *5 oz, fresh or frozen*
EGGS *2*
EXTRA VIRGIN OLIVE OIL *1 tablespoon*
SALT *to taste*

For the filling
SEAFOOD *1 lb (monkfish,*
John Dory, sea bass, etc.)
ASPARAGUS *4*
ZUCCHINI *2*
SPINACH *11 oz, fresh of frozen*
PARSLEY *a bunch*
EXTRA VIRGIN OLIVE OIL *4 tablespoons*
SALT & PEPPER *to taste*

For the sauce
SHRIMP *7 oz*
SHALLOTS *1*
PARSLEY *a bunch*
BALSAMIC VINEGAR *1 tablespoon*
EXTRA VIRGIN OLIVE OIL *4 tablespoons*
SALT & PEPPER *to taste*

1 Prepare the pasta dough. Scald the spinach leaves in a pan with very little salted boiling water for 3-4 minutes, drain and dry well, and chop finely. Sift the flour into a mound on the work surface; make a well in the mound and mix in the spinach, the eggs, the olive oil, and the salt. Work the ingredients until the dough becomes smooth and elastic. Cover the dough with in a towel and let it rest for about 30 minutes in a cool place.

2 In the meantime, prepare the filling. Shell the shrimp, wash all the fish and chop. Cut the hard stems of the asparagus, peel and rinse. Cut the ends of the zucchini, rinse; prepare the spinach, rinse carefully and dry well. Clean, rinse and dry the parsley.

3 Dice the asparagus, the zucchini, the spinach and the parsley; put into a pan with 2 tablespoons of extra virgin olive oil and brown for 7-8 minutes over moderate heat. Transfer the mixture to a mixing bowl. In the same pan, heat the remaining oil, and fry the diced fish over high heat for 1 minute, stirring with a wooden spoon. Add the fish to the prepared vegetable mixture, season with salt and pepper and mix thoroughly.

4 Roll out the pasta in very thin sheets and cut into 4 inch diameter disks. Place 2 tablespoons of the filling in the center of each pasta disk, cover with another disk and press the edges together with fingers or with a fork to seal the ravioli. Steam the ravioli for 7-8 minutes.

5 Meanwhile, prepare the sauce. Peel and devein the shrimp, rinse and cut into round slices. Rinse and finely chop the parsley. Peel and mince the shallot and cook with the oil in a skillet without browning; add the shrimp and brown slightly; drizzle with the balsamic vinegar, salt and pepper and cook for 2 minutes over moderate heat; add the parsley and remove from heat. Serve the ravioli while hot, accompanied by the shrimp sauce.

Ravioli with potatoes and ricotta

Difficulty **medium** • *Time needed* **over an hour** • *Calories per serving* **650**

INGREDIENTS
serves 4

For the pasta
UNBLEACHED FLOUR *1 1/2 cups*
RYE FLOUR *1 1/2 cups*
EGGS *2*
MILK *3 tablespoons*
BUTTER *1 tablespoon*
SALT *to taste*

For the filling
POTATOES *11 oz*
RICOTTA *8 oz*
CHIVES *a bunch*
GRATED GRANA CHEESE *2 tablespoons*
SALT & PEPPER *to taste*

For frying
PEANUT OIL *abundant*

1 Prepare the pasta dough. Melt the butter in a pan; sift the white and the rye flours into a mound on the work surface; make a well in the mound and put in the eggs, a pinch of salt, the milk, the butter and work the ingredients until the dough becomes smooth and elastic. Wrap with a sheet of transparent plastic and let rest for at least 30 minutes.

2 In the meantime, rinse the potatoes, place in a pot, cover with cold water, bring to a boil, salt and cook for 30 to 35 minutes until soft. Rinse the chives, gently dry with a clean kitchen towel and chop finely. Drain the potatoes, remove the skins, pass through a potato masher into a mixing bowl.

3 Add the ricotta, the grated grana cheese, and the chives; season with a pinch of salt and pepper and mix thoroughly with a wooden spoon. Roll out the pasta gradually into a thin sheet; with a round pasta stamp cut into 2 1/2 inch diameter disks.

4 Place a little of the filling in the center of each disk and fold over into a half moon. In a deep pan, heat abundant peanut oil and fry the ravioli until evenly brown; drain on an absorbent paper towel and serve at once.

Vegetable pasta roll

Difficulty **medium** • *Time needed* **over an hour** • *Calories per serving* **890**

INGREDIENTS
serves 4

For the pasta
UNBLEACHED FLOUR *3 cups*
EGGS *3*
EXTRA VIRGIN OLIVE OIL *1 tablespoon*
SALT *to taste*

For the filling
MIXED HERBS *1 lb (nettles, mint, basil, etc.)*
SPINACH *1 lb*
PANCETTA *3 oz, in 1 piece*
ASIAGO CHEESE *4 oz*
EGGS *2*
NUTMEG *to taste*
BUTTER *3 tablespoons*
SALT & PEPPER *to taste*

For the sauce
SAGE *3 leaves*
GRATED GRANA CHEESE *2 tablespoons*
BUTTER *6 tablespoons*

1 Prepare the pasta dough. Sift the flour into a mound on the work surface; make a well in the center; break the eggs into it and pour in the olive oil and the salt. Work the ingredients until the dough becomes smooth and elastic. Cover with plastic wrap and let rest for at least 30 minutes.

2 Prepare the filling. Prepare the herbs and the spinach, rinse carefully, drain, dry and cut into thin slices. Heat the butter in a pan, add the herbs and the spinach and cook for 3-4 minutes, stirring often, until the water is boiled off. Remove from heat, let cool and transfer into a bowl.

3 Remove the crust from the cheese and dice the cheese; then dice the pancetta and brown in a non-stick pan and drain on paper towels. To the herbs in the bowl, add the eggs, the browned pancetta, the diced cheese, the nutmeg, a pinch of salt and pepper and mix the ingredients thoroughly.

4 On a lightly floured cloth, roll out the pasta dough into a sheet a little less than 1/8 inch thick. Spread the filling on the sheet in one uniform layer, leaving about 1 inch free around the edges. Using the cloth, roll the pasta into a log and wrap with the cloth; close the ends with kitchen needles or strong rubber bands.

5 Cook the roll (wrapped in the cloth) in abundant boiling salted water for about 35 minutes. In a skillet, melt the butter and cook the sage leaves. When the pasta roll is cooked, drain, remove the cloth and cut the roll into slices; arrange on a serving plate. Drizzle with the melted butter and sprinkle with the grated grana cheese. Serve at once.

Tortelli with pork, sausage, and salami

Difficulty **medium** • *Time needed* **over an hour** • *Calories per serving* **550**

INGREDIENTS
serves 4

For the pasta
UNBLEACHED FLOUR *3 cups*
EGGS *4*
EXTRA VIRGIN OLIVE OIL *1 tablespoon*
SALT *to taste*

For the filling
GROUND LEAN PORK *8 oz*
MILD SAUSAGE *3 oz*
SALAMI *3 oz, in 1 piece*
EGGS *1*
GRATED PECORINO *3 tablespoons*
EXTRA VIRGIN OLIVE OIL *1 tablespoon*

For the sauce
TOMATOES *1 lb, ripe and firm*
CARROTS *1*
CELERY *1 stalk*
ONIONS *1*
BASIL *1 bunch*
GRATED PECORINO *2 tablespoons*
EXTRA VIRGIN OLIVE OIL *4 tablespoons*
SALT & PEPPER *to taste*

1 Prepare the pasta dough. Sift the flour into a mound on the work surface; make a well in the center; break the 3 eggs into it, pour in the olive oil and the salt. Work the ingredients until the dough becomes smooth and elastic. Cover with plastic wrap and let rest for 30 minutes.

2 Meanwhile, prepare the filling. Peel the sausage and chop it up along with the salami. In a non-stick pan, heat the oil and brown the ground pork briefly, add the chopped salami and the sausage and continue to cook for 2-3 minutes on moderate heat; transfer into a mixing bowl and let cool. Put the egg into a small pot, cover with cold water, bring it to a boil and let it cook for about 9 minutes; drain, cool, immerse in cold water, shell and dice; add to the mixture of ground beef, sausage and salami; finally, add the grated parmigiano and mix until well blended.

3 Return to the pasta dough. Take the dough and roll it into a thin sheet. With an indented cutting wheel, cut into 12 squares about 3 1/2 inches across. Lightly beat the remaining egg and brush one half of each square with the egg; put a small heap of the prepared filling in the center of each square; fold over into a triangle and press the edges to seal the pasta; lay out the ravioli on the work surface sprinkled with flour and let dry.

4 In the meantime, prepare the sauce. Peel the onion; cut the ends of the carrot and peel; remove the large fibers from the celery; rinse the vegetables, dry them and chop finely; rinse the basil, dry and tear up finely. Scald the tomatoes in boiling water, drain, remove the skin, the seeds and the juice and dice, Heat the oil in a skillet and cook the onion, the celery and the carrot without browning; add the tomatoes, season with a pinch of salt and pepper and cook the sauce for 15 minutes; add the basil and cook another 5 minutes.

5 Cook the ravioli in abundant boiling salted water; when al dente, drain and toss with half of the tomato sauce. Place into a baking dish in layers covered with some of the remaining sauce and sprinkle each layer with a little grated pecorino; top with the last of the sauce. Bake in a preheated oven at 350°F for about 15 minutes. Serve at once.

Tortelletti with herbs

Difficulty **medium** • *Time needed* **over an hour** • *Calories per serving* **660**

INGREDIENTS
serves 4

For the pasta
UNBLEACHED FLOUR *3 cups*
EGGS *3*
SALT *a pinch*

For the filling
HERBS *1 1/2 lbs*
RICOTTA *7 oz*
BASIL *a bunch*
PARSLEY *1 bunch*
EGGS *1*
POWDERED CINNAMON *a pinch*
NUTMEG *a pinch*
GRATED GRANA CHEESE *2 tablespoons*
BUTTER *3 tablespoons*
SALT & PEPPER *to taste*

For the sauce
BASIL *a bunch*
PARSLEY *a bunch*
MARJORAM *a branch*
GRATED PARMIGIANO *3 tablespoons*
BUTTER *3 tablespoons*
SALT & PEPPER *to taste*

1 Prepare the filling. Clean the beet tops, rinse thoroughly, drain and dry. Heat the butter in a skillet and cook the beet tops for 3-4 minutes until the water is evaporated; then chop in a food processor. Transfer into a mixing bowl. Clean, drain, dry and chop the basil and the parsley and add to the bowl. Mix in the ricotta, the grated grana cheese, the egg, the cinnamon, the nutmeg, and a pinch of salt and pepper. Mix with a wooden spoon until well blended.

2 Sift the flour into a mound on the work surface; make a well in the center; break the 3 eggs into it, and add the salt. Work the ingredients until the dough becomes smooth and elastic. Form into a ball, cover with a dish towel and let rest for about 30 minutes.

3 Roll out the pasta into a very thin sheet; cut into squares and place a walnut size heap of filling in the center of each. Fold the squares into a triangle, press the edges well to seal the tortelletti, then fold over the long edges of the triangle and squeeze together. Lay them out on the flour sprinkled work surface and let dry.

4 In a pot with abundant boiling salted water, cook the tortelletti for 5-6 minutes. Clean, rinse, drain, dry and chop the basil, the parsley and the marjoram. In a small pan, melt the butter with the basil, parsley and marjoram. When al dente, drain the tortelletti, transfer to a serving plate and drizzle with the melted butter. Add a dash of salt and pepper. Serve sprinkled with grated parmigiano.

Tortelli with fontina in asparagus sauce

Difficulty **medium** • *Time needed* **under an hour** • *Calories per serving* **630**

INGREDIENTS
serves 4

FRESH EGG PASTA DOUGH *12 oz*

For the filling
FONTINA CHEESE *7 oz*
MILK *as needed*
CORN STARCH *1 tablespoon*
EGG YOLKS *3*
EGG WHITES *1*
SALT & WHITE PEPPER *to taste*

For the sauce
ASPARAGUS TIPS *8 oz*
SHALLOTS *1/2*
BUTTER *4 tablespoons*
SALT & PEPPER *to taste*

1 Remove the crust from the fontina, cut thinly, place into a bowl and cover completely with the milk, letting it soak for at least 1 hour; then drain and transfer to a double boiler; save three tablespoons of the milk for soaking to dissolve the corn starch in a small pot; add the dissolved corn starch to the fontina.

2 Add the egg yolks and whisk continually. The fontina will melt, first forming long strings, then becoming almost liquid and finally thickening.

3 Once the sauce is creamy, remove from the heat, add a pinch of freshly ground white pepper, stir and let cool. Roll out the dough gradually into very thin sheets. Lightly beat the egg white with a fork and brush half of each sheet.

4 On the brushed part of the sheet, lay out walnut size heaps of the creamy cheese filling spaced 1 1/2 inches apart and from the edges. Cover with the other half of the sheet, press around the filling heaps to seal the pasta and cut the tortelli with an indented rotary cutter.

5 Rinse the asparagus tips thoroughly and dry. Peel the shallot and chop. In a pot, heat the butter and cook the shallot without browning; add the asparagus tips and brown briefly, stirring with a wooden spoon.

6 Add 2 or 3 tablespoons of water, cover the pot, and continue cooking another 5 minutes over moderate heat; season with salt and pepper. Meanwhile bring to boil abundant water, add salt and cook the tortelli about 5 minutes. When al dente, drain, toss with the asparagus sauce and serve at once.

Tortelli with nettles

Difficulty **medium** • *Time needed* **under an hour** • *Calories per serving* **480**

INGREDIENTS
serves 4

For the pasta
UNBLEACHED FLOUR 5 *cups*
EGGS 4
SALT *a pinch*

For the filling
NETTLES 2 *lbs*
RICOTTA 8 *oz*
ONIONS 1
GARLIC 2 *cloves*
GRATED PARMIGIANO 4 *tablespoons*
EXTRA VIRGIN OLIVE OIL 3 *tablespoons*
SALT *to taste*

1 Prepare the filling: rinse the nettles in running water, protecting your hands with rubber gloves; drain well and boil in salted water for about 10 minutes. When done, drain well, wringing by hand, and chop very finely.

2 Peel onion and garlic and chop together; heat the olive oil in a casserole and cook the onion and garlic for 2-3 minutes, add the nettles and simmer for 5 minutes. In a bowl, mix the ricotta well with a wooden spoon, add the nettles and the parmigiano; mix thoroughly.

3 Prepare the pasta dough: sift the flour into a mound on the work surface; make a well in the center; break the eggs into it, and add the salt. Mix and work the ingredients about 15 minutes until the dough becomes firm and elastic. Roll out into a thin sheet.

4 On 1/2 of the sheet, lay out small heaps of filling 3 inches from one another, cover with the other sheet pressing around the filling and cut into squares. Cook the tortelli in boiling salted water for 8-10 minutes, drain, place in a serving plate; drizzle with melted butter and sprinkle with grated parmigiano or serve with a tomato or other vegetable sauce.

Tortelli with duck in vegetable sauce

Difficulty **medium** • *Time needed* **over an hour** • *Calories per serving* **600**

INGREDIENTS
serves 4

For the pasta
UNBLEACHED FLOUR *2 1/2 cups*
EGGS *2*
EGG WHITES *1*
SALT *a pinch*

For the filling
DUCK BREAST *8 oz*
FRESH SPINACH *11 oz*
ONIONS *1/2*
THYME *a sprig*
PARSLEY *1 bunch*
EGGS *1*
RED WINE *1/4 cup*
EXTRA VIRGIN OLIVE OIL *2 tablespoons*
SALT & PEPPER *to taste*

For the sauce
EGGPLANT *1, small*
ZUCCHINI *2*
STRING BEANS *7 oz*
SHELLED PEAS *5 oz*
CARROTS *1*
BASIL *1 bunch*
BUTTER *4 tablespoons*
SALT & PEPPER *to taste*

1 Sift the flour into a mound and make a well in the center; break the eggs in the middle and add a pinch of salt. Work the ingredients until the dough becomes smooth and elastic. Wrap in a dish towel and let rest for half an hour.

2 Make the filling: peel and chop the onion; heat the oil in a skillet and cook the onion until transparent; remove the skin from the duck breast and dice, then add to the onion; brown evenly, pour the red wine on and evaporate over high heat; remove from heat and let cool.

3 Rinse the spinach and wilt for 1 minute in a pan, chop finely. Clean and chop the parsley and the thyme. Place the meat, the spinach, the thyme, and the parsley in a mixing bowl. Add the egg, the salt and the pepper and mix the ingredients thoroughly.

4 Roll out the pasta into a thin sheet and cut into 2 1/2 inch squares. Whisk the egg white lightly and use to brush the edges of the squares. In the center of half of the squares place a little of the filling, cover with another square and press the edges to seal.

5 Clean and rinse the eggplant, the carrot, the zucchini and the string beans and dice or cut in julienne. Rinse, dry and tear the basil into small pieces. In a small skillet, melt the butter and add the carrot, the string beans, 1/14 cup of water, a dash of salt and fresh ground pepper; cook for 5 minutes, then add the peas; cook another 5 minutes, add the zucchini and the egg plant cooking for 5 more minutes; finally, sprinkle with the basil.

6 In a large pot, boil abundant water, add salt and cook the ravioli. When al dente, drain, transfer into a serving plate and toss with the sauce. Serve immediately.

Tortelli with vegetable ragù

Difficulty **easy** • *Time needed* **under an hour** • *Calories per serving* **700**

INGREDIENTS
serves 4

FRESH EGG PASTA DOUGH *12 oz*

For the filling
RICOTTA *7 oz*
POTATOES *11 oz*
SPINACH *1 1/4 lbs*
EGGS *1*
EGG YOLKS *2*
GRATED GRANA CHEESE *6 tablespoons*
BUTTER *3 tablespoons*
SALT & PEPPER *to taste*

For the sauce
ZUCCHINI *7 oz*
CARROTS *5 oz*
CELERY *1 stalk*
ONIONS *1*
GARLIC *1 clove*
BUTTER *3 tablespoons*
SALT & PEPPER *to taste*

1 Rinse the potatoes, put in a pot full of water, add salt, bring to a boil and cook for about 40 minutes. Drain, peel and strain through a potato masher. Clean the spinach, rinse thoroughly in cold water, drain and brown in a skillet with the butter; season with salt and pepper, boil off all the liquid, remove from heat and chop finely.

2 Put the spinach in a bowl, add the mashed potatoes, the ricotta, the grated grana cheese, the egg, the egg yolks, a pinch of salt and pepper and thoroughly mix the ingredients with a wooden spoon. Roll out the pasta into two thin sheets; on one lay out small amounts of the filling, evenly spaced, and cover with the other sheet, pressing well between the filling to seal the pasta; cut the tortelli into a shape you choose.

3 Let the tortelli rest on the work surface and prepare the zucchini and carrot sauce. Trim the zucchini and the carrot, peel the carrot, remove the large fibers from the celery. Rinse the vegetables, dry and dice; peel the onion, rinse and chop finely. Peel the garlic, rinse and dry.

4 Heat the butter in a pan and cook the chopped onion and the garlic without browning. Add the carrot and the celery and simmer for 3 minutes; add 5 tablespoons of water, season with salt and pepper and cook for 10 minutes on moderate heat. Add the zucchini and continue cooking 7-8 minutes; season with salt and pepper. In the meantime, boil abundant water, add salt and cook the tortelli; when al dente, drain, toss with the sauce and serve hot.

Tortelli with potatoes

Difficulty **easy** • *Time needed* **over an hour** • *Calories per serving* **910**

INGREDIENTS
serves 4

For the pasta
UNBLEACHED FLOUR *3 cups*
EGGS *3*

For the filling
POTATOES *1 1/4 lbs*
PANCETTA *4 oz*
RICOTTA *5 oz*
ONIONS *1*
GARLIC *3 cloves*
GRATED NUTMEG *1 pinch*
GRATED GRANA CHEESE *2 tablespoons*
EXTRA VIRGIN OLIVE OIL *3 tablespoons*
SALT & PEPPER *to taste*

For the sauce
GRATED GRANA CHEESE *4 tablespoons*
BUTTER *3 tablespoons*

1 To prepare the filling, cook the potatoes in salted water for about 40 minutes; peel, mash and put in a bowl. Peel the onion and the garlic and chop finely along with the pancetta.

2 In a skillet, heat the oil and brown the mixture, then add the mashed potatoes with the ricotta, the grana cheese, a dash of fresh ground pepper. and the nutmeg; mix the ingredients thoroughly with a wooden spoon.

3 On the work surface, make mound with the flour and break the egg into the center; mix the ingredients, then knead for 15 minutes until the dough is firm. Roll out into two thin sheets.

4 Place the filling in small heaps regularly spaced on one of the sheets and cover with the other; press around the heaps to seal, and cut the tortelli with a rotary cutter.

5 In a large pot, boil abundant water, add salt and drop in the tortelli; cook until al dente. Melt the butter in a pan. Drain the tortellini, drizzle with the melted butter and sprinkle with the grated grana cheese. Serve immediately.

SUGGESTION
To embellish the tortelli, add a chopped black truffle to the filling or sprinkle with shavings of white truffles just before serving.

Tortelli with ricotta

Difficulty **medium** • *Time needed* **over an hour** • *Calories per serving* **590**

INGREDIENTS
serves 4-6

For the pasta
UNBLEACHED FLOUR *4 cups*
EGGS *4*
SALT *to taste*

For the filling
RICOTTA *11 oz, very fresh*
SPINACH *1 1/4 lbs*
EGGS *2*
GRATED NUTMEG *a pinch*
GRATED GRANA CHEESE *6 tablespoons*
SALT *to taste*

For the sauce
HEAVY CREAM *1 cup*
GRATED GRANA CHEESE *4 tablespoons*
BUTTER *1 tablespoon*

1 To prepare the filling: clean the spinach, rinse and cook in little salted water for about 15 minutes from start of boiling; put the ricotta in a mixing bowl, and work with a fork until creamy.

2 When the spinach is cooked, drain well and chop finely; mix with the ricotta, season with salt and nutmeg, add the grated grana cheese and blend in the egg, mixing well.

3 To prepare the pasta: form a mound with the flour, put the eggs and the salt in the middle and mix well; knead vigorously for about 15 minutes until small bubbles form on the surface of the dough.

4 Roll out the dough into a sheet; on half of the sheet place walnut-sized heaps of filling at regular distance from one another and cover with the other half, pressing the dough well around the heaps; cut the tortelli with a rotary cutter.

5 Let the tortelli rest on a flour dusted surface for 2 hours. Cook the tortelli in abundant boiling salted water for 10-15 minutes. In the meantime, melt the butter in a small pot and blend in the cream.

6 When done, drain the tortelli, transfer to a serving plate, drizzle with the cream and sprinkle with the grana; serve at once, topping with a pinch of nutmeg.

Tortelli with trout

Difficulty **medium** • *Time needed* **under an hour** • *Calories per serving* **440**

INGREDIENTS
serves 4

FRESH EGG PASTA DOUGH *12 oz*
SALT *to taste*

For the filling
TROUT FILLETS *11 oz*
PARSLEY *1 bunch*
SHALLOTS *1*
SPINACH *4 oz*
GARLIC *1/2 clove*
EGGS *1*
EGG WHITES *1*
EXTRA VIRGIN OLIVE OIL *4 tablespoons*
SALT & PEPPER *to taste*

For the sauce
ASSORTED SHELLFISH *3 lbs*
(clams, mussels, sea snails, razor clams, etc.)
TOMATOES *7 oz, ripe and firm*
PARSLEY *1 bunch*
GARLIC *1 clove*
DRY WHITE WINE *1/4 cup*
EXTRA VIRGIN OLIVE OIL *5 tablespoons*
SALT & PEPPER *to taste*

1 Prepare the filling. Trim and rinse the spinach in plenty of cold water; chop finely. Rinse the trout fillets and wipe dry. Peel the garlic; rinse and dry the parsley. Heat the oil in a skillet, add the garlic and the parsley. Put in the trout fillets and brown 2 minutes per side; drain and chop. Peel and chop the shallot and cook in the same pan until transparent.

2 Add the chopped spinach; mix with a wooden spoon and cook for a few minutes to draw off the liquid. Add the fish and mix again; remove from the heat and transfer into a mixing bowl. When the mixture has cooled, season with a pinch of salt and pepper, add the egg and mix the ingredients well.

3 Gradually roll out the pasta in 2 1/2 inch strips and lay out the filling in small heaps 2 1/2 inches apart. Lightly beat the egg white and brush on the strips which you lay on top of the filling; press well around the filling to seal the pasta and cut into tortelli.

4 Prepare the sauce. Peel, rinse and dry the garlic; rinse and dry the parsley and chop both separately. Clean the seafood, wash carefully, put in a wide skillet with the oil, pour the white wine on and add the garlic and a little parsley. Cover the pan over high heat, shaking it from time to time, so the shells will be completely open. Drain, separate the meat from the shells and set apart, eliminating the closed shells.

5 Pass the cooking liquid through a sieve and reduce over high heat. Scald the tomatoes in boiling water, drain, remove the skin, the seeds and the juice and dice the meat; add to the reduced liquid and mix in the shellfish meat. Briefly cook on high heat; remove from heat and sprinkle with the remaining parsley and some fresh ground pepper. Cook the tortellini in abundant boiling salted water, drain when al dente and pour the sauce over the tortellini just before serving.

Tortelli with pumpkin

Difficulty **medium** • *Time needed* **over an hour** • *Calories per serving* **700**

INGREDIENTS
serves 4

For the pasta
UNBLEACHED FLOUR *4 cups*
EGGS *4*
SALT *a pinch*

For the filling
PUMPKIN *3 lbs*
SWEET RELISH *4 oz*
AMARETTI *4 oz, ground*
LEMON *1/2, grated peel*
EGG YOLKS *2*
GRATED NUTMEG *1/2 teaspoon*
BREAD CRUMBS *4 oz*
GRATED PARMIGIANO *6 tablespoons*
SALT *to taste*

For the sauce
GRATED PARMIGIANO *4 tablespoons*
BUTTER *4 tablespoons*

1 Rinse, dry, clean out the seeds and the central fibers and cut the pumpkin into thick slices; bake in a very hot oven 450°F for about an hour. When ready, take out of the oven, remove the skin, dice the pulp and pass through a vegetable strainer.

2 Transfer into a mixing bowl, add the relish, the egg yolks, the ground macaroons, the salt and the nutmeg. Thoroughly mix with a wooden spoon and let rest in a cool place for at least 3 hours (preferably for a whole day).

3 In the meantime, prepare the pasta dough: on the work surface, form a mound with the flour, add the eggs and the salt and knead until the dough becomes smooth and elastic. Roll the dough into a thin sheet and divide into two equal rectangular parts. On one, arrange small heaps of filling about 2 inches apart. Cover with the other sheet and press well around the filling to seal. With a pasta cutting wheel, cut the tortelli into the desired shapes.

4 In an ample pot, bring abundant water to boiling and salt lightly. Drop in the tortelli, stir and let cook for 7-8 minutes. When ready, drain with a perforated ladle.

5 Arrange the tortelli in a soup terrine in layers, alternately drizzling with melted butter and parmigiano, topping with the cheese. Cover the terrine and place in a preheated oven. Turn off the heat and leave terrine in oven for 10 minutes. Serve at once.

Tortelli with squash

Difficulty **medium** • *Time needed* **over an hour** • *Calories per serving* **600**

INGREDIENTS
serves 4

FRESH EGG PASTA DOUGH *11 oz*
EGG WHITE *1*

For the filling
SQUASH *1 lb*
AMARETTI *3-4*
EGGS *1*
NUTMEG *a pinch*
GRATED GRANA CHEESE *7 tablespoons*
SALT & PEPPER *to taste*

For the sauce
SAGE *3 leaves*
GRATED GRANA CHEESE *3 tablespoons*
BUTTER *4 tablespoons*

1 Cut the squash into 1 inch thick slices, arrange in a baking dish and bake in a preheated oven at 450°F for about 30 minutes. Remove from the oven, let cool completely, then pass through a potato masher.

2 Transfer the mashed squash to a mixing bowl, add the grated parmigiano, the ground macaroons, an egg, a pinch of nutmeg, a dash of salt and pepper. Mix thoroughly working the ingredients vigorously with a wooden spoon.

3 Roll out the pasta dough into a very thin sheet; then, with a pasta cutter, cut into 2 inch squares. Beat the egg white lightly and brush the edges of the squares; in the center of each, place a little of the mashed squash, fold the square into a triangle and press the edges well together.

4 Cook the tortelli in a pot of abundant boiling salted water for 5-7 minutes; when al dente, drain and transfer to a serving plate. Melt the butter with the sage leaves in a small pan and drizzle over the tortelli, finally sprinkling with the grated grana cheese. Serve at once.

Tortellini regali

Difficulty **easy** • *Time needed* **less than 30 minutes** • *Calories per serving* **520**

INGREDIENTS
serves 4

TORTELLINI *1 lb*
RICOTTA *7 oz*
PROSCIUTTO *2 oz, in 1 piece*
PARSLEY *1 bunch (optional)*
NUTMEG *to taste*
HEAVY CREAM *1/4 cup*
GRATED PARMIGIANO *4 tablespoons*
BUTTER *1 large dab*
SALT & PEPPER *to taste*

1 Mash the ricotta for several minutes in a mixing bowl with a wooden spoon, add the cream and blend well; mix again a little to incorporate the parmigiano, add a generous dash of grated nutmeg and season with a pinch of salt and a dash of ground pepper. Cut the prosciutto in julienne, heat in a pan with the butter, add the ricotta mixture and keep it hot.

2 Heat the oven to 350°F. In a large pot, boil abundant water, add salt and drop in the tortellini; cook until al dente; drain well and transfer into a lightly buttered baking dish.

3 Pour the prepared sauce over the tortellini; if you wish, sprinkle with cleaned and chopped parsley and mix uniformly with the ingredients. Pass the baking dish into the oven for 4-5 minutes, or until the top is golden (au gratin). Remove from oven and serve right in the cooking dish.

SUGGESTION

If dry tortellini are used, one method to keep them from breaking up is to soak them for a few minutes in cold water, then transfer them to a pot with lukewarm water and then bring to a boil: after this, transfer into another pot with already boiling salted water and cook until done.

Tortelloni Calabresi

Difficulty **medium** • *Time needed* **under an hour** • *Calories per serving* **750**

INGREDIENTS
serves 4

FRESH EGG PASTA DOUGH *12 oz*
EGGS *1*
SALT *to taste*

For the filling
MILD SAUSAGE *5 oz*
FRESH CACIOCAVALLO CHEESE *5 oz*
GRATED PECORINO *4 tablespoons*
EGGS *2*
SALT & PEPPER *to taste*

For the sauce
GROUND BEEF *5 oz*
GROUND PORK *5 oz*
TOMATOES *1 lb, ripe and firm*
PARSLEY *1 bunch*
BASIL *1 bunch*
GARLIC *1 clove*
EGGS *2*
GRATED GRANA CHEESE *4 tablespoons*
EXTRA VIRGIN OLIVE OIL *3 tablespoons*
PEANUT OIL *enough for frying*
SALT & PEPPER *to taste*

1 Prepare the filling. Place an egg in a small pot, cover with cold water, bring to a boil and cook for about 8 minutes; drain, let cool, then shell and chop coarsely. Remove skin and dice the caciocavallo; remove the skin and dice the sausage. In a mixing bowl, put in the diced caciocavallo and the sausage, add the chopped egg, the raw egg, the grated pecorino and season with pinch of salt and a dash of fresh ground pepper; mix the ingredients with a wooden spoon until well blended.

2 Prepare the tortelloni. Gradually roll out the pasta dough into a thin sheet; lightly beat one egg with a fork and brush half the sheet of dough with it; with a teaspoon, arrange the filling in regularly spaced small heaps on the prepared half; cover with the other half sheet and press firmly around the heaps of filling to seal the pasta; cut the tortelloni with an indented oval pasta cutter. Place them on a floured work surface so they do not touch each other.

3 Prepare the sauce. Scald the tomatoes in boiling water, drain, remove the skin, the seeds and the juice and chop. Peel the garlic, and crush; rinse the basil and the parsley, gently dry with a dish towel and chop them separately. Heat the oil in a casserole and cook the garlic without browning; add the chopped tomatoes, a dash of salt and pepper and cook for about 10-12 minutes over moderate heat.

4 Meanwhile, put the ground beef and the ground pork in a bowl, add the grated parmigiano, the chopped parsley, the eggs and a pinch of salt and pepper; mix the ingredients with a wooden spoon until well blended. Form little meatballs about the size of a walnut and fry in abundant hot peanut oil; drain over absorbent paper towels, transfer to the tomato sauce, add the basil and cook for about 5 minutes.

5 In a pot, boil abundant water, add salt and cook the tortelloni; when al dente, drain and mix with the tomato and meatball sauce. Serve hot, sprinkled with as much grana as you like.

Tortelloni with leeks and beans

Difficulty **medium** • *Time needed* **over an hour** • *Calories per serving* **700**

INGREDIENTS
serves 4

FRESH EGG PASTA DOUGH *11 oz*
LEEKS *2*
DRIED BORLOTTI BEANS *7 oz*
BABY CHARD *4 oz*
RICOTTA *7 oz*
ROSEMARY *1 branch*
BAY LEAVES *1*
SAGE *3 leaves*
GARLIC *1 clove*
EGGS *1*
EGG WHITES *1*
HEAVY CREAM *1/4 cup*
GRATED GRANA CHEESE *4 tablespoons*
BUTTER *2 tablespoons*
SALT & PEPPER *to taste*

1 Soak the beans in water for 12 hours; drain, rinse and place in a pot. Cover with water, add the bay leaf, the sage, the garlic clove and the rosemary; salt and bring to a boil. Cook for an hour on moderate heat, then drain and pass in a vegetable mill into a mixing bowl. Clean the chard and cut in julienne. Clean and chop the white of the leeks; brown with the butter in a pan together with the chard for 8-10 minutes and season with salt and pepper. Add 4 tablespoons of the bean purée and cook off the liquid over moderate heat, then remove from heat and let cool. Mash the ricotta in a bowl with a wooden spoon, add a tablespoon of parmigiano, the mixture of leeks and beans, the egg and the salt and pepper.

2 Roll the pasta into a thin sheet and cut into strips 4 inches wide. Brush the edges with the egg white; on half of each strip, place little mounds of filling equidistantly spaced, fold over the other half, press firmly around the filling to seal, and cut the tortelloni with an indented rotary cutter. Put the remaining bean purée in a pot, add the cream, season with salt and pepper and bring to a boil, stirring until dense and creamy. In another pot, boil abundant water, add salt and cook the tortelloni. When al dente, drain and add the sauce, transfer to a baking dish and sprinkle with the remaining parmigiano. Bake at 415°F until golden. Serve at once.

SUGGESTION
If you wish to lighten the sauce for these rich tortellini, you can replace the bean sauce with melted butter and sage, or with roast pan juices.

Tortelli with ricotta and thyme

Difficulty **medium** • *Time needed* **over an hour** • *Calories per serving* **500**

INGREDIENTS
serves 4

For the pasta
UNBLEACHED FLOUR *3 cups*
SPINACH *7 oz*
EGGS *2*
CORN OIL *1 teaspoon*
SALT *a pinch*

For the filling
RICOTTA *7 oz*
THYME *1 sprig*
BABY CHARD *11 oz*
EGG YOLKS *1*
NUTMEG *a pinch*
GRATED GRANA CHEESE *6 tablespoons*
SALT & PEPPER *to taste*

1 Thoroughly rinse the spinach in abundant cold water and wilt in very little boiling salted water for about 2 minutes; drain thoroughly, dry with a dish towel and chop finely. Sift the flower on a work surface, break the eggs in the middle of the flour, add the spinach, the oil and the salt. Mix the ingredients and knead until the dough becomes smooth and elastic.

2 Cover the dough with a towel and let rest in a cool place for about 30 minutes. Meantime, cut the stems of the chard, rinse and cook for 4 minutes in boiling salted water; drain well and chop finely.

3 Transfer the chopped chard to a bowl and add the ricotta, the chopped thyme, the grated parmigiano, the egg yolk, a dash of salt and pepper, and the nutmeg; mix the ingredients well. Roll out the pasta dough into a very thin sheet and cut into 2 inch squares.

4 In the center of each square, place a small teaspoon of filling. Fold the squares over to form triangles; press the edges firmly, bring the two exterior ends together and squeeze together to form the tortelli. Cook in abundant salted water for 5-6 minutes. When al dente, drain and serve with a sauce of your choice.

Baked pasta

Green pepper cannelloni

Difficulty **difficult** • *Time needed* **over an hour** • *Calories per serving* **550**

INGREDIENTS
serves 4

CANNELLONI *12*

For the filling
GREEN PEPPERS *2*
GROUND BEEF *7 oz*
GROUND PORK LOIN *2 oz*
BREAD CRUMBS *1 oz*
MILK *1/2 cup*
GARLIC *1 clove*
ONIONS *1*
RED WINE *1/4 cup*
EGGS *1*
GRATED GRANA CHEESE *3 tablespoons*
NUTMEG *a pinch*
EXTRA VIRGIN OLIVE OIL *3 tablespoons*
SALT & PEPPER *to taste*

For the sauce
TOMATOES *11 oz*
ONIONS *1/2*
BASIL *a few leaves*
SAGE *1 leaf*
MARJORAM *1 branch*
EXTRA VIRGIN OLIVE OIL *2 tablespoons*
SALT & PEPPER *to taste*

1 Prepare the filling. Place the dry bread crumbs in a bowl and moisten with the milk. Chop the garlic and the onion; cut the pepper into strips. In a saucepan, heat the olive oil. Cook half the garlic and onion until transparent. Add the pepper and sauté for a minute. Salt, pepper, lower the heat and cook for 20 minutes. Put mixture in a blender, setting aside a few strips of pepper. In another saucepan, cook the remaining garlic and onion until transparent. Add the ground beef and pork; cook on low heat for thirty minutes. Add the wine and let evaporate on high heat. Set aside to cool.

2 In the meantime, in abundant salted water cook the cannelloni al dente; drain, pass under cold water, drain again well and lay on a dry clean towel. In a large mixing bowl, add meat, pepper mixture, crumbs, egg, grana cheese, nutmeg and salt; mix until well blended. Put filling in a pastry bag and stuff the cannelloni. Preheat the oven to 375°F.

3 Prepare the sauce. Rinse and chop the onion. Scald tomatoes in boiling water, drain, peel, press to remove seeds and coarsely chop. In a skillet, heat olive oil; add onion, half the basil, sage, marjoram; cook until the onion is transparent. Add the tomatoes, salt, pepper and cook for ten minutes, reducing the sauce. Remove from heat. Pass through the food mill. Return to skillet to heat. Chop the remaining basil and add it to the sauce. Distribute half the sauce on the bottom of a baking dish; carefully place the cannelloni on top of the sauce. Pour the remaining sauce over and garnish with the remaining strips of peppers. Cover with aluminum foil and cook in oven for 30 minutes. Five minutes before the end of cooking time, remove the aluminum foil and cook au gratin. Serve very hot.

SUGGESTION
To make these tasty cannelloni easier to digest, you can peel the peppers before using them. This can be done by lightly roasting them on a low flame, or scalding them in boiling water before peeling.

Cannelloni with sausage and beef

Difficulty **medium** • *Time needed* **over an hour** • *Calories per serving* **790**

INGREDIENTS
serves 4

FRESH PASTA SQUARES 8
PEANUT OIL *2 tablespoons*

For the filling
MILD SAUSAGE *7 oz*
GROUND BEEF *7 oz*
ONIONS *1/2*
GARLIC *1 clove*
ROSEMARY *1 branch*
SAGE *4 small leaves*
DRY WHITE WINE *1/4 cup*
WHITE FLOUR *1 tablespoon*
HEAVY CREAM *2 tablespoons*
EGGS *2*
GRATED PARMIGIANO *4 tablespoons*
EXTRA VIRGIN OLIVE OIL *3 tablespoons*
SALT & PEPPER *to taste*

For the sauce
PEELED TOMATOES *1 lb*
ONIONS *1*
BASIL *6 small leaves*
MOZZARELLA *1*
EXTRA VIRGIN OLIVE OIL *3 tablespoons*
SALT & PEPPER *to taste*

1 In abundant salted water, cook the squares of pasta, adding peanut oil. Drain pasta with a slotted spoon and cool on a dry clean towel. Turn on the oven at 375°F.

2 Prepare the filling. Peel the onion and the clove of garlic, rinse them, chop them, put them in a saucepan with the olive oil and cook until onion is transparent. Peel and crumble sausage; add sausage and ground beef to saucepan; brown and season with salt and fresh ground pepper

3 Add the chopped rosemary and sage; mix well. Add white wine and let evaporate on high heat. Lower heat and add the flour through a sifter; mix well. Add heavy cream and cook for 10 minutes, mixing from time to time with a wooden spoon.

4 Turn off the heat. Blend preparation a mixer. Pour in a serving bowl. Add the eggs and the parmigiano, mix well with a wooden spoon. Set aside to cool.

5 Put a long dab of the prepared filling on each square of pasta; roll them pressing edges together. Lightly oil a low oven dish and place the cannelloni next to one another.

6 Prepare the sauce. Peel and chop the onion. In a skillet heat olive oil and cook onion until transparent. Add tomatoes, a pinch of salt and fresh ground pepper. On medium heat, cook sauce for 15 minutes. Add the crumbled basil.

7 Pour sauce over the cannelloni; sprinkle with diced mozzarella and cook in oven at 415°F for 15 minutes. Serve in the oven dish.

Cannelloni all'aretina

Difficulty **medium** • *Time needed* **over an hour** • *Calories per serving* **640**

INGREDIENTS
serves 4

For the pasta
UNBLEACHED FLOUR *5 oz*
EGGS *1*
PEANUT OIL *2 tablespoons*
SALT *to taste*

For the filling
GROUND BEEF *14 oz*
RICOTTA *4 oz*
MOZZARELLA *5 oz*
ONIONS *1*
BASIL *one bunch*
RED WINE *1/4 cup*
NUTMEG *a pinch*
EXTRA VIRGIN OLIVE OIL *4 tablespoons*
SALT & PEPPER *to taste*

For the sauce
TOMATOES *14 oz, ripe and firm*
ONIONS

BASIL *one bunch*
EXTRA VIRGIN OLIVE OIL *5 tablespoons*
SALT & PEPPER *to taste*

1 Prepare the pasta. Sift the white flour on a pastry board into a mound. Make a well in the middle; add the eggs and a large pinch of salt. Work the ingredients thoroughly adding warm water if needed, until the dough is smooth and elastic. Cover with plastic and set aside for 30 minutes. Roll pasta dough until very fine; using an indented pastry wheel, make 8 rectangles 3 by 4 inches (or 8 ovals). Cook a few at a time in abundant salted water, adding the peanut oil; drain, pass under cold water, drain again well and lay on a clean kitchen towel.

2 Prepare the filling. Peel, rinse, dry and finely chop onion. Rinse, dry delicately with a clean towel and chop basil. Heat olive oil in a skillet and cook onion until transparent; add ground beef; pour red wine and let evaporate on high heat. Season with salt, pepper and nutmeg; cook on moderate heat for 20-

30 minutes, mixing from time to time with a wooden spoon. Once cooking is done, put the meat in a mixing bowl and set aside to cool. Add ricotta, 3 oz of diced mozzarella, chopped basil, salt and pepper. Mix well until you obtain a homogeneous mixture.

3 Prepare the tomato sauce. Scald tomatoes in boiling water, drain, peel, press to remove seeds and chop. Rinse, dry delicately and chop basil. Peel, rinse, dry and finely chop onion. Heat 4 tablespoons of olive oil in saucepan and cook onion with some basil until onion is transparent; add tomatoes and the remaining basil.

4 Prepare the cannelloni. Place some filling in the center of each rectangle of pasta and fold them like cannelloni, pressing edges. Brush a baking dish with oil; place the cannelloni in the dish; pour some tomato sauce over; add remaining diced mozzarella. Cook in preheated oven at 415°F for approximately 15 minutes. Serve hot with tomato sauce and remaining chopped basil.

Cannelloni with ricotta

Difficulty **medium** • *Time needed* **over an hour** • *Calories per serving* **810**

INGREDIENTS
serves 4

FRESH PASTA SQUARES *12*
GRATED PARMIGIANO *2 tablespoons*
BUTTER *2 tablespoons*
PEANUT OIL *2 tablespoons*

For the filling
RICOTTA *11 oz*
BEET GREENS *14 oz*
BASIL *1 bunch*
EGGS *1*
GRATED PARMIGIANO *2 tablespoons*
NUTMEG *a pinch*
SALT & PEPPER *to taste*

For the béchamel
WHITE FLOUR *1/2 cup*
MILK *2 cups*
NUTMEG *a pinch*
BUTTER *3 tablespoons*
SALT & PEPPER *to taste*

1 In abundant salted water cook the squares of pasta al dente, adding peanut oil. With the help of a slotted spoon, drain and pass under cold water; drain well and dry on a dish towel.

2 In the meantime, prepare the filling. Trim and rinse the beet greens; put in a skillet and boil with a little lightly salted water. When cooked, drain well and chop them with basil.

3 Put the mixture in a mixing bowl. Add ricotta, egg, grated parmigiano, a pinch of salt, fresh ground pepper and nutmeg.

4 Prepare the béchamel. In a saucepan, melt the butter. Add the flour and, mixing with a wooden spoon, brown; add the cold milk, and always mixing, cook for approximately 10 minutes. Remove from heat. Season with salt, fresh ground pepper and some nutmeg.

5 With a pastry bag or a spoon, spread the filling on the squares of pasta, fold them by pressing the edges. When ready, lay them in a baking dish brushed with oil or butter.

6 With the béchamel still warm, cover the cannelloni, sprinkle with parmigiano and dabs of butter. Cook in a preheated oven at 415°F for approximately 20 minutes. Serve hot.

Cannelloni alla sorrentina

*Difficulty **medium*** • *Time needed **over an hour*** • *Calories per serving **830***

INGREDIENTS
serves 4

FRESH EGG PASTA DOUGH *12 oz*
BUTTER *1 tablespoon*
PEANUT OIL *2 tablespoons*
SALT *to taste*

For the filling
MOZZARELLA *4 oz*
RICOTTA *11 oz*
PANCETTA *4 oz, in 1 piece*
PARSLEY *one bunch*
EGGS *2*
GRATED GRANA CHEESE *4 tablespoons*
SALT & PEPPER *to taste*

For the sauce
PORK *4 oz*
BEEF *4 oz*
LAMB *4 oz*
TOMATOES *14 oz, ripe and firm*
PARSLEY *one bunch*
CARROTS *1*
CELERY *1 stalk*
ONIONS *1/2*
HOT CHILI PEPPER *1*
RED WINE *1/4 cup*
EXTRA VIRGIN OLIVE OIL *3 tablespoons*
SALT *to taste*

1 Prepare the sauce. Scald tomatoes in boiling water, drain, peel, press to remove seeds and chop. Put the beef, pork and lamb in a grinder. Rinse parsley, delicately dry with a dish towel and finely chop. Cut off ends of the carrot and peel. Remove large filaments from celery stalk. Peel onion. Rinse, dry and finely chop all vegetables.

2 In a skillet heat olive oil. Cook celery, onion, carrot and hot red pepper, until onion is just transparent. Add the ground meat and brown on high heat until all cooked. Add 1/4 cup of red wine and evaporate on high heat. Add chopped tomatoes, chopped parsley. Salt. Cook covered on moderate heat for approximately one hour.

3 In the meantime, prepare the filling. Chop the pancetta and brown in a nonstick saucepan, mixing with a wooden spoon. Drain and set aside. Rinse parsley, dry delicately with a dish towel and chop. Dice the mozzarella and drain in a colander for approximately 15 minutes.

4 In a mixing bowl, work the ricotta with eggs, salt and pepper. Add the pancetta, mozzarella dice, parsley and grana cheese. Mix with a wooden spoon until all ingredients are well incorporated.

5 Prepare the cannelloni. Spread the pasta dough and cut rectangles 4 inches long and 3 inches wide. Cook a few at a time in abundant salted water, adding olive oil. Drain, pass under cold water rapidly, drain well and lay on a dish towel. Put some mixture in each rectangle of pasta and fold, forming cannelloni. Place them in a buttered baking dish and pour the sauce over. Cook in preheated oven at 375°F for 15-20 minutes. Serve hot.

Cannelloni with wild herbs

Difficulty **difficult** • *Time needed* **over an hour** • *Calories per serving* **610 circa**

INGREDIENTS
serves 4

For the pasta
UNBLEACHED FLOUR *3 cups*
EGGS *2*
PEANUT OIL *2 tablespoons*
SALT *to taste*

For the filling
WILD HERBS *7 oz*
(wild chicory, watercress, etc.)
BORAGE *7 oz*
BEET GREENS *11 oz*
RICOTTA *4 oz*
ONIONS *1/2*
MARJORAM *one bunch*
GRATED GRANA CHEESE *3 tablespoons*
EGGS *1 (optional)*
EXTRA VIRGIN OLIVE OIL *2 tablespoons*
SALT & PEPPER *to taste*

For the sauce
BECHAMEL *1 1/2 cups*
GRATED GRANA CHEESE *2 tablespoons*
SALT & PEPPER *to taste*

1 Prepare the pasta: Sift flour on a pastry board into a mound. Make a well in the middle; add eggs, a large pinch of salt and 3 or 4 tablespoons of warm water if needed. Work the ingredients thoroughly until you obtain a firm and elastic dough. Cover with a humid dish towel and set aside for approximately 30 minutes.

2 In the meantime, prepare the filling. Clean the herbs, the borage and the beet greens; rinse and brown for 2 minutes in abundant salted water; drain and finely chop. Peel and chop onion. In a skillet, heat olive oil; cook onion until transparent.

3 Add the chopped marjoram and the herbs. Brown for 2 minutes, mixing from time to time with a wooden spoon.

Place mixture in a bowl. Add ricotta, grana cheese, egg, salt and pepper; mix all ingredients until all incorporated.

4 Roll pasta dough very thin and divide it into 3 by 4 inch rectangles. In abundant salted water, cook a few at a time, adding peanut oil. Drain and place on a dish towel.

5 Put the herb mixture in a pastry bag and form long dabs on the rectangles of pasta; fold to make the cannelloni. Carefully set on an oiled oven dish.

6 Pour the béchamel over the cannelloni; sprinkle with grana cheese and a few leaves of marjoram. Cook in preheated oven at 415°F for 15 minutes. Serve hot.

Cannelloni with fish

Difficulty **medium** • *Time needed* **over an hour** • *Calories per serving* **630 circa**

INGREDIENTS
serves 4

CANNELLONI *12*

For the filling
FRESH FISH FILLETS *14 oz*
RICOTTA *7 oz*
BAY LEAVES *2*
EGGS *1*
GARLIC *2 cloves*
PARSLEY *1 bunch*
NUTMEG *to taste*
EXTRA VIRGIN OLIVE OIL *5-6 tablespoons*
SALT & PEPPER *to taste*

For the sauce
PEELED TOMATOES *14 oz*
ONIONS *1*
BREAD CRUMBS *2 tablespoons*
BUTTER *2 teaspoons*
EXTRA VIRGIN OLIVE OIL *4 tablespoons*
SALT & PEPPER *to taste*

1 Prepare the sauce. Peel onion and finely chop. In a skillet, heat 3 or 4 tablespoons of olive oil and cook the onion until transparent. Add tomatoes. Mix well, season with salt and pepper, cover and cook on low flame for approximately 15 minutes.

2 In the meantime, in a saucepan cook the fish with the bay leaf and little, lightly salted water. Drain fish. Chop it and transfer it to a mixing bowl. Beat the egg with a little salt and add to the mixture with the ricotta, some nutmeg and the finely chopped garlic. Mix well adding the chopped parsley.

3 Boil the cannelloni in abundant salted water, adding a tablespoon of oil (to avoid sticking). Drain, place on a dish towel and let cool.

4 Fill the cannelloni, one at a time, with the fish mixture and place them in a rectangular oiled baking dish. Pour tomato sauce over, spreading it well on the cannelloni.

5 Sprinkle with bread crumbs and dabs of butter; put in oven at 395°F until the top is cooked au gratin. Serve hot, and if you wish, sprinkle with fresh ground pepper.

Cannelloni filled with tofu

Difficulty **medium** • *Time needed* **over an hour** • *Calories per serving* **920**

INGREDIENTS
serves 4

For the pasta
UNBLEACHED FLOUR *4 cups*
EGGS *4*
PEANUT OIL *2 tablespoons*
SALT *to taste*

For the filling
TOFU *1 1/4 lbs*
GRATED CACIOCAVALLO CHEESE *7 oz*
PINE NUTS *4 oz*
RAISINS *4 oz*
NUTMEG *a pinch*
VEGETABLE BROTH *1/2 cup*
SESAME SEED OIL *to taste*

1 Sift the flour on work surface into a mound. Make a well in the middle; add a pinch of salt and the eggs. Add some warm water, if needed, and work the ingredients thoroughly until you obtain a firm and elastic dough. With a rolling pin, roll the pasta dough thinly and make 3 x 4 inch rectangles.

2 In two pots, cook a few rectangles of pasta in abundant salted water, adding 2 tablespoons of peanut oil; drain and set aside. In the meantime, prepare the filling. Finely chop the tofu. Soak pine nuts and raisins in lukewarm water; drain. In a saucepan add tofu, half the caciocavallo cheese, some nutmeg, pine nuts and raisins.

3 Cook, adding some sesame oil. Let cool and add the remaining caciocavallo cheese. Place some filling on each rectangle of pasta and fold, making cannelloni. Set them in an oiled oven dish, moisten with the broth and cook in oven at 375°F for approximately 20 minutes. If necessary, add more broth. Serve hot.

Cannelloni with ricotta and fontina cheese

Difficulty **medium** • *Time needed* **over an hour** • *Calories per serving* **900**

INGREDIENTS
serves 4

For the pasta
UNBLEACHED FLOUR *3 cups*
EGGS *3*
EXTRA VIRGIN OLIVE OIL *3 tablespoons*
SALT *to taste*

For the filling
RICOTTA *8 oz*
FONTINA CHEESE *7 oz*
EGGS *1*
EGG YOLKS *1*
PARSLEY *1 bunch*
NUTMEG *a pinch*
GRATED PARMIGIANO *2 tablespoons*
SALT & PEPPER *to taste*

For the sauce
PEELED TOMATOES *1 lb*
GARLIC *1 clove*
THYME *1 branch, or marjoram*
GRATED PARMIGIANO *4 tablespoons*
BUTTER *1 tablespoon*
EXTRA VIRGIN OLIVE OIL *3 tablespoons*
SALT & PEPPER *to taste*

1 Prepare the pasta. Sift the flour on a pastry board into a mound. Make a well in the middle; add a dash of salt, the eggs and a tablespoon of olive oil. Work the ingredients thoroughly until you obtain a firm and elastic dough. Make a ball with dough. Place in aluminum foil and place in a cool environment (not in the refrigerator) for 30 minutes.

2 In the meantime, prepare the filling. Remove crust from the fontina cheese, grate and place in mixing bowl. Add ricotta, grated parmigiano, the egg, egg yolk, the finely chopped parsley, some salt, fresh ground pepper and nutmeg. Mix well with a wooden spoon until all ingredients are incorporated.

3 In a saucepan, heat olive oil. Add peeled garlic clove and brown for a few minutes. Remove clove; add tomatoes, thyme, some salt, fresh ground pepper and let cook for approximately 15 minutes.

4 Roll the pasta dough thinly, then with a sharp knife make 4 inch squares. In a large pot, cook in abundant salted water, adding olive oil for 2-3 minutes. When cooked, drain, pass under cold water and lay on a towel to dry. Place filling on the squares of pasta and fold, forming cannelloni.

5 In a buttered baking dish, place some tomato sauce, then the cannelloni and cover with remaining sauce; sprinkle with parmigiano and dabs of butter. Cook in preheated oven at 415°F for approximately 15 minutes. Serve hot.

Cannelloni with trout and peppers

Difficulty **medium** • *Time needed* **over an hour** • *Calories per serving* **650**

INGREDIENTS
serves 4

For the pasta
UNBLEACHED FLOUR *3 cups*
EGGS *3*
PEANUT OIL *2 tablespoons*
SALT *to taste*

For the filling
TROUT FILLETS *14 oz*
RED PEPPER *1*
YELLOW PEPPER *1*
TOMATOES *3, ripe and firm*
PARSLEY *one bunch*
SHALLOTS *2*
EGGS *1*
HEAVY CREAM *4 tablespoons*
BUTTER *3 tablespoons*
EXTRA VIRGIN OLIVE OIL *4 tablespoons*
SALT & PEPPER *to taste*

1 Prepare the pasta. Sift the flour on a pastry board into a mound. Make a well in the middle; add a dash of salt and the eggs. Work the ingredients thoroughly until you obtain a firm and elastic dough, adding if needed two tablespoons of water. Wrap the dough in plastic and set aside for 30 minutes.

2 Roll the pasta dough thinly; make 8 rectangles 4 inches long by 3 inches wide. Cook for 2-3 minutes in abundant salted water, adding peanut oil. Drain, pass under cold water, let cool and lay on a dish towel.

3 In the meantime, prepare the filling. Scald tomatoes in boiling water, drain, peel, press to remove seeds and thinly slice. Rinse parsley, dry and finely chop; peel shallots, rinse and cut. Peel peppers, remove seeds, rinse, dry and cut in to strips. In a saucepan heat 2 tablespoons of olive oil. Cook the shallots until just transparent. Add pepper strips and cook for 2-3 minutes mixing with a wooden spoon. Add tomatoes, a dash of salt and pepper; cook for 8-10 minutes.

4 In the meantime, rinse the trout fillets, dry, add salt and pepper. Cook with remaining olive oil in a saucepan for 2-3 minutes on each side. Drain, chop and put in a mixing bowl. Add cold pepper mixture, egg, chopped parsley and mix until all ingredients are incorporated.

5 Place some filling in the center of each rectangle of pasta and fold, forming the cannelloni. Butter a baking dish, pour the heavy cream and place the cannelloni; butter top with a brush and cook in preheated oven at 375°F for 10-12 minutes. Serve hot.

Cannelloni filled with ham and mozzarella

Difficulty **medium** • *Time needed* **over an hour** • *Calories per serving* **730**

INGREDIENTS
serves 4

FRESH EGG PASTA DOUGH *12 oz*
PEANUT OIL *2 tablespoons*

For the filling
COOKED HAM *3 oz, in 1 piece*
MOZZARELLA *4 oz*
RICOTTA *11 oz*
BASIL *one bunch*
EGGS *2*
GRATED GRANA CHEESE *4 tablespoons*
BUTTER *1 tablespoon*
SALT & PEPPER *to taste*

For the sauce
TOMATOES *11 oz, ripe and firm*
ONION *1, large*
BASIL *one bunch*
THYME *1 branch*
EXTRA VIRGIN OLIVE OIL *3 tablespoons*
SALT & PEPPER *to taste*

1 Prepare the tomato sauce. Scald tomatoes in boiling water, drain, peel, press to remove seeds and chop. Peel onion, rinse, dry and finely chop. Clean basil and thyme, rinse, dry and chop.

2 In a saucepan, heat olive oil. Cook onion until just transparent. Add tomatoes, basil, thyme, a dash of salt, fresh ground pepper and cook for approximately 10-12 minutes on moderate heat.

3 In the meantime, prepare the filling. Chop ham and set aside. Clean the basil, rinse, dry and chop. Dice the mozzarella and drain for 15 minutes. In a mixing bowl, work ricotta with the eggs; add salt and fresh ground pepper. Add the mozzarella dice, ham, basil and 2 tablespoons of grated grana cheese. Mix with a wooden spoon until all ingredients are well incorporated. Roll pasta dough thinly and cut rectangles 4 inches long by 3 inches wide.

4 In abundant salted water, cook the pasta, a few at a time, adding peanut oil; drain, pass under cold water, drain well and lay on a dish towel. Put a little ricotta-ham filling in each rectangle and fold, forming the cannelloni. Place the cannelloni in a buttered baking dish and pour the tomato sauce over; sprinkle with remaining grated grana. Cook in preheated oven at 415°F for approximately 15 minutes.

Cannelloni with spinach and ricotta

Difficulty **medium** • *Time needed* **over an hour** • *Calories per serving* **610**

INGREDIENTS
serves 4

CANNELLONI *12 or 16*
PEANUT OIL *2 tablespoons*

For the filling
SPINACH *2 1/2 lbs*
RICOTTA *7 oz*
EGGS *1*
GRATED GRANA CHEESE *6 tablespoons*
EXTRA VIRGIN OLIVE OIL *3 tablespoons*
SALT & PEPPER *to taste*

For the sauce
TOMATO SAUCE *7 oz*
BASIL *a few leaves*
EXTRA VIRGIN OLIVE OIL *3 tablespoons*
SALT & PEPPER *to taste*

1 In abundant salted water, cook the cannelloni for approximately 20 minutes, adding peanut oil. Drain, pass under cold water, drain well and lay on a dish towel.

2 In the meantime, carefully peel spinach, rinse and place in a pan; boil, drain well, chop and transfer to a mixing bowl.

3 Add ricotta, whole egg, 3 tablespoons of grana cheese, a dash of salt and fresh ground pepper. Mix well and using a pastry bag, fill the cannelloni with mixture.

4 In a saucepan, heat some olive oil; add tomato sauce, basil leaves, salt and pepper. Cook for approximately 10 minutes. Oil a baking dish; place the cannelloni, pour the sauce over and sprinkle with remaining grana cheese and some olive oil. Cook in preheated oven for about 15 minutes and serve hot.

Cannelloni filled with asparagus and eggs

Difficulty **medium** • *Time needed* **under an hour** • *Calories per serving* **700**

INGREDIENTS
serves 4

For the pasta
UNBLEACHED FLOUR *3 cups*
EGGS *3*
PEANUT OIL *2 tablespoons*
SALT *to taste*

For the filling
EGGS *5*
ASPARAGUS *2 lbs*
HERBS *11 oz*
SHALLOTS *1*
GRATED GRANA CHEESE *3 tablespoons*
BUTTER *4 tablespoons*
SALT & PEPPER *to taste*

For the sauce
BASIL *1 branch*
BUTTER *4 tablespoons*

1 Prepare the pasta. Sift the flour into a mound on the work surface. Make a well in the middle; add a dash of salt and the eggs. Work the ingredients thoroughly kneading for about 15 minutes until you obtain a firm and elastic dough. Cover with plastic and set aside for 30 minutes. Roll the dough thinly and make rectangles 4 inches long by 3 inches wide. In abundant salted water, cook a few at a time, adding peanut oil; drain, pass under cold water, drain well and lay on a dish towel.

2 Prepare the filling. Peel shallot, rinse, dry and finely chop. Clean asparagus removing the tips (setting aside 8 tips for decoration), cut off hard stems and peel. Rinse herbs in cold water, drain and chop. In a saucepan, heat butter. Brown shallot until just transparent. Add asparagus. Cook for 2-3 minutes.

3 Add herbs. Cook for 2-3 minutes. Add salt and fresh ground pepper. Cook for 4-5 minutes on moderate heat, adding if needed 2-3 tablespoons of hot water. Steam the 8 asparagus tips you set aside earlier; drain and set aside. Rinse basil, dry and finely chop. Take 2 tablespoons of butter at room temperature and mix well with the chopped basil.

4 In a mixing bowl, lightly beat eggs; add salt, fresh ground pepper and grated grana. Cook this mixture in saucepan with asparagus and herbs on low heat; stir constantly with wooden spoon, until you obtain a thick cream. Place some of the mixture in each rectangle of the pasta and fold to make cannelloni. Place cannelloni in buttered oven dish; brush with basil butter. Cook in preheated oven at 415°F for 8-10 minutes. Decorate with asparagus tips. Serve hot.

Baked, filled conchiglioni

Difficulty **medium** • *Time needed* **over an hour** • *Calories per serving* **480 circa**

INGREDIENTS
serves 4

CONCHIGLIONI *12 oz*
MILK *4 cups*

For the filling
CHOPPED CHICKEN BREAST *11 oz*
ONIONS *1*
SAGE *a few leaves*
GRATED GRUYERE *4 tablespoons*
EXTRA VIRGIN OLIVE OIL *3 tablespoons*
SALT *to taste*

1 In a pot, boil the conchiglioni with milk and a pinch of salt. Peel and chop onion. In a saucepan, heat 2 tablespoons; brown onion and sage until onion is transparent. Add ground chicken.

2 Cook for 15 minutes, adding if needed a tablespoon of water or vegetable broth. Oil an oven dish with remaining olive oil. Fill cannelloni with chicken mixture and place in dish. Sprinkle with grated gruyere. Cook in preheated oven at 375°F for 30 minutes. Serve hot.

> **SUGGESTION**
> *The chicken can be substituted by carrots and celery, cooked with olive oil and onions.*

Filled conchiglioni au gratin

Difficulty **medium** • *Time needed* **over an hour** • *Calories per serving* **840**

INGREDIENTS
serves 4

CONCHIGLIONI *12 oz*
COOKED HAM *2 oz, in 1 piece*
FONTINA CHEESE *5 oz*
EGG YOLKS *2*
GRATED PARMIGIANO *2 tablespoons*
BUTTER *3 tablespoons*
SALT *to taste*

For the béchamel
WHITE FLOUR *1/2 cup*
MILK *2 cups*
NUTMEG *a pinch*
BUTTER *4 tablespoons*
SALT & PEPPER *to taste*

1 In abundant salted water, cook the conchiglioni al dente; drain and place face down on clean towel. Dice ham. Thinly slice the cheese. Put them in bowl and set aside. Preheat oven to 415°F.

2 Prepare the béchamel. In a saucepan, melt butter. Add flour and pour all cold milk. Boil, mixing with wooden spoon, for approximately 10 minutes. Season with salt, pepper and nutmeg.

3 A minute before removing the béchamel from heat, add fontina cheese and let it melt. Add ham. Remove from heat. Add egg yolks one by one, constantly stirring. Fill the conchiglioni with hot mixture.

4 Place conchiglioni in buttered oven dish. Pour remaining melted butter over. Sprinkle with parmigiano and cook au gratin for approximately 15 minutes. Serve garnished with herbs.

> **SUGGESTION**
> *This healthy dish will be even more appreciated by your guests if you add some truffle paste to the béchamel sauce.*

"Fregnacce," Abruzzo style filled pasta

Difficulty **medium** • *Time needed* **over an hour** • *Calories per serving* **770**

INGREDIENTS
serves 4

For the pasta
UNBLEACHED FLOUR *2 cups*
EGGS *2*
SALT *to taste*

For the filling
SAUSAGES *3*
GROUND BEEF *11 oz*
TOMATOES *1 lb, ripe and firm*
ONIONS *1*
HOT CHILI PEPPER *a pinch*
EGGS *1*
GRATED PECORINO *3 tablespoons*
BUTTER *1 tablespoon*
EXTRA VIRGIN OLIVE OIL *4 tablespoons*
SALT & PEPPER *to taste*

1 Prepare the pasta. Sift the flour on work surface into a mound. Make a well in the middle; add the eggs and a pinch of salt. Work the ingredients until the dough is smooth and elastic. Wrap the dough in plastic and set aside for at least 30 minutes in a cool place (not in the refrigerator).

2 In the meantime, prepare filling. Peel and crumble sausages. Scald tomatoes in boiling water, drain, peel, press to remove seeds and coarsely chop. Peel, rinse and finely chop onion. Cook sausages in a non-stick pan. Drain. Set aside.

3 In a saucepan, heat olive oil. Add ground beef. Cook on all sides. Drain. Set aside. In the same pan, cook onion and hot pepper until onion is transparent. Add beef, sausages and tomatoes. Season with salt and pepper. Cook on moderate heat for 50 minutes, stirring from time to time.

4 Roll the pasta dough thinly and make four 6 inch squares. In abundant salted water, cook pasta squares. Drain well and lay on a dish towel. Pour half beef-sausage sauce in a mixing bowl; add egg, 1 tablespoon of pecorino. Mix well with a wooden spoon, until all ingredients are incorporated.

5 Place filling in the middle of each square. Close like envelopes, making the "fregnacce." Place in buttered oven dish; pour remaining sauce over and sprinkle with pecorino. Cook in preheated oven at 375°F for 10-12 minutes. Serve hot.

Frisinsal de tagliadele

Difficulty **easy** • *Time needed* **under an hour** • *Calories per serving* **640**

INGREDIENTS
serves 4

EGG TAGLIOLINI *14 oz*
GOOSE SALAMI *4 oz, or goose prosciutto*
PINE NUTS *1 oz*
RAISINS *1 oz*
ROSEMARY *1 branch*
SAGE *4-5 leaves*
BREAD CRUMBS *4 tablespoons*
EXTRA VIRGIN OLIVE OIL *5 tablespoons*
SALT *to taste*

1 In a bowl of lukewarm water, soak raisins. Press gently to drain well. In abundant salted water, cook the tagliolini al dente.

2 In the meantime, chop rosemary and sage leaves. Coarsely slice the salami. In a saucepan, heat 4 tablespoons of olive oil; add rosemary, sage and salami. Cook for 7-8 minutes.

3 Drain pasta. In a bowl, season pasta with mixture, pine nuts and raisins. Oil a pie dish and sprinkle with bread crumbs. Add seasoned pasta. Cook in oven at 415°F for approximately 15 minutes. Serve hot.

Frittata with vermicelli

Difficulty **easy** • *Time needed* **under an hour** • *Calories per serving* **700**

INGREDIENTS
serves 4

VERMICELLI *12 oz*
SALAMI *4 oz, in 1 piece*
TOMATOES *14 oz, ripe and firm*
ONIONS *1*
BASIL *one bunch*
PARSLEY *one bunch*
MOZZARELLA *4 oz*
EGGS *2*
GRATED GRANA CHEESE *4 tablespoons*
EXTRA VIRGIN OLIVE OIL *5 tablespoons*
SALT & PEPPER *to taste*

1 In boiling water, scald tomatoes. Drain, peel, press to remove seeds and coarsely chop. Peel onion, rinse, dry and finely chop. Rinse basil and parsley, delicately dry and separately chop.

2 Slice mozzarella; drain for approximately 15 minutes. Peel salami and dice. In a saucepan, heat olive oil; cook onion until transparent. Add tomatoes, basil, salt and pepper. Cook for approximately 15-20 minutes on moderate heat, stirring from time to time.

3 In a bowl, lightly beat eggs with dash of salt and fresh ground pepper. In abundant salted water, cook pasta al dente. Drain. Place in mixing bowl. Add beaten eggs, grated grana, parsley and basil, mixing well

4 Place half the pasta in oiled oven dish. Cover with slices of mozzarella and salami pieces. Cover with tomato sauce and place remaining pasta. Cook in preheated oven at 435°F for approximately 10 minutes. Serve hot.

Pasta gratinée with baby squid

Difficulty **medium** • *Time needed* **under an hour** • *Calories per serving* **490**

INGREDIENTS
serves 4

SHORT PASTA *12 oz*
BABY SQUID *11 oz*
TOMATOES *14 oz, ripe and firm*
PARSLEY *one bunch*
GARLIC *1 clove*
ONIONS *1*
BREAD CRUMBS *1 tablespoon*
EXTRA VIRGIN OLIVE OIL *5 tablespoons*
SALT & PEPPER *to taste*

1 Remove skin from squid, dry and cut in 2-3 pieces. Scald tomatoes, drain, peel, press to remove seeds and coarsely chop. Rinse parsley, dry and chop. Peel garlic and onion, rinse, dry and chop separately

2 In a small bowl, mix bread crumbs with half chopped garlic and parsley. Set aside. In a saucepan, heat 2 tablespoons of olive oil; add squid; cook, stirring often with a wooden spoon. Salt and pepper. Set aside.

3 In a skillet, heat 2 tablespoons of olive oil; add onion and remaining garlic; brown until onion is transparent. Add tomatoes, salt and pepper. Cook on moderate heat for approximately 10 minutes. Add squid and parsley; cook for another 3 minutes.

4 In the meantime, cook the pasta in abundant salted water. Drain. Season with two thirds of tomato-squid sauce. Delicately mix with wooden spoon.

5 Place half pasta in an oiled baking dish; pour tomato-squid sauce over and add remaining pasta. Sprinkle with breadcrumb mixture. Cook in preheated oven at 415°F for approximately 10 minutes. Serve hot.

Pasta gratinée with sardines

Difficulty **medium** • *Time needed* **under an hour** • *Calories per serving* **490**

INGREDIENTS
serves 4

MACCHERONI *12 oz*
SARDINES *8 oz*
TOMATOES *11 oz, ripe and firm*
GARLIC *1 clove*
PARSLEY *one bunch*
MARJORAM *a few branches*
BREAD CRUMBS *1 tablespoon*
EXTRA VIRGIN OLIVE OIL *4 tablespoons*
SALT & PEPPER *to taste*

1 Scald tomatoes in boiling water. Drain, peel, press to remove seeds and coarsely chop. Peel garlic clove, rinse, dry and finely chop. Rinse parsley and marjoram, dry and finely chop.

2 Clean the sardines and remove the heads. Wash under cold water. Delicately dry and cut in pieces. In a skillet, heat olive oil. Place sardine pieces with salt, fresh ground pepper and tomatoes. Add garlic, parsley and marjoram. Add olive oil. Cook on moderate heat for approximately 10 minutes.

3 In the meantime, cook the pasta in abundant salted water; drain. Season with sauce and place pasta in baking dish. Mix bread crumbs with remaining parsley and marjoram. Sprinkle pasta with breadcrumb mixture. Cook in preheated oven at 375°F for 10-12 minutes. Serve hot.

Quick pasta gratiné

Difficulty **easy** • *Time needed* **under an hour** • *Calories per serving* **520**

INGREDIENTS
serves 4

MACCHERONI *11 oz*
MOZZARELLA *1*
BASIL *one bunch*
PARSLEY *one bunch*
MARJORAM *a few branches*
GRATED GRANA CHEESE *4 tablespoons*
EXTRA VIRGIN OLIVE OIL *5 tablespoons*
SALT *to taste*

1 Thinly slice mozzarella. Rinse basil, parsley and marjoram; drain on clean dish towel; delicately dry and chop. In abundant salted water, cook the maccheroni al dente.

2 Drain. Season with 3 tablespoons of olive oil and 2 tablespoons of grated grana. In an oiled oven dish, put half the maccheroni. Sprinkle with grana. Cover with one layer of mozzarella and chopped herbs

3 Add remaining maccheroni and mozzarella. Sprinkle again with grana. Pour olive oil over. Cook in preheated oven at 415°F for approximately 10-12 minutes, until lightly golden. Serve hot

---

SUGGESTION

To cook au gratin well, you can protect the oven dish with another larger oven dish, either empty or with some water.

Lasagna with asparagus

Difficulty **medium** • *Time needed* **over an hour** • *Calories per serving* **670**

INGREDIENTS
serves 4

FRESH EGG PASTA DOUGH *12 oz*

For the sauce
ASPARAGUS *2 bunches*
SPINACH *7 oz*
SMOKED HAM *4 oz, in 1 piece*
BLACK TRUFFLES *1*
SHALLOTS *1*
GRATED GRANA CHEESE *2 tablespoons*
BUTTER *4 tablespoons*
SALT & PEPPER *to taste*

For the béchamel
WHITE FLOUR *2 tablespoons*
MILK *2 cups*
BUTTER *2 tablespoons*
SALT & PEPPER *to taste*

1 Peel the asparagus, remove the stem ends. Set aside the tips and cut stems into strips. Rinse spinach in cold water and drain. Peel shallot and slice. In a skillet, melt 1 tablespoon of butter; add shallot, cooking until it becomes transparent. Add asparagus strips, stirring with a wooden spoon. Add spinach, 1/2 cup of water, salt and pepper. Cook until soft. Pour in food processor and mix.

2 Prepare the béchamel. Melt butter in a saucepan; add flour, constantly stirring with a wooden spoon. Add 1 cup of milk. Bring to boil. Season with salt and fresh ground pepper. Cook for 10-15 minutes, always stirring. Add the asparagus-spinach mixture and mix well. Chop smoked ham. Brush the truffle well and finely chop. Roll the pasta dough into thin sheets and scut circles 3

inches in diameter. In abundant salted water, cook a few circles at a time. Drain, pass under cold water, drain well and place on clean dish towel.

3 Lightly butter an oven dish and add remaining milk. In the center of each pasta circle, place one tablespoon of asparagus-spinach cream, some ham, grana and truffle. Repeat, this time with two pasta circles over the first filled one. Cover with asparagus-spinach cream, ham and truffle. Place the circles in oven dish. Cook au gratin in preheated oven at 435°F for 15 minutes. Cut the asparagus tips in half; sauté in saucepan with some melted butter. Halfway through the cooking, remove and garnish the pasta with the asparagus tips. Serve hot.

Lasagna with mushrooms

Difficulty **medium** • *Time needed* **over an hour** • *Calories per serving* **690**

INGREDIENTS
serves 6

For the pasta
UNBLEACHED FLOUR *4 cups*
EGGS *4*
EXTRA VIRGIN OLIVE OIL *1 tablespoon*
SALT *to taste*

For the béchamel
WHITE FLOUR *1/2 cup*
MILK *2 cups*
NUTMEG *to taste*
GRATED PARMIGIANO *3 tablespoons*
BUTTER *4 tablespoons*
SALT & PEPPER *to taste*

For the sauce
DRIED MUSHROOMS *2 oz,*
or 1 lb of fresh mushrooms
MOZZARELLA *7 oz*
CHOPPED PARSLEY *1 tablespoon*
GARLIC *1 clove*
BREAD CRUMBS *1 tablespoon*
VEGETABLE BROTH *1 cup*
GRATED PARMIGIANO *1 tablespoon*
EXTRA VIRGIN OLIVE OIL *4 tablespoons*
SALT & PEPPER *to taste*

1 Prepare the sauce. In a skillet, heat 4 tablespoons of olive oil; brown crushed garlic; remove garlic. Soak mushrooms in a bowl with lukewarm water; drain well. Add mushrooms to skillet and a little of their soaking water. Cook for approximately 30 minutes. Add parsley, salt and pepper. At the end of the cooking, all liquid should be absorbed.

2 In the meantime, prepare the pasta. Sift the flour on work surface into mound. Make a well in the middle; add the eggs, olive oil and a pinch of salt. Work all ingredients until dough is smooth and elastic. Roll pasta dough thinly. Cut into 3 inch squares. In abundant salted water, cook a few squares at a time. Remove one by one with slotted spoon. Place in a bowl with cold water and one tablespoon of olive oil; drain and place on dish towel.

3 Prepare the béchamel. In a small saucepan, melt butter; add flour, stirring; add milk, always stirring. Season with salt, fresh ground pepper and nutmeg. Finally add the grated parmigiano.

4 Remove béchamel from heat and add cooked mushrooms. In an oiled oven dish, cover bottom with bread crumbs. Place one layer of pasta, one of béchamel and mushrooms, one of mozzarella slices and finally one of grated parmigiano. Repeat until all ingredients are used. Cook in oven at 375°F for approximately 30 minutes.

Baked lasagne

Difficulty **medium** • *Time needed* **over an hour** • *Calories per serving* **1000**

INGREDIENTS
serves 6

DRIED LASAGNE *1 lb*
GROUND BEEF *11 oz*
GROUND PORK LOIN *11 oz*
SAUSAGE *7 oz*
TOMATO PASTE *1 tablespoon*
DRIED MUSHROOMS *1 oz*
CELERY *1 stalk*
CARROTS *1*
ONIONS *1*
THYME *a pinch*
BASIL *5 leaves*
BREAD CRUMBS *to taste*
VEGETABLE BROTH *1 cup*
GRATED GRANA CHEESE *8 tablespoons*
BUTTER *3 tablespoons*
PEANUT OIL *2 tablespoons*
EXTRA VIRGIN OLIVE OIL *6 tablespoons*
SALT & PEPPER *to taste*

For the béchamel

WHITE FLOUR *3/4 cup*
MILK *3 cups*
NUTMEG *a pinch*
BUTTER *6 tablespoons*
SALT *to taste*

1 In a bowl, soak mushrooms in luke-warm water. In abundant salted water, cook lasagne al dente, adding peanut oil. Drain, pass under cold water, drain well and place on a dish towel. Peel and rinse celery, carrot and onion; dry and finely chop. In a pan, heat olive oil and add vegetables.

2 Brown for a few minutes; add peeled sausage and ground meat. Stir well with a fork. Add mushrooms and their cooking water. In a bowl, mix tomato paste with vegetable broth, thyme and whole basil leaves; add to pan. Stir well; lower the heat and boil for approximately 45 minutes, stirring from time to time.

3 Prepare the béchamel. In a small pan, melt butter. Add flour, stirring rapidly; add milk, always stirring. Season with salt and nutmeg.

4 Lightly butter an oven dish. Place one layer of lasagne, covering with 1 or 2 tablespoons of mixture. Sprinkle with some grated grana cheese. Place another layer of lasagne, this time cover it with béchamel and sprinkle with grana.

5 Repeat, alternating, until all ingredients are used. The last layer should be covered with béchamel. Add a tablespoon of meat mixture here and there.

6 Place dabs of butter over. Mix bread crumbs and remaining grated grana cheese together in a bowl. Sprinkle pasta with this grana preparation. Cook in preheated oven at 415°F or until top is lightly golden. Serve hot.

Lasagna with pesto

Difficulty **medium** • *Time needed* **under an hour** • *Calories per serving* **710**

INGREDIENTS
serves 4

FRESH EGG PASTA *14 oz*
GRATED PARMIGIANO *4 tablespoons*
MELTED BUTTER *1 tablespoon*

For the pesto
BASIL *2 bunches*
GARLIC *1 clove*
GRATED PARMIGIANO *2 tablespoons*
GRATED PECORINO *2 tablespoons*
EXTRA VIRGIN OLIVE OIL *3 tablespoons*
SALT *to taste*

1 Prepare the pesto. In a mortar, put peeled garlic, basil, salt, pecorino and parmigiano. Grind until mixture is homogeneous. Little by little, as you mix, add olive oil

2 Cut pasta into squares (or rectangles). In abundant salted water, cook pasta al dente. Drain using slotted spoon and place on dish towel. Add 2 tablespoons of pasta cooking water to pesto and mix well.

3 In a preheated serving plate, brushed with melted butter, one layer of lasagne, a little pesto and grated cheese. Repeat until all ingredients are used. Grill for a few minutes. Serve immediately.

Lasagna with goose ragù

Difficulty **medium** • *Time needed* **over an hour** • *Calories per serving* **1000**

INGREDIENTS
serves 6

For the pasta
UNBLEACHED FLOUR *4 cups*
EGGS *4*
PEANUT OIL *2 tablespoons*
SALT *to taste*

For the sauce
GOOSE *2 lbs, without the skin*
GOOSE LIVER *1*
PROSCIUTTO *4 oz*
TOMATOES *8*
CARROTS *1*
CELERY *1 stalk*
ONIONS *1*
NUTMEG *a pinch*
BEEF STOCK *1 cup*
BREAD CRUMBS *2 tablespoons*
GRATED GRANA CHEESE *4 tablespoons*
BUTTER *3 tablespoons*
SALT & PEPPER *to taste*

1 Cut prosciutto in pieces. Peel onion. Peel, rinse and chop carrot and celery stalk. Scald tomatoes in boiling water for 30 seconds. Drain, peel, press to remove seeds and coarsely chop.

2 Debone the goose. Cut meat in small pieces and place them in a saucepan with butter. Brown for 5-6 minutes. Add prosciutto and vegetables. Lightly lower the flame and cook for 5 minutes. Add nutmeg, salt, pepper and tomatoes.

3 Cook on low heat for approximately one hour, if needed, add the broth little by little. Cut goose liver in small pieces and add to pan 5 minutes before turning heat off.

4 Prepare the pasta. Sift flour on work surface into a mound. Make a well in the middle; add eggs and salt. Work the ingredients well using a fork, starting from the middle. Then use your hands and work dough for 15 minutes. Shape dough in ball; set aside for 30 minutes; roll thinly. Cut pasta into strips 2 inches wide and as long as your oven dish.

5 In abundant salted water, cook pasta strips, adding peanut oil. Drain. In a buttered oven dish, place layers of pasta strips and goose sauce, always alternating. Cover the last layer with sauce, grana, bread crumbs and dabs of butter. Cook at 375°F for 20 minutes. Serve hot.

Lasagna alla bolognese

*Difficulty **medium** • Time needed **over an hour** • Calories per serving **690***

INGREDIENTS
serves 6

FRESH EGG PASTA DOUGH *1 lb*
GRATED GRANA CHEESE *6 tablespoons*
PEANUT OIL *2 tablespoons*
BUTTER *3 tablespoons*
SALT *to taste*

For the sauce
GROUND BEEF *1 lb*
GROUND PORK *5 oz*
PROSCIUTTO *3 oz, in 1 piece*
DRIED MUSHROOMS *1 oz*
TOMATOES *1 lb, ripe and firm*
CARROTS *1/2*
CELERY *1/2 stalk*
ONIONS *1*
GARLIC *1/2 clove*
PARSLEY *one bunch*
MARJORAM *a few branches*
RED WINE *1/4 cup*
WHITE FLOUR *1 teaspoon*
NUTMEG *to taste*
BEEF STOCK *1/4 cup*
EXTRA VIRGIN OLIVE OIL *3 tablespoons*
SALT & PEPPER *to taste*

For the béchamel
WHITE FLOUR *1/4 cup*
MILK *1 cup*
NUTMEG *to taste*
GRATED GRANA CHEESE *2 tablespoons*
BUTTER *3 tablespoons*
SALT & PEPPER *to taste*

1 Prepare the sauce. Soak mushrooms in lukewarm water. Peel onion and garlic. Remove large filaments from celery stalk. Cut off the ends of the carrot and peel. Rinse, dry and chop all vegetables. Chop prosciutto. Scald tomatoes, drain, peel, press to remove seeds and coarsely chop. Rinse, dry and finely chop parsley and marjoram.

2 In a pan, heat olive oil. Brown prosciutto; add garlic, onion, carrot and celery until onion is transparent. Add mushrooms; let simmer for a few minutes. Add ground meat and cook on all sides. Add red wine and let evaporate. Add flour. Cook for a few minutes, stirring with a wooden spoon.

3 Add tomatoes, salt, fresh ground pepper, nutmeg, parsley and marjoram. Add broth. Cook on moderate heat for one hour, adding more broth if needed. In

the meantime, prepare the pasta. Roll dough and cut into 4 inch squares. In abundant salted water, cook a few squares at a time, adding peanut oil. Drain and place on clean dish towel.

4 Prepare the béchamel. In a small saucepan, melt butter. Add flour; stir using a wooden spoon. Add all cold milk and cook on moderate heat for 10 minutes, always stirring. Add salt, pepper and nutmeg. Remove from heat and add grated grana cheese.

5 Butter a baking dish. Place one layer of lasagne, a layer of sauce and grated grana. Repeat until all ingredients are used. Pour béchamel over lasagne, spreading it evenly with a fork. Add dabs of butter. Cook in preheated oven at 415°F for approximately 15 minutes. Serve hot.

Lasagna with prosciutto

Difficulty **medium** • *Time needed* **over an hour** • *Calories per serving* **740**

INGREDIENTS
serves 4

For the pasta
UNBLEACHED FLOUR *3 cups*
SPINACH *4 oz*
EGGS *2*
PEANUT OIL *2 tablespoons*
SALT *to taste*

For the sauce
GROUND BEEF *4 oz*
PROSCIUTTO *4 oz*
TOMATO PASTE
1 tablespoon
CARROTS *1*
CELERY *1 stalk*
ONIONS *1/2*
BECHAMEL *2 cups*
DRY WHITE WINE *1/4 cup*
VEGETABLE BROTH *1 1/2 cups*
GRATED PARMIGIANO *4 tablespoons*
EXTRA VIRGIN OLIVE OIL *3 tablespoons*
SALT & PEPPER *to taste*

1 In a saucepan, heat olive oil; add peeled and sliced onion, carrot and celery, and chopped ham. Cook on moderate heat. Add ground meat; brown, stirring from time to time. Add red wine. Mix tomato paste with broth; add to pan.

2 Add remaining broth to pan. Mix and boil for one hour, adding more broth if needed. Boil spinach in abundant salted water for 30 seconds. Prepare the pasta. Sift the flour on pastry board into a mound. Make a well in the middle; add spinach and eggs

3 Work pasta ingredients until mixture is homogeneous. Cover and set aside for 30 minutes. Then divide dough in half

and roll thinly. Cut in rectangles.

4 In abundant salted water, cook pasta for 90 seconds, adding 1 tablespoon of olive oil. Drain, pass under cold water, drain well and place pasta between 2 clean dish cloths. Set aside.

5 In an oiled oven dish, place a layer of pasta, a layer of sauce, another of pasta and one of béchamel and parmigiano. Repeat until all ingredients are used.

6 Cover last layer of pasta with béchamel and parmigiano. Cook in preheated oven at 415°F for approximately 20 minutes or until top is lightly golden.

Lasagna with basil and walnuts

Difficulty **medium** • *Time needed* **under an hour** • *Calories per serving* **760**

INGREDIENTS
serves 4

For the pasta
UNBLEACHED FLOUR *3 cups*
EGGS *3*
PEANUT OIL *2 tablespoons*
EXTRA VIRGIN OLIVE OIL *2 tablespoons*
SALT *to taste*

For the sauce
PINE NUTS *2 oz*
SHELLED WALNUTS *5*
BASIL *4 oz*
GARLIC *1 clove*
GRATED PECORINO *1 tablespoon*
GRATED GRANA CHEESE *5 tablespoons*
EXTRA VIRGIN OLIVE OIL *8 tablespoons*
BUTTER *3 tablespoons*
SALT *to taste*

1 Prepare the pasta. Sift flour on work surface into a mound. Make a well in the middle; add eggs, salt and oil. Work ingredients thoroughly until you obtain a firm and elastic dough. Cover with plastic and set aside for 30 minutes.

2 In the meantime, prepare the sauce. Rinse basil leaves, lay on dish towel and delicately dry. Put in a mortar with salt. Crush with a pestle.

3 Add peeled garlic, pine nuts and walnuts. Crush with the pestle. When all ingredients are incorporated, add grated pecorino little by little and 2 tablespoons of grated grana cheese. Mix well. Add oil, just enough to obtain a creamy mixture.

4 Roll pasta thinly with rolling pin. With a pastry wheel, cut 4 inch squares. In abundant boiling salted water, cook a few squares of pasta at a time, adding peanut oil. Save cooking water.

Drain pasta squares and set aside on a dish towel.

5 In a bowl, put the basil sauce. Add 2 tablespoons of cooking water and stir well with a wooden spoon. Butter an oven dish. Place a tablespoon of sauce at the bottom, then cover with a layer of pasta and 2 tablespoons of sauce. Sprinkle with grana cheese. Repeat with 2 layers of pasta, sauce and cheese, ending with the sauce. In a saucepan, melt butter. Cover pasta with melt butter. Cook in preheated oven at 415°F for approximately 10 minutes. Serve hot.

SUGGESTION
The sauce can also be prepared by putting pine nuts, walnuts and garlic in a mixer. Then add basil, salt, extra virgin olive oil grated grana and grated pecorino. Blend well.

Lasagna with sausage and mozzarella

Difficulty **medium** • *Time needed* **over an hour** • *Calories per serving* **900**

INGREDIENTS
serves 4

For the pasta
UNBLEACHED FLOUR *3 cups*
EGGS *3*
PEANUT OIL *2 tablespoons*
SALT *to taste*

For the filling
SAUSAGE *7 oz*
TOMATOES *11 oz, ripe and firm*
MOZZARELLA *5 oz*
RICOTTA *7 oz*
SHALLOTS *1*
BASIL *1 bunch*
EGGS *3*
GRATED GRANA CHEESE *2 tablespoons*
BUTTER *3 tablespoons*
EXTRA VIRGIN OLIVE OIL *4 tablespoons*
SALT & PEPPER *to taste*

1 Prepare the pasta. Sift flour on work surface into a mound. Make a well in the middle; add eggs and salt. Work ingredients thoroughly until you obtain a firm and elastic dough. Cover with plastic and set aside for 30 minutes. Roll pasta thinly and cut in rectangles 4 inches long and 3 inches wide. In abundant salted water, cook a few at a time, adding peanut oil. Drain, pass under water, drain well and lay on dish towel.

2 In the meantime, scald tomatoes; drain, peel, press to remove seeds and coarsely chop. Peel shallot, rinse, dry and finely chop. Rinse, dry and chop basil. In a skillet, heat 3 tablespoons of olive oil; brown shallot until transparent. Add tomatoes, salt and fresh ground pepper. Cook on moderate heat for 10-15 minutes. A minute before removing from heat, add basil.

3 Dice the mozzarella; drain for 15 minutes. In a saucepan, heat olive oil; brown sausage, pricking it with a fork. Drain, peel and slice. In a small pot, hard boil 2 eggs for 7-8 minutes; drain, pass under cold water, drain again and slice. In a mixing bowl, beat the third egg with the grated grana cheese, salt and fresh ground pepper.

4 Butter a baking dish. Place one layer of lasagne, one of tomato sauce, mozzarella, ricotta, 1 tablespoon of egg-cheese mixture, a few slices of boiled eggs and sausage. Repeat until all ingredients are used. The last layer should be the lasagna. Brush top with melted butter. Cook in oven at 415°F for 15 minutes.

Lasagna with fontina cheese

*Difficulty **medium*** • *Time needed **over an hour*** • *Calories per serving **580***

INGREDIENTS
serves 4

For the pasta
UNBLEACHED FLOUR *2 cups*
EGGS *2*
PEANUT OIL *2 tablespoons*
EXTRA VIRGIN OLIVE OIL *1 tablespoon*
SALT *to taste*

For the filling
TOMATOES *11 oz*
FONTINA CHEESE *7 oz*
MILK *1 cup*
EGG YOLKS *3*
SAGE *2 leaves*
BUTTER *3 tablespoons*
WHITE PEPPER *to taste*

1 Prepare the pasta. Sift flour on work surface into a mound. Make a well in the middle; add eggs, oil and salt. Work ingredients thoroughly until you obtain a firm and elastic dough. Cover with a slightly humid towel and set aside for 30 minutes in a cool place. Roll pasta dough into thin sheets and cut rectangles 5 inches by 3 inches. In abundant salted water, cook a few at a time, adding peanut oil. Drain and lay on a humid dish towel.

2 Prepare filling. Scald tomatoes in boiling water; drain, peel, press to remove seeds and dice. In a non-stick pan, sauté tomato dice for 2 minutes until all water has evaporated. Remove from heat. Pass tomatoes through a food mill. Set aside in a bowl.

3 Remove crust from fontina cheese; thinly slice; put slices in high and narrow dish; cover with milk for approximately one hour. Drain and melt in a double boiler. Add tomatoes and egg yolks. Beat constantly. The fontina will make long strings, then will become almost liquid before finally thickening.

4 When sauce is creamy, remove from heat. Add fresh ground white pepper and mix well. Butter an oven dish. Place one layer of pasta, then pour half of the sauce. Repeat once, finishing with the pasta. In a saucepan, melt remaining butter with sage leaves. Brush top layer of pasta with butter. Cook in preheated oven at 415°F for approximately 15 minutes. Serve hot.

Curly lasagna with two cheeses

Difficulty **medium** • *Time needed* **over an hour** • *Calories per serving* **540**

INGREDIENTS

serves 4

CURLY LASAGNA *8 oz*
MILD GORGONZOLA *4 oz*
BRIE *4 oz*
GRATED GRANA CHEESE *4 tablespoons*
MILK *1 cup*
TOMATOES *2*
TABASCO SAUCE *a few drops*
SAGE *1 leaf*
DRIED THYME *1/2 tablespoon, ground*
PARSLEY *1 bunch*
DRY WHITE WINE *4 tablespoons*
BUTTER *1 tablespoon*
SALT & PEPPER *to taste*

1 In abundant salted water, cook the lasagna al dente. Drain, pass under cold water, drain again and lay on humid dish towel.

2 In a saucepan, pour milk. Add wine, Tabasco, sage and thyme. Cook on moderate heat. Remove crust from brie. Add gorgonzola pieces and brie to saucepan. Add pepper. Whisk until the cheeses have melted, obtaining a smooth cream. Remove from heat.

3 Butter a baking dish. Place 3 layers of pasta, alternating with cheese cream and grated grana. Keep one tablespoon of grana aside. Cook in preheated oven at 415°F for approximately 10 minutes.

4 Rinse and thinly slice tomatoes. Remove seeds. Place tomatoes on pasta. Sprinkle with chopped parsley and grated grana. Return to oven for 10-12 minutes, until top is cooked au gratin. Serve hot.

Lasagna with artichokes and spinach

Difficulty **medium** • *Time needed* **over an hour** • *Calories per serving* **590**

INGREDIENTS

serves 4

FRESH EGG PASTA DOUGH *11 oz*
ARTICHOKES *4*
SPINACH *1 lb*
LEMON JUICE *1 tablespoon*
WHITE FLOUR *1/4 cup*
MILK *1 1/2 cups*
GRATED GRANA CHEESE *3 tablespoons*
NUTMEG *a pinch*
BUTTER *6 tablespoons*
EXTRA VIRGIN OLIVE OIL *2 tablespoons*
SALT & PEPPER *to taste*

1 Clean the artichokes, cut into thin slices and place into a bowl with water and lemon juice. Peel spinach, rinse well in cold water, drain and cut into strips. In a skillet, melt 2 tablespoons of butter. Brown spinach for 2-3 minutes. Salt and pepper. Drain artichokes. In a saucepan, sauté artichokes with butter. Add 2-3 tablespoons water, salt and pepper. Cook covered for 10 minutes on moderate heat.

2 In another saucepan, melt 3 tablespoons of butter; add flour and cook for 2 minutes. Pour milk and boil. Season with salt, pepper and nutmeg. Cook for 10 minutes, stirring well. Remove from heat. Add spinach strips and slices of artichokes. Set a few slices aside for decoration.

3 Roll pasta into thin sheets and cut 4 inch circles. In abundant salted water, cook a few at a time, adding 2 tablespoons of olive oil. Drain and lay on humid dish towel. Butter an oven dish. Place layers of pasta, alternating them with spinach-artichoke mixture and grated grana. Pour some of the mixture on the last layer and top with the artichokes set aside. Cook au gratin in preheated oven at 415°F for 10 minutes. Serve hot.

Lasagna with savoy cabbage

Difficulty **medium** • *Time needed* **over an hour** • *Calories per serving* **790**

INGREDIENTS
serves 4

For the pasta
UNBLEACHED FLOUR *3 cups*
EGGS *3*
BUTTER *4 tablespoons*
PEANUT OIL *2 tablespoons*
SALT *to taste*

For the filling
SAVOY CABBAGE *2 lbs*
FONTINA CHEESE *5 oz*
SHALLOTS *1*
BAY LEAVES *1 leaf*
VEGETABLE BROTH *1/4 cup*
GRATED GRANA CHEESE *3 tablespoons*
EXTRA VIRGIN OLIVE OIL *2 tablespoons*
SALT & PEPPER *to taste*

For the cream of vegetables
ZUCCHINI *14 oz*
SPINACH *14 oz*
SHALLOTS *1*
BECHAMEL *2-3 tablespoons*
EXTRA VIRGIN OLIVE OIL *3 tablespoons*
SALT & PEPPER *to taste*

1 Prepare the pasta. Sift flour on work surface into a mound. Make a well in the middle; add eggs and salt. Work ingredients thoroughly until you obtain a firm and elastic dough. Cover with plastic and set aside for 30 minutes. Roll pasta dough thinly and cut 4 by 3 inch rectangles. In abundant salted water, cook a few at a time, adding peanut oil. Drain, pass under cold water, drain well and lay on dish towel.

2 In the meantime, prepare filling. Clean cabbage and discard its heart; slice, rinse in cold water and cook in abundant salted water for 2 minutes; drain. Peel 2 shallots, rinse and chop. In a skillet, heat olive oil; cook shallot and bay leaf until shallot is transparent. Add cabbage slices and brown for a few minutes, stirring with a wooden spoon. Salt and pepper. Add broth. Cook on moderate heat for 15-20 minutes. Remove bay leaf.

3 Prepare the cream of vegetables. Cut off zucchini tips, rinse and chop. Rinse spinach in abundant cold water; drain.

In a skillet, heat olive oil; cook third shallot until transparent. Salt and pepper. Add one cup water. Cook for approximately 10 minutes on moderate heat.

4 When the cooking is finished, transfer the zucchini and spinach mixture to the bowl of a food processor and mix well; if the mixture is a little too thin, reduce over medium heat stirring often; pour into a bowl and blend in the béchamel. Cut the crust off the fontina cheese and slice thinly. Butter a baking dish and cover the bottom with sheets of pasta; spread a layer of the spinach and zucchini cream on top, make a layer of the shredded cabbage, a few slices of fontina and sprinkle with a little grated grana cheese. Cover again with lasagna and continue with the same process until the ingredients are used up, finishing with the lasagna; melt the remaining butter in a small pan and brush the lasagna. Put the baking dish into a preheated oven at 415°F for approximately 15 minutes until top is lightly golden. Serve hot.

Lasagna with eggplant and zucchini

*Difficulty **medium** • Time needed **over an hour** • Calories per serving **630***

INGREDIENTS
serves 4

For the pasta
UNBLEACHED FLOUR *3 cups*
EGGS *3*
EGG YOLKS *2*
PEANUT OIL *2 tablespoons*
EXTRA VIRGIN OLIVE OIL *1 tablespoon*
SALT *to taste*

For the sauce
EGGPLANTS *12 oz*
ZUCCHINI *12 oz*
PREPARED BASIL TOMATO SAUCE
1 1/2 cups
GRATED GRANA CHEESE *4 tablespoons*
BECHAMEL *2 tablespoons*
BUTTER *1 tablespoon*
PEANUT OIL *enough for frying*
SALT *to taste*

1 Prepare the pasta. Sift flours on work surface into a mound. Make a well in the middle; add eggs, egg yolks, oil and a pinch of salt. Work the ingredients until the dough is smooth and elastic. Cover with plastic wrap and set aside for 30 minutes.

2 Roll pasta dough thinly and cut 4 by 3 inch rectangles. In abundant salted water, cook a few rectangles at a time, adding peanut oil. Drain, pass under cold water, drain well and lay on dish cloth.

3 Prepare sauce. Cut off the ends of eggplants and zucchini; rinse, dry and slice. Place eggplant slices in colander with salt; drain for 30 minutes.

4 In a saucepan, heat olive oil; add zucchini slices and fry on both sides. Drain on paper towel; sprinkle with salt. Rinse eggplants slices, dry with dish towel; then in abundant oil, fry until lightly golden. Drain on paper towel.

5 Butter a baking dish. Place one layer of pasta, one layer of eggplant slices and one of basil tomato sauce. Sprinkle with grated grana cheese.

6 Place another layer of lasagna, one of zucchini slices, one of basil tomato sauce and finally sprinkle with grana cheese. Repeat until all ingredients are used, finishing with the zucchini and eggplant slices. Add béchamel over. Cook in oven at 415°F for approximately 15 minutes. Serve hot.

Lasagna with sour cream and prosciutto

Difficulty **medium** • *Time needed* **over an hour** • *Calories per serving* **690**

INGREDIENTS
serves 4

For the pasta
UNBLEACHED FLOUR *3 cups*
EGGS *3*
PEANUT OIL *2 tablespoons*
EXTRA VIRGIN OLIVE OIL *1 tablespoon*
SALT *to taste*

For the filling
HEAVY CREAM *1/2 cup*
LEMON JUICE *1 teaspoon*
PROSCIUTTO *4 oz*
THYME *one bunch*
EGGS *1*
GRATED GRANA CHEESE *2 tablespoons*
BREAD CRUMBS *1 tablespoon*
BUTTER *3 tablespoons*
SALT & PEPPER *to taste*

1 Prepare the pasta. Sift the flour on work surface into a mound. Make a well in the middle; add eggs, oil and salt. Work all ingredients until the dough is smooth and elastic. Set aside for 30 minutes. In the meantime, place heavy cream and lemon juice in a bowl; beat well with a fork; store in cool place.

2 Roll pasta dough thinly and cut 4 inch squares. In abundant salted water, cook a few at a time, adding peanut oil. Drain, put in a mixing bowl with cold water, drain well and place on humid dish cloth. Rinse thyme and finely chop.

3 Chop prosciutto. Add egg and grana cheese to mixing bowl. Beat until all ingredients are well incorporated. Butter a rectangular oven dish. Place one layer of pasta; cover with half chopped ham, some thyme, salt, fresh ground pepper and half cream-egg mixture.

4 Place another layer of pasta, one of ham and one of cream-egg mixture. Finish with a layer of pasta. Add dabs of butter and bread crumbs. Cook au gratin in preheated oven at 415°F for approximately 15 minutes.

Lasagna with ricotta and walnuts

Difficulty **medium** • *Time needed* **over an hour** • *Calories per serving* **750**

INGREDIENTS
serves 4

For the pasta
UNBLEACHED FLOUR *3 cups*
EGGS *3*
PEANUT OIL *2 tablespoons*
SALT *a pinch*

For the sauce
RICOTTA *14 oz*
WALNUTS *30*
GARLIC *1 clove*
MILK *1/2 cup*
GRATED PARMIGIANO *6 tablespoons*
BUTTER *4 tablespoons*
SALT *to taste*

1 Prepare the lasagna. Sift the flour on work surface into a mound. Make a well in the middle; add eggs and a pinch of salt. Work all ingredients until the dough is smooth and elastic. Form a ball. Cover with aluminum foil and set aside for approximately 30 minutes.

2 Prepare sauce. Scald walnuts in boiling water; remove skin; place in blender with ricotta, 3 tablespoons of parmigiano, 2 tablespoons of butter, milk, garlic and salt. Blend for a few minutes.

3 Roll pasta dough thinly, adding flour. Cut medium-size rectangles. In abundant salted water, cook a few at a time, adding peanut oil. Drain one by one with a slotted spoon, placing them on a humid dish towel. Keep some of the cooking water.

4 Thin walnut sauce with 2 tablespoons of pasta cooking water. In a buttered baking dish, place layers of pasta, alternating with walnut sauce. Cook in oven at 415°F for approximately 15 minutes. Serve hot with remaining parmigiano.

Abruzzo style lasagna

Difficulty **medium** • *Time needed* **over an hour** • *Calories per serving* **820**

INGREDIENTS
serves 4

LASAGNA *12 oz*
BEEF *5 oz*
VEAL *5 oz*
PROSCIUTTO *1 oz, in 1 piece*
TOMATOES *1 lb, ripe and firm*
SCAMORZA CHEESE *1*
TOMATO PASTE *1 tablespoon*
EGGS *3*
DRY WHITE WINE *1/4 cup*
GRATED GRANA CHEESE *6 tablespoons*
BUTTER *1 tablespoon*
PEANUT OIL *2 tablespoons*
EXTRA VIRGIN OLIVE OIL *6 tablespoons*
SALT & PEPPER *to taste*

1 Scald tomatoes in boiling water; drain, peel, press to remove seeds and coarsely chop. Separately grind beef, veal and prosciutto. Remove crust from scamorza cheese and cut in small pieces.

2 In a saucepan, heat 3 tablespoons of olive oil. Brown the prosciutto. Add beef, cooking well on all sides. Season with salt and fresh ground pepper. Add wine and let evaporate on high heat.

3 In a bowl, mix tomato paste with 2 tablespoons of water. Add tomatoes and tomato paste to saucepan. Cook on moderate heat for one hour, stirring from time to time with a wooden spoon. In the meantime, in a skillet, hard boil 2 eggs for 7-8 minutes; pass under cold water, drain and coarsely chop.

4 In a bowl, place veal, remaining egg, 2 tablespoons of grated grana, salt and pepper. Mix well until all ingredients are incorporated. Make nut-size balls. In a non-stick pan, heat olive oil and brown few balls at a time. Drain, add to sauce and cook for approximately 15 minutes.

5 In abundant salted water, cook the lasagna al dente. Drain, pass under cold water, drain well and lay on clean dish towel. In a buttered oven dish, place one layer of lasagna and then one of sauce. Sprinkle with scamorza cheese; add chopped eggs and grated grana. Repeat until all ingredients are used, finishing with the sauce. Cook in preheated oven at 415°F for approximately 20 minutes. Serve hot.

Lasagna with artichokes

Difficulty **medium** • *Time needed* **over an hour** • *Calories per serving* **530**

INGREDIENTS
serves 4

FRESH PASTA SQUARES 8
ARTICHOKES 8
LEMON *1, the juice*
WHITE FLOUR *1 tablespoon*
MILK *1 cup*
NUTMEG *to taste*
GRATED GRANA CHEESE *4 tablespoons*
BUTTER *4 tablespoons*
EXTRA VIRGIN OLIVE OIL *2 tablespoons*
SALT *to taste*

1 Clean the artichokes, thinly slice and soak in a bowl with water and half lemon juice. In a pot, boil water with salt; add remaining lemon juice and artichokes; boil for 20 minutes, drain well to remove any water and pass through the vegetable mill, over a skillet.

2 In abundant salted water, cook 2-3 lasagna at a time, adding olive oil. Drain with slotted spoon and place on humid dish towel. Preheat oven to 415°F.

3 In the skillet with artichoke cream, add 4 tablespoons of butter; sprinkle with sifted flour and cook on moderate heat for 5 minutes, and constantly stirring, pour milk. Cook for another 5 minutes, then salt as needed and add nutmeg.

4 Butter a baking pan. Place one layer of lasagna and one of artichoke cream; sprinkle with grana cheese. Repeat until all ingredients are used, finishing with cream and cheese. Cook au gratin in oven at 415°F for 20 minutes. Remove, let cool for a few minutes and serve.

SUGGESTION
*You can substitute fresh artichokes with
1 lb of frozen artichokes;
in this case you will not need
to soak them in water.*

Lasagna alla napoletana

Difficulty **medium** • *Time needed* **over an hour** • *Calories per serving* **710**

INGREDIENTS
serves 6

LASAGNA *12 oz*
PORK LOIN *7 oz*
SAUSAGE *5 oz*
MOZZARELLA *7 oz*
FRESH RICOTTA *7 oz*
TOMATO PASTE *2 tablespoons*
CARROTS *1*
CELERY *1 stalk*
ONIONS *1*
LARD *1 oz*
RED WINE *1/2 cup*
EGGS *2*
BREAD CRUMBS *to taste*
GRATED GRANA CHEESE *5 tablespoons*
EXTRA VIRGIN OLIVE OIL *6 tablespoons*
PEANUT OIL *to taste*
SALT & PEPPER *to taste*

1 Peel onion; chop onion, lard and celery stalk. In a saucepan, heat 3 tablespoons of olive oil; brown onion, lard, celery and pork loin. Add wine and let evaporate on high heat. In a bowl, mix tomato paste with 2 cups of water. Add to saucepan. Salt and pepper. Cook covered for 2 hours on low flame, stirring. Add hot water if needed.

2 Thinly slice the mozzarella. Peel and crumble sausage. In a skillet, heat 1 tablespoon of olive oil; add sausage. Push ricotta through a fine mesh sieve, collecting it in a bowl; add one egg and 3 tablespoons of grana cheese. Salt, pepper and mix well of wooden spoon.

3 After 2 hours of cooking, drain pork loin and cut in half. Place half in a pan and cook. Finely chop the other half of pork loin, placing it in a bowl; add egg and 2 tablespoons of bread crumbs. Mix well. Make nut-size balls and in a pan, fry with peanut oil.

4 In abundant salted water, cook lasagna al dente, adding 2 tablespoons of peanut oil. Drain, pass under cold water, drain well and lay on dish towel.

5 Brush a baking dish with 2 tablespoons of olive oil. Place 1 layer of lasagna and 1 of ricotta. Cover with pork loin sauce, mozzarella, sausage and pork balls. Repeat until all ingredients are used, finishing with loin, sauce, mozzarella and grana. Cook in oven at 415°F for approximately 15 minutes.

Lasagna incassettate

Difficulty **medium** • *Time needed* **over an hour** • *Calories per serving* **420**

INGREDIENTS
serves 6

For the pasta
UNBLEACHED FLOUR *3 cups*
EGGS *3*
EXTRA VIRGIN OLIVE OIL *1 tablespoon*

For the sauce
GROUND MEAT *5 oz*
CHICKEN BREAST *1*
CHICKEN GIBLETS *5 oz*
WHITE TRUFFLES *1*
DRY WHITE WINE *1/2 cup*
BEEF STOCK *3/4 cup*
GRATED GRANA CHEESE *3 tablespoons*
BUTTER *1 tablespoon*
SALT *to taste*

1 In a pan, melt butter. Brown ground beef, chicken breast and innards, keeping aside the livers. Stir well. Five minutes later, gradually add the wine; let evaporate. Lightly salt. Add broth and cook for 20-25 minutes, adding the chopped chicken livers a few minutes before removing pan from heat.

2 Prepare the pasta. Sift flour on work surface into a mound. Make a well in the middle; add eggs and oil. Work the ingredients until dough is smooth and elastic. Roll dough thinly and cut strips 3/4 inches wide and the length of the oven dish. In abundant salted water, cook lasagna al dente.

3 Drain lasagna, pass under cold water, drain well and place on dish towel. Butter a baking pan. Place one layer of lasagna then one layer of meat sauce and grana cheese. Repeat until all ingredients are used. Cook in oven at 415°F for 20 minutes. Remove, sprinkle with grated truffle and serve immediately.

SUGGESTION
The use of excellent extra virgin olive oil in the pasta dough will help make it smoother and will give it more taste.

Multicolored lasagna

*Difficulty **difficult*** • *Time needed **over an hour*** • *Calories per serving **520***

INGREDIENTS
serves 4

For the pasta
UNBLEACHED FLOUR *2 cups*
GREEN PEPPERS *1*
EGGS *2*
GARLIC *1 clove*
BUTTER *1 tablespoon*
PEANUT OIL *1 tablespoon*
EXTRA VIRGIN OLIVE OIL *1 tablespoon*
SALT & PEPPER *to taste*

For the sauce
RED PEPPER *1*
TOMATOES *1 1/4 lbs*
PARSLEY *one bunch*
ONIONS *1/2*
GARLIC *1 clove*
EXTRA VIRGIN OLIVE OIL *3 tablespoons*
SALT & PEPPER *to taste*

For the béchamel
WHITE FLOUR *2 tablespoons*
MILK *1 cup*
GRATED GRANA CHEESE *2 tablespoons*
BUTTER *2 tablespoons*
SALT & PEPPER *to taste*

1 Rinse, peel and chop green pepper. Peel and chop garlic. In a blender, mix pepper and garlic. Prepare the pasta. Sift flour on work surface into a mound. Make a well in the middle; add eggs, pepper mixture, olive oil, salt and pepper. Work all ingredients until dough is smooth and elastic. Cover in plastic wrap and set aside in a cool place for 30 minutes.

2 Prepare the sauce. Rinse red pepper, cut in half, peel and chop. Scald tomatoes in boiling water, drain, peel, press to remove seeds and coarsely chop. Rinse and chop parsley. Chop garlic and onion. In a pan, heat olive oil; brown garlic and onion. Add red pepper and cook for 5 minutes, stirring. Add tomatoes and parsley; cook for 25 minutes.

3 Pass in a vegetable mill, then pour in a cooking pan and thicken sauce. Salt and pepper. Cool. Thinly roll pasta dough and cut into 4 inch squares. In abundant salted water, cook a few at a time, adding peanut oil. Drain, pass under cold water, drain well and lay on dish towel.

4 Prepare the béchamel. In a saucepan, melt butter; add flour, stirring for a few minutes with a wooden spoon. Pour cold milk and boil; add salt and pepper. Cook for 10 minutes, constantly stirring. Remove from heat and add grated grana.

5 Butter a baking pan. Place one layer of béchamel, one layer of pasta and one of pepper-tomato sauce. Repeat until all ingredients are used, finishing with pasta. Brush top with melted butter. Cook in preheated oven at 415°F for approximately 20 minutes. Cool for 5 minutes before serving.

Green lasagna with shrimp

Difficulty **medium** • *Time needed* **over an hour** • *Calories per serving* **580**

INGREDIENTS
serves 6

GREEN LASAGNA *1 lb*
SHRIMPS *2 lbs*
PEELED TOMATOES *14 oz*
CELERY *1 stalk*
ONIONS *1, small*
PARSLEY *1 bunch*
NUTMEG *a pinch*
PAPRIKA *a pinch*
CLOVES *1*
DRY WHITE WINE *1/4 cup*
GRATED PARMIGIANO *to taste*
BUTTER *4 tablespoons*
PEANUT OIL *2 tablespoons*
SALT & PEPPER *to taste*

For the béchamel
FLOUR *1/2 cup*
MILK *2 cups*
NUTMEG *a pinch*
BUTTER *4 tablespoons*
SALT & PEPPER *to taste*

1 Peel, rinse and chop celery and onion. Chop parsley. In abundant water, boil shrimps; drain with slotted spoon, keeping cooking water. In a skillet, melt 2 tablespoons of butter; add the shrimps, the celery, the onion, the parsley, the salt and pepper, the nutmeg, the paprika and the clove.

2 When the shrimps change color, add wine and let evaporate. Add the peeled chopped tomatoes and a full ladle of shrimp cooking water. Cook until the sauce has the right consistency.

3 Prepare the béchamel. In a saucepan, melt butter; add flour, stirring well with a wooden spoon. Pour the milk and boil. Salt and pepper. Cook for approximately 10 minutes, always stirring.

4 In the meantime, in abundant salted water, cook lasagna al dente, adding peanut oil. Drain. In a buttered baking pan, place one layer of lasagna. Add the butter and the grated parmigiano. Add one layer of shrimp sauce. Repeat once, then cover with béchamel. Cook in oven at 375°F for 15 minutes. Serve hot.

Lumache with black truffles

Difficulty **medium** • *Time needed* **under an hour** • *Calories per serving* **820**

INGREDIENTS
serves 4

LUMACHE (SNAIL SHELL PASTA) *11 oz*
VEAL *4 oz*
TURKEY BREAST *8 oz*
COOKED HAM *4 oz, in 1 piece*
BLACK TRUFFLES *1*
ONIONS *1*
PARSLEY *1 bunch*
EGG YOLKS *1*
HEAVY CREAM *3/4 cup*
BEEF BROTH *1/4 cup*
DRY WHITE WINE *1/4 cup*
GRATED GRANA CHEESE *6 tablespoons*
BUTTER *2 tablespoons*
EXTRA VIRGIN OLIVE OIL *2 tablespoons*
SALT & PEPPER *to taste*

1 Peel, rinse, dry and finely chop onion. Rinse, dry and finely chop parsley. Dust, rapidly rinse, dry and slice truffle. Slice ham with a sharp knife. Finely cut veal and turkey breast. Set aside.

2 In a saucepan, heat olive oil; brown onion until transparent. Add veal and turkey breast; brown on high heat. Add wine and let evaporate. Add salt and fresh ground pepper. Cook on moderate heat for approximately 20-30 minutes, adding broth if needed. Add ham and parsley.

3 Pour mixture in a mixing bowl. Add egg yolk, 1/2 cup of heavy cream, 4 tablespoons of grated grana cheese and truffle. Stir with a wooden spoon. In abundant salted water, cook the lumache. Drain and lay on dish cloth with opening face down.

4 Butter a baking dish. Pour remaining heavy cream at the bottom of dish. Fill lumache with mixture and place one layer in dish. Butter them with remaining butter and sprinkle with remaining grated grana. Cook in preheated oven for approximately 15 minutes. Serve hot.

Macaroni of the Bourbons

Difficulty **medium** • *Time needed* **over an hour** • *Calories per serving* **600**

INGREDIENTS

serves 4

FRESH EGG PASTA DOUGH *11 oz*
TOMATOES *1 1/4 lbs*
MOZZARELLA *11 oz*
ONIONS *1*
NEPITELLA *or* MINT *1 bunch*
BAY LEAVES *1 leaf*
SAGE *1 leaf*
MARJORAM *1 branch*
SUGAR *a pinch*
GRATED GRANA CHEESE *4 tablespoons*
PEANUT OIL *2 tablespoons*
EXTRA VIRGIN OLIVE OIL *4 tablespoons*
SALT & PEPPER *to taste*

1 Thinly roll pasta and cut in strips 1 1/2 inches wide and 5 inches long. In abundant salted water, cook a few at a time, adding peanut oil. Drain and lay on humid dish cloth.

2 In the meantime, prepare the sauce. Scald tomatoes in boiling water; drain, peel, press to remove seeds and coarsely chop. In a pan, heat 2 tablespoons of olive oil; brown onion, half the nepitella, bay leaf, sage and marjoram until onion is just transparent.

3 Add tomatoes, salt, fresh ground pepper and a pinch of sugar. Cook on moderate heat. Add the remaining nepitella and olive oil. Stir well. Remove from heat. Slice the mozzarella.

4 In an oven dish, place 1 tablespoon of sauce, 1 layer of pasta and cover with sauce. Add mozzarella slices and sprinkle with grated grana cheese. Repeat until all ingredients are used, finishing with a layer of sauce, mozzarella slices and grana. Cook in preheated oven at 415°F for 15 minutes. Serve hot.

SUGGESTION

Nepitella is a wild mint found all over Italy; it has a very mild taste. If you prefer, you can replace the mint with basil.

Maccheroncini with mozzarella and artichokes

Difficulty **medium** • *Time needed* **under an hour** • *Calories per serving* **550**

INGREDIENTS
serves 4

MACCHERONI *12 oz*
MOZZARELLA *5 oz*
ARTICHOKES *3*
ONIONS *1, small*
PARSLEY *1 bunch*
BREAD CRUMBS *to taste*
VEGETABLE BROTH *1/2 cup*
GRATED PARMIGIANO *2 tablespoons*
EXTRA VIRGIN OLIVE OIL *4 tablespoons*
SALT & PEPPER *to taste*

1 Peel artichokes, remove the ends and remove hardest leaves; cut in half and remove hairs; rinse, dry and thinly slice. Slice onion. In a saucepan, heat 3 tablespoons of olive oil; brown onion until transparent.

2 Add artichokes and salt; stir well with a wooden spoon. Add vegetable broth. Cook on low heat for approximately 20 minutes, stirring. Add chopped parsley.

3 In the meantime, in abundant salted water, cook the maccheroni al dente. Drain in a mixing bowl. Season with artichoke sauce. Add diced mozzarella. Stir well. In an oiled baking dish, place bread crumbs then place pasta.

4 Sprinkle with grated parmigiano. Cook in preheated oven at 435°F for approximately 15 minutes or until top is lightly golden. Serve hot.

Baked maccheroni with tomatoes and capers

Difficulty **easy** • *Time needed* **under an hour** • *Calories per serving* **380**

INGREDIENTS
serves 4

MACCHERONI *11 oz*
TOMATOES *4*
CAPERS IN BRINE *1 oz*
OREGANO *1 teaspoon*
BASIL *1 oz*
GARLIC *1 clove*
GRATED AGED PECORINO *2 tablespoons*
EXTRA VIRGIN OLIVE OIL *2 tablespoons*
SALT *to taste*

1 Scald tomatoes in boiling water; drain, peel, press to remove seeds and thickly slice. Soak capers in water to remove salt. Slice oregano and basil. Peel garlic clove; in a saucepan heat olive oil and brown garlic clove.

2 Remove garlic. Add tomato slices. Cook for 10 minutes. Add capers, stir ring well. Cook for another 10 minutes. Add herbs, and cook 10 minutes.

3 In abundant salted water, cook maccheroni al dente. Drain. Season with sauce. Place in an oiled baking pan. Sprinkle with grated grana and cook in oven at 415°F for a few minutes.

Maccheroni alla pesarese

Difficulty **medium** • *Time needed* **over an hour** • *Calories per serving* **900**

INGREDIENTS
serves 4

LARGE MACCHERONI *11 oz*
GROUND VEAL *2 oz*
TURKEY BREAST *5 oz*
CHICKEN LIVERS *5 oz*
COOKED HAM *7 oz*
BLACK TRUFFLES *1*
ONIONS *1*
HEAVY CREAM *1/2 cup*
GRATED GRUYERE *4 oz*
BUTTER *4 tablespoons*
SALT & PEPPER *to taste*

1 In a saucepan, on low heat, brown 1 tablespoon of butter. Add finely chopped onion and ground veal; cook a few minutes. Add salt and fresh ground pepper. Add 1/2 cup of hot water and cook covered for approximately 20 minutes.

2 In abundant salted water, cook maccheroni. Drain. Chop turkey breast, chicken livers, ham and truffle; place in a mixing bowl. Add 2 tablespoons of heavy cream, salt and pepper.

3 Butter a baking dish. Fill the maccheroni with mixture, using a pastry bag. Place one layer of maccheroni in dish, then add sauce and dabs of butter; sprinkle with gruyere. Add another layer of maccheroni.

4 Pour heavy cream and gruyere over maccheroni. Melt remaining butter in pan; add over pasta. Cook au gratin in preheated oven at 415°F for 15 minutes. Serve hot.

Maccheroni gratinée with pepper sauce

Difficulty **medium** • *Time needed* **under an hour** • *Calories per serving* **560**

INGREDIENTS
serves 4

MACCHERONI *11 oz*
PEPPERS *4*
PITTED BLACK OLIVES *3 oz*
GARLIC *2 cloves*
CHOPPED PARSLEY *1 tablespoon*
OREGANO *a pinch*
CAPERS IN BRINE *3 oz*
BREAD CRUMBS *5 tablespoons*
EXTRA VIRGIN OLIVE OIL *6 tablespoons*
SALT & PEPPER *to taste*

1 Rinse, dry and cook peppers in oven for 5-6 minutes; peel, remove seeds and slice. In a large pot, bring water to boil.

2 Peel garlic cloves; chop. In a saucepan, heat olive oil; add garlic and parsley. Soak capers in lukewarm water to remove salt. Add olives, oregano, unsalted capers and pepper. Cook covered for 8-10 minutes, stirring with a wooden spoon.

3 When the water is boiling, add the pasta, and cook al dente. Drain and season with sauce and half the pepper slices.

4 Oil a baking dish. Place one layer of pasta, then place remaining 1/2 peppers and bread crumbs. Repeat until all ingredients are used, finishing with bread crumbs. Oil top with remaining olive oil. Cook for approximately 20 minutes at 415°F. Serve immediately.

Stuffed maccheroni

Difficulty **medium** • *Time needed* **under an hour** • *Calories per serving* **740**

INGREDIENTS
serves 4

LARGE MACCHERONI *11 oz*
GROUND BEEF *11 oz*
SAUSAGE *5 oz*
EGGS *2*
GRATED PECORINO *6 tablespoons*
EXTRA VIRGIN OLIVE OIL *5 tablespoons*
SALT & PEPPER *to taste*

1 In abundant salted water, cook the maccheroni al dente. Drain and lay on dish cloth. In a saucepan, heat 4 tablespoons of olive oil; fry the peeled and crumbled sausage with ground beef. Pepper. Cook for approximately 20 minutes, constantly stirring and adding if needed hot water. Keep some cooking water.

2 Transfer meat to a mixing bowl. In another bowl, pass the sauce through a fine mesh. Hard-boil the eggs, drain and chop; add to bowl with meat. Fill maccheroni.

3 Oil a baking dish. Place layers of maccheroni alternating with pecorino and some of the meat cooking water. Cook in a preheated oven at 375°F for approximately 15 minutes.

> ### SUGGESTION
> *To obtain a more delicate preparation, you can substitute meat with boiled and chopped beets.*

Green cannelloni with ham

Difficulty **easy** • *Time needed* **under an hour** • *Calories per serving* **620**

INGREDIENTS
serves 6

FRESH PASTA SQUARES *12*
GREEN TORTELLINI *11 oz*
COOKED HAM *12 slices*
RICOTTA *5 oz*
HEAVY CREAM *11/4 cup*
GRATED PARMIGIANO *4 tablespoons*
BUTTER *1 tablespoon*
PEANUT OIL *2 tablespoons*
SALT *to taste*

For the béchamel
WHITE FLOUR *1/2 cup*
MILK *2 cups*
BUTTER *4 tablespoons*
SALT & WHITE PEPPER *to taste*

1 In a large pot filled with abundant boiling salted water, cook the tortellini. When al dente, drain and sauté in a pan with heavy cream.

2 Using a separate pot, in abundant salted water, cook squares of fresh pasta, adding peanut oil. Drain and lay on a dish towel.

3 On each square of pasta, place a slice of ham, a spoonful of tortellini and a little crushed ricotta. Fold pasta, forming cannelloni.

4 Prepare the béchamel. In a saucepan, melt butter; add flour, stirring well. Then add milk; boil for 10 minutes, constantly stirring with a wooden spoon. Season with salt and fresh ground pepper.

5 Butter an oven dish. Place a thin layer of béchamel then place the cannelloni. Cover with remaining béchamel and sprinkle with grated parmigiano.

6 Cook in preheated oven at 435°F until top is lightly golden. Serve immediately.

Fagottini with lamb and yogurt sauce

Difficulty **medium** • *Time needed* **over an hour** • *Calories per serving* **510**

INGREDIENTS
serves 4

For the pasta
UNBLEACHED FLOUR *3 cups*
EGGS *3*
SALT *to taste*

For the filling
GROUND LAMB *8 oz*
ONIONS *1*
PARSLEY *1 bunch*
PEPPER *to taste*

For the sauce
YOGURT *1 1/2 cups*
DRIED MINT LEAVES *1 teaspoon*
GARLIC *3 cloves*
VEGETABLE BROTH *1/2 cup*
BUTTER *3 tablespoons*
SALT *to taste*

1 Sift flour on work surface into a mound. Make a well in the middle; add eggs and a pinch of salt. Work all ingredients until dough is smooth and elastic. Roll pasta dough thinly and cut 2 inch squares.

2 Peel, rinse and finely chop onion. Rinse and dry parsley. In a mixing bowl, place onion, parsley, meat and fresh ground pepper. Mix well with a wooden spoon.

3 On each square, place 1 tablespoon of mixture. Fold square over filling. Bring up corners together turning to make lit-tle bags. In a buttered baking dish, place one layer of pasta bags. Cover with enough broth. Cook in oven at 415°F for 20-25 minutes, until broth is ab-sorbed and pasta is golden.

4 In the meantime, prepare the sauce. Peel and rinse garlic cloves. In a mortar, place garlic cloves and a pinch of salt; add yogurt, stirring well. Then pour sauce over the pasta bags.

5 In a small saucepan, melt butter; add mint leaves, stirring well. Pour over pas-ta and serve immediately.

Baked rigatoni

*Difficulty **easy*** • *Time needed **over an hour*** • *Calories per serving **540***

INGREDIENTS
serves 4

RIGATONI *12 oz*
EGGPLANTS *7 oz, small*
ZUCCHINI *7 oz*
TOMATOES *14 oz, ripe and firm*
BASIL *1 bunch*
ONIONS *1*
GRATED GRANA CHEESE *4 tablespoons*
EXTRA VIRGIN OLIVE OIL *6 tablespoons*
SALT & PEPPER *to taste*

1 Cut off the ends of eggplants, rinse, dry well, and with a sharp knife, slice; place in colander, salt and let sit for 30 minutes to drain well. Then pass under running water, drain well once again and dry with a dish towel. Cut off the ends of zucchinis, rinse and slice. Rinse basil, dry and break it in small pieces.

2 Scald tomatoes in boiling water, drain, remove seeds and coarsely chop.

3 Peel onion, rinse, dry and chop. In a pan, heat 3 tablespoons of olive oil; cook onion until just transparent. Add the eggplant and zucchini slices. Cook on high heat for 3-4 minutes, stirring.

4 Add chopped tomatoes, salt and fresh ground pepper. Cook for approximately 15-20 minutes, then add basil.

5 In abundant salted water, cook the rigatoni al dente; drain; season with a third of eggplant-zucchini sauce and grated grana.

6 Place half the pasta in an oiled baking dish; add sauce and grated grana. Cover with remaining pasta and grated grana. Pour remaining olive oil. Cook in preheated oven at 415°F for approximately 10 minutes, or until top is lightly golden. Serve hot.

Orecchiette with lamb and mozzarella

Difficulty **easy** • *Time needed* **under an hour** • *Calories per serving* **590**

INGREDIENTS
serves 4

ORECCHIETTE *11 oz*
LAMB *5 oz*
ROMA TOMATOES *1 lb*
MOZZARELLA *1*
GRATED PECORINO *4 tablespoons*
EXTRA VIRGIN OLIVE OIL *4 tablespoons*
SALT *to taste*

1 Cut lamb in small pieces; in a pan, heat olive oil and cook lamb, stirring well.

2 Rinse tomatoes, scald for a minute, drain, peel, cut in half, press to remove seeds and coarsely chop. When meat is cooked on all sides, add tomatoes; cook covered on low heat for approximately 20 minutes, adding salt before the end of cooking.

3 In abundant salted water, cook the orecchiette al dente; drain and season with lamb sauce and grated pecorino.

4 Thinly slice mozzarella. In a rectangular baking dish, place one layer of orecchiette, one of sauce, one of mozzarella and pecorino, then another of orecchiette. Repeat until all ingredients are used, finishing with a layer of sauce and pecorino. Cook at 375°F for 10 minutes.

Puglia style baked pasta

Difficulty **medium** • *Time needed* **over an hour** • *Calories per serving* **910**

INGREDIENTS
serves 4

ZITI *12 oz*
GROUND MEAT *8 oz (beef, pork)*
SCAMORZA CHEESE *1*
TOMATOES *1 lb, ripe and firm*
TOMATO PASTE *1 tablespoon*
DRY WHITE WINE *1/4 cup*
EGGS *2*
GRATED GRANA CHEESE *3 tablespoons*
BUTTER *1 tablespoon*
EXTRA VIRGIN OLIVE OIL *3 tablespoons*
SALT & PEPPER *to taste*

For the meatballs
GROUND BEEF *7 oz*
EGGS *1*
GRATED GRANA CHEESE *2 tablespoons*
EXTRA VIRGIN OLIVE OIL *3 tablespoons*
SALT & PEPPER *to taste*

1 Remove crust from scamorza cheese and thinly slice. Scald tomatoes in boiling water, drain, press to remove seeds and coarsely chop. In a pan, heat olive oil; brown the ground beef and pork.

2 Season with salt and pepper; add wine and let evaporate on high heat; add chopped tomatoes. In a bowl, dilute tomato paste with 2 tablespoons of water; add to pan. Add salt; cook covered on moderate heat for approximately one hour, stirring from time to time.

3 In the meantime, hard-boil the eggs; pass under water to cool; drain and slice. Prepare the meatballs. Put the beef in a bowl; add egg, grated grana, salt and pepper; mix until all ingredients are incorporated.

4 Form nut-size balls; in a non-stick pan, heat olive oil; brown a few balls at a time; drain, add to sauce and cook for approximately 10 minutes. In abundant salted water, cook the ziti; drain and season with a third of sauce.

5 In a buttered baking dish, place half the pasta; cover with a layer of sauce, a layer of scamorza cheese, hard-boiled eggs and grana. Cover with remaining pasta and repeat until all ingredients are used. Cook in preheated oven at 390°F for 15 minutes. Serve hot.

Baked pasta with meatballs

Difficulty **medium** • *Time needed* **over an hour** • *Calories per serving* **670**

INGREDIENTS
serves 6

FRESH EGG PASTA DOUGH *11 oz*
GROUND PORK *14 oz*
TOMATO SAUCE *24 oz*
(with garlic, oregano and capers)
HARD BOILED EGGS *4, sliced*
EGGS *2*
PROVOLONE *7 oz, diced*
GRATED PECORINO *6 tablespoons*
EXTRA VIRGIN OLIVE OIL *4 tablespoons*
PEANUT OIL *2 tablespoons*
SALT & WHITE PEPPER *to taste*

1 In a mixing bowl, place pork with 3 tablespoons of pecorino, 2 eggs, a pinch of salt and fresh ground white pepper. Mix well with a wooden spoon. Using your hands, shape olive-size meatballs.

2 In a saucepan, heat 4 tablespoons of olive oil; fry meatballs. Drain on paper towels.

3 In abundant salted water, cook the lasagna al dente, adding peanut oil. Drain and lay on humid dish towel. Preheat oven at 415°F.

4 In a small saucepan, heat tomato sauce; cover bottom of a baking dish. In baking dish, place one layer of lasagna, one layer of sauce, meatballs, slices of hard-boiled egg, some provolone and some pecorino. Repeat until all ingredients are used, finishing with grated pecorino. Cook in preheated oven for 30 minutes. Serve immediately.

SUGGESTION
If the meatball mixture is too soft, you can add some bread crumbs. The original recipe calls for pieces of sausage and ricotta cheese.

Casserole with mozzarella and tomatoes

Difficulty **medium** • *Time needed* **over an hour** • *Calories per serving* **650**

INGREDIENTS
serves 4

For the pasta
UNBLEACHED FLOUR *3 cups*
PEANUT OIL *2 tablespoons*
EXTRA VIRGIN OLIVE OIL *1 tablespoon*
SALT *to taste*

For the filling
TOMATOES *1 1/4 lbs, ripe and firm*
MOZZARELLA *11 oz*
ONIONS *1*
BASIL *1 bunch*
BAY LEAVES *1 leaf*
MARJORAM *1 branch*
GRATED GRANA CHEESE *4 tablespoons*
EXTRA VIRGIN OLIVE OIL *4 tablespoons*
SALT & PEPPER *to taste*

1 Prepare the pasta. Sift the flour on work surface into a mound. Make a well in the middle; add oil and salt. Work ingredients, adding water if needed, until dough is smooth and elastic. Cover in plastic wrap and set aside for 30 minutes in a cool place.

2 In the meantime, prepare the filling. Peel, rinse and finely chop onion. Scald tomatoes in boiling water, drain, peel, press to remove seeds; coarsely chop one half, thickly slice the other half.

3 In a skillet, heat 2 tablespoons of olive oil; add onion, chopped basil, bay leaf and marjoram; brown until onion is transparent. Add tomato slices, chopped tomatoes, a pinch of salt and fresh ground pepper. Cook on high heat for approximately 10 minutes. Finally add the remaining basil and olive oil. Mix well. Remove from heat.

4 Thickly slice the mozzarella. Roll the pasta dough thinly and cut 3 by 2 inch rectangles. In abundant salted water, cook a few at a time; drain, pass under cold water, drain well and place on humid dish cloth.

5 In baking pan, pour some sauce. Place one layer of pasta; add some mozzarella; sprinkle with grated grana cheese. Repeat until all ingredients are used, finishing with a layer of tomato sauce and mozzarella. Cook in preheated oven at 415°F for approximately 15 minutes; serve hot.

Casserole with reginette and mushrooms

Difficulty **easy** • *Time needed* **under an hour** • *Calories per serving* **530**

INGREDIENTS
serves 4

REGINETTE *12 oz*
TOMATOES *1 lb, ripe and firm*
DRIED MUSHROOMS *1 oz*
MUSHROOMS *11 oz*
GARLIC *2 cloves*
BASIL *1 bunch*
PARSLEY *1 bunch*
GRATED GRANA CHEESE *3 tablespoons*
EXTRA VIRGIN OLIVE OIL *5 tablespoons*
SALT & PEPPER *to taste*

1 Soak the dried mushrooms in lukewarm water. Clean fresh mushrooms, rapidly rinse in cold water, drain, dry with dish towel and thinly slice. Peel garlic, rinse and lightly crush. Rinse basil and parsley, chop parsley and break garlic into small pieces. Scald tomatoes in boiling water, drain, peel, press to remove seeds and coarsely chop.

2 In a pan, heat 3 tablespoons of olive oil; brown one garlic clove with some parsley; add dried and fresh mushrooms. Cook, stirring with wooden spoon; season with salt and fresh ground pepper. Remove garlic; add remaining parsley.

In a separate pan, heat remaining olive oil; brown the other garlic clove; add chopped tomatoes, salt and pepper. Cook for 5 minutes; remove garlic; add mushrooms from the other pan and some basil; cook a few more minutes.

3 In the meantime, in abundant salted water, cook the pasta al dente; drain and season with half of the sauce. Pour remaining sauce in a baking dish over half the pasta; sprinkle with grated grana and cover with remaining pasta. Cook in preheated oven at 415°F for approximately 15 minutes.

Vegetable casserole

Difficulty **medium** • *Time needed* **over an hour** • *Calories per serving* **440**

INGREDIENTS

serves 4

REGINETTE *11 oz*
EGGPLANTS *7 oz, small*
ZUCCHINI *7 oz*
TOMATOES *7 oz*
ONIONS *1*
BASIL *1 bunch*
GRATED GRANA CHEESE *3 tablespoons*
EXTRA VIRGIN OLIVE OIL *4 tablespoons*
SALT & PEPPER *to taste*

1 Slice eggplants; place in a colander; add salt. Set aside for 30 minutes; drain, pass under cold water and dry with a dish towel. Slice zucchinis. Peel tomatoes and coarsely chop.

2 Peel onion and chop. In a pan, heat 3 tablespoons of olive oil and brown onion until just transparent. Add eggplants and zucchinis. Brown on high heat for 3-4 minutes, stirring delicately. Add tomatoes, salt and pepper. Cook for 15-20 minutes.

3 Add chopped basil before removing from heat. In abundant salted water, cook pasta al dente; drain; season with a third of the sauce and grated grana.

4 In an oiled baking dish, place half the pasta covered with remaining sauce and grated grana. Place remaining pasta and sprinkle with grana. Cook in preheated oven at 415°F for approximately 10 minutes, until top is lightly golden.

Casserole with cauliflowers and zucchini

Difficulty **medium** • *Time needed* **over an hour** • *Calories per serving* **480**

INGREDIENTS

serves 4

FRESH EGG PASTA DOUGH *12 oz*
CAULIFLOWER *2 lbs*
ZUCCHINI *1 lb*
CHICKEN LIVERS *3 oz*
ONIONS *2, large*
BUTTER *4 tablespoons*
EXTRA VIRGIN OLIVE OIL *1 tablespoon*
PEANUT OIL *2 tablespoons*
SALT & PEPPER *to taste*

1 Rinse zucchini and slice. Clean, rinse and chop onions. Rinse cauliflower, separate flowers, steam for 15 minutes, drain and pass in vegetable mill. In a pan, heat olive oil; brown onions and 2 tablespoons of butter; add cauliflower purée; add salt and pepper; let cook for 2 minutes. In a separate pan, melt 2 tablespoons of butter; add zucchinis and cook for 4-5 minutes with salt and pepper. Dice chicken livers. In a saucepan, heat olive oil; brown livers on all sides.

2 Thinly roll pasta and cut 5 by 3 inch rectangles; in abundant salted water, cook a few at a time, adding peanut oil. Drain, pass under cold water, drain again and lay on humid dish towel.

3 Butter a baking dish; place one layer of pasta and then one layer of cauliflower purée; add liver dice and zucchini slices. Repeat, always alternating. Finish with pasta. Brush top with remaining butter; cook in preheated oven at 415°F for approximately 15 minutes. Serve hot.

Austrian style lasagna

Difficulty **medium** • *Time needed* **under an hour** • *Calories per serving* **840**

INGREDIENTS
serves 4

For the pasta
UNBLEACHED FLOUR *3 cups*
EGGS *3*
EXTRA VIRGIN OLIVE OIL *1 tablespoon*
SALT *to taste*

For the filling
PROSCIUTTO *7 oz, chopped*
EGGS *3*
HEAVY CREAM *1/4 cup*
BUTTER *6 tablespoons*
EXTRA VIRGIN OLIVE OIL *2 tablespoons*
SALT *to taste*

1 Sift flour on pastry board into a mound. Make a well in the middle; add 3 eggs, 1 tablespoon of olive oil and salt; if needed, add 1 tablespoon of lukewarm water. Work all ingredients until the dough is smooth and elastic. Shape into ball. Set aside covered with dish towel for approximately 20 minutes. Thinly roll pasta dough and cut 3 by 5 inch rectangles.

2 In abundant salted water, cook lasagna al dente, adding olive oil. Drain and lay on dish towel.

3 In a bowl, beat butter and 3 egg yolks, setting aside the whites. Add ham; mix well. Finally add the whipped egg whites and heavy cream.

4 Oil a rectangular oven dish; place lasagna and cover with a few tablespoons of egg-ham sauce. Repeat, alternating layers with lasagna and sauce until all ingredients are used. Cook in preheated oven at 415°F for 15 minutes. Serve immediately.

Zucchini and carrot lasagna

Difficulty **medium** • *Time needed* **over an hour** • *Calories per serving* **480**

INGREDIENTS
serves 4

For the pasta
UNBLEACHED FLOUR *3 cups*
EGGS *3*
SESAME SEED OIL *3 tablespoons*
SALT *to taste*

For the filling
ZUCCHINI *4*
CARROTS *4*
MOZZARELLA *4 oz*
BASIL *1 bunch*
WHITE FLOUR *1 tablespoon*
VEGETABLE BROTH *3/4 cup*
SALT & PEPPER *to taste*

For the sauce
PEELED TOMATOES *1 lb*
BASIL *1 bunch*
LEMON JUICE *1 tablespoon*
SALT & PEPPER *to taste*

1 Prepare the pasta. Sift flour on pastry board into a mound. Make a well in the middle; add eggs, a tablespoon of oil and salt; mix well until dough is smooth and elastic. Cover with humid dish towel and set aside for approximately 30 minutes. Thinly roll pasta dough and cut 4 inch squares. In abundant salted water, cook a few squares of pasta at a time. Drain and lay on dish towel.

2 Peel, rinse and thinly slice zucchini and carrots; steam. Rinse basil and break in small pieces. Slice mozzarella. In a saucepan, pass broth and flour together through a fine mesh. Cook for approximately 10 minutes, always stirring. Season with salt and fresh ground pepper.

3 Oil a baking dish. Place one layer of lasagna, cover with a layer of zucchinis and carrots, alternating them and overlapping. Add basil, salt and pepper. Repeat layers, finishing with lasagna. Cover with sliced mozzarella; pour broth-flour sauce. Cook in preheated oven at 375°F for approximately 20 minutes.

4 Mix tomatoes with basil, lemon juice, salt and pepper; pour the mixture in a pan and cook until it becomes purée. Serve warm with the lasagna.

Macaroni casserole

Difficulty **difficult** • *Time needed* **over an hour** • *Calories per serving* **850**

INGREDIENTS
serves 6

For the pie dough
WHITE FLOUR *2 cups*
SUGAR *4 oz*
EGGS *2*
GRATED LEMON PEEL
1 teaspoon
BUTTER *6 tablespoons, at room temperature*
SALT *to taste*

For the filling
MACCHERONI *14 oz*
TOMATOES *7 oz*
DRIED MUSHROOMS *1 oz*
CHICKEN GIBLETS *4 oz*
VEAL SWEETBREADS *2 oz*
BLACK TRUFFLE *1, small*
GRATED GRANA CHEESE *2 tablespoons*
EGGS *1*
POWDERED SUGAR *1/2 tablespoon*
MARSALA *1/4 cup*
BUTTER *4 tablespoons*
SALT & PEPPER *to taste*

For the béchamel
WHITE FLOUR *1/2 cup*
MILK *2 cups*
GRATED NUTMEG *a pinch*
BUTTER *4 tablespoons*
SALT & PEPPER *to taste*

1 Rinse tomatoes, peel, press to remove seeds and break into pieces. Soak mushrooms for 20 minutes in lukewarm water; drain. Melt 3 tablespoons of butter in a pan; add sweetbreads and giblets; slowly cook; add salt, pepper and marsala. Let evaporate on high heat, then add mushrooms, 1/2 cup of water and tomatoes; cook on low heat, stirring, for approximately 20 minutes.

2 To prepare the pastry dough, sift flour on pastry board; add sugar, eggs, butter, salt and lemon peel. Rapidly mix, shaping dough in ball; add more flour and let sit for approximately 30 minutes in a bowl, covered with a dish towel.

3 Prepare the béchamel. In a pan, melt 3 tablespoons of butter; add flour, stir continuously and then add cold milk; cook for 15 minutes, always stirring. Season with salt, pepper and nutmeg.

4 Clean truffle and thinly slice. Using a ladle, remove the giblets, sweetbreads, mushrooms and tomatoes from the sau-ce; add them to the béchamel with the truffle. Pour pan juices in a bowl and set aside. In abundant salted water, cook the maccheroni; drain; transfer to a bowl. Pour pan juices over pasta and sprinkle it with grated grana. Toss well.

5 Divide pastry dough in 2 pieces, one bigger than the other; thinly roll pasta dough. Put largest sheet at the bottom of a buttered pie dish; alternating, place layers of maccheroni and béchamel. Cover with second pastry sheet. Close pie tightly. Brush top with beaten egg.

6 Cook in preheated oven at 415°F for 30 minutes. Remove, sprinkle with powdered sugar and serve immediately.

SUGGESTION
If you prefer, you can substitute the chicken giblets with meat sauce.

Vegetable casserole with sherry

Difficulty **easy** • *Time needed* **under an hour** • *Calories per serving* **910**

INGREDIENTS
serves 4

ELBOW MACARONI *12 oz*
MILD SAUSAGE *11 oz*
FONTINA CHEESE *7 oz*
TOMATOES *11 oz, ripe and firm*
CARROTS *1*
CELERY *1 stalk*
ONIONS *1*
SHERRY *2 oz*
DRY WHITE WINE *1/4 cup*
GRATED GRANA CHEESE *3 tablespoons*
BUTTER *1 tablespoon*
EXTRA VIRGIN OLIVE OIL *3 tablespoons*
SALT & PEPPER *to taste*

1 Peel sausage, break into pieces and set aside. Remove crust from fontina, thinly slice and set aside. Cut off the ends of carrots and peel; remove large filaments from celery stalk. Peel onion. Rinse, dry and finely chop carrot, celery and onion.

2 Scald tomatoes in boiling water, drain, peel, press to remove seeds and coarsely chop. In a pan, heat olive oil and brown sausage; drain and set aside.

3 In the same pan, brown onion, celery and carrot until onion is just transparent; add white wine and sherry; let evaporate on high heat. Add sausage and chopped tomatoes; season with salt and pepper; cook on moderate heat for approximately 20 minutes, stirring from time to time.

4 In the meantime, cook the pasta al dente in abundant salted water. Drain and season with two thirds of sausage sauce and 2 tablespoons of grated grana. Place half the pasta in buttered baking dish; add remaining sauce and half slices of fontina; cover with remaining pasta and fontina; finally sprinkle top with grated grana. Cook in preheated oven at 415°F for approximately 10 minutes. Serve hot.

Casserole with spring vegetables

Difficulty **medium** • *Time needed* **under an hour** • *Calories per serving* **640**

INGREDIENTS
serves 4

TORTIGLIONI *12 oz*
COOKED HAM *3 oz, in 1 piece*
SHELLED PEAS *5 oz*
ASPARAGUS *12 oz*
RED PEPPER *1*
ONIONS *1*
BASIL *1 bunch*
GRATED GRANA CHEESE *2 tablespoons*
BUTTER *4 tablespoons*
EXTRA VIRGIN OLIVE OIL *2 tablespoons*
SALT & PEPPER *to taste*

1 Clean asparagus, cut the hard stems, peel, rinse and slice. Remove seeds and white parts from red pepper, rinse, dry and slice. Peel onion, rinse, dry and finely chop. Rinse basil, delicately dry with dish towel and chop.

2 Slice ham and set aside. In a pan, brown half chopped onion with 1 tablespoon of butter, until just transparent; add asparagus, season with salt and pepper; cook on moderate heat for approximately 7-8 minutes. Remove from heat and pass the asparagus in mill, keeping a few whole tips.

3 In a separate pan, brown the other half of the onion with 1 tablespoon of butter, until just transparent; add peas, salt and pepper; add 1/2 cup of water; cook for 8-10 minutes, covered on moderate heat. In a non-stick pan, heat olive oil and cook pepper slices for approximately 6-7 minutes, stirring from time to time. Season with salt and pepper.

4 Add asparagus sauce, asparagus tips and pepper to the pan with peas. Cook for a minute; remove from heat; add ham and chopped basil.

5 In the meantime, in abundant salted water cook pasta al dente; drain and season with a third of the sauce. Place one layer of pasta in a buttered baking dish; cover with some sauce and grated grana; add another layer of pasta; finish with sauce and grated grana. Cook in preheated oven at 415°F for approximately 10 minutes.

Casserole with tagliatelle

Difficulty **medium** • *Time needed* **over an hour** • *Calories per serving* **660**

INGREDIENTS
serves 6

EGG TAGLIATELLE *12 oz*
EGGS *1*
EGG YOLKS *1*
GRATED PARMIGIANO *5 tablespoons*
BUTTER *6 tablespoons*
SALT *to taste*

For the pie dough
WHITE FLOUR *2 1/2 cups*
EGGS *1*
SALT *to taste*

For the béchamel
WHITE FLOUR *1/2 cup*
MILK *2 cups*
BUTTER *4 tablespoons*
SALT *to taste*

1 Prepare the pasta. Sift flour on pastry board into a mound. Make a well in the middle; add egg, salt and a little water. Work ingredients well, using a fork or your fingers, until dough is smooth and elastic.

2 Form 2 balls, one doubled the other. Thinly roll the largest dough ball. Cover the bottom of a buttered pie dish with dough.

3 Prepare the béchamel. In a saucepan, melt butter; add flour, stirring well. Add cold milk, constantly stirring. Boil for approximately 10 minutes, stirring until béchamel is creamy.

4 In abundant salted water, cook tagliatelle al dente. Drain; place in a bowl with beaten egg. Add melted butter, parmigiano and béchamel. Stir and pour this mixture in pie dish.

5 Roll remaining dough ball; cover pie dish; pinch borders of the dough together; brush top with beaten egg yolk. Cook at 415°F until lightly golden. Serve hot.

Baked penne with mozzarella

Difficulty **easy** • *Time needed* **over an hour** • *Calories per serving* **730**

INGREDIENTS
serves 4

PENNE *14 oz*
MOZZARELLA *1 piece, 7 oz*
TOMATOES *14 oz*
SHELLED PEAS *11 oz*
ONIONS *1*
BASIL *1 bunch*
GRATED GRANA CHEESE *4 tablespoons*
EXTRA VIRGIN OLIVE OIL *5 tablespoons*
SALT & PEPPER *to taste*

1 Scald tomatoes in boiling water; drain, peel, press to remove seeds and coarsely chop. Peel and finely chop onion. In a saucepan, heat 4 tablespoons of olive oil; brown onion until transparent; add tomatoes, peas, salt and pepper. Cook for approximately 20 minutes. Shortly before removing from heat, add sliced basil leaves.

2 In abundant salted water, cook pennette al dente. Drain in a bowl; add a third of sauce, 1/2 of the diced mozzarella and grated grana.

3 In an oiled baking dish, place 1/2 of the pennette. Add sauce, mozzarella and grana.

4 Repeat until all ingredients are used. Cook in preheated oven at 400°F for approximately 10 minutes. Serve hot.

Penne au gratin

Difficulty **easy** • *Time needed* **under an hour** • *Calories per serving* **620**

INGREDIENTS
serves 4

PENNE *12 oz*
COOKED HAM *4 oz, in 1 piece*
WHITE FLOUR *1 tablespoon*
MILK *1/2 cup*
HEAVY CREAM *1/4 cup*
NUTMEG *to taste*
GRATED GRANA CHEESE *4 tablespoons*
BUTTER *3 tablespoons*
SALT & PEPPER *to taste*

1 In a saucepan, melt 2 tablespoons butter; add flour, stirring well. Cook for a minute. Add milk and heavy cream; slowly boil, constantly stirring

2 Season with salt, pepper and nutmeg. Cook for another 10 minutes, always stirring.

3 Coarsely chop ham and set aside. In abundant salted water, cook pasta al dente. Drain in a bowl, and add 1/2 of the sauce. Mix well.

4 In a buttered baking pan, place 1/2 of the pasta. Cover with ham, grated grana and remaining pasta.

5 Pour remaining sauce over. Sprinkle with remaining grana. Cook in preheated oven at 400°F for approximately 10 minutes. Serve hot.

Penne with vegetables

Difficulty **medium** • *Time needed* **over an hour** • *Calories per serving* **670**

INGREDIENTS
serves 4

PENNE *12 oz*
ZUCCHINI *2*
CARROTS *2*
EGGPLANT *1*
SPINACH *7 oz*
LEEKS *1*
CELERY *2 stalks*
BOILED CHICKPEAS *7 oz*
FONTINA CHEESE *4 oz*
BECHAMEL *1 cup*
CHOPPED PARSLEY *1 tablespoon*
BASIL *1 tablespoon, chopped*
EXTRA VIRGIN OLIVE OIL *3 tablespoons*
SALT & PEPPER *to taste*

1 Clean leek, discard outside leaves and green part. Chop leek, celery, parsley and basil. In a saucepan, heat olive oil; place chopped leek, celery, parsley, basil, salt and fresh ground pepper. Fry for 10 minutes. Preheat oven at 400°F.

2 In the meantime, cut off ends of zucchini, carrots and eggplants; dice. Rinse spinach, drain and cut in pieces.

3 Add vegetables, chickpeas and 1 cup of hot water to saucepan. Cook covered on moderate heat for approximately 30 minutes, stirring.

4 In abundant salted water, cook penne al dente. Drain; transfer to a mixing bowl with saucepan mixture. Add sliced fontina. Mix well. Transfer to an oiled baking dish. Cover with béchamel and cook au gratin in oven for approximately 10 minutes. Serve immediately.

Penne au gratin with radicchio

Difficulty **easy** • *Time needed* **under an hour** • *Calories per serving* **490**

INGREDIENTS
serves 4

PENNE *14 oz*
RADICCHIO *3 heads*
GARLIC *1 clove*
BREAD CRUMBS *2 tablespoons*
GRATED PARMIGIANO *1 tablespoon*
BUTTER *3 tablespoons*
SALT & PEPPER *to taste*

1 Carefully rinse radicchio leaves and cut them in pieces. Peel and crush garlic clove. In a saucepan, melt butter; add garlic clove and brown for a minute; remove.

2 Add radicchio, mix well and cook on high heat. Season with salt and fresh ground pepper. Cook on moderate heat, stirring well.

3 In abundant salted water, cook penne al dente. Drain; transfer to saucepan. Toss well and add grated parmigiano.

4 Transfer pasta to buttered baking dish; sprinkle top with bread crumbs and dabs of butter. Grill for a few minutes; serve immediately.

Casserole with prosciutto and mushrooms

Difficulty **medium** • *Time needed* **under an hour** • *Calories per serving* **610**

INGREDIENTS
serves 4

PIPE *12 oz*
COOKED HAM *3 oz*
MUSHROOMS *7 oz*
SHELLED PEAS *4 oz*
TOMATOES *7 oz*
ONIONS *1*
PARSLEY *1 bunch*
GRATED GRANA CHEESE *4 tablespoons*
EXTRA VIRGIN OLIVE OIL *5 tablespoons*
SALT & PEPPER *to taste*

1 Clean mushrooms, rapidly rinse, dry with a clean dish cloth and thickly slice. Scald tomatoes in boiling water; drain, peel, press to remove seeds and coarsely chop

2 Cut ham. Peel onion; finely chop half. In a saucepan, heat 2 tablespoons of olive oil; brown finely chopped onion. Add mushrooms and cook for a few minutes on high heat. Drain and set aside.

3 Slice the remaining half of onion. In the same saucepan, heat 2 tablespoons of olive oil; cook sliced onion until trans-parent. Add chopped tomatoes, peas, salt and pepper; cook for 15-20 minutes. Shortly before removing from the heat, add mushrooms and chopped parsley.

4 In abundant salted water, cook the pipe al dente. Drain and transfer to a mixing bowl; add a third of the sauce, some ham and grated grana cheese.

5 In an oiled baking pan, place pasta; cover with sauce, ham and grana. Repeat once. Cook in preheated oven at 400°F for approximately 10 minutes. Serve hot.

Baked ravioli with eggplant, walnuts and ricotta

Difficulty **medium** • *Time needed* **over an hour** • *Calories per serving* **750**

INGREDIENTS
serves 4

For the pasta
UNBLEACHED FLOUR *3 cups*
EGGS *3*
SAFFRON *1 sachet*
SALT *to taste*

For the filling
EGGPLANT *14 oz*
SHELLED WALNUTS *2 oz*
RICOTTA *8 oz*
PARSLEY *1 bunch*
SAGE *1 leaf*
BASIL *1 bunch*
EGGS *1*
GRATED PECORINO *4 tablespoons*
EXTRA VIRGIN OLIVE OIL *4 tablespoons*
SALT & PEPPER *to taste*

For the sauce
PREPARED TOMATO SAUCE *1 1/2 cups*
GRATED PECORINO *2 tablespoons*
BASIL *a few small leaves*

1 In a bowl with 2 tablespoons of lukewarm water, place saffron. Prepare the pasta. Sift the flour on work surface into a mound. Make a well in the middle; add 2 eggs, a pinch of salt and diluted saffron. Work all ingredients until dough is smooth and elastic. Cover with plastic wrap and set aside for 30 minutes.

2 In the meantime, prepare the filling. Peel eggplants, slice, drain, salt and set aside for 30 minutes; rinse, drain and dry with a clean dish towel. In a saucepan, heat olive oil; brown eggplant slices. Drain on paper towel, let cool and chop finely.

3 Rinse parsley, sage and basil; finely chop. Chop walnuts. In a mixing bowl, place ricotta; add grated pecorino, chopped eggplants, egg, walnuts, parsley, sage and basil. Salt and pepper. Toss ingredients well with a wooden spoon.

4 Prepare the ravioli. Thinly roll pasta dough. Brush with remaining beaten egg. Pour filling on one side of pasta sheet. Fold other half over and press between the mounds of filling to extract any air. Cut the dough in squares between the mounds, forming ravioli.

5 In abundant salted water, cook ravioli al dente. Drain. Heat tomato sauce with basil leaves. Transfer ravioli in a baking dish, sprinkle with grated pecorino and cook in preheated oven at 400°F for 10 minutes. Serve hot.

Baked green ravioli

Difficulty **easy** • *Time needed* **under an hour** • *Calories per serving* **800**

INGREDIENTS
serves 4

GREEN RAVIOLI *1 1/4 lbs*
COOKED HAM *4 oz, diced*
SHELLED WALNUTS *4 oz*
EGG YOLKS *4*
EGG WHITES *3, beaten to stiff peaks*
HEAVY CREAM *4 tablespoons*
NUTMEG *a pinch*
GRATED GRANA CHEESE *6 tablespoons*
MELTED BUTTER *3 tablespoons*
SALT & PEPPER *to taste*

1 In abundant salted water, cook the ravioli al dente. Drain, place in a mixing bowl and season with melted butter. In a bowl, beat egg yolks with the heavy cream, a pinch of salt, fresh ground pepper and nutmeg. Mix well. Add to bowl with ravioli. Blend in the egg whites.

2 Butter an oval baking pan. Place one layer of ravioli, then place diced ham. Sprinkle with grated grana cheese and coarsely chopped walnuts. Repeat until all ingredients are used, finishing with the ravioli.

3 Cook in oven at 400°F until top is lightly golden. Serve immediately.

Baked rigatoni with cherry tomatoes

Difficulty **easy** • *Time needed* **under an hour** • *Calories per serving* **530**

INGREDIENTS
serves 4

RIGATONI *14 oz*
CHERRY TOMATOES *14 oz*
PARSLEY *1 bunch*
GARLIC *2 cloves*
GRATED PECORINO *2 tablespoons*
EXTRA VIRGIN OLIVE OIL *to taste*
SALT & PEPPER *to taste*

1 Preheat oven to 400°F. Rinse tomatoes and thickly slice evenly. Remove seeds. On the bottom of an oiled baking pan, place tomatoes.

2 Rinse and chop parsley. Peel and chop garlic. In abundant salted water, cook the rigatoni al dente.

3 Drain. Place pasta in baking pan on top of the tomatoes. Sprinkle with garlic, parsley and grated pecorino. Pour 2 tablespoons of olive oil. Salt and pepper. Cook for 20 minutes. Serve hot.

Rigatoni au gratin

Difficulty **easy** • *Time needed* **over an hour** • *Calories per serving* **800**

INGREDIENTS
serves 4

RIGATONI *14 oz*
GRATED AGED PECORINO *4 oz*
CACIOCAVALLO CHEESE *4 oz*
MILK *2 cups*
WHITE FLOUR *1/2 cup*
NUTMEG *a pinch*
BUTTER *4 tablespoons*
SALT & PEPPER *to taste*

1 In abundant salted water, cook the rigatoni al dente.

2 In the meantime, prepare the béchamel. In a pan, melt butter; add flour, stirring well; add milk, always stirring; bring to boil. Add nutmeg, salt and pepper. Remove from heat.

3 Drain rigatoni; transfer to mixing bowl and add béchamel and pecorino. Mix well. Butter a baking dish; place pasta and cover with thinly sliced caciocavallo cheese.

4 Cook au gratin in preheated oven at 400°F for approximately 10 minutes. Remove and serve immediately.

Baked stuffed rigatoni

Difficulty **medium** • *Time needed* **under an hour** • *Calories per serving* **580**

INGREDIENTS
serves 4

RIGATONI *5 oz*
COOKED HAM *4 oz*
MUSHROOMS *11 oz*
TOMATOES *1 lb, ripe and firm*
MOZZARELLA *4 oz*
ONIONS *1*
BASIL *1 bunch*
BAY LEAVES *1 leaf*
SAGE *1 leaf*
MARJORAM *1 branch*
PARSLEY *1 bunch*
NUTMEG *to taste*
GRATED GRANA CHEESE *6 tablespoons*
BUTTER *1 tablespoon*
EXTRA VIRGIN OLIVE OIL *4 tablespoons*
SALT & PEPPER *to taste*

1 In abundant salted water, cook rigatoni al dente. Drain, pass under cold water, drain well and lay on a dish towel. Peel onion, rinse and finely chop. Scald tomatoes in boiling water; drain, peel, press to remove seeds and coarsely chop.

2 In a saucepan, heat olive oil; brown onion, some basil, bay leaf, sage and marjoram until onion is transparent. Add tomatoes, salt and pepper; cook on moderate heat. Add remaining basil, stirring well and remove from heat.

3 Coarsely slice the mozzarella. Finely slice ham. Rinse mushrooms and finely slice. In a pan, melt butter; brown mushrooms for 3 minutes on high heat, stirring with a wooden spoon.

4 Drain, finely chop and transfer to mixing bowl. Add mozzarella, ham, parsley, 3 tablespoons of grated grana, salt, pepper and nutmeg. Mix well. Place mixture in pastry bag, and fill rigatoni.

5 In a baking dish, place sauce; alternate filled rigatoni, sauce and grated grana. Cover dish with aluminum foil and cook in preheated oven at 350°F for approximately 20 minutes. Five minutes before cooking ends, remove aluminum foil and cook au gratin. Serve hot.

Baked rosette with tofu

Difficulty **medium** • *Time needed* **over an hour** • *Calories per serving* **890**

INGREDIENTS
serves 4

For the pasta
UNBLEACHED FLOUR *4 cups*
EGGS *4*
SALT *a pinch*

For the filling and the sauce
TOFU *14 oz*
TOMATO SAUCE *14 oz*
ZUCCHINI *11 oz*
CELERY *1 stalk*
ONIONS *1*
PARSLEY *1 bunch*
GRATED CACIOCAVALLO *8 tablespoons*
SUNFLOWER OIL *4 tablespoons*
SALT & PEPPER *to taste*

1 Sift flour on work surface into a mound. Make a well in the middle; add salt and eggs. Work all ingredients until dough is smooth and elastic. Thinly roll and cut 2 inch squares. Set aside.

2 Peel onion. Rinse and peel celery stalk and parsley; chop together. In a saucepan, heat sunflower oil; brown onion, parsley and coarsely chopped tofu, stirring well with a wooden spoon. Season with salt and pepper. Add tomato sauce and cook covered for approximately 20 minutes on low heat, constantly stirring. Drain the tofu sauce and set aside.

3 In the meantime, rinse zucchini, peel and thinly slice. In a pan, heat olive oil and fry zucchini on both sides. Drain with slotted spoon on paper towel. Transfer to mixing bowl and add the tofu.

4 In abundant salted water, cook squares of pasta al dente. Drain and place in each a little filling. Sprinkle with caciocavallo and oil. Fold pasta, forming cannelloni. In an oiled baking pan, place the cannelloni, pour cooking water of tofu and cook in preheated oven at 350°F for approximately 20 minutes. Serve hot.

Baked filled maccheroni

Difficulty **medium** • *Time needed* **under an hour** • *Calories per serving* **820**

INGREDIENTS
serves 4

LARGE MACCHERONII *12 oz*
GROUND PORK *8 oz*
SAUSAGE *4 oz, peeled and crumbled*
SALAMI *4 oz*
HARD BOILED EGGS *2, chopped*
GRATED PECORINO *4 tablespoons*
EXTRA VIRGIN OLIVE OIL *to taste*
SALT & PEPPER *to taste*

1 In a skillet, heat 4 tablespoons of olive oil; fry sausage; add pork and salami; brown. Add pepper and cook on moderate heat, mixing well and adding little hot water if needed.

2 In the meantime, in abundant salted water, cook maccheroni al dente. Drain and place on dish cloth. Remove meats from skillet and transfer to a mixing bowl; mix with hard-boiled eggs.

3 Fill maccheroni with this mixture; transfer to a baking dish. Sprinkle meat sauce and pecorino. Cook for some 10 minutes in oven at 400°F. Serve hot.

Pasta sformatini with mushrooms

Difficulty **medium** • *Time needed* **over an hour** • *Calories per serving* **530**

INGREDIENTS
serves 4

FRESH EGG PASTA DOUGH *11 oz*
MUSHROOMS *1 lb*
FROZEN SPINACH *2 lbs, cooked*
SHALLOTS *2*
HEAVY CREAM *1/4 cup*
DRY WHITE WINE *5 tablespoons*
BUTTER *4 tablespoons*
SALT & PEPPER *to taste*

1 Peel shallots and finely chop. In a skillet, melt 2 tablespoons of butter and brown half shallots; add spinach; cook for a few minutes. Add 1/2 white wine and let evaporate. Add 1/2 of heavy cream, salt and fresh ground pepper. Remove from heat and set aside. Rapidly rinse mushrooms, dry and slice. In another pan, melt 2 tablespoons of butter and brown remaining shallots; add mushrooms and brown for 2 minutes. Pour remaining wine and let evaporate; add heavy cream, salt and fresh ground pepper.

2 Preheat oven to 400°F. Thinly roll pasta, and with a cookie cutter, cut 48 disks. In abundant salted water, cook a few disks at a time. Drain, pass under cold water, drain well and place on dish towel. Butter 12 ramekins and cover with disks. On each, place spinach preparation, cover with another disk and place a layer of mushroom preparation. Repeat until all ingredients are used. Finish with a disk and seal sides together. Cook in oven for approximately 7-8 minutes. Serve hot.

Baked capellini sformato

Difficulty **easy** • *Time needed* **less then 30 minutes** • *Calories per serving* **390**

INGREDIENTS
serves 4

CAPELLINI *8 oz*
GARLIC *1 clove*
BROTH *2 cups*
BUTTER *3 tablespoons*
EXTRA VIRGIN OLIVE OIL *2 tablespoons*
SALT & PEPPER *to taste*

1 Rinse garlic clove and dry; do not peel it. In a small pan, bring broth to boil. Separate the capellini in half. In a baking dish or cast iron pan, heat olive oil and butter; add garlic clove and brown; add half of the capellini.

2 Cook for a few minutes, stirring with a wooden spoon; add broth; cover and cook for 6-7 minutes on very low heat.

3 When broth is absorbed, remove garlic; season with salt and fresh ground pepper, stirring well. Cook in preheated oven at 400°F for approximately 10 minutes.

4 When finished cooking, take out of the baking dish, turn over onto the serving plate and serve immediately.

Baked sformato with tagliolini and zucchini

*Difficulty **easy*** • *Time needed **under an hour*** • *Calories per serving **420***

INGREDIENTS
serves 4

TAGLIOLINI *12 oz*
ZUCCHINI *14 oz*
EGG YOLKS *2*
VEGETABLE BROTH *1/2 cup*
GRATED PARMIGIANO *3 tablespoons*
EXTRA VIRGIN OLIVE OIL *1 tablespoon*
SALT *to taste*

1 Rinse zucchini, cut off the ends and cut in julienne. In abundant salted water, cook tagliolini and zucchini slices for 5 minutes. Drain and transfer to a mixing bowl.

2 Beat egg yolks with broth and parmigiano; add to mixing bowl, tossing well. Place mixture in an oiled baking dish and cook in preheated oven at 400°F for approximately 10 minutes..

SUGGESTION
This sformato of tagliolini can also be made with other vegtetables; if you use green leaves, like beet tops, cut them in strips and scald them in boiling water for 30 seconds and then add the pasta. If you use carrots, cut them in julienne and boil in water for 10 minutes, like the zucchini.

Baked tagliatelle and spinach

*Difficulty **medium*** • *Time needed **under an hour*** • *Calories per serving **590***

INGREDIENTS
serves 4

TAGLIATELLE *12 oz*
SPINACH *14 oz*
RICOTTA *4 oz*
HEAVY CREAM *to taste*
NUTMEG *a pinch*
GRATED PARMIGIANO *4 tablespoons*
BUTTER *4 tablespoons*
SALT *to taste*

1 Tear off the stems from all spinach leaves. Clean well, dry and coarsely chop. Twist them in a towel to eliminate all water.

2 In a non-stick pan, cook spinach for 3 minutes to remove excess water. Set aside. Preheat oven at 400°F. In a large pot, bring water to boil, adding salt. In a bowl, mix ricotta and heavy cream until you obtain the consistency of a béchamel; season with nutmeg, add spinach and season with salt.

3 In the large pot with salted water, cook the tagliatelle al dente.

4 Drain. Transfer to a buttered baking pan. Cover with spinach preparation. Sprinkle with grated parmigiano and dabs of butter.

5 Cook in oven for 10 minutes, until top is lightly golden. Serve immediately.

Tagliatelle baked with artichokes

Difficulty **medium** • *Time needed* **under an hour** • *Calories per serving* **610**

INGREDIENTS
serves 4

For the pasta
UNBLEACHED FLOUR *3 cups*
EGGS *3*
SALT *to taste*

For the sauce
ARTICHOKES *4*
LEMON *1, the juice*
PARSLEY *1 bunch*
SHALLOTS *1*
GRATED EMMENTAL *5 oz*
BUTTER *1 tablespoon*
EXTRA VIRGIN OLIVE OIL *4 tablespoons*
SALT & PEPPER *to taste*

1 Prepare the pasta. Sift the flour on work surface into a mound. Make a well in the middle; add eggs and salt. Work all ingredients until dough is smooth and elastic. Cover with plastic wrap and set aside for 30 minutes.

2 In the meantime, prepare the sauce. Clean artichokes, removing hard leaves and tips; cut in half; remove hairs. Thinly slice. Transfer to a bowl with cold water and lemon juice.

3 Rinse parsley, dry with dish towel and chop. Peel shallot, rinse, dry and finely chop. Drain and dry artichokes. In a saucepan, heat olive oil; brown shallot until transparent; add artichokes, salt and pepper; cook covered for 7-8 minutes, stirring well. Add parsley.

4 Prepare the tagliatelle. Thinly roll pasta dough; with a sharp knife, cut tagliatelle. In abundant salted water, cook al dente. Drain and transfer to mixing bowl with two thirds of sauce; add half the grated emmental and mix well.

5 Butter a baking dish; place half tagliatelle, remaining artichokes and sprinkle with grated emmental; finish with tagliatelle. Sprinkle with remaining emmental. Cook in preheated oven at 400°F for approximately 10 minutes. Serve hot.

Buckwheat tagliatelle baked with tofu

Difficulty **medium** • *Time needed* **under an hour** • *Calories per serving* **470**

INGREDIENTS
serves 4

BUCKWHEAT TAGLIATELLE *11 oz*
TOFU *6 oz*
ONIONS *1*
CARROTS *1/2*
CHOPPED PARSLEY *2 tablespoons*
LEMON RIND *to taste*
SOY MILK *1/2 cup*
WHOLE WHEAT FLOUR *2 tablespoons*
EXTRA VIRGIN OLIVE OIL *5 tablespoons*
SALT *to taste*

1 Peel and slice onion. In saucepan, heat 2 tablespoons olive oil; brown onion until just transparent. Peel and slice carrot in julienne. Dice tofu. Add carrot and tofu to saucepan. Sauté for 3-4 minutes and salt.

2 In a small pan, heat a little olive oil and add whole wheat flour; stirring constantly, cook for a minute; gradually add soy milk; cook on low heat, until sauce is creamy, always stirring; add salt.

3 In abundant salted water, cook tagliatelle al dente. Drain and transfer to an oiled baking dish. Pour tofu sauce and olive oil over.

4 Cook in preheated oven at 350°F for approximately 20 minutes until top is lightly golden. Remove and serve hot. This dish can also be served cold, sprinkled with chopped parsley and lemon peels, cut in strips.

Tagliolini au gratin with herbs

Difficulty **easy** • *Time needed* **under an hour** • *Calories per serving* **520**

INGREDIENTS
serves 4

EGG TAGLIOLINI *11 oz*
BASIL *1 bunch*
PARSLEY *1 bunch*
MARJORAM *a few branches*
ONIONS *1, small*
WHITE FLOUR *1/4 cup*
MILK *1 cup*
NUTMEG *to taste*
GRATED GRANA CHEESE *4 tablespoons*
BUTTER *4 tablespoons*
SALT & PEPPER *to taste*

1 Peel onion, rinse and finely chop. Rinse basil, parsley and marjoram; dry and chop. In a small saucepan, melt butter; brown onion until just transparent.

2 Add flour, stirring constantly with wooden spoon. Add milk and boil; add salt, pepper and nutmeg. Cook for 10 minutes, always stirring.

3 Remove saucepan from heat; add herbs and 2 tablespoons of grated grana cheese. In the meantime, in abundant salted water, cook tagliolini al dente, drain and add to saucepan. Toss well.

4 In buttered baking dish, place tagliolini. Brush surface with remaining melt butter and sprinkle with grated grana cheese. Cook au gratin in preheated oven at 400°F. Serve hot.

Tagliolini with truffles in puff pastry

Difficulty **medium** • *Time needed* **under an hour** • *Calories per serving* **880**

INGREDIENTS
serves 4

FRESH TAGLIOLINI 8 *oz*
PUFF PASTRY DOUGH 8 *oz*
TRUFFLE PASTE 1 *tablespoon*
ZUCCHINI 5 *oz*
STRING BEANS 5 *oz*
CARROTS 5 *oz*
LEEKS 5 *oz*
EGGS 1
GRATED GRANA CHEESE 3 *tablespoons*
BUTTER 3 *tablespoons*
SALT & PEPPER *to taste*

For the sauce
CHIVES 1 *bunch*
HEAVY CREAM 1/4 *cup*

For the béchamel
WHITE FLOUR 1/4 *cup*
MILK 1 *cup*
NUTMEG *a pinch*
BUTTER 3 *tablespoons*
SALT & PEPPER *to taste*

1 Cut off ends of carrot and peel. Clean leeks, discard outside leaves and green part. Cut off ends of zucchini and green beans. Rinse vegetables. Cut green beans in small pieces. Cut carrots, leeks and zucchini in big strips. Scald vegetables separately in boiling water. Drain. In a skillet, melt butter; add vegetables and brown for 3-4 minutes. Season with salt and fresh ground pepper.

2 In the meantime, prepare the béchamel. In a saucepan, melt butter. Add flour, stirring with wooden spoon. Add cold milk, salt, pepper and nutmeg; cook for approximately 10 minutes. Transfer to a bowl; add vegetables and truffle paste; mix well.

3 In abundant salted boiling water, un-dercook the tagliolini, harder than al dente. Drain well and add to the béchamel and vegetables, and toss well. Add grated grana, salt and pepper. With a rolling pin, roll out a thin layer of puff pastry. Cut out 4 circles. In the center of each, place a portion of the pasta mixture, close in little pouches.

4 Brush surface with beaten egg. Cover with leaf dough and brush with beaten egg. Brush cookie sheet with water. Place purses on cookie sheet. Cook in preheated oven at 350°F for approximately 15 minutes. Rinse chives, dry and finely chop. In a saucepan, reduce heavy cream on moderate heat; add chives, pinch of salt and pepper. Serve hot with chives sauce.

Vegetable casserole, Puglia style

Difficulty **easy** • *Time needed* **under an hour** • *Calories per serving* **530**

INGREDIENTS
serves 4

SHORT PASTA *11 oz*
TOMATOES *1 lb, ripe and firm*
POTATOES *2*
ONIONS *1*
CELERY *1 stalk*
CHILI PEPPER *1*
OREGANO *a pinch*
BREAD CRUMBS *1/2 tablespoon*
GRATED PECORINO *6 tablespoons*
EXTRA VIRGIN OLIVE OIL *5 tablespoons*
SALT *to taste*

1 Peel potatoes and onion, rinse, thinly slice and scald separately in boiling water for a minute. Drain and set aside. Remove large filaments from celery stalk, rinse and slice. Scald in boiling water and drain.

2 Scald tomatoes in boiling water; drain, peel, press to remove seeds and coarsely chop. In abundant salted water, cook the pasta for 6 minutes; drain; season with 2 tablespoons of olive oil.

3 In an oiled baking dish, place one layer of pasta; cover with half the tomatoes, celery, potatoes and onions; season with salt; add chopped hot pepper and oregano; sprinkle with grated pecorino and add olive oil.

4 Repeat once, finishing with potatoes and tomatoes. Add olive oil and sprinkle bread crumbs. Cook in preheated oven at 350°F for approximately 15 minutes. Serve hot.

Pasta baked with asparagus and peas

Difficulty **easy** • *Time needed* **under an hour** • *Calories per serving* **610**

INGREDIENTS
serves 4

SHORT PASTA *12 oz*
ASPARAGUS *12 oz*
SHELLED PEAS *5 oz*
FONTINA CHEESE *4 oz*
ONIONS *1*
GRATED GRANA CHEESE *2 tablespoons*
BUTTER *7 tablespoons*
SALT & PEPPER *to taste*

1 Remove crust from fontina and thinly slice. Clean asparagus, remove hard stems, peel, rinse and chop, keeping aside some whole tips. Peel onion, rinse and chop.

2 In a skillet, melt 3 tablespoons of butter; brown half onion until just transparent; add asparagus, season with salt and pepper; cook covered on moderate heat for approximately 7 minutes. Remove from heat. Blend asparagus, keeping aside some tips.

3 In a saucepan, melt remaining butter and brown remaining onion until transparent; add peas and brown a few minutes. Add a tablespoon of water, salt and fresh ground pepper. Cook covered for approximately 10 minutes on moderate heat, stirring. Add asparagus mixture and the asparagus tips.

4 In the meantime, in abundant salted water, cook pasta al dente. Drain and transfer to asparagus-peas preparation.

5 In a buttered oven pan, place one layer of pasta; cover with fontina cheese; sprinkle with grana cheese and cover with another layer of pasta. Repeat until all ingredients are used. Cook au gratin in preheated oven at 400°F for approximately 10 minutes. Serve immediately.

Baked tordelli with mixed meats

Difficulty **medium** • *Time needed* **over an hour** • *Calories per serving* **670**

INGREDIENTS
serves 6

FRESH EGG PASTA DOUGH *12 oz*
EGGS *1*
BUTTER *1 tablespoon, for pan*

For the filling
LEFTOVER MEATS *11 oz (beef and pork)*
BREAD CRUMBS *2 oz*
MILK *1/2 cup*
EGGS *1*
NUTMEG *a pinch*
POWDERED CINNAMON *a pinch*
HEAVY CREAM *1/2 cup*
GRATED GRANA CHEESE *3 tablespoons*
SALT & PEPPER *to taste*

For the sauce
GROUND BEEF *14 oz*
TOMATOES *1 lb, ripe and firm*
DRIED MUSHROOMS *1 oz*
CARROTS *1/2*
CELERY *1/2 stalk*
ONIONS *1*
GARLIC *1/2 clove*
BASIL *1 bunch*
RED WINE *1/4 cup*
BEEF BROTH *1/4 cup*
GRATED GRANA CHEESE *6 tablespoons*
EXTRA VIRGIN OLIVE OIL *4 tablespoons*
SALT & PEPPER *to taste*

1 Prepare sauce. Soak dried mushrooms in lukewarm water. Peel onion and garlic. Remove large filaments from celery stalk. Cut off ends of carrot and peel. Rinse, dry and chop vegetables. Scald tomatoes in boiling water; drain, peel, press to remove seeds and coarsely chop.

2 Rinse basil, dry and finely chop. In a skillet, heat olive oil; cook garlic, onion, carrot and celery until onion is transparent. Drain and chop mushrooms. Add to skillet and cook for a few minutes. Add ground beef and cook on all sides.

3 Add wine and let evaporate on high heat. Add tomatoes, salt and pepper; cook for a few minutes. Add broth and basil; cook on moderate heat for one hour, adding more broth if needed.

4 In the meantime, prepare the filling. In a bowl, place bread crumbs and milk. Let soften. Chop meat and place in mixing bowl; add egg and grated grana. Drain bread crumbs well and add to meat mixture; add heavy cream, salt, pepper, nutmeg and cinnamon. Mix well, stirring with a wooden spoon until mixture is homogeneous.

5 Prepare the tordelli. Thinly roll pasta dough. With a pastry wheel, cut 2 inch circles. Brush with beaten egg. On each pasta circle, place a little filling; fold pasta, forming a half-moon.

6 In abundant salted water, cook tordelli al dente. Drain. Mix with two thirds of meat sauce and 3 tablespoons of grana. In a buttered oven pan, place a third of pasta. Cover with meat sauce and grana. Repeat until all ingredients are used. Cook au gratin in preheated oven at 400°F for approximately 10 minutes. Serve hot.

Maccheroni timballo

Difficulty **medium** • *Time needed* **over an hour** • *Calories per serving* **430**

INGREDIENTS
serves 6

MACCHERONCELLI *12 oz*
GROUND BEEF *11 oz*
TOMATOES *1 lb, ripe and firm*
DRIED MUSHROOMS *1 oz*
PROSCIUTTO *2 oz*
EGGPLANTS *2*
CARROTS *1/2*
CELERY *1/2 stalk*
ONIONS *1/2*
GARLIC *1/2 clove*
BASIL *1 bunch*
PARSLEY *1 bunch*
MILD SCAMORZA CHEESE *3 oz*
NUTMEG *to taste*
RED WINE *1/4 cup*
BEEF BROTH *1/4 cup*
BUTTER *1 tablespoon*
EXTRA VIRGIN OLIVE OIL *3 tablespoons*
SALT & PEPPER *to taste*

1 Scald tomatoes in boiling water; drain, peel, press to remove seeds and coarsely chop. Soak mushrooms in lukewarm water. Chop prosciutto. Rinse and chop parsley. Rinse and finely chop carrot, celery, onion and garlic.

2 In a saucepan, heat 2 tablespoons of olive oil; brown prosciutto. Add celery, onion, carrot and garlic, stirring. Drain and chop mushrooms; add to saucepan. Add meat and brown. Add wine and let evaporate on high heat. Add tomatoes, nutmeg, parsley, salt, pepper and broth. Cook uncovered on moderate heat for at least one hour. Add more broth if needed. At the end of cooking, add chopped basil.

3 Thinly slice scamorza cheese. Cut off ends of eggplants and rinse; with the help of a potato peeler, cut skin into long strips; scald strips in boiling water; drain and dry on paper towel.

4 Thinly slice the peeled eggplants. In a non-stick pan, heat olive oil and brown eggplants on both sides. Butter an oven dish. Cover bottom with strips of eggplant, alternating with strips of peel. Let the strips go over sides of dish. Keep a few strips aside.

5 In abundant salted water, cook pasta al dente; drain and add meat sauce. Place sauce, scamorza slices and pasta in oven dish. Repeat until all ingredients are used, finishing with meat sauce.

6 Fold strips over sauce. Cover with strips you set aside earlier. Cook in pre-heated oven at 400°F for approximately 15 minutes. Serve hot.

Maccheroni pie

Difficulty **medium** • *Time needed* **over an hour** • *Calories per serving* **770**

INGREDIENTS
serves 6

For the pie dough
WHITE FLOUR *2 cups*
SUGAR *2 oz*
EGG YOLKS *2*
LEMON *1, rind*
BUTTER *6 tablespoons*
SALT *to taste*

For the filling
MACCHERONI RIGATI *14 oz*
PREPARED MEAT SAUCE *1 cup*
BREAD CRUMBS *to taste*
GRATED GRANA CHEESE *6 tablespoons*
BUTTER *1 tablespoon*
SALT *to taste*

For the béchamel
WHITE FLOUR *1/2 cup*
MILK *2 cups*
NUTMEG *1 pinch*
BUTTER *4 tablespoons*
SALT *to taste*

1 Prepare pastry dough. In the bowl of a food processor, mix sifted flour, sugar, cold butter cut in small pieces, grated lemon peel and a pinch of salt, pulsing until the mixture resembles coarse meal. Add egg yolks and continue mixing at high speed until dough is smooth and forms a ball, cover with plastic wrap and set aside in refrigerator for 45 minutes to an hour.

2 Prepare the béchamel. In a saucepan, melt butter. Add flour, stirring well; cook for a few minutes. Add cold milk, constantly stirring. Add salt and nutmeg; cook for 5 minutes, continuing to stir until sauce is creamy.

3 Remove pastry dough from refrigerator. In abundant boiling salted water, cook maccheroni al dente, drain and let cool. Butter a baking pan and cover bottom with bread crumbs. Divide pastry dough in 2 balls, one double the other. Thinly roll the largest; cover bottom and sides of pan. Place several layers of maccheroni, béchamel, meat sauce and grana cheese. Repeat until all ingredients are used.

4 Roll remaining pastry dough ball and cover pasta, carefully bringing together the sides. Cook in oven at 400°F for approximately 40 minutes. Serve hot.

Tortellini in a pie

Difficulty **difficult** • *Time needed* **over an hour** • *Calories per serving* **840**

INGREDIENTS
serves 6

TORTELLINI *1 lb*
FROZEN PUFF PASTRY DOUGH *1 package*
GROUND BEEF *4 oz*
SAUSAGE *4 oz*
PEELED TOMATOES *8 oz*
DRIED MUSHROOMS *1 oz*
ONIONS *1*
CELERY *1 stalk*
CARROTS *1*
DRY WHITE WINE *to taste*
GRATED PARMIGIANO *to taste*
BUTTER *3 tablespoons*
EXTRA VIRGIN OLIVE OIL *2 tablespoons*
SALT & PEPPER *to taste*

For the béchamel
WHITE FLOUR *1/2 cup*
MILK *2 cups*
NUTMEG *a pinch*
GRATED PARMIGIANO *to taste*
BUTTER *4 tablespoons*
SALT & PEPPER *to taste*

1 Thaw puff pastry dough. Soak mushrooms in lukewarm water. Peel and crumble sausage. Peel, rinse and chop onion, celery and carrot.

2 In a saucepan, heat 2 tablespoons of olive oil and a dab of butter. Brown chopped vegetables. Add ground meat and sausage; cook for a minute. Add wine and let evaporate.

3 Drain and slice mushrooms. Peel tomatoes. Add mushrooms, tomatoes, salt and pepper. Cook on low heat for 45 minutes.

4 Prepare the béchamel. In a skillet, melt butter; add flour, stirring well. Add cold milk and continue to stir. Add salt, pepper, nutmeg and 1 tablespoon of grated parmigiano.

5 In abundant salted water, cook tortellini al dente, drain and transfer to mixing bowl with half the sauce and parmigiano. Butter and flour a springform. Cover bottom and sides with puff pastry dough.

6 Place one layer of tortellini in springform, one of béchamel, one of sauce and parmigiano. Repeat until all ingredients are used, finishing with parmigiano. Cook in oven at 400°F for 30 minutes. Remove from oven, transfer to a serving plate and serve immediately.

Ditalini au gratin

Difficulty **easy** • *Time needed* **under an hour** • *Calories per serving* **450**

INGREDIENTS
serves 4

DITALINI *7 oz*
STRING BEANS *7 oz, boiled*
MILK *3 cups*
EGGS *1*
BREAD CRUMBS *to taste*
GRATED GRANA CHEESE *4 tablespoons*
BUTTER *3 tablespoons*
SALT & WHITE PEPPER *to taste*

1 Preheat oven at 400°F. In a pot, boil milk, salt and fresh ground white pepper. Add pasta; cook al dente, stirring well; almost all milk should be absorbed. Remove from heat. Cut green beans in small pieces. Add green beans, 2 tablespoons of grana cheese and the

egg to pot.

2 Mix well. In a buttered baking dish, cover bottom with bread crumbs. Add preparation; sprinkle with remaining grana cheese. Cook in oven until top is lightly golden. Serve immediately.

Pesara style cannelloni

Difficulty **medium** • *Time needed* **under an hour** • *Calories per serving* **800**

INGREDIENTS
serves 4

CANNELLONI *11 oz*
GROUND VEAL *2 oz*
TURKEY BREAST *5 oz*
COOKED HAM *7 oz*
CHICKEN LIVERS *5 oz*
BLACK TRUFFLES *1*
ONIONS *1*
HEAVY CREAM *2 tablespoons*
GRATED GRUYERE *4 oz*
BUTTER *2 tablespoons*
SALT & PEPPER *to taste*

1 Peel and finely chop onion. In a saucepan, melt butter; cook onion until transparent; add ground veal and cook until meat starts to brown. Add 1/2 cup of water, salt and pepper. Cook on low heat until all juices have reduced by half.

2 Finely chop together turkey breast, chicken liver, truffle and ham; pass in a blender. Transfer mixture to a mixing bowl. Add 2 tablespoons of heavy cream, salt and pepper. Mix well, using a wooden spoon, until homogeneous.

3 In abundant salted water, cook canneloni al dente for approximately 10 minutes; drain. Fill with mixture, being careful not to break them. If you wish, you can use a pastry bag to completely fill the pasta.

4 Butter a baking dish. Place one layer of filled pasta. Cover with veal sauce, a dab of butter and grated gruyere. Cook in oven at 400°F for approximately 15 minutes, until top is lightly golden. Serve hot.

Lasagna alla marchigiana

Difficulty **medium** • *Time needed* **over an hour** • *Calories per serving* **640**

INGREDIENTS
serves 4

FRESH EGG PASTA DOUGH *11 oz*
CHICKEN BREAST *11 oz*
CHICKEN GIBLETS *5 oz*
DRIED MUSHROOMS *1 oz*
BLACK TRUFFLES *1*
CARROTS *1*
ONIONS *1*
DRY MARSALA *2 tablespoons*
BEEF BROTH *1/4 cup*
GRATED GRANA CHEESE *2 tablespoons*
BUTTER *3 tablespoons*
PEANUT OIL *2 tablespoons*
EXTRA VIRGIN OLIVE OIL *2 tablespoons*
SALT & PEPPER *to taste*

For the béchamel
WHITE FLOUR *1 tablespoon*
MILK *1 cup*
BUTTER *1 tablespoon*
SALT & PEPPER *to taste*

1 Peel onion. Cut off ends of carrot and peel. Rinse and chop onion and carrot. Soak mushrooms in lukewarm water, drain well and chop. Brush truffle and coarsely chop. Wash, dry and separately dice chicken innards and chicken breasts. In a skillet, heat olive oil; brown onion and carrot until onion is transparent. Add innards (keeping aside the livers) and brown for a few minutes.

2 Add dry marsala and let evaporate on high heat; add mushrooms and truffle. Cook for a minute. Add chicken breasts and cook on high heat, stirring with a wooden spoon. Add broth; cook covered on moderate heat, adding if needed some boiling water. Approximately 2 minutes before the end of cooking, add chicken livers.

3 In the meantime, prepare the béchamel. In a small saucepan, melt butter. Add flour, stirring for 2 minutes; slowly add the milk mixing constantly. Add salt and pepper. Bring to boil and cook for approximately 10 minutes, stirring. Remove from heat; add to skillet and mix well. Thinly roll pasta and cut rectangles of 4 by 8 inches.

4 In abundant salted water, cook a few at a time, adding peanut oil. Drain, pass under cold water, drain well and lay on dish cloth. Butter a baking pan; place one layer of pasta and then one layer of sauce. Repeat until all ingredients are used, finishing with a layer of pasta. In a saucepan, melt remaining butter. Brush top of last layer with melted butter. Cook in preheated oven at 400°F until top is lightly golden. Serve hot, with grated grana cheese.

Sicilian style zite

Difficulty **medium** • *Time needed* **over an hour** • *Calories per serving* **540**

INGREDIENTS
serves 4

ZITE *11 oz*
EGGPLANTS *14 oz*
TOMATOES *1 lb*
ONIONS *1*
GARLIC *1 clove*
BASIL *1 bunch*
GRATED GRANA CHEESE *2 tablespoons*
GRATED PECORINO *2 tablespoons*
EXTRA VIRGIN OLIVE OIL *6 tablespoons*
SALT & PEPPER *to taste*

1 Rinse eggplants, dry, cut off ends and slice. Drain, salt and set aside for one hour. Peel tomatoes, press to remove seeds and coarsely chop. Peel and chop onion. Peel garlic.

2 In a saucepan, heat 2 tablespoons of olive oil; brown onion and garlic. Add tomatoes and chopped basil. Season with salt and pepper. Cook for 20 minutes, stirring. In abundant salted water, cook zite al dente. Drain and add 2 tablespoons of olive oil.

3 Pass eggplants under cold water and dry. In a pan, heat olive oil; cook eggplants until both sides are golden. Drain and set aside. Place half in an oven dish, covering with tomato sauce. Add half eggplants and sprinkle with cheese.

4 Repeat until all ingredients are used. Keep aside 3 slices of eggplants. Cook au gratin in preheated oven at 400°F for approximately 10 minutes. Remove from oven, add the 3 slices of eggplants on top and serve.

Index

Indice by ingredients